6/98

The Great Pox

Jon Arrizabalaga, John Henderson and Roger French

The Great Pox

The French Disease in Renaissance Europe

Yale University Press
New Haven and London

Set in Bembo by Best-set Typesetter Ltd, Hong Kong
Printed in Great Britain by St Edmundsbury Press

Library of Congress Cataloging-in-Publication Data
Arrizabalaga, Jon.
    The great pox: the French disease in Renaissance Europe/Jon
  Arrizabalaga, John Henderson, and Roger French.
    Includes bibliographical references and index.
    ISBN 0-300-06934-0 (alk. paper)
    1. Syphilis—Europe—History—16th century. I. Henderson, John,
  1949–   . II. French, R. K. (Roger Kenneth)   III. Title.
  RC201.6.A1A77   1997
  614.5'472'09409031—dc20   96–23453
                                                        CIP

A catalogue record for this book is available from the British Library.

10 9 8 7 6 5 4 3 2 1

Contents

Plates, Figures, Tables

Plates

Figures

Tables

Acknowledgements

During the long gestation of this book the authors have incurred a debt of gratitude to a number of individuals and institutions. In the first place our colleagues in Italian universities, libraries and archives have proved very generous in their willingness to help well beyond their normal call of duty. This was particularly the case in Rome, where the research on the records of the Spedale di San Giacomo in Augusta could not have been completed by John Henderson in the short time at his disposal. In this respect two people should be especially mentioned, Claudio Schiavone and Vittorio Malvagna, as well as the staff of the Archivio di Stato di Roma. We should also like to thank the archivists of the Archivio di Stato in Bologna, Ferrara, Florence, Modena and Siena as well as of the Archivio Diocesano in Ferrara and the Archivio Segreto Vaticano. We are also grateful to Professor Alessandro Pastore of the University of Verona, who expedited a number of matters in relation to the records of the Incurabili hospital in Bologna. We are also grateful to the staff of a number of libraries. In Florence: Villa 'I Tatti', The Harvard University Italian Center for Italian Renaissance Studies, Biblioteca Nazionale Centrale, Kunsthistorisches Institut; in Rome: Biblioteca Apostolica Vaticana, Institut Français; Biblioteca Civica di Ferrara; Barcelona: Biblioteca de Catalunya, Institución Milà i Fontanals (CSIC); Madrid: Biblioteca Nacional; London: British Library, Warburg Institute, Wellcome Institute Library; Cambridge: University Library, Whipple Library.

We are also grateful for financial support from a number of institutions. The support of the University of Cantabria (Santander) and of the Basque Government made it possible for Jon Arrizabalaga to stay for twenty months in Cambridge and four months in Florence between 1985 and 1987. For further shorter periods he has been subsidised by the DGICYT (Spanish Ministry of Education and Science) and the British Council, the British Academy and the CSIC. From 1987 his research for this book has been partly funded by the research fellowships PB86-0639, PB89-0066, and PB92-0910-C03-03 of the Spanish DGICYT.

John Henderson's research in Italian state archives (Ferrara, Florence and

Rome) was funded first by a Wellcome Trust Research Fellowship and then by a British Academy Travel Grant; further periods of research have been financed by the Wellcome Trust. John Henderson is also grateful to the American Academy in Rome for the privilege of staying there as a Visiting Scholar.

Thanks are also due to a number of scholars who provided invaluable suggestions on reading all or part of the manuscript: above all to the anonymous reader of Yale University Press, but also to Jane Bridgeman (for her guidance on the history of sixteenth-century Italian dress), Andrew Cunningham, Luis García-Ballester and Juan A. Paniagua. We also owe a considerable debt to Dr John Dawson and the staff of the Literary and Linguistic Computing Centre of the University of Cambridge for all their help in the processing, preparation and analysis of the patient records of the Spedale di San Giacomo in Rome. We are also grateful to the librarians and archivists who have granted us permission to reproduce the photographs listed on pages ix and x, and to Deborah Howard for her helpful advice. Especial thanks are due to the staff of the following institutions for their help: Archivio Fotografico, Castello Sforzesco, Milan; Biblioteca Comunale Augusta, Perugia; and the Centro Minorile, Venice. Finally we should like to thank our families who have given us support during the long gestation of this book.

Preface

This book is about the appearance of the French Disease in renaissance
Europe and the reactions of the doctors and other people to what was
perceived by the majority as a new disease. Inevitably, given that research on
the subject is still in its infancy in many countries, we have had to restrict our
coverage to a series of interrelated case studies. Our main emphasis is on
renaissance Italy, but detailed comparisons with other parts of Europe have
helped to show what was common and what special to the reaction of several
of the countries of the Old World. The main historical argument of this book
rests on the surviving written evidence about what people thought and did
when the disease arrived and during the subsequent hundred years. Their
thoughts and actions often had enough in common for us to see groups of
people with some characteristic reaction to the disease. These groups and
their reactions raised a number of questions which we have tried to answer in
this book. These questions derive essentially from a single query: what made
a particular reaction characteristic of the group that displayed it?

Of course, these groups were not mutually exclusive, for a doctor was a
citizen of this or that town and may have belonged to a religious
confraternity, but as a medical man, as a citizen and as a member of a pious
association he had purposes, interests and beliefs in common with other
members of those groups. The purposes, interests and beliefs of groups had
some bearing on how they reacted to the French Disease; and within a group
the reactions of the individual reflected his other allegiances.

In the first place, what were the concerns of the learned doctors in the
society of the time that made them agree on aspects of the French Disease,
and what led them to disagree? However much they disagreed among
themselves, they agreed in disagreeing totally with the other kinds of practitioners. Did the other practitioners have a characteristic response that derived
from their position? Since the doctors were learned and rational, their characteristic action was to try to understand the French Disease. Undoubtedly
they believed that understanding the disease was the surest way to treating and
preventing it. But equally clearly it gave them a competitive edge in the

medical marketplace: what relationship was there between the commercially useful image of the learned doctor and the content of his theoretical medicine?

Similar problems arose with men and women without medical training. Religious confraternities were clearly defined groups; they thought charitable thoughts and acted in charitable ways, including building hospitals. But were these the only reasons that hospitals for poxed patients were built? (And how charitable was compulsory admission to a hospital?) Did the perception of the pox by laymen who were responsible for public health differ from that of the learned doctors? Centrally, to what extent did they agree on how a person contracted the disease and how therefore it was transmitted? How characteristic of them as a whole was the reaction of the city authorities?

The confraternity, the hospital, the urban administration, the medical faculty were all in some sense institutions. The biggest institution of the time was of course the Church, and we explore in the following pages how the Church as a spiritual, political and very strong social force tackled the problems generated by the new disease. As an institution the Church was composed of smaller groups. One important charitable arm consisted of the religious orders. How, then, did the newer orders such as the Jesuits or the Capucin fathers take on and develop the example of the Observants in caring for the poor in general and the sick poor in particular?

Indeed, the biggest social group to be affected was the urban poor, if only because there were more of them. It had been the same in the Black Death, a century and a half before, and in the epidemics of 'plague' which afflicted Europe every ten to fifteen years thereafter. The poor were noticeable in urban centres, and it was here that public health measures first evolved and also where civic authorities turned to the university physicians for advice. But the medicine of the university-trained physicians was not designed to cope with epidemics that were sudden, widespread, acute and fatal in the case of the plague, or chronic, disabling and disgusting, as with the French Disease. It was based on Greek and Arabic sources and was geared towards the long-term care of the class of citizen who could pay a physician's fees. We explore contemporary perceptions of how the pox affected the different social classes and what kind of medical help was available for them. Directly related is the question of how far experience of two great epidemics changed the attitudes and actions of the city authorities, towards public health in general and towards that of the poor in particular. Furthermore, how did plague and pox ultimately change European medicine as a whole?

As for cultural groupings, a doctor in a papal or princely court or a medical faculty might give his primary allegiance to Greek or to Arabic authors and so think and behave differently. Despite being dispersed across several European countries, the hellenists were very conscious of being a group with common aims. They therefore had a characteristic reaction to the French Disease. How did this reaction work out in the practice of medicine? To what extent were the humanists a coherent group throughout Europe with common ideals that might influence the way they perceived the pox?

Few would have disagreed that the arrival of the French Disease was an act of God. This was thus part of the nature of the disease and part of its contemporary perception. To invoke the image of St Job and to exercise piety and charity might seem the characteristic reaction of a major group, the whole of Christendom. But northern Europe practised a different religion after the Reformation. Did these changed affiliations of the new group affect its perceptions of the French Disease?

These issues are studied in the following chapters. Disputations in a faculty and a princely court make the allegiances of the disputants clear. When learned physicians are competing for the favours of a pope or ducal patron, their strategies are revealed. The death of a cardinal at the hands of his doctors highlights the dangers of administering mercury. The administration of a large hospital generates paperwork that reveals a great deal about the patients. All this accumulated experience formed contemporary perceptions of the disease, the answer to our *quaestiones disputatae*: what did people think and do about the disease?

Since the manuscript of this book went to press the following works have appeared which we have been unable to incorporate in our discussion: W. Schleiner, *Medical Ethics in the Renaissance*, Washington DC, 1995, esp. ch. 6; and D. W. Amundsen, *Medicine, Society, and Faith in the Ancient and Medieval Worlds*, Baltimore and London, 1996, esp. ch. 11.

Chapter One

Syphilis and the French Disease

Introduction: medicine and history

This is a history of the French Disease; or, in the English vernacular, the pox. It is not a history of syphilis. The difference is an important one and is reflected in the kind of historical analysis we have adopted in writing this book. This is not the only kind of way to write about the history of a disease, but the nature of the pox makes the issues involved in investigating the history of diseases particularly clear.

By 1905–6, when the venereal syphilis treponeme[1] was isolated and the first serological procedure (the Wassermann reaction) for the diagnosis of syphilis was invented, a great change had overtaken Western medicine. It was a change doubly important for the theme of this book. First, and simplest, the means of overcoming a great scourge were potentially at hand. The causal organism of other dangerous diseases, cholera, tuberculosis and plague, had already been discovered. From 1909 to 1912 venereal syphilis became the target of the first successful aetiological drug ever developed against a bacterial disease.

Second, medicine's success against bacteria changed medicine and medicine's perception of itself. It may not be an exaggeration to say that for the first time in its history Western medicine supported its reputation by obvious success in the process of cure. A powerful new tool was now added to the other strategies the doctor had long employed to generate authority for himself and his profession. When the doctor came to look at the history of medicine, his view was coloured not only by his professional authority but by the nature of the new medicine.

Laboratory Medicine and the New Ontology of Infectious Disease

In earlier periods, before the laboratory and the germ theory, the relationship between cause, disease, symptom and sign had been different in different systems of medicine, as we shall see in the course of this book. Often the nature of the relationship was discussed in learned and theoretical treatments, and often in practice the doctor found it unnecessary or undesirable to 'diagnose' a specific disease. Causal systems generally agreed that there was a hierarchy of causes ramifying through a world where macrocosm was closely related to microcosm. There was a 'first cause', perhaps celestial, and a chain of secondary causes down to the 'immediate cause'. A single cause might lead to a number of different diseases and a single disease might arise from a number of different causes. It was widely agreed that there were 'mixed' diseases and that one disease could change into another. The nosologists constructed schemes of classification that subdivided groups of diseases into genera and species, and quarrelled with each other over the details.[2]

During the nineteenth century most diseases that modern medicine recognises 'crystallised in the form of specific entities'.[3] Central to this event was the development of a new medicine based in the laboratory.[4] It was here that complex doctrines of causality whose origins were ultimately Greek and ancient were abandoned in the construction of a wholly new pattern of causality.[5] We will focus on infectious diseases, the group to which syphilis belongs. When it was understood that the infective micro-organism was the cause of the disease, a new ontology arose. By 1910 it was clear that the essence of these infectious diseases was always an external pathogen or causative agent. This was a natural species, was alive and reproduced its kind. In all the shifting picture of symptoms and clinical descriptions the one constant was the pathogen. Only when, in the laboratory, the pathogen was identified in the tissues or fluids of the patient was a diagnosis confirmed. Variable (and therefore unreliable) symptoms became secondary in the processes of explanation and diagnosis. Although some specific diseases had had names and had prompted discussion about disease entities in the Latin tradition, particularly from the sixteenth century onwards, the germ theory of infectious diseases in the nineteenth century transformed the way in which people thought about them.

But all this did not represent confusion, for confusion is a muddling of extant categories, and our categories did not then exist. In solving their own problems in their own ways these doctors serve to highlight the great change that came over medicine after the laboratory and the germ theory. Their perceptions were so different that we cannot insist on the identity of diseases before and after. 'We are simply unable to say whether they were the same, since the criteria of "sameness" have been changed'.[6] Yet the new authority of the doctor and his technical expertise in knowing about pathogenic organisms made it natural that he should be thought of as the best qualified to look at the history of medicine. The new ontology of disease seemed to provide a scientific yardstick to measure the attempts of people in the past to understand and treat diseases.

Doctors knowledgeable about the germ theory did in fact begin to write histories of infectious diseases in the last decades of the nineteenth century. They believed that the germ theory had provided 'the first successful understanding of these diseases' and had 'replaced the old, unsuccessful and misguided attempts'[7] at achieving this aim. One of the purposes of writing about the past is to win present battles, and the medical bacteriologists faced a good deal of opposition at first.[8] But they won their battle and the history they wrote was rapidly and widely diffused. It was a constructed history, legitimating the position of its authors by selecting and championing men like Fracastoro, Leeuwenhoek, Redi, Spallanzani and Semmelweis as microbiologists and bacteriologists *avant la lettre*. And they introduced themselves as products of their own history, 'successors to those far-sighted men whose fate had inevitably been not to have been appreciated in their own day'.[9]

In other words, we can see elements of construction in historical accounts, both after and before the germ theory. Our own attempt to write a history of the pox will be seen in clearer perspective if we examine in more detail how others have done so.

The Historiography of the Pox

It is recognised that physicians from the Greeks to the Enlightenment turned to the medical past for three major reasons. One was to enhance the dignity of their profession by giving it a distinguished ancestry. A second, related tactic was to seek credibility for novel systems by claiming that the ancients knew something of them. The third reason was to improve directly their own knowledge of medicine and therefore its practice. While introductions to medical works often reflected (and sometimes still do) the first of these reasons for looking at medical history – giving it the dignity of age – the technical stuff of medicine was drawn from the old authorities, which gave medicine epistemological support. Up into the nineteenth century, large editions of the old authorities were intended for medical rather than historical use.

In parallel, the ever more rapid accumulation of European medical literature in early modern times added substantially to the problems of handling large amounts of technical literature. Two techniques for coping with this were biography and bibliography prompted by humanist scholarship and changes in historiographical practice outside medicine. Broadly, they formed new genres of literature, but within medicine served the subsidiary purpose of categorising and analysing the technical literature. Because the major ancient authors did not date, and indeed attracted much new scholarship, the ancient literature added to these problems.

A determined attempt to solve these problems was made in the Enlightenment. Separate intellectual concerns from the fields of history and textual criticism were drawn together to produce medical historiography in the strict sense. The result was that simple chronology ceased to be the main criterion for the arrangement of the medical past. While the ancient authors were still consulted for the technical content of medicine, there could be no strict distinction between historical and technical texts; but the new historical awareness gave rise to the first historico-critical reconstructions of the medical past. This in turn influenced the textual, biographical and bibliographical traditions and began to make new distinctions. By the mid-nineteenth century these had come to follow two alternative patterns, medical documentation and medical history.[10]

The French Disease was being studied while these changes were going on. We can see in what was written about it the changes that were occurring in medical historiography as a whole. The three traditional patterns that we in fact see in it can be called the textual, the bio-bibliographical and the historical. These three traditions changed over time and (as we shall see) were often combined. No exhaustive analysis is in order here, but a brief glimpse at these traditions will help to locate both the customary account of 'syphilis' in the past and our own treatment of the pox.

The Textual Tradition

The textual tradition was dominant until well into the eighteenth century and was maintained for direct medical purposes at least until the end of the century. Thereafter it was slowly transformed, but kept vigorous for the purposes of medical history. Very many of the studies that have fuelled this tradition have actually focused on works from the late fifteenth and early sixteenth centuries, when the French Disease attracted most attention. Thus for nearly five centuries the pox itself has been a centre of attention from both historians and medical men, for different reasons.

From the second decade of the sixteenth century, the European printing presses began to issue a series of collections of medical works (up to six authors) dedicated to the French Disease. Many went into subsequent editions, and the individual works themselves appeared many times. Among the most popular of the collections were those published in Pavia and Venice in 1516, another of unknown origin in 1532, one more from Venice in 1535 and a collection published in Basel and Lyon in 1536.[11] They centred on a core collection of works by Joan Almenar, Nicolò Leoniceno and Angelo Bolognini, to which different editors added according to preference from a looser group of tracts by Sebastiano dall'Aquila, Antonio Scanaroli, Nicolò Massa, Ulrich von Hutten, Pietro Andrea Mattioli, Lorenz Friese and Nicolaus Pol.

This tradition culminated in the collection made by Luigi Luigini (b. 1526), who in 1566–7 gathered together the works of no less than fifty-nine authors.[12] As the lengthy title of the collection itself proclaims, Luigini's aim was to be exhaustive and to collect every extant work, whether already in print or not. For him his final published collection was a documentary corpus that would help the medical men of his time to fight what they saw as a new scourge more ferocious than any faced by their predecessors. It attacked the main organs of the body, they said, the heart, liver and brain; it corrupted the blood and putrefied the spirits, crippling the vital actions; it demanded the most powerful remedies the doctors could secure in their attempts to cure it. Luigini's purpose was less to allow his readers to compare these texts by reason of their proximity than to make it possible to learn from them the true nature of the disease, 'To discern silently all that is valuable to contemplate upon'.[13] In other words he was acting as an 'aggregator' who collected the views of authors and authorities following the epistemological tradition that held medical knowledge to be cumulative, collaborative and progressive. The publisher, Jordanus Zilettus, thought so too, and in his brief foreword claimed that the collection was 'the best way of making it possible for every scholar to read so many authors and achieve knowledge of, and the cure of, the French Disease'.[14] While the technique of 'aggregation' was well established in medical circles in the middle ages, Luigini treated it in a humanist way, editing out the 'numerous and abominable' errors introduced by printers into earlier editions of the various tracts.[15] What he did not say was that he suppressed sentences and even paragraphs which he considered irrelevant.

Luigini's collection retained its utility down to the eighteenth century, when it was re-edited (1728) by the 'teacher of Europe', the Leiden professor Herman Boerhaave.[16] His purpose, like that of Luigini, was medical. The cumulative knowledge that the collection contained was for him a *perfectissimam historiam*, a 'complete description', where *historia* means a sort of generalised case history of the disease, with overtones of empirical description of the Hippocratic kind. Boerhaave's editorial improvements on the collection consisted of marking the references off from the text by the use of italics, inserting medical receipts and textual references and reordering the sequence of texts. This and his alleged correction of dangerous errors was for the medical use of the 'cultivators of medicine' whom he addresses in his preface.[17] The disease by now had a new technical name – *lues venerea*. The accumulated lore within the collection could be seen to support Boerhaave's own notion of a *radicalis curatio*: cure by the mercury method.[18] Inevitably there is a chronological component to Boerhaave's *historia*. It was not only that support for the mercury treatment was to be derived from a practice that was now over two centuries old, but that the old accounts of its beginning and the symptoms showed that in the intervening period the disease itself had changed. Consequently, its treatment had to be different: history was of direct medical use.

Despite the changes in the disease, no one doubted that the old *Morbus Gallicus* was the same as the eighteenth-century *lues venerea*. To trace its origins and changes was to discover the natural history of the disease, and a knowledge of its natural history was preliminary to a knowledge of its cure. So thought Christian Gottfried Gruner (1744–1815), who in 1789 published a new collection of texts, which he introduced as additional to those of Luigini's collection in Boerhaave's edition. It was bigger – sixty-four authors from 1495 to 1556 – and included material on the disease from non-medical sources. To this he added 'vestiges' of the disease from a further seventy-two authors from the ancient period (Greek, Latin and Hebrew) and the middle ages (Arabs and their Latin followers).[19] His scholarly apparatus is more elaborate than Boerhaave's, as Boerhaave's had been more so than Luigini's. His additional historical information and bibliography, together with the new rare or unknown texts, were designed to recover the fullest possible memory of the human experience with the disease: 'Only by the means of the guide and teaching of history can one dispel the darkness and illuminate with its light anything dubious, uncertain and obscure. Who follows it without anger or bias can scarcely deceive or be deceived.'[20]

But in fact Gruner's techniques of presentation were also designed to support his own rather peculiar ideas about the origin of the disease, for he maintained that it had first appeared among the *Marrani*, a term he used to cover both Jews and the Arabs who had been expelled from Spain in 1492. With this in mind Gruner continued his programme of work and four years later published another volume with twenty-seven more early works, medical and non-medical, on the French Disease.[21] The same instinct that made sixteenth-century Italians call the disease French and citizens of France call it Neapolitan, now made Gruner elaborate on the alien origin of the disease among the *Marrani*. He claimed that his new collections of texts supplied a complete natural history of the disease in which its origins, mode of transmission and changes all pointed to a Marranic source. Gruner also had in mind that a historical treatment of the disease as detailed as his not only would directly improve the medicine of the learned practitioner, but also would enhance his reputation as learned, an image so useful in the traditional competitive battle with the unlettered practitioner.[22]

Gruner's was the last attempt to provide a general history of the disease within the textual tradition that saw history of direct use to practice. Later studies were more narrowly conceived. In 1843 the professor of pathology Conrad Heinrich Fuchs (1803–55) put together a collection of thirteen Latin and German medical works on the *Lustseuche*, the pox in Germany. He focused on the first fifteen years of the disease, beginning in 1495, and on German writers. The collection was intended to be of service to German readers and it rested on the assumption that the disease had been epidemic during its first fifteen years, thereafter changing its nature.[23] Indeed, he held that the pox had changed in that time more than any other disease, and in that sense he was reporting historically rather than medically. This is why he excluded non-German and later authors from his account, for the disease they handled in their patients was different. Surely Fuchs had taken some historiographical assumptions from the Romantic movement, for he criticised Gruner's method of editing and thought that the meaning of works from the past could be understood only by giving them the colour of a precise context of historical circumstances. To this end, he added to his collection a number of bio-bibliographical accounts of the authors of the tracts, a short historical account of 'epidemic syphilis' in Germany and over seventy short pieces of information, extending the picture of the disease up to 1590.

Once the early tracts had been republished in the simpler, general histories of the disease, there was more reason to concentrate – with more elaborate editing techniques – on national histories. As Fuchs had done for Germany, so Alfonso Corradi (1833–92) wrote a historical treatment of the pox for his own country, Italy.[24] Like Fuchs too, Corradi concentrated on a short chronological period, from the late fifteenth to the early sixteenth century, from which he published again fifty documents. His work differed from earlier collections in including his interpretative study of the documents. Corradi saw himself in a tradition of pox-writers that itself had a history: all the old texts had now been republished, he said, and attention now had to be given to more detailed histories of the pox in different countries and to problems that remained to be solved. The particular difficulty that he saw was to explain why the disease had suddenly become a dangerous epidemic with different manifestations in late fifteenth- and early sixteenth-century Europe. That is, while he accepted that some form of general or 'constitutional' pox existed in ancient and medieval times, identifying the causes that changed it so radically now became a problem to be tackled through local studies. As in the case of Fuchs, this was partly a historical study in that the disease at their time was (they held) very different from that of the historical period they were studying.

To the extent that these accounts are historical, it was history written by physicians. This continued as editions and translations of the works of fifteenth- and sixteenth-century doctors on the pox continued to appear from the middle of the nineteenth century to the 1940s. Many of them had a particular interest in venereal diseases and some were dermato-venereologists. Their work had the effect of dignifying their own specialty with a historical lineage and of identifying their perceived forerunners as the heroes of the discipline. The same historical writing was also used to give credit to specifi- cally national developments within the specialty. This is illustrated by German authors like Alexander Seitz, whose text was re-edited by A. Moll in Stuttgart in 1852, and Ulrich von Hutten, translated from Latin into German by H. Oppenheimer in Berlin in 1902. They are paralleled by the French: Jacques de Béthencourt's tract was translated into French by A. Fournier in Paris in 1871 and Jean Fernel's by L. le Pileur in Paris in 1879. Foreign authors could also be appropriated to the new specialty, and there were English translations of Spanish and Italian authors (G. Gaskoin translated Francisco López de Villalobos in 1870; W. C. Wright produced an English version of Fracastoro's works on contagion in 1930), German translations of Spanish authors and French of Italian. There have, of course, been many translations and editions of Fracastoro's poem *Syphilis*.

The textual tradition culminated in the work of Karl Sudhoff (1853–1938). By now too the historical component of it, which we have glimpsed in earlier authors, had become important. Indeed, Sudhoff was writing in the first quarter of this century, when the causal micro-organism of syphilis had been discovered and the practical medical value of studying old accounts of diseases was diminishing. Sudhoff made, perhaps too easily, the assumption that venereal syphilis and the *Morbus Gallicus* were to be identified and developed a wide and critical project to present again the earliest textual sources. Convinced that syphilis existed in the Old World before the New had been discovered, he sought out every documental 'fact'[25] and published them in accordance with the most rigorous historiographical standards of the time.[26]

It was Charles Singer who in adapting Sudhoff's works for English readers revealed in an extreme form the power of the natural-scientific image of medicine after its success against bacterial disease, and the consequent positivist view of historical method. In terms reminiscent of sixteenth-century wrangles between hellenists and Arabists, Singer singled out the 'stutterings' and 'bunglings' of the old writers on the French Disease, and begged 'the reader's most charitable interpretation' for what he called the early monuments of science.

> The 'Experimental Method', in which we have been trained, was as yet no part of the philosophical system of the day. These pamphlets are but as the poor flights of weak fledglings, unaccustomed to the use of what will one day grow into mighty wings. Their authors had no such teachers as Vesalius and Harvey, Galileo and Kepler. . . . Judge gently of them, kind reader, as you would be gently judged![27]

The Biographical and Bibliographical Traditions

The quantity of medical literature on the French Disease is second only to that on the plague. Those who wrote biographically had a splendid example in the eighteenth century in Astruc's study, and the method reached its peak in the late nineteenth century in the works of Proksch. It was only in the nineteenth century that we see the full development of the bibliographical method, in the indices of men like Choulant, Haeser and, again, Proksch and in the *Index Catalog*.

Jean Astruc (1684–1766) published his *De Morbis Venereis libri sex* in Paris in 1736. It went through a second edition four years later, when Astruc took the opportunity to add three more books (it appeared in Paris in two volumes).[28]

Astruc's interest was primarily historical. He sought to give an exhaustive account of what earlier physicians had thought and done about the *lues venerea* and his efforts were directed towards intellectual recognition of his forerunners rather than towards improvement in practice. Of course, his understanding of the natural history of the disease did not rule out benefit that might accrue to practice, particularly since the changes that he thought the disease had undergone since its first appearance could well include a change back to its first savage form.[29] He thought, in fact, that the *lues venerea* was a generic name and covered a number of specific diseases like gonorrhoea, venereal buboes, genital sores and warts. These were *lues venerea incipiens*, initial stages, while the 'confirmed' or 'universal' disease included venereal pain, glandular and lymphatic tumours and functional lesions. All kinds of *lues venerea*, according to Astruc, were caused by a *virus venereum* (where *virus* is 'slime' or 'poison').

Astruc confidently identified the disease described in this way as the French Disease (a name he naturally did not use extensively) despite the fact that it had, he believed, gone through major changes as it passed through six periods since its arrival from America. It was, he held, declining in severity to the extent that it looked as if it would become extinct. He also held that medicine had improved, so that paradoxically the early severity of the disease had prompted medical development, just as warfare stimulated the art of fortification. In this way the perceived changes in the disease itself and in medicine meant that the information Astruc was providing was of historical rather than clinical importance. He begins his work with an account of the origins of the disease and three books deal with the strictly medical aspects of it. The remaining books consist of a wide bio-bibliographical index of medical and surgical works devoted to the disease from the late fifteenth century to Astruc's day. He sketched the lives of previous authors and summarised the main points of their works. This index was tripled in size in the second edition, from 180 to 550 authors.[30]

The same desire for an exhaustive treatment lay behind the historical work on venereal diseases published in 1895 by the Viennese doctor Johann Karl Proksch (1840–1923).[31] Proksch was able to fill the first of his two volumes (which totalled more than 1,300 pages), the first one referring to the traces left by venereal diseases in ancient and medieval literature. The second volume contained material from the late fifteenth century onwards: he, like Astruc, divided the history of venereal diseases into broad periods, but more than Astruc he held that medical knowledge was cumulative. It was therefore also progressive, and progress had led to the medical thought of his own day, so very different from that of the late fifteenth century. Needless to say, Proksch was mostly concerned with syphilis, which he assumed was identical to the French Disease. In his day, the spirochete of syphilis had not yet been discovered, but medical men had already split gonorrhoea and chancroid conditions from the common trunk of venereal disease. He divided the history of the disease into five periods: from the earliest *Syphilographen* to Fernel; from Fernel to Astruc; Astruc to Hunter; Hunter to Ricord; and finally Ricord and his contemporaries. His treatment is uniform and significant. He gives a biography of each of the authors, summarises their major arguments and from them synthesises what he took to be the major medical ideas for each period. He was, like others we have met, selective, and, in choosing to highlight the progressive stages through which medical knowledge had reached its level of achievement in his own times, he was in fact choosing his own heroes and predecessors as good venereologists and syphilographers.

This historico-medical positivism was widespread by the middle of the century. General indices of historical medical literature were published by Choulant and Haeser[32] during the second third of the century, and prompted the vast specialised bibliographical index with which Proksch completed his work on the history of syphilis.[33] It appeared in three volumes from 1889 to 1900 and covered (in the first volume) topics like prostitution, marriage, the armed forces, secret and folk medicines, poems, hospitals, geography, statistics and contagion. It was exhaustive in its use of the old literature, and again Proksch's medical purposes are seen in the medical topics (in the second and third volume) of therapeutics, semeiology, sterility, 'rheumatism' and so on of the specific venereal diseases. Choulant and Haeser, the founding fathers of historico-medical positivism (both of whom devote sections to syphilis), contributed to a climate that produced not only Proksch's final index but also the *Index Catalog*, which first appeared in Washington in 1880.[34] Syphilis claimed sections in its five series, those of the first three being extensive; the first, in line with common historiographical thinking, presented history along with the technical literature.

The Historical Tradition

We have seen, then, that in the historiography of the French Disease we can discern a textual tradition, in which the main voice to be heard was that of the text; and another in which access to the greatly growing amount of medical literature – these texts indeed – demanded indices and critical evaluation of authors. A third 'tradition' – or at least a uniformity of treatment – is seen in the historical, where 'history' is both descriptive and chronological. We have seen that this mode of treatment did not emerge until the eighteenth century. It was an attempt to discover the essence of the disease by looking at its origins, and so covered the first years of the French Disease.

Most historical constructions of the early years of the French Disease were associated with contemporary controversies and can be understood only in conjunction with them. It takes at least two opposing groups to make a controversy and here we can identify, on the one hand, the physicians and,

on the other, a less homogeneous group of natural historians, natural philosophers and theologians. We shall look first at the non-medical things they
argued about, and then at the medical. The non-medical controversies died
out after the middle of the nineteenth century, but it would not be an
exaggeration to say that the medical-controversy tradition still survives. This
is no place to examine these controversies minutely, but a glance at them
helps to indicate why we have chosen our particular approach to the French
Disease in this book.

The non-medical controversy was a form of the 'decay of nature' argument, now exercised in the so-called dispute of the New World. As Gerbi has
splendidly shown, in the mid-eighteenth century the French naturalist the
Comte de Buffon (1707–88) declared that nature in the New World was
'weak' or 'immature'. It was a doctrine that was used often in the years after
the 1760s as the dispute continued. It derived from Buffon's observations on
the scarceness of quadrupeds in North America and was elaborated into his
Eurocentric theory that all animals were created in the Old World and
degenerated as they migrated to the New. The New World dispute began in
about 1768 as essentially an ethnographical-natural-historical contention at a
time when European culture was expanding rapidly and confidently. Europe
had reached so high a degree of consciousness of itself that non-Europe – that
is, the rest of the world – was not merely seen through European eyes, it *was*
Europe as well, a part and offprint of Europe. This was particularly so in
America, where Europeans were more openly expressing their faith in their
civilising mission. The dispute lost its original natural-history character as the
Romantic movement and the political conflict engendered by the independ-
ence movement of the American colonies combined to push the controversy
to a historical and theological level.[35]

In this context we can see that there were cultural factors affecting the
continuing debate about the nature and origins of the French Disease. It was
precisely because many people held that the pox had come from the New
World that more general arguments about the decay of nature there could be
useful to them.[36] The French Disease in fact was often used as an example of
the degeneration of American nature; probably first by the Dutch pastor
Cornelius de Pauw (1739–99).[37] His *Recherches philosophiques sur les Américains*
(1768–9) reveals its author's admiration for the works of Buffon and often
expresses the doctrine that American nature was degenerate and corrupt and
weak and inferior to European nature. The result, said Pauw, was that
harmful animals like insects and snakes were more numerous, bigger and
more dangerous in America, to the detriment of the quadrupeds (including
reptiles), which were accordingly fewer, smaller, weaker and ill-bred. No
wonder that Pauw held that the French Disease had originated in America
(and had come to Europe with Columbus' sailors).[38] More than that, Pauw
repeated the legend that the disease would be contracted by anyone eating the
meat of the American iguana.

Rather than identifying 'cultural factors' affecting the question of the French Disease, we should perhaps think of the question as itself a cultural phenomenon. As we shall see in Chapter Two, from the earliest chroniclers the one constant feature of all accounts of the French Disease was that it did not arise among the group to which the author belonged.[39] It seems important for a culture that diseases come from somewhere else, another country or another race. As in the outbreak of AIDS, which because of its similarity has stimulated new interest in the history of syphilis, the question of the source of the disease is partly a cultural one, rising almost to xenophobic belief that diseases always come from elsewhere. In the fifteenth and sixteenth centuries the French wriggled desperately to avoid the label the 'French Disease' and tried to pin the pox on to the Neapolitans, or to find a neutral name for it.[40] The rise of European consciousness in the eighteenth century convinced Europeans that the pox had come from outside Europe and had arisen there among outsiders, who were generally perceived as less civilised if not actually degenerate. This made the theory of a New World origin of the pox attractive; it also made it possible to believe that it originated among others seen as outsiders, like the Jews and Arabs who had been expelled from Spain at the end of the fifteenth century.

This cultural attitude shapes most of the accounts of the pox that compose what we have called the historical tradition. We shall look at these accounts in a little more detail below: first we must think again of eighteenth-century Europe. We have seen that a feature of Enlightenment thought about nature was that living things could change. All over Europe natural historians were thinking about the origin of natural species and the changes they underwent: natural history related animals to their environment and natural historians collected and arranged specimens of living and non-living natural kinds. Now, in the Enlightenment, this gave added interest to earlier attempts to see the pox as a 'natural kind'. As we shall see later in this volume, since the 1540s most physicians came to believe that the pox was not just a humoral imbalance but had a specific external cause, a 'seed' or a poison-like *virus*, which was a new element in the traditional causal system. This implies the development of an ontological view of the disease, which was seen as a sort of natural species with a vital cycle of birth, growth, maturity, decline and death. To the eighteenth century (and sometimes before) this looked like the business of natural history. Certainly the 'natural history' of the French Disease had been sought for medical reasons since the time of Luigini and his collection of pox-tracts, that is, to best diagnose and treat it, and to predict its future in broad terms. This developed in the late seventeenth century into an antiquarian interest in the pox in some physicians, but it was not until Astruc had his own collection of pox-tracts that what we call a historical treatment of the topic was apparent.

This moment coincided, as we have observed, with the new natural history and a high-point in European self-consciousness. Not perhaps surprisingly

Jean Astruc (he was a royal physician) in a well-documented introduction to his influential *De Morbis Venereis* (1736) claimed that the place of origin of the pox was the West Indian island of Santo Domingo. Here, he thought, it was endemic before the arrival of Columbus in 1492, from whose sailors it spread to Italy and France, the other European nations, and finally to Africa and the rest of the world. Those who somewhat later believed in the degeneration of American nature of course found Astruc's views significant. Here, it seemed, was technical medical evidence that supported their Eurocentric position.

Astruc and the argument for an American origin of the pox were opposed by those with different cultural connections, mostly geographical and ethnic. One of the first to oppose Astruc was the Portuguese Jew Antonio Nunes Ribeiro Sanches (1699–1783) in a work first published in English in 1751 (and in French in the following year).[41] Using the same evidence as Astruc, Sanches argued that the pox had begun, before June 1495, in Italy. He was clearly sensitive to national attitudes and accused Astruc the Frenchman of being afraid of giving the pox the name by which it was known to the Portuguese, the Germans and the Italians, namely the French Disease.[42] Probably, as a Portuguese, Sanches saw Italy as sufficiently distant, geographically and culturally, to be an appropriate birthplace for the pox. Possibly, as a Jew, he felt himself to be a little distant from European culture as a whole.

Certainly other opponents of Astruc, Pauw and the American-origin theory had non-European cultural ties. Above all, Pauw was opposed by those who were themselves American or had lived long enough in America to feel ill-disposed to accept that American nature was degenerate and the natural source of the pox. By the end of the eighteenth century there were many who felt more American than European. Pauw and European authors who supported him, like William Robertson (in 1777), Herder (1784), Hegel (1842), were opposed by men like the Benedictine Antoine Joseph Pernety (1770), the naturalist George Forster (1777), M. Drouin de Bercy, who colonised Santo Domingo, the pox-island itself (1818), and above all the Jesuit Francisco Javier Clavijero (1731–87).[43] Using medical and non-medical works produced since the fifteenth century, he devoted the ninth dissertation of his *Storia antica del Messico* (1780–1) to a systematic rebuttal of the opinions of Pauw and Astruc about the origins of the pox, by means of medical and non-medical works produced during the fifteenth century.

The disease thus continued as always to be seen as originating at a great distance from the cultural centre of the groups articulating opinions. Non-Europeans saw no difficulty in Europe being the distant place in which the French Disease had arisen. Europeans replied as we would expect them to have done. Sanches, the Portuguese Jew, was opposed point by point by Christoph Girtanner (1760–1800), who restated the Columbian theory.[44] Even those who accepted a European origin of the disease (like Philip-Gabriel Hensler [1733–1805]) had to accept that some major change had taken place at the end of the fifteenth century (Hensler thought that the disease had changed from 'sporadic' to 'endemic').[45] Two ancient societies in particular, those of the Arabs and of the Jews, were seen as marginal by the Europeans, both geographically – across the Mediterranean in North Africa and the Near East – and culturally. Moreover, European culture had been traditionally hostile to them for centuries, and the Jews had been driven out of a number of countries before the final expulsion of Muslim belief from Spain. The Arabs and Jews therefore made a useful target for some Europeans seeking to locate the blame for having originated the French Disease. Thus in 1789 Gruner, as we saw above, grouped together the Arabs and Jews expelled from Spain in 1492. As we shall see in Chapter Two, he followed contemporary chroniclers by calling them *Marrani*. His argument was that the French Disease was not a sudden transmutation of a pre-existing disease, nor an import from the New World, but had appeared in Italy suddenly in 1492 or 1493 at the same time as the *Marrani* expelled from Spain arrived there.

Gruner's use of the term *Marrani* was pejorative, even xenophobic, but not untypical of Europeans' views of people of other continents. 'Always something new out of Africa' was a proverb for the Romans, and Pliny and Strabo provide abundant evidence of Roman notions about the disgusting habits of the strange people at the fringe of the Empire.[46] In Gruner's time Africa was seen in a similar way as the motherland of all skin diseases, and he believed that the pox (with its obvious cutaneous symptoms) had ultimately originated there. It was, he held, endemic in the *Marrani*, but had been unknown to the Spanish because the two societies were secluded from each other. Only the dislocation of the *Marrani* turned it from a racially endemic disease to a European epidemic: once among the French military, it spread quickly to the Italian cities and ultimately back to Spain.[47] Gruner claimed that the disease had at first been pestilential and had spread like a plague, but that it was mainly propagated by *impurus coitus* – certainly adulterous liaisons and perhaps also inter-ethnic ones. Gruner added to his picture in 1793, when he explained that the *Marrani* were a 'very libidinous' people and that this was the reason why the disease was endemic among them.[48] He now had a rather different account of the disease, for what was endemic among the libidinous *Marrani* was, he said, a leprous miasma, *miasma leprosum*. Claims that the pox was a form of leprosy had been made since the sixteenth century,[49] and Gruner is also drawing on old explanations in stating that his leprous miasma was the 'tinder' of the disease, its *fomes*.[50] But in historical usage 'miasma', having disease-specific characteristics, is a new, nineteenth-century term. In medical discussions of the previous centuries the more general 'corrupt air' was used: it was not until Sennert in the seventeenth century (as we shall see) that 'miasma' was used by doctors. Gruner's new theory was that this endemic miasma had, when the *Marrani* reached Italy, mixed with epidemic plague – *pestis epidemica* – which ignited its tinder and generated the French Disease, seen as an epidemic plague.

Although differing in much, authors like Hensler and Girtanner agreed that the question of the origin and nature of the French Disease could best be answered by the writing of monographs. These were neither indices to the literature nor biographical studies and in collecting together all relevant information they constituted a new genre of literature, the historical. One of the earliest practitioners of this genre was Julius Rosenbaum (1807–74), a belated follower of Hensler, who projected a three-volume history.[51] The only volume to appear (in 1839) was the first, dealing with the pox in the ancient world (it was often re-edited, down to the beginning of this century). He explained that the virulence of the disease in the renaissance was due to something else:

[I] arrived at the surprising result, that the Venereal Disease of the XVth century owed its terrible characteristics solely and entirely to the contemporary exanthematic-typhoidal Genius Epidemicus, which made itself known in the South of Europe by petechial fevers and by the Sudor Anglicus (English Sweating-fever) in the North. I concluded further that the disease was not epidemic at all, merely liable to arise under epidemic influence; and must consequently have been already extant before the arrival of the said Genius Epidemicus.[52]

This new approach, said Rosenbaum, exonerated 'honourable nations . . . from the shameful reproach of fathering this Complaint'. Perhaps he was thinking of the French, who had much resented the label 'French Disease'; or perhaps he was Jewish and objected to Gruner's theories about the *Marrani*. By showing how the disease was variable under external circumstances, Rosenbaum could also explain why the so-called specific remedies for the disease were unreliable.[53] His point is that a *historical* treatment in these ways reveals a great deal of the 'Proteus-like' disease,[54] but he recognised that the method 'hardly corresponds with the taste of the present day', and he complained about the lack of interest in historico-medical topics in the medical faculty of Halle, where he taught.[55]

Rosenbaum's interest in the history of venereal disease was exceptional at this time. But after the middle of the century medical controversies over the origins and nature of these diseases began to be rearticulated.[56] They were of course expressed in the terms of the time, and it was a time of positivism in both the scientific and historical disciplines. Moreover, the controversies were led by physicians with historico-medical interests who attempted to illuminate the topic with the new theories, concepts and methods of the new medicine. Thus medical events like the division of the category 'venereal diseases' into specific morbid species and the later identification of the causal germ in each case had a major influence on historical work in the area. The same may be said of the recognition of the kind of treponematoses, the development of pathology and the emergence of palaeopathology, which continue to influence historical work. Additionally, scientific developments in national contexts involved nationalist and even imperialist ideologies in discussions about diseases so stigmatising as syphilis – and this continues to be the case.[57]

The Columbian Question

For a century and a half the controversy over the origins of venereal disease has been dominated by the particular question of whether 'syphilis' existed in the Old World before the return of Columbus from the New World. There have been additions to the ever-growing collection of documentary materials, medical, lay and iconographic, and new material evidence, since the late nineteenth century, based on developments in palaeopathology.[58] The result has been to extend rather than settle the dispute, for 'in claiming that present-day venereal syphilis was already known and had been described under several different names before or after the Europeans' arrival in America, historians have produced the kind of contradictory conclusions that serve only to keep [the controversy] alive'.[59] This is, in other words, part of the very process of historical construction which has formed the image of syphilis and of which the earlier part is the subject of this book.

Secondly, as a result of the development of molecular biology after the Second World War, the question of the origin of venereal syphilis and the germ responsible for it has increasingly been framed within the broad context of the biological and economic history of all human treponematoses by integrating results provided by palaeopathology and historical epidemiology. Attractive and promising as some resulting hypotheses are, no definitive conclusions have yet been reached.[60]

Thus the question of whether venereal disease is pre- or post-Columbian itself has a history, going back to the beginning of the sixteenth century. It may one day be possible to answer it, if we are thinking in terms of syphilis and its pathogen. But with present evidence it is a tired as well as an old question and this book is not an attempt to answer it. But we do not intend here to discredit other approaches. We are not seeking to deny that the modern trepanome, or some very close ancestor of it, was in Europe in 1494 or even before. It might even be possible to reconstruct some of its physical history by the techniques of palaeopathology, and conceivably in the future to identify the pathogen in human remains by methods of molecular genetics. But that would be material for another book.

Conclusion

We have seen, then, that knowledge in the past – including knowledge of the pox – was contingent upon other knowledge, whether pre- or post-germ theory. It is a historical truism to insist that 'knowledge' was relative, to accept that what a person knew was knowledge, through the very fact that he or she knew it, irrespective of whether we think that it was true or not. Few historians would now want to persist with the image of fifteenth- and sixteenth-century physicians struggling against ignorance and confusion in their search for truth and health, but failing. But in medical history it is often difficult to live up to the truism in practice for the temptation to look for what was 'really' the case (like the existence of a pathogen) is great. We have tried to resist this temptation and to tell a story of a construction of the image of pox beginning in the fifteenth and sixteenth centuries as a result of contemporary concerns. Looking at the subject in this way, we can even see that often the doctor's knowledge of the French Disease made him *successful*. The success of the doctor depended on the expectations of the patient and of those in whose interest it was that the doctor should continue to practise. Expectations are cultural things too, and part of the doctor's job was to make sure that they were fulfilled. The doctor knew, for example, that expensive remedies worked better than cheap ones, simply because they were expensive; and that princes would be angered by the offer of anything but the priceless. They knew that the inevitability of a disease could be attributed to astrological causes, in the face of which medicine could only prevent things from becoming worse. They knew that the patient was often to blame, by having the wrong style of life, by promiscuity, by disobeying the doctor and above all by going to the wrong kind of practitioner, the empiric. It was the doctor's job to make sure that the patient also knew this so that he shared that part of the doctor's knowledge which confirmed the patient's expectations.

Since the historian is concerned largely with words we must be careful about the kind of assumptions we make (and without which history would be impossible). In dealing historically with words we are in effect making a kind of translation, from the past to the present. Everybody familiar with a second language recognises the dangers of facile translation. Some words simply do not have an adequate partner in the other language. It is easy to see that there are cultural reasons for this. The same difficulty of translation is evident in translating from the culture of the past.

In translating anatomical terms for example we recognise that, while there are simple terms meaning 'nose' or 'toe' in our language and, say, Latin, terms used for 'ventricle' or 'valve' or even something so general as 'flesh' implied something very different to people in the past in terms of physical delimitation and, even more important, of function. The difficulties of translating names of disease entities is even greater. Sometimes the name changes, so that if we are looking at the history of tuberculosis we soon have to start using 'scrophula' instead. But scrophula meant a lot of things that tuberculosis does not; and further back still even scrophula disappears.[61] This loss of the name means that, to keep the entity of the disease as we search historically, we have to rely on descriptions of it. But these too slide through our fingers. Many early descriptions of the French Disease are brief to the point of obscurity. Others could equally well apply to other diseases. Where more detailed descriptions survive they rarely coincide with modern descriptions. To insist on the modern identity of a disease in the past, without a name or a description, would be like the famous owner of a hammer who thought it was the same hammer despite having replaced the head once and the handle twice.

The dangers of historical mistranslation are evident in the practice of historians. Most of them use the term 'syphilis' for the disease we deal with in the present book. This is the name given by the Italian humanist and physician Girolamo Fracastoro in 1530 to the disease suffered by the hero of his poem. It was not a term that became popular before the late eighteenth century; and ironically it was the germ theory itself that showed that 'syphilis' was not a useful historical term, for it demonstrated that traditional 'syphilis' was a group of diseases. One of them was given the name 'venereal syphilis'. Even when historians have distinguished between the diseases of the group they have not agreed on their respective prevalence in the past. The standing of this modern category is such that it has enabled those who use it to build a history for it; that is, to diagnose retrospectively and apply the term 'syphilis' to what most fifteenth- and sixteenth-century Europeans called the French Disease (*Morbus Gallicus*). Even when the term 'venereal disease' (*lues venerea*) began to replace the older term in the later sixteenth century and when the collective term *morbi venerei* dominated in the eighteenth century, historians have assumed an underlying entity of venereal syphilis. Moreover, those historians who have claimed that the disease goes back in time in Europe to before Columbus' return from the New World, have insisted on identifying the disease with earlier descriptions of genital and skin conditions taken from medical authorities both within and without Europe.

Seeing knowledge in the past as contingent, and looking for mechanisms that direct perception and construction of a disease, we are departing from the traditional practice of historians and commentators who have striven to grasp the quiddity or essence of the French Disease. The doctors hoped to distil some essence of the disease from the accumulated experience of all those who had written on it. The same is true of the writers of the time, whose efforts were concentrated on understanding the disease the better to treat it. The post-germ-theory doctors looked for a historical manifestation of a quiddity they now knew about. They too were constructing the disease in the image of their culture.

Our interest is in how the quiddity arose from the society and culture of the time. We have accordingly given attention to circumstances in which knowledge of the disease was built up. Sometimes this was a formal institution, like a medical faculty within a university, with detailed rules about how knowledge was obtained and verified, whether by lecture, reading or disputations. Sometimes the institution was less formal but more powerful, like the court of a pope, emperor or prince. Here knowledge might be governed by the interests or even the suffering of the patron. It mattered indeed who was ill and whether the concern of those with political power was restoration of health or removal of disgusting people from the streets. It mattered that the disease was associated with promiscuous sexual activity, and in some cases knowledge about the disease was accordingly suppressed. The hospital was another institution that to some extent governed the kind of knowledge that was generated inside it, for it was here that the physician could see many cases together and here too that he was able to conduct post-mortem examination by dissection. What he expected to find was governed by his largely theoretical knowledge of the way the disease took hold of the body, and this in turn depended on his education and other cultural circumstances. Knowledge was also generated in the city or town, where those in power had to judge between the theories of the doctors and experience of contagion. Knowledge of the disease included how it could be cured or prevented and it reflected the differences between people and institutions that the answer might be mercury, guaiac wood or avoiding prostitutes. Knowledge of the disease also included why God had sent it. Perhaps it was a direct punishment, or to test one's faith. But perhaps God (as He often did) had put a simple remedy close to the origin of the disease so that physicians or the patients themselves could experience God's mercy at the same time as His anger. It was cultural forces like this that made one remedy sometimes preferable to another; and it was a matter of culture that the merchants attempted to monopolise the trade in remedies, that some doctors preferred Greek medical authorities and others Arabic, that in some places religious confraternities were formed to bring help to the sick and that in others poems were written about the disease.

Chapter Two

The Arrival of the French Disease in Renaissance Italy: initial impact and lay reactions

Introduction

The appearance of Mal Francese in Italy in 1496 was one of a series of crises which afflicted the peninsula in the last decade of the fifteenth century. The association of this disease with the French points to contemporary reactions to the disruption caused by the invasion of Charles VIII in 1494. The political status quo was challenged as many city-states divided in their allegiance between those who sought to oppose and those who welcomed the French troops. This in turn helped to create an atmosphere of uncertainty which fuelled the millenarian visions of a figure such as Girolamo Savonarola, whose very success depended on the expectations and fears aroused by the proximity of the end of the century.

Contemporary chroniclers were only too anxious to record any further events which might be interpreted as apocalyptic with the approach of the third half-millennium since the birth of Christ.[1] There were natural disasters in the form of floods, earthquakes, pestilences and famines and then the invasion of King Charles VIII of France in 1494. These sources, and especially those of north and central Italy, stressed as especially dramatic the months after October 1494, when the French army retreated.[2] During the autumn and winter of 1495–6 weather conditions were very severe all over Italy. The combination of intense cold, severe snowstorms and sudden temperature changes provoked serious flooding when many of the largest rivers burst their banks. In some places there were also severe earthquakes. These natural disasters in a land already under the strain of war made food scarce and led to serious dearth followed by an outbreak of many pestilential diseases.[3] The outcome of these circumstances was described dramatically by the Florentine physician Antonio Benivieni:

> During the year 1496 almost all Italy was stricken with such widespread and enormous hunger that everywhere many people died in the streets and public squares, and many others fell prey to various diseases as a result of having

consumed bad and unhealthy food. . . . We also saw women who passed away along with, and because of, the infected children they nursed.[4]

Even if descriptions of people dying in the streets is a familiar topos of accounts of food shortage, the situation was genuinely serious for the city authorities. Florence was flooded in this period with large numbers of hungry *contadini* and food supplies did run very low.[5] Furthermore, while there was also nothing new in contemporary accounts of the link between war and disease, what was new in the 1490s was the kind of disease that followed the war. Throughout 1496 local sources began to record a disease that most Italians perceived as new, loathsome and incurable. The laity called it Mal Francese, or, in Latin, *Morbus Gallicus* – a designation that most university physicians disliked as inappropriate. At all events, both groups agreed that it had been brought to Italy by the French invaders.[6]

Reactions to the appearance of the French Disease must also be seen within the social and economic context. This was particularly true of its impact on the poorer classes, who, as during any epidemic, were the worst affected. The 1490s represented one of the lowest points in fifteenth-century standards of living. The series of bad harvests combined with growing demand from an expanding population had led to a shortage of resources, exacerbated by the disruption of local commerce caused by the French invasion. As if this was not bad enough, trade between states was further interrupted by the appearance of plague in many parts of Italy. All these factors provide the background to the hardening of official attitudes towards the poor from the late fifteenth century.[7] These new policies have been seen as stemming partly at least from the impact of plague; but, as we shall see, another important contributory factor was the impact of Mal Francese.

Chronicles and Mal Francese in the 1490s

In contrast to later chapters on the medical disputes about the nature of the pox, this chapter looks at the reactions of non-medical men to the French Disease. This will involve initially examining how the laity viewed the nature of this disease, and then in later chapters how this informed the policies which were put into practice both by city governments and by Church-inspired charitable foundations, most important of which were confraternities and hospitals.

The main sources in this first section on the 1490s are chronicles written in Italy at the time of the first appearance of the French Disease. It is important to determine the date when a particular commentator was writing in order to distinguish the initial as opposed to later reactions to this disease. Some contemporary chroniclers sat down to describe these events only after many years, and others, with hindsight, later changed earlier passages to incorporate more up-to-date information.[8] Thus the famous passage on Mal Francese in Francesco Guicciardini's *Storia d'Italia* is often cited when discussing how contemporaries first viewed the appearance of the disease,[9] despite the fact that Guicciardini was only ten at the time of the invasion of Charles VIII. Moreover because he wrote from the vantage point of the late 1530s he was able to provide a historical overview of the development of the pox.[10]

The best collection of the earliest Italian non-medical sources to deal with Mal Francese is still the article of 1884 by that tireless nineteenth-century physician-turned-medical-historian Alfonso Corradi.[11] Some of the sources consulted by Corradi have been published over the past hundred years; others still remain in manuscript. With the addition of a few obvious omissions, his collection will form our point of departure to examine contemporary reactions to the pox in order to understand better the non-medical perspective.[12]

A number of general points emerge from an examination of this collection, which although not complete probably includes most of the chronicles which record contemporary reactions to Mal Francese in late fifteenth- and early sixteenth-century Italy. In the first place the vast majority come from northern and central Italy. This is perhaps hardly surprising given that this was the most highly urbanised part of the peninsula, although in contrast to the impression given by most historians it should be emphasised that not every contemporary writer made a point of commenting on the appearance of Mal Francese. It is significant that, when one examines the geographical origins of those chroniclers who provide the most detailed descriptions of reactions to the impact of the French Disease, there is a surprisingly close correlation with the subsequent foundation of the specialised Incurabili hospitals or at least the establishment of specialised wards within general hospitals to treat this ailment. This may be sheer coincidence, but it may also have reflected a strong local perception of the necessity to deal with the disease, which in turn provided the incentive to found a specialised centre for treatment. Ferrara, which will be examined in more detail in Chapter Three, is a case in point. Two Ferrarese chroniclers writing in the 1490s discussed the appearance of Mal Francese in some detail (Bernardino Zambotti and an anonymous diarist),[13] and a confraternity dedicated to St Job, the patron saint of pox sufferers, was set up in May 1499. We know that from at least 1502 the company saw as one of its main missions the establishment of a hospital 'in which to treat those infected with the Morbo Gallico'. However, there is no evidence that the hospital was actively in operation before 1525.[14]

As we shall see, there were two main reasons why Ferrara cannot be taken as an entirely representative city in its reactions to Mal Francese. First, the members of the ruling Este family were themselves infected with the disease and were therefore particularly interested in the pox.[15] Secondly, an important public debate took place in Ferrara under their patronage among the medical profession concerning the nature and origins of Mal Francese. But Ferrara was not the only centre where such debates occurred in Italy. Bologna saw the same phenomenon, this time apparently under the auspices of the university. It can be no coincidence that this publicity and interest led no fewer than four contemporary Bolognese chroniclers to mention the appearance of the disease, and yet another, the Augustinian friar Cherubino Ghirardacci, to record the event when he was writing the annals of his city as late as 1570.[16] Once again local interest led to local action. The existing general Spedale di S. Maria dei Guarini was changed into a hospital specialising in the treatment of our disease and rededicated to San Giobbe. This took place as early as about 1500 and was hence one of the first of its type to be established in the peninsula.[17]

Many other contemporary chroniclers who commented on the appearance of Mal Francese came from cities which later set up specialised hospitals to treat this disease. These include Brescia, Venice, Modena and Florence in northern–central Italy and Rome in the south.[18] Once again this may be a coincidence. Other cities, including Como, Cremona, Foligno and Ravenna in the north, and Orvieto, Perugia and Siena in the centre, had chroniclers who recorded the arrival of Mal Francese, but here there were no local initiatives to establish separate Incurabili hospitals.[19] This may not mean very much; work on the records of many Italian hospital archives remains in its infancy. Further research may reveal that specialised wards were set aside for looking after the *mal franciosati* and that there was therefore a much wider institutional reaction than has been concluded by historians who have tended to concentrate on the Incurabili hospitals (see below). An important case in point is that of Milan. We know that the duke, Lodovico Sforza, was obviously concerned about the new epidemic from its first appearance. In 1495 he received a special report on Mal Francese from the physician Nicolò Squillaci when he was on a diplomatic mission to the Spanish court. Then we learn that by 1508 – and probably well before – the Spedale del Brolo in Milan had been designated as the main hospital for the treatment of Mal Francese.[20] This is not an event which appears in the majority of surveys of the Incurabili hospitals in Italy. Although the Brolo was fulfilling this role in practice, it had not been established by a Company of Divine Love, which was the way the majority of these hospitals came into being and why they have therefore attracted most historical attention.

The first chroniclers to record the appearance of Mal Francese came from a variety of backgrounds and included a ducal officer of supplies, a notary, two apothecaries, a papal secretary and two patricians.[21] Each of these men obviously had a different perspective and motivation in writing his account of the events of their day, but even so they shared much in their descriptions of the arrival and impact of the disease. Their accounts are differentiated by the amount of detail they provided, which in turn depended on their reasons for writing. Thus the civic chronicler tended to record information concerning events which glorified his city. In the case of Bologna, for example, the chroniclers were able to show that the threat of Mal Francese had been dealt with successfully by the establishment of an Incurabili hospital.[22] There are also examples of more personal accounts, as in the case of the daily diary of the Florentine apothecary Luca Landucci. He recorded the arrival and impact of the disease with a few examples of people who had contracted it.[23] But most detailed was the man with a very personal interest in Mal Francese, the Orvietan canon Ser Tommaso di Silvestro, who actually contracted the disease himself.[24]

Mal Francese as a New Disease

Virtually all of these chroniclers recorded the first appearance of pox as one of the main events of 1495–6. The majority described it as a new disease, thus coming down quite firmly, as we shall see in Chapter Four, on the revisionist medical side of the Ferrarese and Bolognese debates concerning its novelty. Indeed chroniclers from both these cities declared that it was 'unknown to any doctor'.[25] From the very beginning the disease was associated with the French and its most common name was therefore Mal Francese or Mal Francioso, on the grounds that the French army was responsible for bringing this, among other calamities, to Italy. For example, the two Florentines, Landucci and the patrician Parenti, recorded that the disease was known as 'French boils' (*bolle franciose*) or the 'French itch' (*rogna franciosa*).[26] Later a more geographically specific name also came into usage: 'Mal Napolitano' or 'Mal de Naples'. On the one hand, this was encouraged by the French, who disliked the association of the disease with themselves. On the other hand, this echoed another current belief, that the disease had first been brought to Italy from Spain, through the long-standing political and commercial connections between the Spanish Crown and the Kingdom of Naples. In fact, the Roman chronicler Sigismondo dei Conti recounted that the specific way Mal Francese was transmitted was by the Jews, who had been driven out of Spain by King Ferdinand and collected together in Naples. Conveniently this also provided for Sigismondo what sounded like Biblical authority for his belief; he saw a parallel between the arrival of pox in Italy with the introduction of leprosy by the Jews when they were driven out of Egypt.[27] This theme, as we have seen in the previous chapter, was then taken up and developed by Gruner in the late eighteenth century.

　　If the motivation behind assigning these labels was to blame your enemy for your misfortunes, the search for the origins of the disease went further. The contemporary Genoese chronicler Senarega recorded, for example, that 'many say it came from Ethiopia'.[28] The 'Indies' as a source of Mal Francese was underlined by, among others, Cirillo Bernardino Aquilano and Francesco Guicciardini in his *Storia d'Italia*, written between 1537 and 1540, in which he blamed the Indians for having infected the Europeans, thus allowing him to downplay the influence of the French.[29] However, this is not a subject which we can discuss in detail here; our concern is principally with examining reactions to the disease once it had become epidemic in Europe.[30]

Even if the chroniclers regarded Mal Francese as new, some also attempted to explain it in relation to existing diseases. The Bolognese Fileno dalle Tuatte associated it with leprosy, the 'lebra di San Job', and the Roman chronicler Sigismondo dei Conti, as we have seen, likened the introduction of Mal Francese to Naples to the introduction of leprosy to Spain. However, in both cases they were clearly using leprosy as an analogy rather than suggesting they were the same disease. For Dalle Tuatte the symptoms of the two illnesses had something in common, given that both led to the destruction of tissue and even bone.[31] Two other chroniclers, the Roman Raffaello da Volterra and the Genoese Senarega, recorded another contemporary opinion, that it was associated with *elephantiasis*.[32] But the doubts within the medical profession concerning the novelty of Mal Francese were not reflected among our chroniclers, even in the diaries of the two apothecaries, Jacopino de' Bianchi of Modena and Luca Landucci of Florence.[33]

The reasons why some physicians wished to make the association with an existing disease were both theoretical and practical. As we shall see in Chapter Four, one school of academics would not believe that any disease could appear which was not described within the canon of accepted medical belief, namely within the writings of Galen and Hippocrates. This was not simply professional obduracy. It had implications for treatment, given that in describing the disease the ancients would then provide a clear idea of the symptoms and therefore a guide to the best remedies. These two subjects will be examined here through the eyes of our lay chroniclers in the following sections.

Symptoms

The descriptions of the symptoms of Mal Francese recorded by chroniclers writing in the 1490s or early 1500s have much in common, but they are not all the same. For, as the Orvietan canon Ser Tommaso di Silvestro remarked, 'The said sickness appears in different ways: there is he who is with pains in his arms and in the legs, he with terrible sores with pains, and he who has sores without pains and he who has pains without sores.'[34] This variety underlines the need to avoid adopting too rigid a picture of the disease, which clearly changed over the years, and to remember that Mal Francese may also have been used on occasions as a catch-all term to denote a wide collection of symptoms.

Certain symptoms were mentioned by the majority of chroniclers. The first were the pains, which usually attacked the joints and sometimes were associated with fevers. The papal secretary, Sigismondo dei Conti da Foligno, tells us that sometimes the pain was so intense that patients 'screamed day and night without respite, envying the dead themselves'.[35] Francesco Matarazzo from Perugia recorded that some were driven to suicide: 'many men through desperation went to drown themselves in the river'.[36] But more noteworthy to the observer were the terrible sores and swellings, known variously as *bolle*, *brozole* and *buboni*. They spread all over the body, leaving scabs which turned from red to black.

As if these symptoms were not bad enough, as the sickness progressed it began to destroy the body. The Bianchina chronicler of Bologna talks of it having 'eaten [away] the nose and half the face', while Sigismondo dei Conti says that these pustules and ulcers 'gnawed away as far as the marrow'.[37] Matarazzo talks too about the body rotting inside. Indeed one Perugian merchant is supposed to have been so 'consumed by this disease between the thigh and torso such that it was possible to see everything he had inside his body and there was such a great hole that it would have been possible to introduce an "ancrestana" inside'.[38]

Finally, people in this condition clearly became unbearable to encounter in the streets because, as Piero di Marco Parenti remarks of those in Florence, 'this putrefaction stank and [it was] a most awful filth'.[39] Here we have a reference to the relationship between disease and poverty and the more general preconditions for epidemics. For putrefaction and rotting material – whether waste matter or human flesh – were seen as producing a stink which in itself could generate disease. But it was further believed that if the poor were reduced to a very inadequate diet during periods of shortage this could actually lead to the putrefaction of their humours, which in turn led to putrefaction of the air when exhaled and this could lead to an epidemic.[40]

These represented the worst cases; not everybody appears to have been so badly affected. Ser Tommaso di Silvestro has left his own personal account of what it was like to suffer from a somewhat lighter version of Mal Francese. He first began to suffer the symptoms at Christmas 1496 when he felt 'certain pains in his knees' and then in January 'went into a great decline' and felt 'certain pains on the top of the left shoulder and in the kidneys and buttocks'. These symptoms lasted until May when they apparently disappeared, only to recur again a year later.[41] In April 1498 he began to feel pains in his penis and gradually the sickness worsened daily:

> And all my head became covered with blemishes [*bruscialime*] or scabs, and the pains appeared in my right and left arms . . . from the shoulder to the joint with the hand, the bones ached so that I could never find rest. And then my right knee ached, and I became covered with boils, all over my front and back, *adeo* that Corpus Christi, I received treatment and medicines and blood-letting, and then they anointed me for the pains and for the boils that I had. And Frate Olivetano who lived at Benano treated me. I remained six days continuously in bed, and at the end of the seventh . . . that was the last day of June, I was

washed with a bath of wine and many herbs, such as *amaro*, rue, mint, *trasmerino*, *lionoro*, sage and other herbs. And on Sunday I began to go outside the house, that is on the first day of July. Item, I was left with a very bad mouth, that lasted for thirty-six days so that I could hardly eat cooked bread, nor anything else; and on the fourteenth day the pain in the arm and the sores went away. My mouth remained very bad and on the 22nd of July I had a great flux which lasted . . . days, from which I could have died. And then from the month of November very terrible pains began to recur in my leg.[42]

As far as we know, this is the earliest and most detailed account of the course of Mal Francese in Italy drawn from the personal experience of a non-medical man. In common with descriptions of other contemporary chroniclers, Ser Tommaso experienced pains in his joints and boils and scabs all over his body. But, as other commentators were to mention only later in the sixteenth century, these torments were not continuous; patients had periods of remission. However, what Ser Tommaso fails to make explicit is whether he made a complete recovery from his disease. His silence on the matter suggests that he did get better; the chronicle continued for another fifteen years, but he failed to mention his symptoms again. Therefore they probably ceased, especially given his interest in sickness evident in his punctilious accounts of the causes of death of virtually everybody who died in Orvieto in the period covered by the diary.

Ser Tommaso's account of his experience of Mal Francese raises a number of important points. In particular, how far his contemporaries in late fifteenth- and early sixteenth-century Italy regarded the disease as curable or incurable and therefore whether or not they perceived its treatment as efficacious. This leads one to the highly problematic question of whether it is possible to measure the mortality of pox in its initial epidemic form, given the paucity of reliable and continuous causes of death in this period.

Curable or Incurable?

Chroniclers within the first ten years of the appearance of Mal Francese were divided in their opinions about whether or not the disease was curable. Even those writing at the same time in the same city failed to agree: this was the case in both Bologna and Ferrara, the locations of the debates in the medical world about the nature of Mal Francese. In Bologna Gaspare Nadi and Fileno dalle Tuatte stated that few had died and that for those who fell ill it 'lasted for one year or a year and a half'.[43] Friano degli Ubaldini and the anonymous 'Cronica Bianchina' stated that 'few were cured from it'.[44] To the latter it was, moreover, 'quasi inchurabile', an opinion shared by the Ferrarese notary Bernardino Zambotti.[45]

These contradictions could be repeated, but how can they be explained?

There is probably a range of reasons. In the first place it may have depended on whether the chronicle remained unaltered after the initial draft or was later updated. If it was changed this might explain the differences between, for example, the two Bolognese chroniclers, Gaspare Nadi who died in 1504 and Friano degli Ubaldini who died in 1513.[46] The former said that those who contracted Mal Francese 'stavano assae a guarire' and the latter recorded that 'the majority of the people [with Mal Francese] die in the long term'.[47] The answer may also lie in the personal circumstances of the writer and his experience of either knowing somebody with Mal Francese or having been annoyed by the sight of the poor sick on the streets of his city.

It may very well be that Mal Francese had a differential impact on different strata of society. Those, like the majority of our chroniclers, who came from a similar social background would have received better care, as we have seen in the case of Ser Tommaso di Silvestro. Indeed this may explain the apparent contradiction in his *Diario*. On the one hand, he described Mal Francese as 'almost incurable', yet he himself apparently recovered for, as he said, 'he who did not die of this illness remained sick [for] one, two, three and four years'.[48] The poor, on the other hand, in contrast to the more affluent, would have been more likely to have languished without proper care and even to have died from other complications. For example, Ser Tommaso cites the case of a certain Giuliano, brother of Bruscho, who 'had had the Mal Francese for a good four years, and was almost cured . . . [when] he went outside the district [and] got heated and then cooled [*se rescaldo e refredo*] and he died of that'.[49] The question, of course, arises of whether Giuliano would have died had he not left Orvieto and therefore whether the treatment he was receiving was efficacious.

Treatment of Mal Francese

The vast majority of the earliest chronicles were sceptical of the medical profession's ability to treat the disease satisfactorily. Fileno dalle Tuatte from Bologna stated quite categorically that 'nobody has found doctors who know how to provide a remedy', and Landucci from his point of view as a supplier to physicians recorded that 'one cannot find medicines'.[50] The papal secretary, Sigismondo dei Conti da Foligno, who must have been able to observe closely the effects of Mal Francese on the papal court in general and on his employer Pope Julius II in particular, is even more specific: 'no remedies, no ointments, nor other drugs of physicians and of doctors [have any effect on Mal Francese]'.[51] And that was from the circle of men able to afford to pay for the most up-to-date remedies and physicians, who included many of the leading practitioners of the day, such as, for example, Gaspar Torrella and Pere Pintor.

Within the medical profession many admitted the intractability of the disease. The papal physician Gaspar Torrella reported that at the beginning Mal Francese was seen as incurable by his colleagues, although he himself disagreed. Furthermore, the 1497 Ferrara disputants did not manage to agree about its nature or treatment. But Jacopo Cattaneo of Genoa noted that if it was treated early then it could be more easily cured and vice versa; all realised it could relapse easily.[52]

None of these views stopped a wide variety of empirics and physicians from offering courses of treatment and their patients from seeking a cure. We have seen that a certain friar in Orvieto treated Ser Tommaso, who claimed it was successful. This included blood-letting, ointments and baths of wine and herbs. These did him some good for apparently the day after the bath he was well enough to leave the house.[53] Indeed empirics offered a variety of remedies which were more or less successful. In nearby Perugia, Francesco Matarazzo recorded the arrival of a Spaniard who prescribed a treatment combining 'a certain unction' with heat, which after three to four days 'cured' the sick. His success, both medical and financial, was immediate, but he left town quickly because his patients soon grew worse again. He was followed by two 'doctors' who employed a similar recipe. They met with little enthusiasm from the Perugians. Although Matarazzo recorded that this was attributable to the cynicism of his fellow citizens, a subtext is the chronicler's own scepticism about their training. As a university professor himself, he regarded them as not properly trained since they did not wear the insignia of the doctorate. Another treatment was then introduced by a local merchant who was close to death from Mal Francese. His system involved purgation and a recipe including mercury, which apparently 'cured' him.[54]

Although we shall leave to a later chapter (Chaper Six) a detailed discussion of medical theories about the nature and treatment of Mal Francese, it is nevertheless necessary to outline very briefly at this stage the earliest methods of treatment recommended by physicians in order to understand better the remarks on the subject by the chroniclers writing within the first few years of the start of the epidemic.

The main aim in all treatment was to remove the morbid matter from the body of the patient, for this was regarded as the main cause of the disease. There were, as we have seen in the few cases cited above, a series of procedures recommended by physicians. Some of these methods were illustrated in a series of remarkable watercolours, painted by an anonymous artist in the mid-sixteenth century.[55]

The first procedure can be seen in Plate 2.1, which shows the letting of blood by a surgeon, as had been performed on Ser Tommaso in Orvieto. The patient is shown with a ligature above the elbow and his left arm, head and legs in bandages, suggesting probably a man in the more advanced stages of Mal Francese. The aim of this procedure was to remove directly from the humour the corrupt or morbid matter, the same principle which was behind purgation, the next stage in the treatment.

Plate 2.1 'The letting of blood during the treatment of Mal Francese' in mid-sixteenth-century Italy

Elimination of corruption from within the sick man or woman would also have been behind their bathing in various substances with medicinal properties, as in the case of Ser Tommaso's bath of wine and herbs. Another alternative employed was olive oil; either this was used in a hot bath or the patient was fully immersed, as was recorded in Venice in 1498. In September of that year the Sanità, or Health Board, prohibited the resale of 'wretched oils and of a very bad quality in which people who had or have Mal Francese have been immersed, for as a result of these bodies being in these said oils there has been found much filth, scabs and filth and dirt'.[56] Heat was regarded, however, as particularly efficacious in the elimination of corrupt matter. This explains the popularity of the so-called 'dry stove', an enclosed space, such as a large barrel, which could be easily heated and in which the patient was placed to sweat for as long as he could endure the heat.

Fire was another important element used in the treatment of Mal Francese, as can be seen in Plates 2.2 and 2.3. The first is a vivid picture of a young man yelling in agony as a particularly intractable sore is removed from his foot through cauterisation. Plate 2.3 shows instead the patient seated close to a fire in order to induce sweating. But the heat was also probably designed to help the ready absorption of a mercury unguent which would have been placed on the sores caused by Mal Francese.

Plate 2.2 'The removal of a Mal Francese sore through cauterisation'

Plate 2.3 'The sweating of a Mal Francese patient'

Indeed, as we have seen, the main treatment in Perugia which had allegedly led to good results was the use of unguents containing mercury. Both
Torrella and Pintor recommended a course of between five and thirty days
with these mercury ointments. The patient was normally placed in a heated
room to encourage the sweating out of morbid matter. In 1512, as we shall
see in more detail in the next chapter, it was this treatment which was
probably prescribed for Francesco Gonzaga by a number of physicians, including a certain Ferrarese doctor, who 'had placed on the sores certain things
which had led to a great burning sensation'.[57] This treatment had unfortunate
side effects in the shape of ulcers in the mouth, of which our Orvietan canon
complained, as did Francesco Gonzaga.[58]

Despite the claims of some doctors that they had considerable success in
treating patients – Maestro Batista da Vercelli, who offered his services to
Gonzaga in 1514, said he had cured 400 people in Florence[59] – we have seen
that this was no guarantee that the Mal Francese did not return after a period
of remission and then finally kill the patient. Evidently, though, the length of
time a pox-sufferer survived depended to a large degree on his social standing.
Francesco Gonzaga or even Ser Tommaso di Silvestro clearly received better
treatment than the poor, whose plight might mean they were unable to work,
even lose their lodgings and be forced to beg and live on the streets. We
know nothing about what caused the death of the Orvietan canon, although
he was still in good health twenty years after he had contracted Mal Francese.
The survival time of others higher up the social scale varied considerably. For
example, Francesco Gonzaga died of the disease in 1519, twenty-three years
after the initial symptoms showed themselves. While Cardinal Francesco
Soderini was rumoured to be suffering from venereal disease in 1510, he died
fourteen years later 'because he is old'.[60]

Mortality

The differential social impact of Mal Francese may also help to explain the
curious contradictions when our chroniclers talk about mortality.[61] It consequently remains difficult to assess how many died from this disease in late
fifteenth- and early sixteenth-century Italy, especially among the poor. Even
when contemporaries did suggest that mortality was high they tended to do
so in the most general terms, as in Ser Tommaso's remark, 'in every city and
region, it is said, there were many sick people and many died of it'.[62] He is,
then, citing other people's opinions rather than his own, even though he was
assiduous in making a note of the cause of death of many people who died
in Orvieto in this period. It is not clear from the *Diario* whether every death
was recorded, although in 1497 he did note all deaths between 16 July and 17
October during a plague epidemic.[63] In fact, his diary, which is the only
surviving source from which we can judge the level of mortality caused by

Mal Francese in Orvieto, suggests that very few people are actually recorded as having died specifically from this disease. During the four years from the beginning of January 1497, when he first mentions it, until the end of 1500 only thirteen people were buried in Orvieto with a diagnosis of Mal Francese. This was a fraction of those who were diagnosed as having died from plague in the same period.

Although Ser Tommaso may not have recorded all those who died of Mal Francese during these years and not everybody who eventually succumbed to the disease may have been diagnosed as such, it is at the very least interesting that all these people were adults, as appears to have been the case according to the early sixteenth-century mortality records of the city of Milan.[64] Furthermore, only three of the ten deaths were female. The males were all older men, with the exception of Cesare, son of Eusebio dell'Avedute, described as 'a gallant young man' of about twenty-two years old, who had been sick from Mal Francese for about eighteen months with terrible sores all over his face, back and venereal area.[65]

The contrast between the number who died from what are normally regarded as two of the major epidemics in this period raises some very interesting questions. Can it be that much of the recorded reaction was simply literary hype, and that, as Ann Carmichael has suggested, mortality from Mal Francese increased significantly only after 1500?[66] Or is it more complicated? A major problem may have been posed by the very novelty of the disease; physicians viewing it for the first time may not have recognised the symptoms, and therefore the figures cited by Ser Francesco were simply an underestimate of the real mortality in Orvieto. The comparison with plague is also instructive, but we should remember that perhaps we are not comparing like with like. Plague often had a very sudden and dramatic impact on a population because it visited an area for a limited period, during which a large number of people could die from its effects. The pox, on the other hand, had a much longer time-fuse.

All these earliest chroniclers, whether they believed that Mal Francese could or could not be cured, stressed that patients suffered over a long period. For example, those like Friano degli Ubaldini, who thought that the disease was fatal, stressed that 'the majority of people died after a long time'.[67] In these circumstances most chronicles cease to be a useful source in assessing mortality since they did not have a long-term perspective of the effects on patients of such chronic diseases. This is why Ser Tommaso's evidence, though impressionistic, is valuable, given that he had a particular interest with his own personal experience of Mal Francese. It is hoped that a more systematic account will emerge with the publication of further research on sources such as the Milanese city burial registers, which contain detailed causes of death.[68]

The vast majority of chroniclers failed to return to the subject of the French Disease after they had recorded its initial impact in 1496 and were not concerned to provide more accurate information than was based on hearsay. There was no dramatic new wave of infection as with plague, producing large numbers of new deaths. Instead it rumbled on and caused a long-term problem for the poor in particular and the authorities in general.

Conclusion: the lack of an official response

It was in fact the chronic nature of this epidemic which appears to have left Italian city authorities somewhat confused over what course of action to adopt in the face of this new threat. The problem was that, unlike plague, it did not kill off its victims rapidly. Instead those afflicted by the disease, and especially the very poor, remained to clutter up the streets and molest passers-by. This confusion is attested by the Bolognese chronicler Friano degli Ubaldini, who must have expressed a general feeling when he characterised Mal Francese as 'strange and horrible'. The descriptions of the symptoms cited above certainly reflect the chroniclers' horror and disgust at the disfiguring effects of the disease. In time, as they came to discover, this created a problem for public health, especially as the disease apparently affected substantial numbers of people, leaving them 'tutti manzati per la persona', as Friano so graphically puts it.[69]

Official initiatives by communal and princely governments within the first few years of the appearance of Mal Francese were lacking, despite the suggestions of even the papal physician Gaspar Torrella, who wrote in 1500 that:

> Leaders like the Pope, the Emperor, kings and other lords should send matrons to investigate the disease, especially among prostitutes who, if they be found to be infected, should be confined to a place designated for this purpose by the community or the lord, and treated by a physician or surgeon paid to do so.[70]

Some historians writing about the French Disease in this period have taken this reference to prostitutes to mean that from the very beginning all contemporaries made the assumption that this was an exclusively venereal disease.[71] Italian society in this period is represented as being particularly immoral and licentious, a situation largely caused, so they argue, by the large numbers of prostitutes assumed to have thronged major cities such as Rome and Venice. This theme would seem to be further corroborated by the remarks of contemporary chroniclers. Thus Giovanni Portoveneri of Pisa stated quite categorically that 'it is spread through having sex with women who have these sicknesses, and especially with prostitutes',[72] or the Venetian Marin Sanudo's comment: 'And this sickness begins first in the area of the genitals; and in coitus it is contagious, otherwise not.'[73] Furthermore a whole genre of popular literature emerged in this period which took a moralistic line, linking

Mal Francese with sex and prostitution, as Francesco Matarazzo records: 'Songs, stories and moral sonnets were made about this disease.'[74]

But sexual activity was never regarded as the exclusive method of transmission of *Morbus Gallicus*, especially during the first decade of its appearance. Only half of the sixteen earliest chroniclers mentioned the association between sexual activity and catching Mal Francese. The Orvietan canon Ser Tommaso di Silvestro, perhaps for obvious reasons, made no comment about how either he or his fellow Orvietans contracted the disease, merely recording that he had been 'infected' the year that the French troops passed by Orvieto on their way to Naples.[75] As we shall see in Chapter Six, a number of cardinals were also infected by the disease. However, it is some reflection of the wider influence of the debates in Bologna and Ferrara that most of the contemporary chroniclers of these two cities linked coitus and the disease. The Bolognese Bianchina chronicler states quite categorically, 'And the majority catch it through coitus.' But it is significant that he left his options open – 'the majority catch it' – suggesting that there were also other forms of transmission. Indeed his co-citizen Friano degli Ubaldini was prepared to entertain an even broader range of possibilities: 'it is passed on . . . through eating and through drinking and through sexual relations'.[76]

Even if some chroniclers such as Sanudo make definitive statements about the contagious nature of the disease, we should be cautious in interpreting contemporary concepts of contagion. Thus for Girolamo Fracastoro, whose name is now associated closely with the 'contagion theory' of Mal Francese in the sixteenth century, it was quite possible to hold concurrently other views about modes of transmission of disease. Indeed it is especially important when examining reactions to Mal Francese to remember that for Fracastoro, as for his contemporaries, contagion could also mean transmission through the air. As we shall see in more detail in Chapter Six, this was understood in terms of his theory of 'seedlets of contagion', which were seen as an infective agent, not in the sense of a germ theory but rather as corrupting the air and reactivated within an individual by food of poor quality. More generally, there was also the more traditional view which saw contagion as a synonym for staining, both in a literal sense of the air and in a more metaphorical sense of moral pollution.[77]

Given that the medical profession held a variety of theories about transmission, it is hardly surprising that they should be shared by the laity. This explains the variety of contemporary views about ways of catching Mal Francese, from sleeping in the same bed as a patient or using the same bathwater or even exchanging a kiss.[78] In Florence the canons of the cathedral, fearing that they might catch 'French boils and the French Disease' from communicants, requested in 1504 a new cupboard from the Operai so that they might keep separate the 'chasuble, chalices and liturgical vestments' used in public.[79]

This range of ideas about how an individual might catch Mal Francese underlines why it is wrong to adopt a mono-causal interpretation of contemporary concepts of transmission by concentrating exclusively on the sexual act. This in turn should make one sceptical about the frequently reiterated belief that prostitutes were seen as the main carriers of the disease and should make one cautious when placing too much weight on statements such as that of the chronicler Fileno dalle Tuatte of Bologna that 'many prostitutes were thrown out of Bologna and from Ferrara and other places'.[80] While there is no reason to doubt that this did happen, one has to place this action within a wider context. The expulsion of prostitutes was not uncommon at times of emergency caused by epidemic disease, especially plague. The aim was to remove corrupt matter from the city; for just as rotting meat produced foul-smelling vapours, so prostitutes were seen as polluting the moral atmosphere, hardly conducive to allowing God to forgive them for their sins. There is no evidence that this action was repeated elsewhere in Italy later in the sixteenth century nor that prostitutes were treated as scapegoats in this early period.[81]

A recognition that it was possible to hold a multiplicity of ideas about transmission helps us to understand the lack of any common programme which could be dignified with the term 'government policy' in Italy during the first decade or so after the onset of this new disease. This was not so true of measures taken in this period in other European cities. These included the banning of pox-victims from the Hôtel-Dieu in Paris, although this does not appear to have been very successfully implemented, and the setting aside of two houses near the Abbey of Saint-Germain-des-Prés for sick Parisians. At the same time in Paris, as in other parts of both northern and southern France, pox-sufferers from elsewhere were driven from the city.[82] In Scotland, when the town authorities of Aberdeen issued a proclamation in April 1497, they ordered the loose women of the town to abandon their vice and take up honourable work, on pain of being branded and expelled. Later in the same year a similar but more severe decree in Edinburgh ordered that all those with the disease – and those who claimed to be able to cure it – should be banished to an island in the Firth of Forth. Banishment was not only punishment, but an attempt at preserving the health of the remainder of the citizens.[83]

Interest seems to have centred around bathhouses in France as well as in the Imperial cities of southern Germany; some were sporadically closed down and others, along with inns, were forbidden to accept people with the disease.[84] North of the Alps, particularly in Germany, there were also some attempts to create an institutional response to the problem of the pox in the late fifteenth and early sixteenth centuries. In south-west Germany, special hospitals known as *Franzosenhäuser* or *Blatternhäuser* were founded from as early as 1495–6, as in the cases of Augsburg, Frankfurt-am-Main, Freiburg im Breisgau, Nuremberg, Strasbourg and Ulm.[85]

While *Blatternhäuser* were established by Imperial German cities, no parallel movement can be ascribed to Italian secular authorities in this period, even following Torrella's suggestion that the *mal franciosati* be placed in a separate house or hospital. But if the men who ran Italian states did not themselves attempt to put this measure directly into practice, pious and charitably minded lay men and women began to take the initiative in first Genoa and then Bologna. They organised themselves into fraternities which established hospitals to treat those suffering from Mal Francese. Very rapidly they received the approval and support of governments, underlining the traditional dependence of local authorities on this type of independent lay religious group, which had been responsible for much of the relief of the sick and poor in late medieval Italy.[86] However, as we shall see in Chapter Seven, it is important not to draw too strict a dividing-line between public and private. Those who ran governments and the leaders of these charitable movements were often members of the same families who made up the elite which dominated most secular and religious corporations within each city-state. This was particularly true of princely states such as that of Ferrara, to which we shall turn in the next chapter.

Chapter Three

God's Punishment: lay perceptions of the French Disease in Ferrara

Introduction

Contemporary opinion and knowledge about the French Disease were formed in a variety of ways, including direct experience and written and oral reports of both medical and non-medical commentators. In the previous chapter we surveyed the reactions of lay chroniclers throughout Italy. In this chapter we shall continue this process within the context of one particularly well-documented place, Ferrara, which will provide the context for the subsequent discussion of the medical debate at the ducal court. Once again we shall confine ourselves to the earliest reactions to the disease.

Religion, as we shall see, was an important element in the perception of Mal Francese. While doctors had a specialist body of doctrine on which to draw, others understood the pox in the absence of medical learning but with a set of detailed religious and moral beliefs about the world and how it worked. We have seen the millenarian interpretations of the natural disasters of the 1490s. It was natural, then, that the coming of the French Disease should be seen as a moral and religious event and the disease itself as much more than a medical business. It is easy for us, with our world-view, to focus on the infective organism and see that moral and religious questions would follow the onset of the disease. But for fifteenth-century Italian laymen it was the other way round: the essence of the disease was God's displeasure, and the mechanisms which He had chosen to inflict the disease on mankind were secondary. This was a view which many doctors shared. Our focus here is on the ducal court, and particularly on Duke Ercole I d'Este, through whom religion played its part in determining the nature and stability of civil life. Ercole was advised by Girolamo Savonarola, who pushed the religious framework in a particular direction.

Much of our information comes from contemporary Ferrarese diaries and chronicles, including those we discussed in the previous chapter. The two most important diaries are that of the notary Bernardino Zambotti and another which was compiled by several unknown authors, among them in this period an anonymous ducal officer of supplies. The radically different social positions of the writers of both diaries led them to reflect different aspects of the Ferrarese reality: while the anonymous diary reported a great deal of information of day-to-day life in Ferrara as a result of the diarists' close contact with it, Zambotti's diary says little about the life of the city, from which he was often absent, but is full of information about the court.[1] Further sources include internal and external correspondence of the Estense court[2] and the letters between Duke Ercole d'Este and the Dominican friar Girolamo Savonarola.[3]

Ercole d'Este and Girolamo Savonarola

To understand the power of the court and how religious questions played a distinctive role in the lay reaction to the pox in Ferrara we need to go back a little in time. Located in the north-east of Italy, Ferrara was, at the end of the fifteenth century, with its 30,000 inhabitants, the main city in the Po delta. It was also the principal town of a small dukedom which had been ruled over by the Este family since 1332, although it occupied a territory permanently claimed by the papacy. Surrounded by powerful neighbours (the great dukedom of Milan and the republic of Venice to the north; the republic of Florence and the Church states to the south), the lords of the Este had always known the essence of discreet and shrewd politics. During more than three centuries (1267–1598) they managed to keep Ferrara and its region under control by means of astute politics which were based upon a prosperous rural economy, the benefits of their mercenary participation in the military campaigns of other European powers, a series of wise marriages, and the support of an efficient and loyal team of public servants who were in charge of the state administration.[4]

During the fifteenth century Ferrara became a major trading and industrial centre which took advantage of its strategic position in the middle of important land, river and sea communication routes to achieve rapid economic development. With the support of a prosperous and increasingly influential urban patriciate (including Jewish bankers), the lords of the Este – particularly Duke Ercole I (1472–1505) – undertook major projects of public works which transformed what had been a mere medieval town into an elegant renaissance city. In the late fifteenth and early sixteenth centuries the dukedom of Ferrara went through its most splendid days. Its main creator was Duke Ercole himself, a clever and sensitive man who generously patronised religion, arts and all branches of knowledge and transformed the University, or *studio generale*, of Ferrara into one of the most prestigious in Italy at the time.[5]

Ferrara, in common with the rest of Italy, suffered from the impact of Charles VIII's invasion. But, in contrast to other political powers, the house of the Este survived and was even reinforced by the disaster because of the political astuteness of Duke Ercole, who remained neutral in the face of the invasion, although secretly well disposed towards it.[6] In short, a great deal of power lay in the duke's hands. What he thought and did was important for his citizens. What kind of religion he practised and what he did about the French Disease mattered to those over whom he had political influence. Ferrara appeared to be at its height when the series of natural disasters mentioned in the previous chapter seemed to threaten everything. The French Disease was one of these disasters and cannot be separated from them in contemporary perceptions. We need to look in some detail at contemporary happenings in order to understand those perceptions.

However successful he was, Ercole d'Este had little influence over the extreme climatic conditions, from floods to earthquakes.[7] As we would expect, these adverse and uncontrollable natural conditions increased social sensitivity to extraordinary phenomena, which were interpreted as presaging further calamities in the light of the prophecies which proliferated everywhere.[8] The anonymous diary referred to a natural portent having happened in a forest of the Romagna on 11 December 1495.[9] On 2 January 1496 it also reported a miraculous apparition of the Virgin Mary announcing that Italy would suffer that year from 'the greatest famine, war, and shortages that had ever happened in the world before'.[10] A friar of the order of St Lazar who preached on this theme at Ferrara on New Year's Day warned that only those who participated in a penitential fasting, such as the general one which Pope Alexander VI had presided over at Rome some days before for the same reason, would be saved from these misfortunes. According to the chronicler, Duke Ercole decreed for the following day a general fasting of water and bread, in which he took part 'along with all his court'.[11]

Doubtless, Ercole d'Este's involvement in this initiative was stimulated by his readiness to accept that all the troubles suffered were due to divine intervention and that they portended others even greater. He seems to have paid particular attention to the information that a monster had appeared at Rome on the banks of the Tiber after the floods of December 1495, which was seen as presaging imminent new calamities.[12] All this has to be seen within the context of Ercole's sincere piety, which became more accentuated with the passage of time, and was evident in many ducal initiatives. He turned religion into so relevant a part of daily life in the court and city of Ferrara that Church and state were inextricably entwined in the domains of the Este family during his rule.[13]

The climate of moral and religious pressure rose to a climax in Ferrara during the last decade of the fifteenth century. This was to a great extent due to the influence on Ercole d'Este of the messianic leader of Florence in the 1490s, Girolamo Savonarola. By the middle of 1495 Ercole had become a fervent follower of the Dominican, whose profound influence came to be felt in both the Estense court and the city of Ferrara. And Savonarola's influence on Ercole even survived his execution on 23 May 1498.[14]

Savonarola, who had proclaimed King Charles VIII of France as the new Cyrus leading his triumphant army all over Italy without breaking a lance or encountering any resistance, had become after the fall of the Medici regime at the end of 1494 the most outstanding spokesman of the new Florentine republic. At the time, Savonarola gradually transcended his initial apocalyptical pessimism in prophesying the imminent arrival of the world's end and of divine punishment for the sinfulness of the Italians. Now more optimistic and markedly millenarian, his teaching began to proclaim, on the contrary, that Florence under the new regime was the New Jerusalem and the New Rome, the place selected by divine inspiration. He also proclaimed himself as God's envoy to warn Italians of the tribulations awaiting them and to rescue them from their predicament.[15]

Ercole's deep concern about Savonarola's prophecies can be followed through two channels of correspondence. First, the letters (no less than eighteen, all of them in friendly terms and showing great reciprocal esteem) in which Ercole and Savonarola addressed each other between May 1495 (that is, six months after the fall of the Medici) and August 1497 (that is, three months after the Dominican was excommunicated by Pope Alexander VI). The second channel was Ercole's correspondence with the Estense orator at Florence, Manfredo Manfredi, whose role appears to have been essential not only in putting the duke and the friar in touch, but also in keeping open the lines between them after August 1497, when it became politically too risky for Duke Ercole to correspond directly with Savonarola.[16] This is expressed clearly in the last paragraph of Manfredi's letter to Ercole on 1 September 1497.[17]

It was probably after Manfredi's letter to Ercole on the 5 November 1494 that Ercole began to be interested in the preaching of the Dominican.[18] Savonarola, in turn, was impressed by Ercole's piety,[19] and, urged by the duke's orator Manfredi, soon began a correspondence with Ercole.[20] This opening letter has not survived, but it must have been written to Ercole on 20 or 21 May, since in a letter of 26 May the duke thanked the friar for his advice and took note of the proposed 'remedies', promising to put them into practice. He also reminded Savonarola to send him a book.[21] It came in August: Savonarola's *Compendio di rivelazioni*, the Latin version of which Ercole also received in October. This work, newly printed, summarised the friar's prophecies and soon circulated extensively.[22]

Although during the following months Manfredi continued to inform Ercole about Savonarola's preaching and what he was publishing,[23] it is obvious that from May 1495 the duke and the friar corresponded extensively with each other. The main subject of most of Savonarola's letters was obsessively the same as in his other contemporary writings: the imminent *tribulazione et flagelli preparati a tuta Italia*, almost always summarised in the triad war–pestilence–dearth that God would send Italians because of their *mal vivere*. Savonarola urged them to repent and behave. Ercole's replies demonstrate his close study of Savonarola's writings and sermons, and his diligence in putting into practice every measure dictated or inspired by the friar and directed towards greater piety and the moral reform of Ferrara. To read this correspondence between the two men is to enter the atmosphere that Savonarola's prophecies created in late fifteenth-century Ferrara, and to understand better how the French Disease was perceived when it arrived.

Still sharing the anxious mood in Ferrara created by the serious and widespread floods of late 1495 (a mood clearly reflected in the contemporary of *The Flood* now in the Rijksmuseum, Amsterdam – see Plate 3.1), Savonarola announced to Ercole on 10 January 1496 the imminence of the *tribulatione* of Italy, of Christianity and of the entire world, and exhorted him to be diligent with divine things, 'and above all to cleanse the city from wicked men and to put civil duties into the hands of the good ones, to provide them with authority and to remove it from wicked and infamous men, since the latter greatly provoke the rage of God'.[24] Ercole's reaction was not long delayed: on 3 April he addressed a long edict (*grida*) to his subjects, including numerous injunctions about good behaviour and strict penalties for offenders. His aim was to eradicate from his domains 'all the vices' and to sow in them 'all the virtues', in order to placate the rage of God, who was punishing mankind by sending to the earth 'famines, earthquakes, plagues, wars, water and fire'. The edict also enumerated the 'crimes' which would be particularly prosecuted: blasphemy, sodomy, games of chance, concubinage, prostitution and pimping – precisely those quoted obsessively by Savonarola in his sermons and writings.[25]

In his letter to Ercole on 27 April 1496 Savonarola praised the severe measures the former had taken, calling them the only effective remedy 'against the imminent tribulations and scourges prepared for the whole of Italy'.[26] Four months later, on 28 August, Savonarola reminded Ercole that his prophecies would be confirmed: 'there will definitely soon be the greatest scourge of war, pestilence and dearth, and things like this are already beginning to happen now. . .'.[27]

Ercole and Savonarola continued to correspond, even (in August 1497) three months after Savonarola's excommunication. Indeed, on 1 August Savonarola exhorted Ercole not to be concerned that his prophecies had not yet been realised. He asserted:

God is not like man, variable and impatient. On the contrary, in His things, particularly in those of justice, He walks firmly and slowly in order to prove the faith of His elected, as well as to make more manifest the wickedness of the damned, who, the longer these things are delayed (although the punishment is inevitable), become worse and mock them more. Not even Jews believed in

Plate 3.1 *The Flood*, school of Ercole de' Roberti, Ferrara

what their prophets foretold since they thought that what was prophesied was distant; and they remained deceived even until their last destruction by Romans.[28]

At the end of his letter, Savonarola urged Ercole to take these prophecies seriously and to act on them, administering justice and continuing to 'live virtuously' (*ben vivere*). He also urged him to read and to make others read the books of Jeremiah and Ezechiel, since they reflected circumstances which were very close to those of his own time.[29] Again, Ercole replied swiftly. He denied that he had hesitated at all in accepting Savonarola's prophecies. Yet he regretted that Charles VIII had not been able to accomplish the expectations that his invasion had created because of his 'delay and negligence' and of his carelessness 'about his honour and the good of his own people'.[30]

There were no more letters between Ercole d'Este and Girolamo Savonarola after the end of August 1497. But Ercole's correspondence with Manfredi, who remained in Florence, reflects the Duke of Ferrara's serious concern about the friar's increasing difficulties in the months leading up to his execution in May 1498, which Ercole did his best to prevent. He also records that he kept faith with Savonarola's dictates and prophecies even after the latter's death.[31]

The atmosphere created by Savonarola's prophecies and their apparent fulfilment through natural disasters formed the background against which news of the latest scourge, Mal Francese, arrived and spread in Ferrara and many other Italian cities. It soon became reality, striking at the heart of the city, the court. Before the end of 1496 the disease already seems to have afflicted Ercole's son-in-law Francesco Gonzaga, the Marquis of Mantua. During the following year the calamities intensified at the Este family: Ercole's daughter Beatrice and daughter-in-law Anna Sforza died, while the latter's husband, the ducal heir Alfonso d'Este, was so ill from the French Disease that he even felt unable to attend the burial of his young wife. In the following years, two other sons of Duke Ercole also became afflicted by the disease. It must have seemed that the prophecies of Savonarola were becoming a grim reality. The French Disease was a punishment from God visited upon the powerful as well as on the people.

Mal Francese Overtakes Ferrara

As in most Italian cities, there is no information in our sources about *Morbus Gallicus* in Ferrara until late 1496. The earliest evidence from this city was a ducal payment order on 13 October of four Lire Marchesine to the master surgeon Giovanni Giusti 'as a stipend for curing and liberating from the French Disease'.[32] The fact that this order came from the duke's treasury strongly suggests that the disease was very close to the ducal family.[33]

By the end of the year the disease had become apparent to the chroniclers and diarists of Ferrara. According to the *Cronaca Estense* of the Carmelite friar Paolo da Lignago, 'the French Disease started at Ferrara' in December 1496.[34] At about the same time the *Diario Ferrarese* of Bernardino Zambotti also referred to Mal Francese for the first time:

> [1496] December, on the day. . . . The French Disease began to be discovered in many people in this region, and also everywhere in Italy; this disease [*male*] seems to be incurable since it is the disease of St Job [*male de Santo Job*]; and it springs from men who do it with women in their vulva [*mona*]. As a result of it most of these men die; they suffer from pains in bones and nerves, and very big pustules [*brozole*] all over the body.[35]

This passage reflects the atmosphere of alarm in Ferrara in the face of an unknown disease which, as we have seen, spread quickly through the region of Ferrara and the whole of Italy. Zambotti also stressed its apparent incurability, and he pointed out that the new disease had a high mortality rate. In addition, he called attention to its more remarkable clinical features.

By 4 February 1497 the pox had forced itself on the attention of the anonymous writer of the other Ferrarese dairy:

Monsignor D'Aubigny, French, arrived at Ferrara [from the kingdom of Naples] being ill from a certain disease [*male*] called French Disease [*male franzoso*], which causes very severe pains and hard buboes [*bognoni duri*] all over the body, so that it is a very serious disease which already has been afflicting its victims for slightly more than one year, and physicians do not know what to do when faced with this disease.[36]

The report could not be more expressive: the first identified victim of the French Disease at Ferrara was a high-ranking officer in the invading army. He was Bernard Stuart (c. 1447–1508), third lord of Aubigny, who had been designated governor of Calabria and lieutenant-general of the French army by Charles VIII in 1495.[37] D'Aubigny, who was mentioned by Francesco Guicciardini in his *Storia d'Italia* as victim of a *lunga infermità* for most of the duration of the French campaign in Italy,[38] started the retreat of the French rearguard from Calabria at the end of 1496 through Florence, Bologna, Modena, Ferrara and Milan. Several contemporary eyewitnesses recorded his passing through all these cities, and coincidentally stressed his bad health. Furthermore, unlike Guicciardini, most of them did not hide the cause of his sufferings, which they referred to as the French Disease. D'Aubigny, who was for ten days the guest of Duke Ercole d'Este at Ferrara, eventually departed for France from Milan in late March.[39]

The tone of this description suggests that the disease was totally unknown to the writer of the anonymous diary. Although he apparently spoke about it from hearsay, he seems to have been well informed, since he knew about its severity, about the fact that Mal Francese had attacked its earliest victims more than one year before, and about the perception of the helplessness of university medicine in the face of it.[40]

While the anonymous diarist does not seem to have been acquainted with Mal Francese until February 1497, two months after D'Aubigny's reported arrival at Ferrara, in early April the diary recorded that 'in Ferrara there is a great profusion of a disease called the French Disease or the disease of St Job, which physicians do not know how to treat'.[41] Furthermore, he insisted that the new disease caused notorious bewilderment among physicians. This was also the first time that the anonymous diarist had identified Mal Francese with the *Male de Santo Job*, in contrast to Zambotti, who had made this association since the beginning.

Some days later, on 11 April, the anonymous diarist announced that the corpse of someone accused of murder and robbery who had been hanged in Ferrara had been given over 'to physicians in order to be dissected [*per fare nothomia*] for the purpose of seeing where the French Disease came from, since he suffered from this disease'.[42] To the best of our knowledge this was the earliest documented autopsy of a victim of the Mal Francese in Ferrara. Although no more details were provided, this post-mortem examination could only have been made with the permission of Duke Ercole,[43] and was probably the one performed at the request of the contenders at the medical disputation held at Ferrara. Evidently Ercole d'Este, increasingly worried about the spread of *Morbus Gallicus* in his court and dominions, had decided to invite several professors of the medical faculty of Ferrara to dispute on this disease. This medical debate was to shed light on the nature and treatment of such a strange disease that spread so quickly and the apparent incurability of which plunged university practitioners into bewilderment. The aim of the dissection was to discover whether the French Disease also caused lesions to 'internal members', as one of the participants in the disputation had argued.[44]

The earliest reference in any contemporary diary to a victim of the French Disease among the members of the Estense family was delayed until early November 1497. The anonymous diary reported that Alfonso d'Este, the first-born son of Ercole and his heir to the dukedom, suffered from that 'disease, extraordinary and unknown to physicians', which afflicted 'very many people all over Italy'.[45] Whether Alfonso had just caught the French Disease or had suffered from it before, this information confirmed that by then the nature of his illness had become public in Ferrara. More than a year had elapsed since the ducal payment to a master surgeon for his services for the French Disease had suggested that the new disease had begun to attack the Estense court. A month later (3 December 1497) the diary of Zambotti – who had been promptly informed by his cousin Zaccaria Zambotti about the private affairs at the Estense court – recorded that Alfonso had the stigma of suffering from Mal Francese. Alfonso had been absent from his wife's funeral 'as a result of his being seriously ill from Mal Francese and quartan fevers, to the extent of hardly maintaining a human appearance so covered as he is with pustules [*impiagato de brozole*]'.[46] Obviously, after Alfonso's absence from such a public occasion, the identity of his illness was a secret to none in Ferrara.

The anonymous diary agreed with Zambotti that the French Disease was fatal to all sufferers: 'whoever contracts it, dies because of it'. As the anonymous diary also made clear, some sections of the population of Ferrara believed that this disease was contracted through sexual contagion: 'the man who suffered from it, gave it to a woman when he made use of her; equally, the woman to the man when she suffered from it, and made use of the male'.[47] Apparently, the perception that Mal Francese was individually transmitted through sexual intercourse by a man suffering from it to a healthy woman, and vice versa, contrasts with that held by Bernardino Zambotti, for whom catching *Morbus Gallicus* always had moral connotations.

During 1498 and 1499 several sources outside the Estense court echoed the persistence and severity of Alfonso's Mal Francese. Indeed, the Venetian ambassador Marin Sanudo, supported by direct and reliable testimony, noted in his diary that at the beginning of February 1499 Alfonso's health was pitiful as a result of this disease. Sanudo emphasised that physicians were greatly worried by the state of the patient's hands, concluding that they 'will be seized with leprosy or cancer [*lepra o cancharo*]'.[48]

A month earlier (January 1499) the anonymous diary had reported that three sons of Duke Ercole, Alfonso, Ferrante and Sigismondo, were already suffering from Mal Francese. The same source reported again the helplessness of 'physicians and their medicines' in dealing with a disease whose victims 'for almost four years are unable to escape from it', and which 'the whole world seems full of, as is well known [*ut palam dicitur*]'.[49] Further on, the same source reported that Sigismondo d'Este had just arrived at Ferrara from Milan 'totally full of Mal Francese' on 13 March 1499.[50] Again, in late December that year the anonymous diary referred to the same son of Duke Ercole as being 'ill with Mal Francese'.[51]

These entries from 1499 concerning Mal Francese are the last in both Ferrarese diaries. In spite of continuing to cause widespread anxiety and medical bewilderment, four years after its outbreak the new disease seems to have become usual enough at Ferrara no longer to appear exceptional. In other words, it had passed from being a serious and embarrassing private affair and became just another public calamity. Even if contemporaries faced the problem with growing resignation, the authorities in Ferrara, as in other Italian states, came to realise increasingly that this was a new threat to public health. Thus in May 1501 a medical practitioner, Maestro Ferrante da S. Domenico, was employed 'to operate on many and diverse diseases, above all on the disease of those who have been infected through lower parts'.[52] Four years later at least one medical practitioner resident at Ferrara was engaged by the Duke of Este as a 'specialist' on the French Disease (Zan Jacomo da Padoa, 'medico del Mal Franzoso').[53]

Furthermore, in March 1502 Duke Ercole gave a patent to a religious confraternity dedicated to the Biblical patriarch Job, to collect funds throughout the whole dukedom with the purpose of erecting a hospital for the sufferers from the French Disease and of paying for their care. This patent was ratified in March 1505 by Alfonso d'Este, soon after he had become duke; he had personal reasons for being acutely aware of the French Disease.[54] We shall return to the story of this hospital in Chapter Seven.

The Ailments of the Este Family

When the great and the good fall ill, the world takes more notice than it does of ordinary folk. Their illness also generates more historical evidence. Private correspondence of the Estense family directly or indirectly dealing with the health of Ercole's sons Alfonso, Ferrante and Sigismondo, and of his son-in-law Francesco Gonzaga, has survived.[55] It includes many clinical descriptions of their illnesses and shows Ercole's deep concern about the health of his sons, particularly in the case of his heir Alfonso. But, surprisingly enough, Mal Francese and other related terms were absent from these descriptions.

Like the diaries, this correspondence apparently reflects the advance of the

of the disease. The earliest information we have concerns the Marquis of
Mantua, Francesco Gonzaga. On 19 October 1496 he arrived in Ferrara from
Naples – where he had fought against the French army along with the
Aragonese troops – seriously 'ill from anguish, fever, and flux'.[56] Affection-
ately welcomed by Ercole d'Este, whose daughter Isabella he had married,
Francesco Gonzaga remained in Ferrara for two days before continuing his
journey back to Mantua.[57]

Ten days afterwards (29 October) the physician Zaccaria Zambotti, then in
Mantua, acknowledged receipt of an oil-based preparation which Ercole had
sent to Francesco, and which had seemingly proved to have wonderful
analgesic effects. Zaccaria Zambotti had taught practical medicine at the *studio*
of Ferrara between 1470 and 1474, was one of Ercole's most trusted physicians, and was often kept at Mantua as a secret informer.[58] Zambotti notified
Ercole of the success of the remedy, as well as of the angry reaction of
Francesco Gonzaga against his physicians, whom he upbraided for their useless
remedies. The letter also specified that the strong and continuous pain in his
jaw ('ala barba sua'), which his physicians were not able to mitigate
for two days and three nights, had stopped six hours after Ercole's oil had
been applied; the marquis ordered that it should be kept safe as a valuable
possession.[59]

In spite of its length and detailed description, Zambotti's letter was not
more precise about the identity of the disease from which Gonzaga suffered.
Nevertheless, the clinical features of the pain and its intractability to remedies
from academic medicine strongly suggest that Francesco Gonzaga could well
have been ill from Mal Francese.[60] Not even Zambotti's letter said anything
about the contents and origin of this oil. It was probably some secret remedy,
perhaps the same for which Ercole had paid four *Lire Marchesine* to the master
surgeon Giovanni Giusti.[61] In fact, as we have already seen in the previous
chapter and will see again in more detail in the chapters that follow, the
failure of traditional remedies that university physicians used to cure the
French Disease made it an excellent target for local remedies, quite often of
unknown composition, which practitioners successfully employed to calm the
sufferers' pains and to clean their skin of pustules and sores. But even if
the effects of such treatment could be spectacular in the short term, as in the
cases recounted by Francesco Matarazzo in Perugia, in the long term these
remedies could have very grave consequences, even leading to the patient's
death. University physicians took advantage of these serious side effects
to level against inexperienced empirics serious charges of malpractice and
professional intrusion.

Even if no further correspondence survives from the Estense court concerning Francesco Gonzaga's complaints, there is a record of the very poor
health of his brother-in-law and the ducal heir, Alfonso d'Este, between 1497
and 1499. In three letters Alfonso told his father of the course of a seemingly
long disease and of the treatment prescribed to him by the ducal physician,

Lodovico Carri. In the first letter Alfonso described his own disease as not serious, which Carri had related to the fact that he had slept uncovered at night during a time of intense heat, presumably in the summer of 1497.[62] On 29 March 1498 Alfonso reported to Duke Ercole that following the advice of Carri he had just had his hair cut 'as I am prepared to do everything that physicians prescribe me for my liberation'.[63] Nevertheless, this unusual remedy does not seem to have proved efficacious, as on 22 August 1499 Alfonso urgently asked Ercole for an effective analgesic oil made of turpentine, cloves and storax, which he knew his father had, to calm 'a certain pain . . . under my left knee . . . that does not let me rest a moment all day and night'.[64] This was probably the same oil that Ercole had sent to Francesco Gonzaga in 1496.

In addition to the letters sent to his father, on 30 April 1498 Alfonso wrote another to thank his brother Ippolito d'Este, the Cardinal of Milan, for the latter's helpful arrangements with the great Duke of Milan, Lodovico Sforza. Knowing that Alfonso was seriously ill, Sforza had immediately sent to Ferrara his personal physician Luigi Marliani to look after his brother-in-law. Alfonso reported that, after the treatment prescribed by Marliani, the 'fever has diminished very much and the suffering I had at my throat is almost cured, and now is so little that I hardly feel it'. At the same time, Alfonso asked after the state of health of the cardinal, who had also been ill for several days.[65]

Although contemporary court sources are still less specific concerning Ippolito's health, we know that he felt suddenly indisposed 'with a certain laxity, and alteration, although without fever' on Holy Saturday, 14 April 1498, and that his personal physician Agostino Benzi had prescribed a two-day purge. Ten days afterwards Cardinal Ippolito was still ill, although his health had improved, as Benzi reported to Duke Ercole on 24 April 1498.[66] What was Ippolito's illness, which caused so much concern among his relatives? Two months before, on the way to Milan to take possession of its archbishopric, Ippolito, along with his brother Sigismondo, stopped in Mantua, where they were guests of Francesco Gonzaga, and enjoyed the last two days of the carnival.[67] It is certain that Sigismondo contracted Mal Francese during the Mantuan carnival or soon afterwards in Milan. Indeed, from the anonymous diary we know that when Sigismondo came back from Milan a year later he arrived at Ferrara 'totally full of Mal Francese',[68] and that he was still sick from this complaint at the end of 1499.[69] Sigismondo's life was seriously restricted by this disease until he died in 1524, since, as Bonaventura Pistofilo wrote, 'in finding himself crippled by Mal Francese, there was little he could do to strive to show his bravery'.[70]

Yet private court correspondence again remains silent about the identity of his complaint; it is possible to assert only that in October 1499 he felt seriously ill, although he had not lost the hope of a quick recovery. Two physicians, Lodovico Carri and a Magistro Palomarino, looked after him, the latter remaining at his bedside every night.[71]

A Significant Silence

Thus members of the ducal family of Ferrara, the Este, were infected with the French Disease, a fact well known to the chroniclers. But private correspondence remained strangely silent about the nature of the complaint suffered by the sons of Duke Ercole. This silence is highly significant, and is explained by the moral and religious connotations of Mal Francese in late fifteenth-century Ferrara, which in turn had serious political implications, given that the ducal heir Alfonso suffered from such a stigmatising disease. We shall seek to understand the importance of these connotations to contemporaries through the following three themes.

God's punishment for the sins of mankind

We have already pointed out that the new disease was unanimously given, in Ferrara as in the rest of Italy, the name of the invading army, whose head, King Charles VIII, had been announced by Girolamo Savonarola as the new Cyrus – the instrument of divine intervention to compel the religious conversion of Italy. The Ferrarese court physician Coradino Gilino[72] did not hesitate to blame the outbreak of *Morbus Gallicus* on God's direct punishment of the Italian people:

> We also see that the Supreme Creator, now full of wrath against us for our dreadful sins, punishes us with this cruellest of ills, which has now spread not only through Italy but across almost the whole of Christendom. Everywhere is the sound of trumpets; everywhere the noise of arms is heard. How many devices of bombardment and machines of war are being made! What unheard-of iron weapons are now constructed to replace stone balls! The very Turks are being called to Italy. How many fires, how much devastation and how much slaughter of miserable mortals do we see: how much more will we see! O that I were a liar! Let us say, with the Prophet in the sixth psalm, 'Lord, do not censure me in your anger nor in your wrath afflict us.' This I believe is the cause of this savage plague.[73]

From the apocalyptic panorama Gilino depicted in this paragraph it is obvious that he perceived Mal Francese as a plague primarily sent by God to punish Italians for their many and serious sins, not the least of which were the widespread preoccupation with war, the increasing use of new lethal arms and the political utilisation of Turks by Christian princes.[74]

Mal Francese and sinful sexual activity

We have already seen that the earliest reference to Mal Francese in Zambotti's *Diario Ferrarese* recounted, among other things, that 'this disease [*male*] seems to be incurable since it is the disease of St Job; and it springs from men who do it with women in their vulva'.[75] The question of Job will be dealt with below, but what concerns us here is Zambotti's perception of the causes of the French Disease. There are three possible interpretations, all of them gynophobic, which could be given to his statement that Mal Francese 'springs from men who do it with women in their vulva'.

First, assuming that in Venetian dialect the word *mona* means the female genitals, the woman's vulva or *natura*,[76] the words of Zambotti's diary (*per li homini hanno a fare con donne in mona*) taken literally seem at first sight to refer to simple sexual intercourse. But, if so, it would seem to be redundant, since contemporary sources – tactful and modest as they were in dealing with such a topic – usually resorted to euphemistic expressions, such as 'make use of a woman' and 'do it with a woman', or to words from the medical and Latin vocabulary, like *coitus* and equivalents of 'intercourse'. The placing of the action in the female external genitals suggests a particular variety of oral sexual practice prohibited by Christian morality as 'unnatural'.[77]

Secondly, it is possible that the word *mona* (that is, vulva) was used here as a figure of speech for referring to a function, that of menstruation. If so, it could be considered as an attempt to attribute the new disease to the same cause to which leprous babies' birth was traditionally ascribed, namely that their mothers had had sexual contact while they were menstruating.[78] It would mean that the French Disease was caused by breaking a religious taboo long established in the Jewish–Christian tradition and so outside its boundaries.[79]

A third interpretation relates to the fact that phrases like *andare in mona* and *mandare in mona* mean 'go' and 'lead [someone] to material or moral ruin', respectively.[80] This would imply that the new disease was contracted only by men who had sexual contacts with 'morally ruined women' (*donne in mona*).[81] Evidently, though, in the midst of growing reactions by civil and ecclesiastical authorities in many parts of Europe against what was perceived then as a crumbling moral system, contemporaries extended their identification of these 'ruined women' to include not just public prostitutes and courtesans, but also elegant and flirtatious women. Anyhow, the control of prostitution became a major issue in the search for a new emerging moral order.[82] In this respect, we may recall that in the *grida* addressed to his subjects on 3 April 1496 containing many provisions for the sake of decency, and harsh punishments for offenders, Duke Ercole d'Este included prostitution among the most severely persecuted crimes along with blasphemy, sodomy, games of chance, concubinage and pimping.[83]

Therefore, to the notary Bernardino Zambotti, catching *Morbus Gallicus* always had moral connotations since he related it to illicit sexual contacts. At this point there is a remarkable contrast between the gynophobic attitude held by Zambotti, who always saw women as the origin of the Mal Francese, and the handling of the problem by the ducal officer of supplies, to whom both sexes could infect each other with the disease through venereal contagion.[84] Zambotti's gynophobia not only was in accordance with Aristotelian–Thomist natural philosophy so widespread in Europe at the time, but seems to be the ultimate expression of the feeling that disasters like epidemics always come from somewhere else: from another world, indeed, either the celestial or the New World; more directly from another nation or state, the 'French', 'Neapolitan' and Ethiopian sources of the disease; from an ethnic group – the Jews – who might be closer to home but who behaved like foreigners; and finally from people who shared everything but gender with the writer.

The disease of St Job

Another important religious and moral dimension of the French Disease as perceived in late fifteenth-century Ferrara was its identification with the *male de Santo Job*. This association was readily made, despite the epidemic proportions of the disease. Most lay people saw Mal Francese as afflicting only a series of specific individuals, largely by person-to-person contagion, and not the entire population in a rapid and dramatic spread. Thus, those who saw this disease as a scourge sent by God tended to identify it with an individual disease such as the mysterious one suffered by the Old Testament patriarch Job, rather than (as Gilino did) with one of the many Biblical plagues that struck the people of Israel or their enemies. Its unknown nature, apparent incurability and unpleasant, long-lasting and recurrent consequences also constituted good evidence for this identification.

The figure of the Biblical patriarch Job possessed an immensely evocative power in both the Jewish and Christian traditions.[85] The influence of Job's story on Christianity largely derives from his having been the Old Testament patriarch closest to the figure of Jesus in relation to a core issue in Christian moral theology, namely that of innocent suffering and of undeserved grief.[86] Long widespread all over Europe, the cult of St Job culminated in the sixteenth century. For several centuries Job was invoked as the patron saint by sufferers from worms, leprosy, cutaneous complaints, affliction and melancholy. But it was plague in some Italian cities on the Adriatic coast that led to his canonisation, despite his having lived before the Christian era.[87]

As we have noted in Chapter Two, the Ferrarese diaries along with chronicles from Bologna and Cologne were among the earliest to identify Mal Francese with the *Male de Santo Job*.[88] As we shall see, in 1499 a religious fraternity dedicated to the Biblical patriarch Job, who was invoked to protect the city of Ferrara from trouble and disease, was established in Ferrara and gained the support of the d'Estes.[89] Also at the beginning of the sixteenth century the Fraternity of Santa Maria dei Guarini in Bologna and the hospital it governed were rededicated to San Giobbe, because it specialised in treating those suffering from Mal Francese.[90]

Plate 3.2 'The sick Job tempted by the Devil and annoyed by two musicians', a woodcut reflecting an apocryphal tradition of the Book of Job

When looking at the Book of Job as a source for Christian inspiration, one must bear in mind that the divine origins of Job's numerous calamities implied a dilemma. This dilemma was to decide whether Job's troubles were divine punishment of an individual's sins or undeserved calamities sent by God to an innocent person to prove the sincerity of his Christian faith. The tension brought about by this dilemma led to inconsistencies, the most significant being the contrast between the image of Job as just and God-fearing in the prologue and epilogue to the Book of Job, and that of Job as defiant and even as a blasphemer in the rest of the book.[91] These inconsistencies became increasingly clear in the three medieval Christian traditions of the story of Job: that is, the Biblical, ecclesiastical and apocryphal, which were reflected in literature and art.[92]

For those who identified Mal Francese with the *male de Santo Job*, the drama of Job suffering from a terrible and incomprehensible illness was reborn in the case of the earliest victims of the French Disease, and along with it the subsequent dilemma between the two opposite ways of perceiving the cause of this disease. The same applies to several aspects of these three traditions which were reflected with their inconsistencies in the way *Morbus Gallicus* was perceived in late fifteenth-century Ferrara. Thus one of the Ferrarese chroniclers (Zambotti) identified Mal Francese with the *male de Santo Job*, and at the same time related the disease to sinful sexual practices.

Both Ferrarese diaries base their claims for the identity of Mal Francese with the *male de Santo Job* on the incurability of the disease from the medical viewpoint.[93] However, the Vulgate version of the Old Testament Book of Job did not refer anywhere to the incurability of the disease of Job,[94] although it was definitely described as serious, painful and loathsome. Indeed, this book recounted that after Job had lost all his sons and possessions Satan was permitted by God to afflict Job with a 'malignant sore covering [him] from the sole of his feet to the top of his head'. Job was sitting down on a dunghill and cleaned his sore with a tile.[95]

If the idea of Job suffering from an incurable disease did not appear in the Book of Job, what was the origin of the double identity established by the Ferrarese diaries, that is, that Mal Francese was both incurable in medical terms and therefore was the *male de Santo Job*? From an examination of some of the commentaries on the Book of Job most widespread in Western Europe before 1500,[96] only that of Aquinas identified in its literal *explicatio* the phrase 'very bad sore' (*ulcere pessimo*) of the Vulgata with 'ugly, detestable, incurable, and painful wound' (*turpi et abominabili vulnere incurabili et doloroso*).[97] Yet this double identity could also be inferred from the contents of another passage of the Book of Job that referred to God as someone who 'injures and cures, strikes and heals with His hands'.[98] If it were only God who had allowed Job's disease, only He could cure it; therefore, it was incurable by physicians and by their medicines. Furthermore, there is one passage underlining the same idea in the apocryphal Testament of Job, a pseudo-epigraphical work which circulated widely in the middle ages.[99] It related that, when Job was visited by one of the kings while he was ill, he refused the offer of a royal physician to look after him, saying: 'My healing and treatment come from the Lord who created even the physicians.'[100]

If it is only by means of divine remedies that a disease caused by God can be healed, one might expect the use of divine remedies to treat Mal Francese – a condition that physicians felt unable to heal with their natural remedies. This seems to be the case when at a seemingly critical moment of Alfonso d'Este's long complaint the ducal physician Lodovico Carri prescribed for him a singular and drastic remedy for a nobleman, that is, to have his hair cut – advice which Alfonso followed without delay. This bizarre therapeutical measure remains undocumented in contemporary medical texts. However, right at the beginning of the Book of Job there is a passage where it is recounted that Job, after discovering that he had suddenly lost all his sons and belongings, stood up, tore his clothes and cut his hair, before hurling himself to the ground and adoring his God.[101] Furthermore, the *Moralia in Job* of St Gregory the Great – the best-known and most authoritative medieval commentary on the Book of Job – interpreted Job's decision to have his hair cut as a sign of grief when faced with so much adversity, allegedly accepted with humility and piety. At the same time it emphasised to later ages the symbolism of this act in the sacrament of the Christian priesthood.[102] The religious nature of this therapeutic measure is also consonant with the fact that Lodovico Carri, who prescribed it, was then a devoted follower of Savonarola at the Estense court, and was seen by the Dominican friar as a trustworthy person.[103]

Conclusion

Lauro Martines has said that 'the life of the Italian people, as a story cast around self-determining city-states, came to an end in 1494' as a result of the invasion by King Charles VIII of France.[104] Although in those days no contemporary could imagine the magnitude of the external dangers confronting Italy, such a foreign invasion did take place in the middle of a deep and generalised crisis of which Italians were well aware. It is in this serious crisis that we must look for clues to help us to understand the profusion of reports and reactions about the many calamities in Italy at the time, not least the French Disease.

Why did the two male Ferrarese diarists have such a different perception of the French Disease? There are two possible answers. First, it should not be forgotten that Duke Ercole d'Este kept himself neutral in relation to the French invasion, which he privately greeted with satisfaction. It is quite certain that the writers of both diaries knew about this neutrality, and shared it to a greater or lesser extent.[105] But, while the favourable feelings of the ducal court and its circle to the French invasion cooled off only when its final fiasco was obvious to them, the popular mood within the Estense dukedom was never unanimous, since the people bore all the consequences of allowing a mercenary army to cross the ducal territory. Indeed, the anonymous diary reported several items of information directly or indirectly related to this issue: the hiding of crops and forage by Modenese and Reggian peasants; the execution of a ducal crossbowman blamed for the killing of a French soldier in the Reggian region; and the killing of a butcher by Venetian soldiers after he had told them they were going to die if they went to fight the French army.[106] Secondly, there is the question of the increasingly moral climate at the Ferrarese court in the late fifteenth century. This attitude, which spread outwards from the court, influenced contemporaries to a greater or lesser degree, as we have seen in the cases of Zambotti and the anonymous diarist of Ferrara.

Chapter Four

The Medical Dispute at the Court
of Ferrara

Disputations and Disputes

We have seen that the French Disease was viewed as a punishment from God.
This did not mean it was impious to try to seek relief from it or cure it.
Learned physicians often stressed the godliness of their calling and it was
commonly held that God's mercy had provided remedies in the natural world
for many illnesses. The university-trained physician often began his treatment
with an invocation for God's help and an injunction to the patient to confess
to what contemporaries called their 'spiritual doctor'.[1] In Ferrara the piety of
the duke was a model for his citizens: necessarily so, for he insisted on it. His
practical efforts to find a treatment for the disease involved finding the best
doctors and the most effective medicines. In this quest he turned to the
experts, the university-trained physicians, and caused them – or at least
allowed them – to decide among themselves by disputation. This was the
accepted method of generating and validating knowledge in the university,
the place where learned and rational medicine was taught and learned.

We shall look later within the context of Leipzig at the form of the
academic disputation, but first we need to understand how a courtly disputation might differ from an academic one. This difference is significant. It was
not only that in a court, unlike a medical faculty, there were no statutes, no
graduation and less need for a formally structured disputation, but that it was
in the courts that cultural movements like hellenism flourished.[2] The
hellenists thought that the medical curriculum badly needed reform and that
the medieval Latin commentators and Arabic authors alike would be replaced
by Greek authors, ideally taught in the Greek language. Ferrara was a
particular centre of medical hellenism; and for these reasons we may call what
happened at Ferrara a 'dispute' rather than a formal disputation. We shall see
that its nature depended on the attitudes of the antagonists towards the
reforms attempted by the hellenists as well as on the reform programme itself.

That a dispute took place at Ferrara in the late fifteenth century on the
nature and causes of the French Disease is well known to medical historians.

But this picture is distorted in two ways. First, historians have been concerned primarily with the work on the French Disease by Nicolò Leoniceno, the professor of the medical school of Ferrara, since he was the only well-known participant. The precise circumstances of the dispute, including participants, place, dates and aims, have been relatively obscure, and we are concerned here to consider its actual contents and context. In this way we can attempt to answer central questions about it: what was the dispute about, and why did it take the form it did? Why did the contenders meet and dispute on this particular topic at that particular time and place?

The second distortion of the picture is that medical historians have tended to adopt Karl Sudhoff's picture of the earliest medical works published by university physicians on this disease.[3] This has tended to turn historians' attention away from the dispute of Ferrara to another and more formal medical disputation in Bolognese university medical circles, generated by the publication of Leoniceno's work.[4] Thus the Ferrara dispute has usually been presented as one more episode in the alleged academic war between humanist and Arabist or scholastic physicians. As part of this picture, its main contenders were seen to be the humanist Leoniceno, who opened fire, the Arabist Natale Montesauro, who replied to him, defending Avicenna, and the former student of Leoniceno, Antonio Scanaroli, who counter-attacked in defence of his old master.[5] We shall reassess this picture by reconstructing as far as possible the dispute, which is generally accepted to have had a key influence on the perceptions and reactions of university-trained physicians to the French Disease in northern Italy and the rest of Europe in the late fifteenth and early sixteenth century.[6]

The Circumstances of the Dispute

Between late March and early April 1497, a number of men met to discuss the pox in a palace in Ferrara belonging to the dukes of Este. They included Leoniceno, Sebastiano dall'Aquila, who was another professor in the medical faculty of Ferrara, and probably the Estense court physician and former lecturer at the *studio* of Ferrara, Coradino Gilino. They all referred to the event as a *disputatio* and so recognised their discussion as similar to the more formal meetings within the universities. Undoubtedly they accepted academic procedures as proper for arriving at knowledge, but our evidence for the event is what the participants committed to paper afterwards and circulated. To this extent the dispute came to resemble the majority of renaissance disputes, which in all probability were literary polemics carried on through epistolary exchange. When the contents of these documents spread – increasingly as a result of the printing press – very often other people joined in and gave new meanings to previous disputes. There is no available archival documentation of the event to allow a full reconstruction; the only indirect evidence comes from the works of some of the earliest medical writers on the French Disease: Leoniceno, Montesauro, Scanaroli and Dall'Aquila.[7] They agree that the *disputatio* was about what was commonly, though not medically, called the 'French Disease', *Morbus Gallicus*. The dispute in Ferrara was not an isolated event, for Coradino Gilino referred to the 'several disputations on the French Disease that have been and will be among physicians', because it was an 'unknown disease among the moderns'.[8]

We know that the dispute in Ferrara did not take place at the faculty of medicine or in any other part of the local *studio generale* from the work Sebastiano dall'Aquila dedicated soon after the dispute to Lodovico Gonzaga, the Bishop of Mantua: 'I have decided to report to you what has been disputed on the disease which people call "French Disease" at the house of our princes during the past days. . . .'[9] This source also makes it possible to date the dispute, for it refers to a post-mortem practised on the corpse of 'somebody who in life suffered from this disease'.[10] This event coincided in time with the autopsy of an alleged thief and murderer who was hanged on 11 April 1497.[11]

The essential feature of a courtly rather than an academic dispute was patronage. The patron could raise matters of interest or concern to himself or those connected to him. His clients would be resident experts, in this case the court physician Gilino and, by extension, those subject to his influence, as the physicians of the *studio* must have been. Whom the patron chose could clearly affect the outcome, and his choice constituted a route whereby different kinds of medical men (hellenist, surgical, Latin 'establishment')[12] could reach a wider audience for their views. The staging of disputes at court on the most diverse topics was a familiar ingredient of the culture of renaissance princes, who in doing so very likely imitated the intellectual usages of university elites. The court of Este was no exception. In fact, it had already been the scene for theological disputes, which had been promoted by Duke Ercole himself with the participation of Dominican and Franciscan friars, and sometimes even of Jewish rabbis, in 1477, 1487 and 1488.[13] In the case of the disputes on the pox, nowhere is the identity given of which of 'our princes' convened it, but it was probably the head of the Este family, Duke Ercole I. His brother Sigismondo probably shared this initiative, since he was the addressee of Coradino Gilino's printed medical work on the French Disease.[14]

The Basics of Medicine

So far we have looked at laymen's reactions to the French Disease. In this and subsequent chapters we examine the reaction of the medical men, which was a more technical business. Although medical men varied among themselves a good deal in their opinions about the pox, they all shared certain basic beliefs about the nature of the body and its diseases. We must briefly set out these beliefs to make this and the following chapter in particular accessible for the non-specialist reader.

Doctors and all educated men held that the world in general was made up of mixtures of the four elements, earth, air, fire and water. Each element was characterised by a pair of qualities. These were also four in number, hot, wet, cold and dry, so that fire for example was hot and dry, and water cold and wet. Hot and dry were the active qualities, and most natural change resulted from action and reaction of opposite qualities.

In the body the four elements and qualities formed particular mixed bodies, the four humours. These were blood, hot and wet; red (or yellow) bile, hot and dry; black bile (melancholy), dry and cold; and phlegm, wet and cold. Blood was the nourishment of the body and the other three humours were by-products of the processes of concoction and purification that generated the blood and governed the body. In health, the humours were in due proportion. But they could become unnatural, either by corruption or by excess or deficiency of quality.

Since the blood was generated directly from food, it was obvious to the doctor that diet played a great part in maintaining and restoring health. In his therapy the doctor relied first on regimen, the control of the patient's activities and diet. The basic principle was the antagonism of opposites, so that, for example, a patient who was plethoric with an excess of blood would be treated either by the application of cooling and drying medicines (because blood was hot and wet) or by blood-letting (to reduce the quantity of blood and regain balance). The other humours could be encouraged or evacuated by special drugs that purged, sweated or vomited the patient or promoted his urine. Disease, on the Galenic model, was primarily disordered bodily function, the result of a poor regimen or innate weakness. The pox was seen as a disastrous breakdown of this bodily activity.

The Disputants

Who were the contenders at the dispute in Ferrara? Of the aforementioned physicians (Leoniceno, Dall'Aquila, Montesauro and Scanaroli) who referred to it in their contemporary works on the French Disease, only Leoniceno and Dall'Aquila, both of them residents at Ferrara and professors in its medical faculty at the time, expressed themselves in a way that suggests their direct participation. Indeed, Dall'Aquila claimed to have written his work to inform his protector and patron, the bishop Lodovico Gonzaga, of the matter of the dispute held at the house belonging to the Este dukes. And, in his dedication to Gianfrancesco Pico della Mirandola, Leoniceno took for granted his own active participation in the 'disputation on the disease that people call French Disease, which has recently taken place at Ferrara, and which I committed to paper afterwards'.[15] At first sight Leoniceno's *Libellus* might seem to suggest that the number of disputants was as many as six. In fact, in facing the intellectual problem of the nature of the French Disease Leoniceno proceeded by exclusion, that is, by discussing and rejecting one after another different (and presumably extant) nosological interpretations of the disease. As current practice in the schools demanded, before giving his own views on this issue Leoniceno ruled out the alternative views, namely that the new scourge was identifiable with one or more of the five clinical labels known as (and in this order) *elephantiasis, lichenas, asaphati, pruna* and *ignis persicus*, all of which were well known and described by the medical authorities. Defenders of any of these five labels can be easily found within the earliest medical literature on the French Disease, and Leoniceno was practising the rhetorical and dialectical technique of strengthening his own views by the destruction of as many opposing views as possible, not necessarily just those presented at the dispute. As he said in the preface of his *Libellus*,

> I myself have proposed to refute with my weak intelligence, not only the main opinion defended at Ferrara, but also the many others that I know flourish elsewhere, as well as to confirm eventually my view with the support of examples, reasons and the authority of very noble physicians.[16]

And further on, in concluding his first refutation (of the clinical label *elephantiasis*), he added: 'And certainly we have discussed those questions about this first view in a more prolix way – maybe longer than is convenient – because it was mainly about it that the dispute was held at Ferrara.'[17] Therefore, although Leoniceno aimed to rule out every single clinical label that to the best of his knowledge the French Disease had received in other places, his primary purpose was to refute the identification of this disease with Galen's *elephantiasis*. This claim, which according to Leoniceno enjoyed great prestige at Ferrara and had constituted the core of the dispute, coincides entirely with the position held by Sebastiano dall'Aquila. We may therefore with some confidence assume that Dall'Aquila was Leoniceno's principal adversary; indeed, to the extent that it was a formal dispute, there could only be two people involved, the man who defended the thesis and the man who attacked it. Each interchange between the *defendens* and *opponens* was part of the sequence of syllogism and authority with a single goal of attacking or defending the thesis. Leoniceno's preoccupation with rejecting Dall'Aquila's views is further evidence of this.

The Ferrarese court physician Gilino is a possible third contender, either giving his views informally or his known views forming a target for Leoniceno. Indeed, in the work on the French Disease which Gilino addressed to Sigismondo d'Este soon after the dates of the dispute, he vaguely referred to the many disputations that the new disease had provoked among physicians, and defended the clinical identification that Leoniceno had attacked at the end of his refutations – that it was the same disease as that called *ignis sacer* by Celsus and *ignis persicus* by late medieval university physicians.

Thus the dispute in Ferrara was primarily a debate between Nicolò Leoniceno and Sebastiano dall'Aquila, with Coradino Gilino as a likely third contender. It is possible that the dispute included more contenders who remain unidentified, but more probably the remaining clinical labels Leoniceno decided to refute simply corresponded to current opinions in Italy and the rest of Europe. In order to understand the dispute in the particular historical context of late fifteenth-century Italian university medicine, we need to provide biographical sketches of the three main contenders, especially of Leoniceno, who was by far the most influential.

Nicolò Leoniceno

Leoniceno (1428–1524) is an important figure for us. He was the arch-hellenist. He was waging a war for Greek medicine of which the dispute at Ferrara was a battle, and the hellenist call for the reform of the medical curriculum found a strong advocate in him. He was both famous and notorious for his attacks not only on Avicenna, the great authority of the establishment university physicians, but also on Pliny, a giant for the Latin humanists. The essential antagonisms of the time were not between humanists and scholastics in the medical world – a picture, as we said above, that is distorted – but between the hellenists and the others, in this case the medical men whose subject had absorbed as much humanism as it could take and who now found themselves defending a Latin culture and a professional medicine that was part of it. These cultural attitudes were fundamental to the way in which their protagonists tackled the question of the French Disease.

In Italy in particular, part of the hellenists' strategy for reform was to win over the politically important. This is why the courtly dispute at Ferrara is important in the story of how cultural attitudes helped to shape reaction to the French Disease. In Leoniceno's example we can see two things: many of the circumstances that might make a hellenist of someone; and the strategies adopted by the hellenists in their reform programme. Both are reflected in the dispute over the French Disease in Ferrara.[18] First, the circumstances: Leoniceno had been born into Latin culture before the fall of Constantinople; he had been young when the Council 'of Florence' first met in Ferrara, where the Greeks, under intense pressure from the Turks, tried to secure military help from the Italian cities against them. He was still young when the Turks destroyed Constantinople and drove even more Greeks to Italy, with their new and fascinating interpretation of Plato and a clear sense of cultural superiority. Just as their Roman ancestors had done when faced with Greeks, some of the Latins were dazzled and fell into an orgy of emulation, while others in reaction regrouped around their own culture and tried to find fault with the newcomer. Leoniceno, in contact with native Greek speakers, was a powerful advocate of the superiority of Greek knowledge, *prisca scientia*. Unlike many of his hellenist persuasion, he brought his beliefs to bear on the technical subjects of medicine and natural philosophy.

The strategies employed by Leoniceno during a long career in the hellenist campaign were three: his university teaching at the faculties of arts and medicine of Ferrara and Bologna,[19] his translation of many ancient authors, and his participation in learned disputations on medical and natural-philosophical subjects. That he also acted as a court physician at an early stage of his career enhanced his position as an apologist for hellenism.[20] As a university teacher in Ferrara he was in a position to promote hellenism among those who would later be opinion-formers in the community and who might patronise hellenists. As a translator he was himself subject to patronage and at first rendered into Italian from Greek and Latin historical and military works that interested Duke Ercole.[21] Later (from 1489 to 1524) he pursued his own programme for hellenising medicine by translating eleven works of Galen from the Greek. Some of these were the standard contents of the *Articella*, which had been the university medical textbook since the thirteenth century,[22] and Leoniceno's translations were a first attempt to improve a medieval text in a hellenist manner. In fact the *Articella* in its later editions (particularly those of 1523 and 1527) became a vehicle for the hellenists' attempted reform of the medical curriculum, for it carried so many Greek works as to deserve the title of the 'hellenist *Articella*'.[23] Not long after Leoniceno's death, the publication history of the *Articella* came to a sudden end. Despite its hellenist accretions, it remained irreducibly medieval in its traditional components, and in killing it off the hellenists had partly won their battle for reform of the medical curriculum.

Almost all Galen's works that Leoniceno translated were already available in other Greek–Latin versions.[24] Clearly Leoniceno felt that these translations were inadequate; only hellenistic scholarship could provide sound texts. But the hellenist battle in medical circles was fought against great odds. Leoniceno found it necessary to write long forewords to justify his work, and his translations provoked some objections which obliged him to publish new works with the sole purpose of defending himself.[25] Nor was courtly patronage for medical translations so readily forthcoming as it had been for military, and the official Estense acknowledgement reached Leoniceno almost at the end of his days: there is no evidence of any financial reward for his work until the academic year 1521–2, when he was given an annual salary of 400 *Lire Marchesine* at the expense of the *studio*, 'for translating from Greek to Latin the works of Galen for the sake of the world, so that by means of his excellence very rare and excellent works come into light in translation'.[26] 'For the sake of the world' encapsulates Leoniceno's own hellenistic programme within medicine: the schoolmen, the medievals, the Latin-culture men were not merely old fashioned or barbaric, they were *wrong*: their texts were inadequate, their understanding of proper medicine faulty. As in the case of Pliny and Avicenna, so in the case of those who wrote about the French Disease, misunderstanding medicine was dangerous in a practical way. Those who could not name the disease or find its ancient description were bound to treat it wrongly and so injure their patients. To Leoniceno it was axiomatic that proper medicine was Greek medicine, and this determined how he approached the French Disease.

So, translation was the second of Leoniceno's hellenist strategies, and it provided materials for his third, the disputation. The dispute on the French Disease was indeed a particular application of general hellenist principles and materials; the hellenists *needed* such materials and principles because, as we have seen, they were fighting against greats odds and needed to agree on tactics. To return for a moment to the educational strategy of the hellenists, we can listen to the manner in which another hellenist addressed Leoniceno in a late edition of the *Articella* which contains Leoniceno's translations. Here are the hellenistic principles that formed part of the intellectual baggage that Leoniceno was to bring to the dispute on the pox. Our second hellenist is Luigi Bonacciuoli, who by 1505 enjoyed courtly patronage as one of the family doctors of Lucrezia Borgia, the second wife of Alfonso d'Este and Duchess of Ferrara.[27] Bonacciuoli praises Leoniceno for his attacks on contemporary medicine and its errors, and looks forward to its destruction. But the enemy are numerous: they are *neroniores*, more and worse than Nero, who forced suicide on his teacher Seneca and on Lucan, and who ordered the death of his mother Agrippina. Their books are full of errors and 'the contagion of deceit'. Bonacciuoli uses language that was almost a code encapsulating hellenist views.[28] He saw Leoniceno's translations of Galen as the principal way out of a subject beset with 'barbarous and false' translations, by allowing Galen's pristine 'eloquence' to stand in the light. These also are hellenist codewords for the superiority of Greek over Latin (it is by Leoniceno's 'good arts' that polluted fruit is cut out, and the profane removed from the vestibule of sacred letters).

Of course, hellenists did not have a monopoly of fulsome dedications, but what they wrote to each other and to their patrons does follow a pattern. In the preface of the translation of Galen's *Ars Parva* that Leoniceno dedicated to Alfonso d'Este, Duke of Ferrara, Leoniceno himself addressed Alfonso in a way that makes it clear how useful was the patronage of powerful figures in the hellenists' campaign for reform. He flatters the duke, suggesting a comparison with the ancient Caesars, and admiring his patronage of the best (that is, hellenist) arts. Neither fire nor the anger of Jove can destroy the immortality that attaches to the cultivation of good letters, Leoniceno assures his patron; and 'good letters' here is the proper study of the old medicine, 'which once enjoyed the brightest light, but which now lies buried in shadows in the books of the barbarians'.[29] He urges Alfonso to help.[30] It is clear from Leoniceno's commentary on the three doctrines of Galen that the 'neoterics' (moderns) include the medieval Latin commentators, of whom few hellenists would have approved. Leoniceno in particular objected to the work of Pietro Torrigiano (Turisanus) and Pietro d'Abano, known respectively as Plusquam Commentator and Conciliator. These are the *iuniores medici* whose work was vitiated by barbaric translations and was marked out by Leoniceno for destruction. In the same edition of the *Articella* Leoniceno presented a preface intended to cover all his translations of Galen. It gives detailed examples of how his new translations were intended to achieve the hellenist programme of reform, and it tells us of the opposition he expected to meet. We can recognise it as the opposition of the medical establishment, which did not like being patronised by presumptuous hellenophiles. No doubt, says Leoniceno,

> Some philophaster will come to me, representing those who hate good letters because they do not possess them, and who therefore cannot talk straight or philosophise properly, and will argue in this kind of way: 'Your [Leoniceno's] kind of argument is taken from the rules of speech and, rather than belonging to the philosophers or medical men, is proper only to grammarians and dabblers in rhetoric and pedagogy; we in contrast look for wisdom rather than eloquence'.[31]

This of course is just what the establishment doctors *did* say, often seeing the hellenists as avoiding the technicalities of philosophy and medicine in their search for 'eloquence'.[32] Leoniceno surely believed that, after his exhaustive and technical analysis of the problem of Galen's three doctrines, no one could accuse him of avoiding the difficult issues: this work must have helped to show that hellenism could deal with what the *scholastici* were proud to be masters of, and must have helped towards the eventual victory of the hellenists.

The hellenist principle that bad texts mean bad medical practice is illustrated by Leoniceno by a passage from Aristotle's *History of Animals*, where Aristotle appears to say that only man catches rabies from a mad dog. Other principles of hellenist scholarship appear: if Aristotle is to be defended here at all, says Leoniceno, it must be by a minimal change to the Greek text. He makes such a change. He categorises errors of transcription and translation. If lost words had to be supplied, he said, then it was best to supply as few as possible and of a kind as close as possible to the Greek. This is what made medieval Latin and Arabic commentaries and textual emendations barbaric, because they supplied alien neologisms for Greek lacunae. Taking the commentary of Haly Rodoan (Ibn Ridwan) on Galen's *Ars Parva* as an example, Leoniceno says that Haly's repair of a defective part of the text is 'violent', not only in supplying Arabic words but in offering something contrary to Galenic principles. The discussion by Plusquam Commentator was barbaric in its Latinity: Galen would never have stuttered – *balbutisset* – like this. Part of the problem with Arabic and medieval Latin – and Leoniceno is doing a very hellenist thing in lumping them together – is that the very nature of the words lacked clarity and made the discussion obscure. Plusquam Commentator, Nicolò Falcucci, Avicenna, Serapion and Averroes were all barbaric (according to Leoniceno) even when not departing from Galen's intentions; what seems to be in Leoniceno's mind too is that words themselves carry significations about meaning and that it is an improper use of language to employ words from another language, or invented words.

As for the third hellenist strategy, Leoniceno took part in no less than three medical and natural-philosophical disputations – or rather controversies – during the decade of 1490.[33] All centred on the identity of ancient things: how a correct name indicated the essence of a thing, and what learned men should do about it. We look at the dispute on the pox below and need note only briefly how the others shared this characteristic. The first followed Leoniceno's work on the errors of Pliny in December 1492 and involved Angelo Poliziano, Ermolao Barbaro and Pandolfo Collenuccio; as a controversy it was still alive in the first decade of the sixteenth century. Leoniceno claimed that in his *Naturalis Historia* Pliny, the Roman, had dangerously confused the names of several anatomical parts and natural medicinal substances. With this work Leoniceno attempted to show how much knowledge on these topics had fallen into decay since ancient Greece through the translations of the Romans, Arabs and Latin medieval Europeans. The relevance of his criticisms of Pliny lay in the breach that they opened in the bosom of the humanist movement, since he attacked one of the authorities whom Latin humanists claimed as a part of the intellectual legacy of the antiquity that should be recovered.[34] Each of these features was to be repeated in the pox dispute: men in the wrong medical camp had misidentified the disease, with dangerous results, and had not recognised the textual sources of error nor returned to the real *prisca medicina*.

We know of the second dispute only through Leoniceno's publication of *De tiro seu vipera*, printed in Venice in 1497 by Aldo Manucio. This pamphlet was concerned with the *tyrus*, a classical ingredient of the well-known remedy theriac, and again it was a question of identity. As Leoniceno himself commented in his preface, *De tiro* was but the enlargement of a chapter of his earlier work on the errors of Pliny – and it was therefore, like the earlier attack on Pliny, a part of his hellenistic programme of reform. *De tiro* was only concerned, however, with Leoniceno's claim that the classical *tyrus* was actually the viper, a snake prevalent in Italy, and not another species carried from Syria, as some Venetian doctors claimed (it is very likely that they made the claim for commercial reasons, as sixteenth-century Italian pharmacists often did).[35]

The third and latest dispute took place, as we have already seen, in the same year as Leoniceno published *De tiro seu vipera*, and compelled him to write his tract on the pox, the *Libellus de epidemia quam vulgo morbum gallicum vocant*, which was printed twice before the end of 1497.[36] Before the end of the century, Leoniceno's *Libellus* came to be printed at the German university city of Leipzig about 1499/1500, where, as we shall see, it prompted a new dispute. In the *Libellus*, Leoniceno extended his strategy, derived from the same hellenistic principles, into a new field, that of diseases. By applying the same methodology, he claimed to have established the identity and therefore the nature of the *Morbus Gallicus* after having rejected several other interpretations. Again, he assumed that he had found the truth in Greece: Greek medical knowledge had been – he said – lost or corrupted in earlier times by the translations of the Romans, Arabs and Western medieval Europeans, so that medicine had become a dangerous and fallacious practice which mistook diseases, and therefore applied dangerous remedies.

Leoniceno seems to have felt a particular urgency about the medical implications of his hellenist programme. As we noted above, he was unusual among the hellenists in engaging fully in the technical businesses of natural philosophy and medicine, and was fully alive to the practical consequences of misidentifying a medicine or a disease like the pox. While hellenists like Aldo Manucio were occupied in bringing major Greek authors to the press – Manucio's project of the 1490s was to present Aristotle to the public, and Leoniceno was involved in it – medicine does not seem to have been high on their list of priorities. Certainly Manucio published Leoniceno's *Libellus* and *De tiro*, but this seems to have been at the urging of the author, his old friend, probably as a return of favours.[37] Perhaps it was their practical importance in Leoniceno's eyes that made him publish his books on the French Disease and the *tyrus* before even his translations of Galen.

Sebastiano dall'Aquila

Doubtless it is because the 'Interpretation and Treatment of the French Disease' (*Interpretatio Morbi Gallici et Cura*, Pavia, 1509) by Sebastiano dall'Aquila (c.1440–c.1510) was not printed until twelve years after the dispute in Ferrara that only an obscure biographical dictionary of illustrious Aquilan people published in the mid-nineteenth century connects him with this controversy.[38]

Sebastiano Foroli was born in the Abruzzo city of L'Aquila in southern Italy about 1440 and died about 1510.[39] He may have studied medicine at the university of Naples and lectured there after taking his degree.[40] By 1489 he appears to have settled in northern Italy. In June that year magister Sebastianus de Aquila acted as the 'promoter' (*promotor*) of a candidate for a doctorate of arts and medicine at the university of Ferrara. This strongly suggests that Dall'Aquila was lecturing at this *studio* by the academic year 1488–9.[41] We know little of his life afterwards until January 1495 when he appears as a promoter of another medical candidate for the doctorate. On this occasion, Dall'Aquila was referred to as an *ordinarius lector* of philosophy at the same *studio*. To judge by the many doctorates – twenty-eight – to which he promoted candidates from 1494 to 1500, he probably continued to lecture at the university of Ferrara until the end of the academic year 1499–1500, although he had turned his lectureship of philosophy into medicine by January 1498.[42] During the academic year 1500–1 Dall'Aquila lectured in medicine at the university of Pavia,[43] but he may have come back to the university of Ferrara during 1501–2, when he was *promotor* for two doctorates (May and August 1502), before his final disappearance from the records.[44]

Dall'Aquila wrote at least five medical works, two of which were printed before he died, while the other three remain unpublished. The first two are the work on the French Disease and an academic *quaestio* on 'blood fever'. Both of them were published for the first time in Pavia in 1509 as part of a collection of works on practical medicine headed by Marco Gattinara's commentary on Book IX of Rhazes' *Ad regem Mansorem*.[45] This collection of medical works enjoyed a great success in the sixteenth century to judge by the number of editions – no less than fifteen between 1509 and 1604, twelve of which included Dall'Aquila's works.[46] His other three works not yet published are typically 'scholastic', consisting of a brief compilation of physicians' and natural philosophers' views on the recurrent topic of what the subject of medicine was, and two *quaestiones*. The first, which he signed as ordinary lecturer in medicine at the university of Ferrara, deals with the supposed hegemony of one of the 'main members' of the body over the rest; the second, which appears to have been debated in Pavia, deals with the causes of the cyclical movement of humours. All three are included in a codex of the Biblioteca Nazionale of Turin, along with his *quaestio* on blood fever, which the copyist rhetorically introduced here as 'addressed to his students' by Dall'Aquila, who 'obtained in his time the foremost chair of medicine in Italy'.[47]

There is abundant evidence that Dall'Aquila was a busy and successful teacher of school medicine. But he was more than that. The earliest piece of additional evidence introduces him as an active propagandist in favour of Neoplatonism in Ferrara by 1498. It is a letter sent in January by the young Lodovico Ariosto (1474–1533) which mentions the lectures on Plato's *Timaeus* that Sebastiano dall'Aquila offered at Ferrara. These had apparently been given before a large audience on feastdays and not in Dall'Aquila's capacity as professor at the local medical faculty.[48] Feastday lectures in the medieval university were traditionally an opportunity to teach something not in the main course of lectures – *ordinarius* – and here they seem to have been an opportunity for the introduction of Dall'Aquila's brand of hellenism. His lectures were appreciated and we know that Ariosto was moved to order Platonist books from Aldo Manucio to satisfy the intellectual curiosity awakened in him by the Platonic lectures of Dall'Aquila, a 'diligent cultivator of good letters, who professes the Academic Dogma'.[49] The second letter suggests that the ducal heir of Ferrara, Alfonso d'Este, found Dall'Aquila intellectually stimulating: in December 1499 Alfonso vividly asked his father to

protect Dall'Aquila, who had just been badly injured by an assailant, 'for the
sake of your subjects' learning' since 'magistro Sebastiano, because of his
learning, should be favoured'.[50] Again, patronage by the powerful was also an
avenue for the advance of hellenism. As Dall'Aquila circulated among the
great on the strength of his medical reputation, so his hellenism became better
known. Another letter was written by Cesare Borgia – Alfonso's brother-in-
law – in October 1501, praising Dall'Aquila's successful medical care of his
personal secretary,[51] and there are other sources of information referring to
the great esteem in which other Italian noble people held Dall'Aquila as a
physician. In August 1502 the wife of a Mantuan courtier successfully treated
by Dall'Aquila recommended his services to the Marchioness of Mantua,
Isabella d'Este, for the case of the sculptor Gian Cristoforo Romano (c. 1470–
1512), who had been seriously ill for several months.[52] Last but not least, there
is also the praise of Dall'Aquila, brief but expressive, which the humanist and
Estense courtier Giovanni Sabadino degli Arienti passed on to Ercole d'Este:
'a virtuous man who should not be denigrated, a person second to none in
his discipline'.[53]

In short, hellenism, Neoplatonism and other cultural and intellectual movements grew by word-of-mouth recommendations and patronage. Dall'Aquila
seems to have had his own patron: we have already noted that he dedicated
his *Interpretatio* of the French Disease to Lodovico Gonzaga (1459–1511), the
Bishop of Mantua (from 1483), probably an early sufferer from the disease.
After serious family conflicts over a cardinalate, Lodovico, known as a patron
and lover of letters, went off in 1496 to live in his refuge of Gazzuolo, where
he surrounded himself with a little court and devoted himself to the collection
of antiquities.[54] Everything suggests that Dall'Aquila as well as the Latin poet
Nicolò Lelio Cosmico,[55] whom Dall'Aquila mentioned twice in the foreword
of his *Interpretatio*, belonged to this court.

Coradino Gilino

We know still less about Coradino Gilino (*fl.* 1468–99). A native of Ferrara,
he was the son of the notary Dominicus de Gilino. He studied arts and
medicine at the Ferrarese *studio*, where he took his doctorate in 1468. This
suggests that he might have been born about 1445, so that he was more than
fifty years old at the time of the dispute. During the period 1471–4 Gilino
lectured on medicine on feastdays at the university of Ferrara, for which he
received the modest annual stipend of 25 *Lire Marchesine*. Afterwards he may
have lectured at the faculty of arts and medicine at Ferrara at least during the
periods 1488–9, 1490–1, 1492–4 and 1498–9.[56] Gilino wrote his *De morbo
quem gallicum nuncupant* in 1497, soon after the dispute,[57] and dedicated it 'to
the illustrious Sigismondo d'Este', who must have been Duke Ercole's sixty-
four-year-old brother.[58]

These then are the ascertainable details of the contenders in the dispute.

We must next set them into their context and then see how their beliefs led them to their differing interpretations of the pox. To do so, let us first recall the different styles of medical thinking which we met briefly above with Leoniceno. At the time of this dispute the majority of university medical professors all over Europe, and therefore also university-educated physicians, identified themselves with the late medieval medical tradition, with its emphasis on Avicennan Galenism (which we can call the 'Avicennan tradition'). In contrast to this was a new intellectual tendency, 'Latin medical humanism', which developed during the fifteenth century mainly as a result of the recovery of the *De medicina* of Cornelius Celsus, whose followers considered him to be 'the physicians' Cicero' (*Cicero medicorum*) and who took his work as a model of Latin writing.[59] Some people found compromises between these two intellectual tendencies. This reflects the fact noted by Paul Oskar Kristeller, that by the mid-fifteenth century the influence of the humanist movement in Italy was no longer confined to the *studia humanitatis*, but had extended to the whole university culture, including natural philosophy and medicine.[60] It was in about 1480 that the third movement, medical hellenism, emerged among the Italian humanist physicians. This radicalised the humanist postulates, advocating a return to the *prisca medicina* of the ancient Greeks, which they claimed to be the real source of medicine. We have seen that Nicolò Leoniceno was one of the propagators of these ideas at the university of Ferrara, and it spread from there to other medical faculties in Italy and the rest of Europe. Little wonder that he claimed that *Morbus Gallicus* had been already described by the Greek Hippocrates. Sharing many aspects of the hellenist programme, but in the last analysis a separate intellectual tendency, 'medical Neoplatonism' can be seen as the extension of the Neoplatonist programme to medicine. Its supporters, who included many outstanding members of the Florentine Neoplatonist circle like Pierleone da Spoleto, were strongly influenced by the medical works of Marsilio Ficino.[61]

In this context we can distinguish between the intellectual concerns of Leoniceno and Dall'Aquila. They were both active hellenists, so what made them differ? From the years of his studies in arts and medicine at the university of Padua, Leoniceno remained deeply influenced – albeit in a critical and independent way – by the 'Paduan Aristotelianism', a leading medical and philosophico-natural tradition which developed in this university from the thirteenth to the seventeenth century.[62] Leoniceno constantly praises Aristotle, the *summus, consultissimus philosophus*[63] on natural things. Dall'Aquila, on the contrary, actively campaigned in late fifteenth-century Ferrara for Florentine Neoplatonism – the *pia philosophia* of Marsilio Ficino – which was clearly opposed to the tendencies of contemporary Aristotelianism.[64]

It may not be too speculative, then, to imagine that behind the intellectual confrontation between Leoniceno and Dall'Aquila in the dispute in Ferrara there were different projects for the reform of medical teaching and practice. Indeed, both of them represented distinct professional patterns: Nicolò

Leoniceno, the learned university professor, deliberately distanced himself from the atmosphere of the Estense court and from medical practice in order to devote himself more fully to the theoretical study of medicine; he confronted the challenge of Sebastiano dall'Aquila, a successful medical practitioner in several Italian courts (Ferrara, Mantua and Rome), who had even achieved a respectable academic position in Ferrara, and whose Neoplatonist 'siren songs' captivated the souls of the youngest members of the Ferrarese urban patriciate.[65]

All this means that the dispute in Ferrara should essentially be considered as an intellectual confrontation between Nicolò Leoniceno and Sebastiano dall'Aquila, although without ignoring Coradino Gilino as a possible third contender. It also means that the dispute cannot any longer be considered as an episode of the academic war between 'humanist' and 'Arabist' physicians but must be viewed rather as a controversy between two professors of the faculty of medicine and arts at the Ferrarese *studio*, both of them medical hellenists. In spite of the fact that the university of Ferrara was one of the earliest places where medical hellenism flourished – at the hands of Leoniceno himself – at the time of the dispute, the hellenists continued to be a minority faced with an academic establishment founded on the Latin Avicennan tradition. Some people found compromise positions between these two intellectual tendencies. Just as the 'humanist' and 'Arabist' polarity now looks inappropriate, so does the long-standing historical distinction between 'scholastic' and 'humanist'. By the mid-fifteenth century, even natural philosophy and medicine had become as humanised as their nature would allow,[66] and especially in these technical disciplines the *scholastici* were those who relished the discipline of scholarship. In medicine this included knowledge of Avicenna. Gilino was a supporter of compromise between the establishment *scholastici* and Latin humanism; he identified *Morbus Gallicus* with the disease that Celsus, Galen and Avicenna knew as *ignis sacer* or *ignis persicus*.

The Substance of the Dispute

The dispute at Ferrara was the earliest major debate on the French Disease. Its purpose was to throw light on the nature of the malady, which plunged university medical practitioners into bewilderment because of its novelty, rapid spread, serious symptoms and incurability. The contenders in the dispute tried to solve what was first a practical medical problem, that is, to decide on the proper treatment once the nature of the disease had been established. Although a practical matter, it immediately led to questions about the theory of medicine, that is, the part of medical learning belonging to natural philosophy.

The first step in the dispute was to establish the nature of the new disease.

The contenders, like so many university physicians who faced and tried to understand the French Disease in the late fifteenth century and early sixteenth, attempted to solve this problem by giving answers to two major questions: what is the actual identity of this apparently new disease? And what is the most appropriate name for it? Both questions were expressively summarised in a formulation which was traditional in scholastic medicine and natural philosophy, *quid nominis et quid rei?* – 'what is the name and what is its essence?'

If the disease was really new and entirely unknown to medical authorities, they had to give it a name more in agreement with its actual nature than simply the 'French Disease', which did not look serious enough to most physicians and meant little. If, on the contrary, it was a disease already known and well described by authorities, then they had to identify it and to show who had described it and where. Although according to most of the earliest medical perceptions the French Disease had features different from other known diseases, the idea of recognising the existence of a really new disease seems to have been unacceptable to most contemporary Latin physicians for three main reasons. First, for epistemological reasons, since it was hard for them to imagine that medical authorities had ignored the existence of a particular disease. Secondly, for cosmological reasons, given that the idea of a single Creation, in which most of them believed, seems to have been at odds with that of the appearance *ex novo* of diseases in different places and times. And thirdly, for professional reasons, for a university medical practitioner to admit that he did not know the identity of a disease and how to treat it shed doubt on his learning and professional skills.

No wonder, then, that none of the three contenders at the dispute at Ferrara nor any physician who wrote on the French Disease during the first ten years of its existence (1495–1504) dared to assert that it was a radically new disease. On the contrary, all of them related the disease to one or more of those already described by the medical authorities, though their own differing responses reflected their different intellectual backgrounds and medical training. Leoniceno opposed those 'many' who claimed that 'this plague [*luem*] was new, never seen by the ancients and, therefore, described neither by the Greeks nor by the Arabs among the diverse kinds of diseases'.[67] Assuming that there was a single Creation, he claimed that *Morbus Gallicus*, as any other disease, must have afflicted mankind from the beginning. He said:

> when I see that men are endowed with the same nature, born under the same heavens and brought up under the same stars, I tend to think that they have always been subjected to the same diseases, and my mind is not able to understand that this scourge, suddenly appearing, has infected our times, and never before. And, if somebody thinks the opposite, what would he say it is? What revenge of the gods? Actually, if one examines natural causes, the same thousand have existed since the beginning of the world.[68]

In contrast, Dall'Aquila alleged that, while not absolutely new, *Morbus Gallicus*, even under different circumstances, 'has never appeared before in our region nor has ever been previously described by the ancients'. Nevertheless he asserted that this ignorance did not destroy the power of medicine to investigate the disease and that Galen's doctrine was 'the way to find the appropriate species' of disease.[69]

For his part, Gilino claimed that 'medical doctors have not overlooked this disease, but have categorised it, for the praise of God': his concern was partly at least to make plain that its treatment was the exclusive concern of university practitioners, and to warn the sufferers of the risk of being treated by ignorant people (*imperitis*) who pretended to cure this universal disease only by means of particular remedies.[70] It was a claim for authority in the medical marketplace.

In short the two hellenists agreed that the disease was not new and that an approach to it must lie through the Greek authors. All three contenders identified the French Disease with diseases described by the medical authorities closest to the intellectual traditions that they preferred. However, in order to examine their views in more detail, we must first look at them within their intellectual context.[71]

Leoniceno and Hippocrates' diseases of summer

In his dedicatory letter addressed to Gianfrancesco Pico della Mirandola, Leoniceno declared that he had written the *Libellus* at Pico's request, adding that only his enormous debt to Pico could justify such an 'arduous and almost rash effort'.[72] But why had Leoniceno taken part in the dispute in the first place? He declared himself sceptical about the value of such things, 'disputations of great contention laboured by physicians and philosophers', most of which 'are not promoted to find truth and generally end with quarrels and uproar'.[73] Yet despite this alleged scepticism this was neither the first nor the last occasion in his long life that Leoniceno succumbed to the temptation of participating in such an event; nor even was his aim now different from that which had encouraged him to be a contender in previous disputes. Certainly now for the first time he applied his philological criticism to the field of diseases, but this was a new technique in a continuing programme of medical reform based upon the restoration of Greek *prisca medicina* that he had begun five years before with his work on the errors of Pliny. Like other hellenist physicians, Leoniceno claimed that this programme was the way to liberate university medical tradition from the numerous errors into which not only Arab and late medieval physicians but also ancient Romans had fallen. As a result, he applied systematic and implacable criticism to every non-Greek medical authority, although with particular intensity in the case of Avicenna.

Evidently Leoniceno expected that his criticism would be answered by equally emphatic responses, for he asked 'those who are going to read this to look favourably upon it, and not to judge me as immodest and insolent because I have dared to attack authorities of such a great name'.[74] He asserted that he did so 'following the example of many ancients, above all the greatest philosopher Aristotle, who sought for truth so much that in order to defend it he even wrote against his master'.[75] Entirely self-confident about what he claimed, he arrogantly added:

> We are saying this for malignant and imprudent people, some of whom urged by their envy have censured even what they tacitly approve, and this only because they themselves had neither written nor made discoveries. Others, on the contrary, like stupid people who always follow somebody else's footsteps, attribute nothing to their own opinion and everything to others'; and if sometimes they have adhered to any authority they think without reason that his authority is reason. But whatever has been the opinion of all those about our writings, so the lesser agreement we get from them, the greater we expect to achieve from the virtuous and learned, and particularly from you who follow the footsteps of your uncle Giovanni Pico through the path of all the virtues. . . .[76]

We have already said that Leoniceno entirely ruled out the possibility that *Morbus Gallicus* could be a really new disease. He found that it had been described (albeit without a name) in some Hippocratic writings, and in the commentaries on them by Galen, whom he considered Hippocrates' main interpreter.[77] There were a number of advantages of looking in the Hippocratic works for ancient knowledge of the pox. First, it was known that they were older than Galen, who was partly a commentator on them (he found it was necessary to explain the archaic terms used by Hippocrates), and this added force to Leoniceno's argument that the pox was not a new disease. Second, while Galen was celebrated for his rationality, Hippocrates, generally regarded as the greater of the two, was admired for his acuteness of observation and depth of experience. It would have been embarrassing for a reforming hellenist to have admitted that the disease was unknown to Hippocrates. Leoniceno concluded his description of the disease by asserting in a challenging way that 'whoever thinks he knows more than Hippocrates should try to define better the French Disease'.[78]

Leoniceno placed *Morbus Gallicus* in the general framework of those diseases derived from a warm and humid 'intemperance' of the air, very frequent (he said) but not exclusively in the summer. He claimed that the French Disease had broken out after an excessive humidity had lasted for over a year, as Hippocrates had described in *Epidemics*, book 3.[79] Leoniceno wondered:

> Who does not recognise from Hippocrates' words a similar epidemic in our times? I need not remind you – since all these things have been obvious

enough to make an account of them unnecessary – how many suffered from oral ulcers and 'herpes' which sometimes corroded their lips; black sores similar to carbuncles which sometimes caused them an unbearable itch, and many other tubercles which sometimes even invaded their eyes.[80]

If *Morbus Gallicus* was not a new disease, Leoniceno wondered why it appeared as such to many contemporaries. He explained this by invoking reasons similar to those which had driven Pliny the Elder to assert wrongly (said Leoniceno) that the *lichenas* had never existed in Italy nor in the rest of Europe before Tiberius Claudius' principate.[81] Contradicting Pliny's claims, Leoniceno stated that the *lichenas* had been very common among Greeks and had already been described in many Hippocratic works, and that it was even possible that they had scourged Italy long before Tiberius, when Rome had not yet extended its empire over other nations. During this period this disease would have lacked its name because Rome was still frequented by very few Greek physicians, who were actually its 'name-givers' (*nomenclatores*). Only after Tiberius, continued Leoniceno, when Greek medicine and arts became dominant in Rome, did the *lichenas*, also named *mentagra*, come to be better known.[82]

The giving of names was a significant business. It has been suggested above that for Leoniceno the hellenist part of the purity of the Greek language was that its terms carried some signification of their meaning and that foreign words, while they could be used without error, were never as meaningful. With his feeling of cultural superiority, Leoniceno thought of himself as a sort of honorary Greek; and the image of the Greeks giving names to Roman diseases, with the result that they could be now brought into the realm of meaningful medical and philosophical dicussion, was no doubt a pleasing one. It was sharpened perhaps by Pliny's quite different view of the Greeks and their medicine. Pliny's treatment of the Greek doctors ranged from sarcasm to anger: their theories, he said, were smoothly plausible imposture, hiding a practice that was at worst a deliberate attack on the persons and lives of the staunch men who had brought the *pax Romana* to the world and who stood at the heart of the empire. No hellenist doctor could read Pliny with sympathy, and Leoniceno seems to have enjoyed pointing out his medical errors and showing once more how real medicine was Greek.

Nor could Leoniceno accept the most popular denomination ('French Disease') of the disease, because it was vernacular and meant little more than the accidents of geography surrounding its recent appearance. Leoniceno notes that the 'true name' of the disease had not yet been given to it by contemporary physicians.[83] The true name, for Leoniceno, would have been either that given by the ancients, or one that carried some greater degree of meaning. Most of the contemporary physicians identified it with *elephantiasis*, deceived (says Leoniceno) by the similarity between the diseases.[84] But Leoniceno did not give a new name to *Morbus Gallicus*. He restricted himself to defining it as 'sores which begin at the pudenda, immediately occupy the whole body, and mainly the face, and almost always cause extreme pain, not to mention hideousness'.[85] These sores were generated 'as a result of the corruption of several humours, mainly provoked by an excessive warm and humid intemperance of the air'.[86]

It is obvious that Leoniceno included the French Disease among the *epidemiae*, by which he understood 'diseases wandering from people to people'.[87] Since it derived from a qualitative change of the air, an 'epidemic' became apparent through many simultaneous clinical appearances, could potentially hurt all the creatures on earth, and was frequently preceded or accompanied by a number of other natural calamities like floods, earthquakes and destruction of crops. We have seen that natural disasters added to millenarian anxieties as the year 1500 approached and were sometimes taken to presage greater troubles, of which the French Disease was an example. For medical men the same association of events could have a basis in natural philosophy. Leoniceno is an example: although he noted the causes of epidemics suggested by theologians and astrologers, he distanced himself from them by including himself among the medical men, a group that was concerned about 'causes closer to nature'. He was known to his close friend Giovanni Pico della Mirandola as deeply sceptical about astrological prophecies, which in the best of cases he saw as clever tricks used by astronomers 'to captivate princes' souls and make them lovers of this art'.[88] Therefore, instead of 'divine wrath' or planetary conjunctions, he chose to relate *Morbus Gallicus* to 'certain intemperances of the air',[89] especially the warmth and humidity of the Italian summer. The lands of Italy were full of humidity and stagnant water as a result of the heavy rains of the winter of 1495–6 and the following spring, and the subsequent floods caused by the overflowing of the main Italian rivers, most seriously at Rome, Bologna, Ferrara, Mantua and Venice.[90] Loyal to his Aristotelian–Galenic medical and natural-philosophical background, Leoniceno considered that this warm and humid intemperance was the 'mother of every putrefaction'.[91] Thus (with the authorial support of two historical cases taken from Flavio Biondo (1392–1463) and Bartolomeo Platina (1421–81)), he was able to explain in natural-philosophical terms the appearance not only of floods and pestilences, but also of famine and earthquakes. At this point, Leoniceno connected the unusual intensity of the earthquakes of that year at Ferrara and neighbouring cities to this humidity of the atmosphere.[92]

A troublesome question in the university-trained doctors' attempt to understand the nature of the French Disease was whether it was a single disease or a compound disease. Such things determined how a course of treatment would run, but they depended on a theoretical handling of medical knowledge. Leoniceno decided that *Morbus Gallicus* was a single generic disease, although it consisted of several species,[93] depending upon the humour or group of humours which were morbid in each case. This allowed him to explain within a single framework the diversity of the external manifestations of the disease: a single peccant matter provoked the most characteristic symptoms of *Morbus Gallicus*, namely pains and sores. According to him, joint pains were caused by the morbid matter accumulated there; and sores either in the skin or in the 'internal parts' were but 'certain buds [*germina*] of the superfluities that in large numbers infest human bodies'.[94]

Based on these assumptions, Leoniceno answered two *quaestiones* posed repeatedly by the earliest medical writers on the French Disease. They referred to the way and the order in which its symptoms appeared. Why should sores appear first at the genitals and then in the rest of the body? Why should *Morbus Gallicus* cause an inhuman (*saevum*) pain to some people? As to the first question, Leoniceno, leaning upon Galen's authority, asserted that the genitals were more exposed to putrefaction because of their natural heat and humidity, so that they might even be hurt by little changes in the air. Nevertheless, as there had been an 'excessive intemperance of the aestival air', sores had not been limited to those parts, but spread out to the rest of the body.[95] As to the second *quaestio*, after having noticed that 'those with very few or no sores at all in the skin suffered from bigger torment', Leoniceno asserted (again resorting to Galen's authority) that sometimes the patient's nature was unable to expel the morbid humour because of its weakness. This made it possible for the humour to take refuge in joints and nerves, where it caused a severe (*ingentem*) pain. As additional proof of his interpretation, Leoniceno alleged that post-mortem examinations of corpses of victims of *Morbus Gallicus* had shown that those without external sores had similar internal abscesses associated with greater pain.[96]

In contrast to his careful study of the identity and causes of *Morbus Gallicus* and to his refutation of those who did not agree with him, Leoniceno scarcely dealt with the remedies for this disease. He merely assumed that, as the French Disease was a multiform disease, it required a manifold treatment, whose detailed exposition he considered would have been not only too prolix, but also redundant since almost all medical works had plenty of descriptions of specific remedies to treat the several kinds of sores. Nevertheless, he discouraged physicians from trying 'to cure the French Disease always by means of the same remedies', as well as from resorting to 'astringent ointments' before having purged the body of superfluities – a practice to which 'many impostors' resorted, and which made the morbid matter return inside the body and worsen the course of the disease.[97] Without entirely ruling out the use of external remedies, Leoniceno did not hide his preference for internal ones, all of them with the aim of expelling the morbid matter from inside the body: phlebotomy, that is blood-letting, when the humour implicated was blood, and other evacuative remedies (unspecified) for any other humour (yellow bile, melancholy and salt phlegm).[98] Finally, he added only some brief considerations about diet. They were focused on the idea that one had always to prescribe foods 'that by no means are inclined to generate bad humours or humours tending to fall into putrefaction; in short foods whose nature is entirely opposite to the causes of the disease'.[99]

Dall'Aquila and Galen's *elephantiasis*

Dall'Aquila's views on the French Disease at the dispute in Ferrara can be reconstructed from the contents in his *Interpretatio morbi gallici et cura* (although the headings of its chapters are quite misleading).[100] He agreed with Leoniceno in calling Galen the 'prince of physicians'. Yet, while to Leoniceno Galen was but an interpreter of Hippocrates (albeit the greatest one), to Dall'Aquila Galen was the *only* authority from whom true medical knowledge could be derived. Consequently, he depended closely on Galen's 'doctrine' (*doctrina*) all through his work on the French Disease, and he insisted up to the hilt on Galen's authority. Dall'Aquila's obvious commitment to the Neoplatonist tradition makes this position perfectly understandable. For Ficino saw Galen as his model of a Platonist physician. Indeed, in the dedication of his *De triplici vita* to Lorenzo de' Medici, Ficino said,

I, the least of priests, have had two fathers: the medical Doctor Ficino, and the Medici's Cosimo. From one I was born, from the other reborn. One commended me to Galen, first as a doctor, then as a Platonist; the other, however, consecrated me to the divine Plato. Both of them destined Marsilio for a doctor's life: Galen was a doctor of bodies, while Plato was the doctor of souls.[101]

In his work on *Morbus Gallicus*, Dall'Aquila was very concerned to abide by the 'very exact way' of diagnosis followed by Galen. Therefore, in order to establish the identity between this disease and Galen's *elephantiasis*, he followed closely Galen's rational or mediate way of diagnosis, which he considered the supreme (if not the only) method of diagnosing any disease the identity of which was immediately obvious to sense perception. It consisted of achieving knowledge of the disease essence by means of reason. Yet Galen assumed that even in this case sense perception should invariably provide the physician with relevant information to this purpose in order to avoid medical knowledge drifting into mere speculation. Thus anatomical dissection played a very important role in Galen's method of mediate diagnosis.[102]

All these aspects were directly reflected by Dall'Aquila's approach to this issue. Relying on several Galenic works[103] Dall'Aquila started by recalling the three major groups of signs or accidents from which a Galenic physician could both establish whether anybody is healthy or ill and diagnose the disease; then he insisted on the Galenic idea that a generic knowledge of any disease should at least be achieved, in order to leave 'open the way to grasp the appropriate species'; and finally he brought to mind Galen's concept and generic classification of disease.[104] Dall'Aquila placed the French Disease within the Galenic conceptual framework he had previously recalled in two successive stages. In the first, he concluded that this disease was identical to Galen's *elephantiasis*; in the second he intended to prove this assertion.[105]

To understand Dall'Aquila's strategy here we should recall that one of Galen's definitions of disease was 'disordered function'. But function was different in different parts of the body. Galen recognised the homogeneous parts, like 'flesh', as 'similar' parts, which had simple actions, mostly of a qualitative nature. 'Organic' parts, such as the stomach or eye, were made up of similar parts and had elaborate functions in the body. It followed that for Galen diseases of the two kinds of part were different, and he regularly divided diseases into those of the similar and those of the organic parts. To Dall'Aquila, the French Disease above all damaged the composite organic members, making 'many bodily parts become thinner, others thicker'. Therefore, it was according to Galen (said Dall'Aquila) a compositional disease, that is, a disease resulting from a bad and unnatural composition of the organic members.[106] Next, Dall'Aquila placed the French Disease within the genus of organic diseases 'of the form', since it involved the corruption of the 'due or natural form' of many organic members.[107] Finally, he identified it with Galen's *elephantiasis* from four medical signs, all of them well known, namely (1) thickening of the members; (2) pustulous skin 'so thick that it looks like the skin of an elephant'; (3) wasting of many other bodily parts; and (4) stiffness of sufferers' faces, 'so that they resemble satyriasic bodies'.[108]

Next Dall'Aquila tried to prove that his interpretation was correct by arguing that such an identification was consistent with each of the three major groups of signs or accidents Galen had used to characterise the healthy or ill condition of anybody, and where appropriate also to define any disease. Dall'Aquila's insistence on repeated resort to Galen's authority to reinforce the claims he made from reason and from his own sense experience becomes still more obvious at this stage.

He first focused on the signs and accidents which were inherent in the essence of this disease, that is, those provoked by its causes.[109] Here he examined the sores and their emissions, paying attention to the main features (colour, shape, primary qualities, consistency and smell). From these signs he established the morbid humour (melancholic blood, black bile and greasy phlegm) which was responsible for the French Disease in each case. Finally, he concluded that the 'material or subject cause' (*causam materialem sive subiectivam*) of the disease lay in the skin, since 'these sores scarcely enter the skin, and most of them remain at its surface'.[110] Since the merely cutaneous condition of the sores, he argued, had been shown by sense experience itself (*ad sensum*) in the post-mortem examination of the corpse of a sufferer from the French Disease mentioned above, no rational demonstration (*probatione*) was required.[111] Such a dissection, he added, had also provided irrefutable evidence of the causal involvement of the 'greasy phlegm' in one of the varieties of the French Disease, since it had made it possible to see directly an unusually large amount of 'viscous phlegm' in the corpse's knees.[112]

Then Dall'Aquila proceeded to examine Galen's second group of signs of disease, namely, those derived from the morbidity of damaged function.[113] He asserted that every sufferer from the French Disease made it possible for everyone to recognise the signs through the senses (*sensibiliter*) during the disease (if not at its beginning): this is what Galen had claimed in numerous passages to be the case with *elephantiasis*. Indeed, as expected with any organic disease of the form, the natural bodily harmony (*pulchritudo*) was replaced by the deformity (*deformitas*), including the same patent signs Galen had described for *elephantiasis* (it was dreadful to look at, and produced a deformed shape).[114] As to the third Galenic group of signs, that constituted by the symptoms themselves, Dall'Aquila confined himself to illustrating – always relying upon Galenic accounts of sufferers from *elephantiasis* – only those accidents occurring by qualitative alteration, which were perceptible through the senses.[115]

From his review of the three groups of Galenic signs Dall'Aquila eventually concluded that the identity of *elephantiasis* with the French Disease 'is clear to everybody who has been concerned about this question with a healthy mind', and briefly referred to what ancient medical authorities (Celsus, Pliny the Elder, Quintus Serenius Sammonicus) had said about *elephantiasis* in order to reinforce his own claims.[116]

After having discussed at length the actual identity of *Morbus Gallicus*, Dall'Aquila briefly dealt with the question which, as we saw in the case of Leoniceno, was very controversial among the earliest medical writers on the French Disease: whether this disease was simple or compound, being manifest in two or more Galenic categories. One of the points at issue was that the disease had two principal symptoms, the acute pains and the skin lesions. The question was to what extent were these two connected? Did they share a common cause or did they have their own? Although Dall'Aquila was conciliatory towards those who considered it a compound disease, he thought of it as a simple disease from which all the symptoms derived. Therefore, both the skin lesions and the terrible pains – afflicting its sufferers even after the skin lesions had disappeared – were accidents derived from a common cause, and did not make separate diseases, as many contemporaries claimed.[117]

The question of causality was central. In the theory of medicine the theory of causes was elaborate and had a recognised place in the natural-philosophical treatment. Causes were parts of definitions, and Dall'Aquila extensively set out the definition, causes, accidents, treatment and prevention of the French Disease in a systematic and logical way that his readers would identify. Not surprisingly as a Galenist he claimed that 'it is impossible to find the method of healing a disease without having previously defined the disease that has to be healed'. Galen's description of *elephantiasis* did not entirely guide Dall'Aquila's medical exposition, which was nevertheless a close adaptation of Galen's doctrines. Dall'Aquila's deductivism and close dependence upon

Galen made him, for instance, effectively get rid of the term 'French Disease' by merely referring to the definition of *elephantiasis* by Galen.[118]

Dall'Aquila's causal interpretation of the French Disease entirely fitted in with the three-fold Galenist model. This was an elaborate piece of medical theory that reminds us both that the renaissance physician had professional reasons for being elaborate and that disease causality before the germ theory was very different indeed from that after it. Broadly, Galen had described three causes of increasing proximity to the sick body, the primitive, ante- cedent and conjunct causes. As to the antecedent and conjunct causes, he confined himself, once more, to the humours (thick phlegm, melancholic blood and black bile) that according to Galen determined the several species of *elephantiasis* (white, reddish and blackish) as well as their variable malignity (increasing from the first to the last species, respectively).[119]

Dall'Aquila's account of the primitive cause, the most distant and general, was more complex. He saw two ways in which the French Disease spread in relation to this category of cause, namely 'from the infection of the air itself', and 'from what physicians call contagion',[120] though he claimed, against Leoniceno's views, that contagion, mostly by direct or indirect touch, was the most usual way in which the disease was spread. Dall'Aquila stressed three modes of contagion for *Morbus Gallicus*: first, by sexual intercourse with a sufferer from *elephantiasis*; secondly, by frequently sharing a bed; and, thirdly, by being suckled by a woman ill from this disease. As we shall see, the pope's physician Gaspar Torrella thought much the same.[121] Dall'Aquila left his views on the alternative way in which the French Disease was spread (that is, the general infection of air) in second place, though he did not entirely rule it out. The limited role that this alternative view played in his causal interpre- tations was in contrast to its central role in Leoniceno's theories.[122] Dall'Aquila accepted a concurrence of 'a certain infection of the air' and recognised that the outbreak of this disease had been preceded by very humid weather, but he denied the supposedly immoderate state of the heat which followed such a humidity.[123]

Like Leoniceno, Dall'Aquila extended his interpretation of *Morbus Gallicus* by answering some *quaestiones*. His answer to one question (why do these diseases described by Hippocrates and Galen begin at the genitals?) entirely coincided with Leoniceno's.[124] To the question of why on most occasions the sores begin at the face and the front part of head, Dall'Aquila replied that it was because of the abundant humidity of the head, particularly in its frontal part.[125] Humidity was also the answer to the question of why the disease was more easily caught through sexual intercourse: in copulation the genital parts become over-heated, which directed more humidity to a place already full of it. This humidity (he concluded) became corrupt very quickly so that its 'corrupt vapours' promptly rose from the womb and penetrated through the pores open at the penis.[126] This is why Dall'Aquila recommended sufferers from the French Disease, as well as the healthy, to avoid sexual intercourse entirely, and particularly urged the healthy not to engage in it with sufferers from the disease.[127]

From Dall'Aquila's larger and more detailed treatment of the cure of *Morbus Gallicus* it is obvious that he was much more concerned about medical practice than Leoniceno. But there is not much that marks out his suggestions as characteristic of the French Disease, since his treatment mostly consisted of measures common within Galenist therapeutics. Treatment began with the canonical gradation of diet and regimen called by Galen 'the six non-naturals', that is, the things that were external to the nature of the body (the nature of the body included its parts and powers). Dall'Aquila's description of treatment then went on to pharmacy and to surgery; his status as a rational physician lies behind his assertion that the cause should have been eliminated before the treatment of accidents began.[128] In his dietetic prescriptions, the most striking thing was perhaps that, apparently in consonance with his commitment to Neoplatonism, he paid a great deal of attention to the accidents of the soul, not only with regard to the sixth of the non-naturals, but also when referring to exercise. Relying always upon Galen, Dall'Aquila recommended enjoyable exercises, stressed the fact that many had recovered from disease by mere enjoyment and referred to playing with a ball as an ideal exercise.[129] As to the 'accidents of soul', Dall'Aquila's commentaries referring not only to Galen but also to the Neoplatonists Iamblichus and Synesius cannot be more expressive about his Neoplatonist background:

> How much the accidents of the soul do is obvious to anyone who reads Galen's books *De sequela potentiarum anime* and *De ludo parve sphere*. How powerfully the fantasy can provoke changes outside as well as inside is more than evident for those who have deeply meditated on [*incubuere*] the works of the divine Iamblichus and Synesius. Also for those who could understand what Galen meant by the controlling power or by natural heat. But on these things I prefer to remain silent at present leaving them for another time.[130]

As far as pharmacy is concerned, Dall'Aquila resorted to remedies both external and internal, in accordance with his assumption that *Morbus Gallicus*, that is, *elephantiasis*, was a 'greasy and pustulous' disease. His aim was to prepare the morbid matter for expulsion by means of remedies that softened, digested and attracted; to expel it by means of evacuatives (drugs if the morbid matter was greasy phlegm or black bile, phlebotomy if it was melancholic blood); and to make the skin recover its good colour by means of cleansing medicines. He suggested additional remedies in order to mitigate the pains allegedly caused by the expulsion of the morbid matter. Here Dall'Aquila makes reference to the three separate Galenic ways of treating pain, which we describe when dealing with *Morbus Gallicus* at the Roman court, currently in use in cases of the French Disease. He warned however against using 'stupefying' remedies, 'except for a case of urgent need'.

Particularly sceptical about the use of an ointment containing quicksilver which 'many people wishing to be soon liberated from this disease' resorted to for five days, he alleged that there were 'sophistical rather true things' in this ointment, since almost all of the patients had relapsed.[131]

Gilino and the *ignis sacer* or *persicus*

Although Coradino Gilino's participation at the dispute in Ferrara is not actually documented, it is probable that he was there and it will be useful to examine his views on the French Disease in the little book *De morbo quem Gallicum nuncupant* he supposedly wrote to commit to paper the claims he had previously made at the dispute.

Gilino was a clear example of that group of Italian university physicians who supported a compromise between late medieval and Latin humanist traditions. He identified *Morbus Gallicus* at once with the 'malignant ulcer' that Cornelius Celsus had called *ignis sacer* and with the 'apostema' known as *ignis persicus* in the Galenic and Avicennan works which circulated among Latin medieval physicians.[132] Moreover, consistent with his Avicennan conceptual framework, he pointed to the frequent association between this aposteme and another one called *formica*.[133]

Apparently relying upon the Avicennan passage that says that sometimes the *ignis persicus* as well as other related conditions was caused by pestilence, Gilino conceived of *Morbus Gallicus* as a pestilential disease.[134] He accordingly described it in a dramatic way in the first lines of his work: he referred to it as 'disease' (*morbus*) and as a 'plague' (*pestis*), which he qualified as 'unknown', 'contagious', 'pernicious', 'very cruel' and 'horrifying', and reported that from 1496 onwards it had quickly spread over Italy and beyond the Alps, damaging very many people.[135]

Gilino asserted that *Morbus Gallicus*, like any other pestilence, was brought about by both superior and inferior causes. He thought it unnecessary to deal with the latter as he assumed that they were 'the same ones generating plague, alopecia, leprosy, scabies and the remaining sores' and they had been sufficiently studied by 'our ancestors'.[136] However, he dealt at length with its superior causes, both theurgic (that is, those related to the intervention of God) and astrological.

As to the astral causes, he assumed that two recent planetary conjunctions were related to the outbreak of the disease. The first was that of Saturn and Mars on 16 January 1496, 'indicating mortalities among human bodies'. The second conjunction was that of Jupiter and Mars in a hot and humid sign on 17 November 1494, as a result of which the air became altered and corrupt so that it generated the 'corrupt and burned humours' causing these mortalities. Then, after having reported two significant passages from Avenzoar and Avicenna where both considered the outbreak of certain diseases, usually epidemic, as God's scourges to punish mankind's sins, Gilino did not hesitate to blame the outbreak of 'this very cruel plague' – as he called *Morbus Gallicus* – on a theurgic cause.[137]

In his description of the French Disease, Gilino underlined three of its 'accidents', namely its beginning at the genitals, its sores and its pains at the joints. To him this disease was generated from the 'burned red bile mixed with melancholy', and could take seat at any member from the 'flesh' to the joints, ligaments and 'nerves'. As the morbid humoral mixture was thinner, so more often the disease took its seat in the flesh and, therefore, emerged from the skin more quickly and so ended. The thicker it was, the more it tended to take its seat in the nerves and other internal members and, therefore, the more insidious it became. In the first case, the disease manifested itself through the appearance of sores on the skin which either took the shape of a 'grain of millet' or successively passed through the stages of ulcer, vesicle and crust. In the second case, the patient suffered from 'pains in the ligaments, nerves and joints', and sometimes there appeared no sores at all at the skin.

In order to explain why this disease sometimes began with 'sores and ulcers' appearing at the pudenda or less dense members, like testicles, vulva, virile member or penis and anus, Gilino resorted to Galen's and Avicenna's description of 'cancer'. He declared that 'as thicker and more burned the matter [of disease] becomes, so quicker it goes to the rarefied and soft members, and not to the tough ones'.[138] For this reason, and also because he assumed that it was a 'contagious' disease, Gilino recommended men to avoid mixing together at festivals with men and women who suffered from this 'pernicious disease' and, particularly, to avoid sleeping with them. He also assured the reader that he had seen 'those having been infected in this way suffering from the worst torments'.[139] In dealing with the treatment of the French Disease, Gilino claimed that sexual intercourse was a very risky practice except for 'those well complexioned, the young and the well habitu-ated' to it. The latter could copulate without risk provided that they did not do it too often.[140]

We have already referred to Gilino's admonition against the ignorant (*imperitis*) who tried to cure a universal disease like this by means of exclu-sively local remedies.[141] As we can expect from his status as university physician, he suggested a treatment for the French Disease in three successive stages, first, a regime according to the 'six non-naturals' (that is, by paying attention to the patient's air and environment, eating and drinking, exercise and rest, sleep, inanition and repletion, and 'accidents of the soul'); secondly, some purgative measures (starting with phlebotomy as the universal evacuative) to eliminate the morbid humour; and, thirdly, several topical remedies (baths, lotions, ointments and liniments, among others) to calm pains in the joints and nerves, as well as to eliminate the ulcers, sores and crusts on the skin. This third group of remedies included mercurial prepara-tions.[142] At the very end of his work, Gilino reported a somewhat striking remedy, by means of which he claimed to have cured every patient whose throat (*gula*) was affected by the French Disease. It consisted of applying an 'actual or potential cautery on the coronal suture' (that is, on the top of the head), in order to stop the multiplication of the morbid matter of this disease on the head.[143] Such a drastic therapeutic measure, unknown elsewhere, could well have been designed to avoid the over-salivation produced by mercury, as Sudhoff suggested. The theoretical basis for it may lie in the Galenist assumption that the brain was the source of phlegm (one of the humours which could be involved in the French Disease), and that this suture was the most appropriate place for topical remedies to be applied to the brain.[144]

Controversial Issues

The rules of the university disputation meant that a conclusion was reached. Normally the thesis was successfully defended, and within the university this meant that knowledge had been defended, refined or even generated. We are here of course taking 'knowledge' to mean what the men of the late fifteenth century 'knew', in their terms, not in ours, and with their principles of the establishment and confirmation of knowledge. In a courtly dispute the same rules may not have applied, and if they did they were certainly abandoned in the pamphlet war that followed. Each of our three authors in the Ferrara dispute was in any case giving *post hoc* rationalisations of what was said, or perhaps of what they wished they had said. In reviewing this literature, only one thing is obvious: that no one who had read it at the time would have been clearer in his mind about what the pox was (or what to do about it).

The complexity of the situation is this: each of our three authors had a preferred ancient model for what he conceived the pox to be, and this model had been chosen in accordance with the beliefs of the tribe to which he belonged (whether Hippocratist, Platonist or establishment). The three protagonists of the three diseases could best establish their case by destroying the cases of the others; and this was best done by proving, or denying, that there was an identity between any of the three diseases and either of two others, *lepra* and *elephantiasis*, which had been discussed by ancient and medieval authors (who were tribally renowned or defamed). Three authors, five diseases, a dozen authorities, all independently variable and linked syllogistically, make for a large number of possible combinations. It would be tedious and unnecessary to go into them and almost certainly no one at the time attempted a dispassionate appraisal of the documents produced by the Ferrara dispute. But what was important was that the sudden appearance of pox in the late fifteenth century served to highlight the different approaches to medicine that had come into existence, some of them not long before. While it seems to have been the case that such attitudes – medical hellenism, Neoplatonism and the Latin humanist reaction – predisposed various authors to seek authority from authors selected by the different tribes, the endless argument and counter-argument must have been increasingly divisive in the crisis precipitated by the disease. Hellenists thought they could cut through it all by referring only to Greek authors, whether ancient or Byzantine. The medical establishment thought no one so professional and authoritative as Avicenna, whom they successfully retained in the medical curriculum until the seventeenth century. The medical humanists who defended the *res Latina* with Celsus likewise survived the onslaught of the hellenists. Celsus remained a model of Latinity (and was used as late as the eighteenth century as an authority for eye operations). In other words, in each of the three cases not only did tribal presumptions contribute to the confusion, but the confusion encouraged tribal cutting of the Gordian knot.

The result was attractive in all cases. Leoniceno and the hellenists could claim that the *elephantiasis* of Galen and Paul of Aegina was the same disease (because both were Greek and authoritative). Leoniceno could also claim that this was to be identified with the *lepra* of Avicenna. He was obliged to consider Avicenna here because his opponents, whose arguments he had to destroy, also mentioned him; and it is at least implicit that Avicenna is already in the wrong for using an alien name (whatever the Arabic original of the Latin *lepra* was) instead of a Greek name. Leoniceno's argument was partly that none of these named diseases was to be identified with the unnamed pox, which was to be found only in Hippocrates and therefore in none of the diseases identified and named by his opponents.

Leoniceno naturally gave his attention to Greek authors, including those represented by his own translations and in his collection of manuscripts. In contrast Gilino made exclusive use of the medieval Latin Galen, preferring translations made from the Arabic. Gilino also remained faithful to Avicenna, whom he repeatedly (on eight of the eleven times his name was mentioned) called 'the prince of physicians'.[145] This was a title reserved by the hellenist end of the spectrum of medical opinion for Galen, as Gilino must have known. It was probably a reaction against hellenism that made him appropriate Galen's title for Avicenna, for he was happy enough to accept Galen's authority. Nor was Gilino lacking humanistic appreciation of the Latinity and authority of Celsus, in which, once more, Gilino was quite at odds with Leoniceno, who condemned Celsus for not using Greek names for diseases.[146] Gilino's solution to the problem of the identity of the pox was to rely not only on Avicenna but on Pliny, the twin targets of Leoniceno's hellenism. Gilino's argument is that the same remedy (human blood) was famously used to treat both *lepra* and *elephantiasis*, which must therefore be the same disease, and could not be the pox.[147] Leoniceno also savagely attacked Gilino's use of cautery, because it was a surgical and Arabic technique, unattractive to a philologising hellenist. He noted that some physicians, influenced by the authority of Avicenna, applied this remedy to the sufferers from this disease to treat the sores all over their body. In accordance with his hellenist views, he challenged these physicians to find where Galen had prescribed this remedy

for this kind of sore.[148] There is little doubt that this criticism was addressed
to Gilino, who in the last paragraph of his work highly praised the application
of this remedy to the coronal suture of any sufferer from the French Disease.
It is clear that the views of Leoniceno and Gilino were irreconcilable because
the circumstances made their authorities irreconcilable. There was hardly
enough common ground for a discussion, and in the end circumstances
eroded the authority of Pliny and the hellenists became more powerful.

There was more common ground in the case of Dall'Aquila. While he kept
an eye open for new hellenist translations and Greek originals, his main
authority was apparently the printed *Opera Galieni* of 1490, that is, the
culmination of the Latin medieval Galenic tradition. Dall'Aquila's Platonised
Galen was the single medical authority for him, while Leoniceno's Prince of
Physicians, newly translated from the Greek, would have been, as many
others also declared, 'second only to Hippocrates'. Unlike Gilino, Dall'Aquila
could agree with Leoniceno that the authority of Galen (although they drew
their image of him from two different traditions) was such that it was
impossible for him to have overlooked the disease called *lepra* (which was so
important in the naming and identity of the pox).[149] Dall'Aquila was ready
with a reason for Galen's apparent silence on the topic: 'since not every
medical work of Galen has reached our hands, and since he wrote many
books specifically dedicated to distinct diseases (for instance, on the healing of
the stone, and of jaundice, among others), he might well have written a book
on lepra' not yet found.[150] If this were not enough, Dall'Aquila did not
hesitate to proclaim his Galenic faith when he admitted that he would
disregard those who defended the identity of Galen's *elephantiasis* and
Avicenna's *lepra*, 'unless they are able to prove it from Galen and Hippocrates,
as we planned from the start';[151] and by citing God as a witness he claimed
that 'if we should have Galen's works, as it is right that we should, all those
medical writers faithful to him will be superfluous (apart from Hippocrates,
the master of all of them) even though many of them were right in what they
wrote'.[152] At the same time, Dall'Aquila had some common ground with
Gilino in accepting the authority of the Arabs Avicenna, Avenzoar, Mesue
and Rhazes (on the identity of *elephantiasis*), excusing apparent inconsistencies
as a 'mistake of translators' who ended up by identifying one disease with the
other.[153] Leoniceno did not agree, holding that the Arabs were wrong in
matters of fact, not merely by accidents of translation.[154] It was of course
because they were Arabs rather than Greeks. Leoniceno broadened his
hellenism from the ancient writers to those of Byzantine vintage, including
Paul of Aegina and Aetius of Amida, and maintained that there was a Greek
tradition of knowledge extending Galen's doctrines to later ages. Dall'Aquila
thought it was sanctimonious nonsense to revere such figures simply because
they wrote in Greek, and he maintained that in fact they diverged sharply
from Galen on the identity of *elephantiasis*.[155]

It is probable that some such complex conflict of views occurred whenever there was a prolonged dispute on the nature of the pox. The disagreements arose from the differences between the groups of university-trained physicians and the different authorities to which they gave their allegiance. Resolution of these differences dialectically in a pamphlet war was impossible and in the resulting confusion of opinion a sweeping reform must have had considerable attractions for the hellenists.

Conclusion

In this and the previous chapters we have tried to show how contemporaries' perceptions of Mal Francese were conditioned by the culture in which they lived and the events they endured. Their picture of the disease was a construction, not an unveiling, of a medical entity. In the case of Mal Francese we have stressed the moral and religious character of the earliest perceptions of the disease and reactions to it, underlining the obvious point, that every disease-entity, past or present, is the cultural product of a precise historical context. The issues are particularly clear in the case of the French Disease: in late fifteenth-century Italy it was not a mere 'medical' event.

In other words, the way Mal Francese was recorded cannot simply be 'read off' as medical information, since it was experienced by contemporaries in the same sort of manner as that series of frightening events which the Florentine historian Francesco Guicciardini would later call *le calamità d'Italia*. This point has been underlined in our analysis of two problems. The first concerns the picture of Mal Francese as it appeared in contemporary chronicles and diaries. Can we in fact 'trust' (in the sense of a modern medical diagnosis) anything at all about the symptoms and presentation of Mal Francese reported by the chronicles? If we take the parallel with the disease of Job, did they see Mal Francese as producing boils all over the body because they first had Job's disease in mind on religious and moral grounds? In other words, to what extent did they believe that this disease, like the French invasion, was sent as punishment for sin and that therefore they saw the boils irrespective of their actual relevance? The second instance refers to the perceived causes of Mal Francese. Was the transmission of this new disease seen as sexual because of Savonarola's attacks on sexual permissiveness, and the link he made between sexual licence and social collapse?

Chapter Five

The French Disease in Northern Europe:
the case of Germany

Introduction

We have seen in the previous chapters that the arrival of the French Disease in Italy had different effects on different groups within society. The same is true of Europe further north. Here too the learned physicians had intellectual problems with the disease and professional problems with empirics; the humanists battled with the school-doctors in explaining the nature of the disease; there were disputations and there were astrologers. But, unlike in Italy, in Germany the religious component of the crisis developed in a new direction. In the early years of the disease the volume of publication from German-speaking countries was second only to that of Italy, and it will be worthwhile to examine this case history of the differences and similarities of the arrival of the French Disease in another society. As before, we shall explore how people *understood* the disease. We shall find that what constituted their knowledge related to aspects of their professional and national culture. Understanding was a necessary preliminary to treatment and prevention, and we shall examine it in academic, intellectual, religious and cultural terms.

The French Disease spread over Europe north of the Alps with rapidity. It reached Lucerne and Zurich in May 1496. By the summer it was in the northern Imperial cities of Frankfurt and Nuremberg.[1] Reaction to it in German-speaking countries was equally swift, certainly in terms of publication. This literature was of various kinds, and reflects the mechanisms at work in society that resulted in some degree of agreement about what the pox was and what to do about it. One such mechanism was the simple pronouncement by leaders of society, political and religious. It was pronounced at the Diet of Worms in 1496 that the pox was God's punishment for the current excess of blasphemy. Plate 5.1 shows the Christ Child as the instrument of God's wrath throwing bolts at women who were regarded as the main transmitters of disease and at their unfortunate victim, a prostrate man covered with deadly pustules. Note that the supplicant ruler is rewarded.

Another ruler, Philip, Elector to the Palatinate, instructed his physician to

Plate 5.1 'The Virgin Mary with the Christ Child punishing people affected with the Pox'

draw up a *consilium* against the pox. A *consilium* was normally written advice from a doctor to a distant patient; when a monarch asked for one, it could apply to his subjects. Konrad Schellig (*fl.* 1495) accordingly did so, advising the people on the causes, prevention and treatment of the disease.[2] The humanist Wimpheling, in a prefatory address to the reader, explained that although God had punished blasphemy in this way He had also provided remedies that could be conveniently used by the doctors and people. As a humanist, he would not allow that the pox was a new disease.

Schellig's *consilium* argued that the contagious pustules which characterised the disease arose from a disturbance – partly 'adustion' (excessive heating) and partly putrefaction – of the humours. Arguing that it was the bile that was primarily affected, Schellig identified the pox with various names and descriptions given by earlier writers, notably Guy de Chauliac (c.1300–68) and Avicenna. But his main concern was to provide a means of avoiding and curing the pox. Since he believed that the disease was seated in a disturbance of the humours and a corruption of their elementary qualities, he prescribed a moderate diet that would not lead to excessive production of humours, consisting of bland foods without pronounced qualities. The details are many and sometimes interesting, but since similar courses of action were applicable to any disease arising from humoral disturbance, there is little that is specific to the pox. It is notable that here, so soon after the appearance of the pox, Schellig's advice to abstain from sexual relations was designed only to conserve the strength and avoid disturbance. Transmission of the disease was held to be either directly from the pustules or indirectly (through some vehicle).

In other words, in this early reaction we see that, as in Italy, the disease although new elicited old responses in attempts to understand and control it. We should not expect anything else, for society's resources were those that were perceived to have been successful in earlier situations. But we shall see later in this book that, as European medicine gained more experience of the features that distinguished the French Disease from others, strategies to deal with it were formed which reflected the unique features of the pox.

Disputation

Reaching an understanding of the nature and treatment of the pox involved other mechanisms too. One device available to the doctors was that characteristic procedure of the schools, the disputation. Many disputations were conducted as people succumbed to the pox across Europe, and we have seen how a disputation was conducted at the court in Ferrara. But most disputations have left little documentary evidence. It is unusual that from surviving material we can reconstruct the disputation that was held in the schools of Leipzig in 1496, the year after the pox reached the town. Disputations were not only pedagogic devices designed to sharpen students' rhetoric and logic skills, and were more than ceremonial displays of learning at graduation: they were in fact – and particularly the masters' disputations – modes of enquiry, ways of establishing the truth. It was only by exposing a question to the full logical rigour of a scholarly analysis and bringing the weight of the learned tradition to bear upon it that the truth of a thesis could be established or destroyed. In a medical question, as in the other higher discipline of law, a solution to a question arrived at by disputation in the faculty would have practical consequences in civil practice, where the faculty exercised a number of privileges. It was the faculty that decided what was good and licit practice; and, if the town wanted advice on how to handle an epidemic, it turned to the faculty. Disputations were also public, and a resolved question had a wide audience. By defending a series of related questions, either directly or through a pupil, a university teacher could establish a whole doctrine on a topic. Disputations, then, had a number of features that made them an important mechanism for the establishment of a consensus.

Let us look at this in a slightly different way. In Chapter One we discussed the question of in what sense the late fifteenth-century doctor *knew* the pox. We will argue that his perception of it was conditioned by a number of other things in his mind, largely culturally determined, but it is important to repeat here that what he knew was for him knowledge. It is with this knowledge that we are concerned, not with some kind of intellectual activity that we may want, with hindsight, to label 'opinion' or 'error'. The fifteenth century had modes of evaluating knowledge that were elaborate and self-conscious, and the disputation was one of them. Because it was central to the intellectual 'reception' of the pox, let us briefly examine the protocol of generating and validating knowledge by means of the disputation.

The normal procedure was for the 'defendant' in the disputation to publish his thesis in advance, perhaps by pinning it to the door of the university church (as Luther did). This gave the 'respondent' time to prepare his attack, which would be either on the logical form of the thesis and the arguments he thought the defendant would use, or on the defendant's use of authority. The thesis itself might begin, for example, with a *quaestio disputata* or a 'doubt', *dubium*, like those extracted from medical commentaries, or a new opinion, and proceed through brief arguments to an affirmative statement of the original question.

The disputation at Leipzig was at the magisterial rather than student level. It began in 1496 with the posting of a thesis on the French Disease by Martin Pollich von Mellerstadt (c.1450–1513).[3] The thesis was simply the disputed question 'Whether the French Disease, a pestilential and invasive illness, is caused by corruption of the air.' That is, Pollich took for granted that the disease was imposed from without and upon large numbers of people. These two suppositions were related, because diseases of individuals were generally accepted to arise from within, by corruption of the humours, and to be conditioned by the individual's own humoral complexion. The classical authorities amply supported all this. The question, then, revolved round the question of the immediate agent of the disease – was it corrupt air?

Pollich prepared his argument by introducing his first *conclusio* – not a 'conclusion' in our sense but a statement of general principle that can explain this particular case (that is, something that must be 'included within' the argument). Here it is assumed that changed dispositions of the air do indeed generate diseases, and that by the power of the sun and stars the air weakens the human body and changes it to its own nature. Again, much support could be found in the Hippocratic and Galenic sources for such a principle. Pollich followed this principle immediately with his first corollary, which was a device to use the general principle in the particular case in hand: whenever the air becomes putrescent, the body is changed. The second corollary refined the particular picture, observing that not all bodies, because of their previous disposition, were changed in the same way.

His second 'conclusion' played the same role, introducing the general principle (it is Hippocratic) that all parts of the body mutually communicate and respire. And, again, the first corollary of this conclusion was the particular application, in the case under discussion, of this general rule. This corollary is that corrupt air reaching the brain (through the body's communicating respiration) caused spasms; reaching the heart, it caused fevers; and, reaching the liver, it caused the pox, which was thought to be a species of the genus *male morigeratum*. The second corollary of this conclusion was that the pox (because the regular means of its generation were now clear) was not a new disease. Pollich added that it was known to medical men by its 'form and disposition', that is, by its appearances (and not by its name).

The third conclusion and its first corollary deal with the means whereby the disease is spread between individuals (it is a question of air, form and the soul, not of personal contact).[4] The second corollary restates the disputed question in an affirmative way.

This form of argument, and the role of the conclusions and corollaries, was general (it was followed elsewhere by Pollich and by his opponent, Pistoris) and any attack upon the truth it revealed had to obey the same rules. Since the general principles embodied in the conclusions were taken from the ancients, a possible mode of attack would be a different selection of ancient authority. Another would be the manner in which the particular case expressed in the corollary was drawn from the general principle of the conclusion. There was room here for the process of logical 'distinction' in which different and perhaps inappropriate meanings were drawn from an opponent's logical terms.

Probably nothing would have come of the disputation that followed this thesis had not Nicolò Leoniceno taken part in a similar disputate in Ferrara. We have seen that this took place at an aristocratic court, not at a university, but it had the same purpose of discovering the nature of the disease. Leoniceno wrote up the disputation and published it in the same year, 1497. An edition of this was published in Leipzig, and Pollich soon read it.[5] It prompted him either to defend another thesis or to offer lectures ('in public with academic certainty' are his words) in support of Leoniceno.[6] His new 'position' (a thesis with its ancillary arguments was often called a *positio*) was challenged in the following year, 1498, by the Leipzig physician and member of the faculty, Simon Pistoris (1453–1523).[7]

Pistoris' *quaestio disputata* asked whether the change in the air that caused the pox was a change in the manifest elementary qualities of the air – its wetness and warmth – or an appearance of a hidden (*occulta*) property of the air. In setting up his question, Pistoris assumed that the French Disease was *not* to be identifed with *male morigeratum*. Indeed, his first conclusion and its corollaries deal with the absence of the pox from old and new categories of disease. Likewise, his second *conclusio* is that the pox is not among the diseases listed by Hippocrates in the third section of the *Aphorisms*, which is where Hippocrates lists those diseases caused by changes in the quality of the air. Pistoris' corollary is that a manifest change in the elementary qualities of the air could not on its own be a cause of the pox. Nor – on their own – could general celestial causes: it followed that an occult property of the air was the principal cause of the French Disease. Finally, Pistoris threw in the 'unrelated conclusion' and its corollary that astrology is not subsumed within medicine but is uncommonly useful to the prognosticating doctor.

Martin Pollich did not like being contradicted. A war of pamphlets followed,[8] and by reading them we can reconstruct some of the actual arguments that took place during the disputations: this is unusual, for it is usually only the theses, conclusions and corollaries that have survived. At the technical level, these are arguments for and against an origin of the pox in an occult quality of the air, for and against astrological causality and whether the disease was new or not. But, at another level, the argument was between people of widely different cultural backgrounds, and the way they handled the arguments – the 'reception' of the pox – was largely determined by that culture.

Humanism

The cultural feature that served to distinguish Pollich from Pistoris also distinguished northern Europeans from southern. Pollich was a humanist,[9] Pistoris a man of the schools; but Pollich's humanism was German, and it differed in a number of ways from that of the south, particularly of Italy. German humanism[10] was a thing of the universities and so differed from the 'civic humanism' of the Italian cities. It did not dwell so much as the Italian on the pagan nature of the classical civilisations and seemed to its proponents more pious. The German humanists could not claim direct ancestry from the Romans, as the Italians could, and looked instead for a corresponding golden age of German history. They could however claim that the political power of the old Roman Empire had passed legally to the Christian and German Holy Roman Empire: the Emperor was a Caesar and had claims upon Italy. Generally the German humanists resented the cultural snobbery of the Italians; and in their piety they resented the Italian aspects of the Church in Germany.

But, like their Italian counterparts, the German humanists saw themselves as a small cultural elite in their own country. In their written works they addressed each other with 'eloquence' in the preferred form of classical Latin verse, and deplored the sea of barbarism in which they found themselves. They formed themselves into groups for mutual support. Jakob Wimpheling (1450–1528), who had prefixed an address to the reader to Schellig's *Consilium* against the pox, is an example: he had his own humanist group, the *Sodalitas litteraria Argentinensis*, of which the poet Sebastian Brant (1458–1521) was a member. Brant wrote a verse *Eulogium* on the pox: to write verse in the classical way was almost to identify oneself as a humanist, whatever the topic of the poem. Wilibald Pirckheimer (1470–1570) wrote an ode to gout; and the arch-humanist Johann Reuchlin (1455–1522) ('Capnion') does not seem to have felt it inappropriate to be the recipient of Brant's poem on the French

Disease. Many German humanists felt, perhaps correctly, that their native names were less graceful than classical names, and they accordingly 'transnominated' themselves, choosing a name of equivalent meaning from the classical languages.[11]

Wimpheling was a 'humanist' in seeking a strict, almost stoical moral code from antiquity. He was a priest who had been brought up as a boy by the Brethren of the Common Life, and his ideal was to employ his moral code in countering the corruption he saw within the Church. He thought the Italian humanists preferred to take from antiquity entertaining fables rather than instructive and useful history; he also suspected that they preferred paganism to Christianity. He certainly disliked their cultural affectations and resented German money leaving the country for the Roman Church.

Pollich too was a humanist. A member of the *Sodalitas litteraria Rhenana* of Conrad Celtis (1459–1508), he was addressed by his admiring humanist contemporaries as *lux mundi*, the 'light of the world'. He was physician to Frederick the Wise. From such a lofty cultural height Pollich looked down with irritation at Simon Pistoris, the Leipzig doctor who so stubbornly disagreed with him on the nature of the pox. For Pollich, Pistoris was a mere *scholasticus*, a term he uses with all the pejorative sense used by later humanists for their contemporaries in the schools. Pistoris does not seem to have resented the term and may even, like others,[12] have taken pride in being a thorough scholar, a 'scholastic' who knew his business. Pistoris emerges in the dispute as a businesslike medical man and teacher, not widely read outside his own field, but convinced of its autonomy and utility. For Pistoris the proper jury for settling the question of the nature of the pox was his own faculty and its dean – under whose auspices his thesis had been disputed – and indeed medical faculties anywhere. (Pistoris uses the medieval term *studium* for 'university', while Pollich uses the renaissance *gymnasium*.) Such a procedure as disputation he said, represented, 'scholastic certainty' (where Pollich pre-ferred 'literary form'). Pistoris believed such a procedure to be preferable to being judged by a tight coterie of humanists. 'I prefer', he said, 'to be thought a pious physician than a precise grammarian or a plausible orator.'[13] He constantly refers the case to his professional colleagues, the doctors, and belittles the medical skill and knowledge of Pollich and his Italian heroes, particularly Giovanni Pico della Mirandola (1463–94). Indeed, Pistoris describes Pollich as being swept along by the prose of Pico and 'your Leoniceno'[14] and thus ignoring the substance of the argument, forgetting the thing in a search after names. Pistoris' insult to Pollich is to treat him as a dilettante doctor with only 'two patients, if you have so many'. To his own long and professional acquaintanceship with the Hippocratic works, Pistoris compares Pico's lack of a medical education, and, by implication, a lack of medical seriousness in Pollich. He treats Pollich simply as a philosopher, and, although agreeing that medicine is subalternated to philosophy, he asserts that medicine is an autonomous field, with its own principles, mostly derived from long experience and practice.[15] Here Pistoris is tapping an argument made since the middle ages[16] that such things as the actions of drugs (their grades and doses, he says) can be known only by experience, and cannot be expressed in words.

Language and names were central to the argument. Pollich uses the term 'excellent eloquence' when referring to the prose of Pico's work against astrology. This was humanist code across Europe for 'classical usage'; the hellenists used it as code for 'Greek'. Pollich sneers at Pistoris by saying that for him, the *scholasticus*, 'eloquence' meant, in practice, 'difficult to read' and he patronisingly offered to render the discussion into simple language for Pistoris' benefit. The real significance behind these differences, however, lay in the business of finding a name for the pox. Everyone (including the Italians) agreed that the 'French Disease' was its common or vulgar name. It was a vernacular term, historically accidental, meaning nothing more than that it had first happened to the French troops in circumstances that were universally known. A *real* name, in contrast, would have been classical and would have meant a great deal more. It would have meant that the disease had *identity* and could be found among the authors. That would have been the key to understanding it: that is, knowing its causes, nature and treatment; in other words its place in the whole network of rational medicine. The hellenists could not believe that the Greeks had failed to describe the disease: what must have happened, they thought, was that the barbarism of the intervening ages had corrupted or destroyed the old texts, so that the name and the description of the disease had vanished. Hellenists (here too Leoniceno is an example) gave special emphasis to the belief that the same causes of diseases were in operation in antiquity as now, and consequently that the same diseases existed.

Many of these aspects of German humanism are to be seen in Pollich's tract, prompted by Pistoris' thesis and the subsequent disputation, in favour of Leoniceno's account of the pox. Addressed to the doctors of Leipzig, Pollich throughout calls Leoniceno 'the master', whose doctrines need to be spread throughout the profession; Pollich must mean in Germany, for he observes that Leoniceno was by then celebrated by the whole of Italy. But spreading them was hampered by the public disputation of a 'sophist' (Pistoris, unnamed throughout), motivated, said Pollich, by spite, armed with a loose tongue, and giving rein to savage delirium, not only in the disputation where both Pollich and Pistoris were present, but by Pistoris' gossip in surgeries and apothecaries' shops. The normal invectives of personal attack become more informative when Pollich expresses his own feeling of affronted superiority in humanist sneers at Pollich. Let us summarise and interpret these sneers: Why, O Sophist, do you use names so barbaric that they are unknown to our doctors? (We can translate this as Why do you use the Arabic terms that we are trying to suppress?) Your chosen term, this *anthimata epidemialia*, is a goatish deer in a category of nightmare monsters and deaf chimaeras. (Translation: How

barbaric!) Follow Leoniceno! (Translation: Be eloquent!) Where Pollich has
to discuss another of Pistoris' preferred names for the pox, *alhumera*, he can
bring himself to do so only by 'putting it in the first declension and making
it feminine', that is, by making it decline as if it were a real Latin noun and
so not offensive to a fastidious humanist. By such means and other elegances
Pollich contrasted his own eloquence with the 'stuttering' and 'muttering' of
Pistoris.[17] Other signs of Pollich's claim to cultural superiority are clear.
Almost as an antidote to Pistoris' barbaric words, Pollich litters his text with
elegant classical tags. While Pistoris' preferred 'piety' seems to have been the
Christian kind, Pollich's prose is full of the classical pantheon; he explains
'epidemic' not as related to 'demotic', or 'visited upon the people', but
'because it goes beyond *demia*', that is, beyond the knowledge of the godlike.
'For Demia is a goddess, as Festus Pompeius writes. . . .' Pollich's respect for
the Italian humanists is often evident. Not only is Leoniceno the Master, but
the best compliment Pollich can pay to a German humanist (Bohuslaus de
Hassentain) is to call him 'the Pico of the Germans'.

The pamphlet war between Pollich and Pistoris continued. We have
glanced above at some of the features of Pistoris' reply (of 1500) to Pollich's
defence of Leoniceno, and we must equally briefly examine Pollich's counter-
attack. His humanist colours are flying bravely as he manoeuvres into position. His first salvo is a hexastichon addressed to Leoniceno, calling him to
action, just as hellenists called to hellenists in Italy, above the primordial sea
of barbarism and rusticity. Will you remain silent, most learned of poets?
Arise and use Mars against the opposing gods! It may be doubted whether the
old Leoniceno was roused by such words to enter a Germanic squabble, but
Pollich was beside himself, combing classical Latin for insults and firing them
off in a language which anger and literary pretension combine to make often
unintelligible.

> What man, studious of letters, would not become hot enough to explode when
> he sees a man of little learning or erudition attack the illustrious Pico della
> Mirandola, the Preserver of Good Arts, the lonely light, the strong president,
> the unbroken fulcrum; or Leoniceno, the great translator, the most learned of
> doctors . . . ?[18]

Pollich thus seems to have seen the light of culture as shining from Italy, and
he identified more with the Italian hellenists than with the other German
humanists. Even Pistoris, discussing recent writers, mentions the Italians and
French, but not the Germans. It seems too evidence of the German's respect
for Italian culture that Pollich chose not only to address Leoniceno, but to
write, with an account of the affair and the relevant papers, to Giovanni
Manardi (1462–1536).[19] He received in reply a reassuringly humanist letter in
which Manardi calmly discussed – in reply to Pistoris' declaration that he was
more interested in the reality of things than in names – the importance of

getting the names of things right. He did so in terms that recall (but do not mention) Leoniceno's attack on Pliny and Avicenna, which we met in Chapter Four. To the efforts of Pico he adds, perhaps out of politeness for Pollich, the author of 'Capnion' (Reuchlin). The dangers of interpretation of names, says Manardi, is as great in the New Testament as in medicine: Manardi sweeps into a typical hellenist critique of the present state of medicine as filthy, uncultivated and positively Punic in its barbarity, and muddied by the evil words of those who do not want to drink from the pure founts of ancient knowledge. It is in these terms that Manardi expresses the view that the medievals and especially the commentators (like Pietro d'Abano [1250–c.1315], on whom Pistoris depended for his view of astrology) are to be avoided because their ignorance of Greek simply multiplied errors.

Pistoris escaped the battle with Pollich by leaving the faculty to become personal physician to Joachim I of Brandenburg. He did not return until 1508, when Pollich had removed to Wittenberg.[20] In his absence at least, it must have looked as though the humanist–hellenist axis had triumphed. It was also by such occurrences that a consensus in medical thinking came about.

In following the dispute between Pollich and Pistoris, we have stepped over another aspect of the German reaction to the pox. This was not medical, but literary, and it equally illustrates the cultural patterns of the time. It is again a story of the difference between northern and southern Europe.

Pox and Literature

Erasmus and Melanchthon agreed that Rudolf Agricola (1443/4–85) had been the first to bring a better study of letters from Italy to Germany.[21] Thereafter the Tour of Italy became a desirable part of the education of culturally ambitious Germans. Agricola's student Reuchlin met Pico during his Tour,[22] and like Pico developed (from the 1480s) an interest in the cabbala. The attraction was in finding a source of knowledge even older and so more authoritative than that of classical antiquity. Cabbalistic studies offered the promise that the knowledge of Moses himself had been passed down orally until committed to writing in the cabbala. It was an added attraction that Pythagorean knowledge was also represented in this tradition, and that Platonism too seemed to partake of it. It is said that Reuchlin undertook to make Pythagoreanism – the eastern *Ur-Philosophie* – a German philosophy as Marsilio Ficino (1433–99) tried to make Platonism Italian and Jacques Lefèvre d'Étaples attempted to make Aristotelianism French.[23]

German humanists announced themselves by joining a sodality and by publishing. The preferred form was verse, based on classical models. Natural philosophy in verse was based on Lucretius; and as we have seen Pirckheimer, who suffered from it, wrote an ode to gout, based on Lucian's *Tragopodagra*. Sebastian Brant's verse on the pox, written in 1496 and dedicated to

Reuchlin, comes into the same category.[24] Brant is very conscious of his
nationality and of being part of a cultural elite. The result was to make his
verse difficult to read. At least, so thought Joseph Grünpeck (c.1473–c.1532),
who reproduced it, together with a simpler explanation, a few weeks after
Brant had sent it to Reuchlin. Grünpeck became (a year after writing this
tract) court historian to Maximilian,[25] and was not a medical doctor.[26] His
tract on the pox is a moral and religious declamation on the fate of man. His
humanist classicism (he spent some time in Italy before the pox arrived) allows
him to talk of the pox as one of the weapons hurled at man, not by God, but
by the gods of the classical pantheon.[27] With poetic licence he speaks of the
four elements as 'soil, waves, fire and air', where *humus* and *unda* replace the
natural philosopher's *terra* and *aqua*, 'earth and water'. We should therefore
not expect here the closely argued dispute of the philosophers on the nature
of the elements and whether their qualities can become corrupt in the
generation of the pox.

In another allegory Grünpeck describes how he laboured to discover the
nature and origin of the pox, consulting physicians, philosophers and all
manner of wise men; his task was to cross a 'river flowing from the centre of
Egypt', that is, to acquire hermetic knowledge. He made little progress and
decided that his only course was to visit 'the *gymnasium* of the Egyptians'
themselves. Although terrified of the crystalline waves of the enticing river,
he entered it and was greeted by the sight of the great men of old discussing
the nature of the pox. Some gave it the name and identity of diseases
recognised in the old literature; others described how it occupied first – for
reasons of temperament – the bodies of the French and then spread to
Germany, eastern Europe, Bohemia, Thrace and Britain. The ancients instructed Grünpeck in the astrological circumstances of the appearance and
spread of the pox, and faded from sight. Grünpeck returned to his city,
amazed, enlightened and ready to write it all down.

In other words, Grünpeck's attempt to understand the pox involved astrology and hermeticism. Other people had different means of understanding it;
but when it came to practical action, in this case giving advice, the agreed
structure of medicine imposed a similarity on most efforts. Diseases were
disruptions in the balance of humours. Grünpeck blames the sharpness of
black bile and inflammation of the red bile. His style was that of an educated
layman, but uses the doctor's stock armoury with confidence. Regimen was
to be based on foods that did not generate these humours to excess, and on
evacuations. Since the contagion was carried in the air, prevention was largely
a case of lighting fires made aromatic by the addition of myrrh, white
frankincense and juniper berries.[28] He normally describes contagion using the
poetic image of arrows, although the frontispiece of his book shows the
Christ Child delivering bolts (see Plate 5.1). He also occasionally descends to
a discussion based on changes in elementary qualities.[29]

We should glance briefly at one more fifteenth-century tract on the pox, that of Johann Widman (1440–1524), published in Rome and Strasbourg in 1497. Widman was a medical man, and here addresses his pupil, J. Nell. Nell replied in flatteringly humanistic terms, and it is clear that Widman, like other German humanists, was no hellenist. At a time when Leoniceno was discovering dangerous errors in Pliny's fragments of medicine, it is to Pliny that Widman turns, rhetorically, as evidence of the large number of diseases afflicting mankind 'even without counting the new diseases'. In some sense the pox was a new disease to Widman, born of God's will through astrological secondary causes. (But Widman recognised descriptions in the old authors as corresponding closely enough to the pox to be useful.) As in Grünpeck's case, having once established that it is a disorder of the humours (he agrees that black bile is principally affected), standard medical theory provided the regimen of cure and prevention. As Widman says, the doctor does not cure through ultimate causes – the astrological situation and subsequent change in the air – but through his understanding of bodily causes, the temper and complexion of the solid parts and the elementary qualities of the humours.

Unusually among these northern literary sources, Widman says that the severity of the disease is such that sufferers are separated 'from civil conversation'[30] until cured. The clear implication is that the sufferers were taken into quarantine or put together in a hospital; but it is not clear whether he meant hospitals in northern Europe or the south. Since Widman was in correspondence with his pupil in Rome, where this tract was published, it may be he was referring to the situation in Italy. Widman's connections with Italy are clear – he was educated partly in Pavia,[31] he published in Rome and his pupil furthered his education in Rome – and it may be that he was familiar with Gaspar Torrella, some of whose views on the pox were similar to his own and who worked in the papal court in Rome, as we shall see in the next chapter. In particular Torrella advocated rounding up the prostitutes into a hospital.

Reform

As we have seen, Widman was not the only German to have links with Italy, for many German humanists shared some ideals with their Italian counterparts. But to publish simultaneously in Rome and Strasbourg, as Widman did, was soon to become an unlikely occurrence as the religious and cultural differences of the Reformation became apparent.

The Reformation and the French Disease came together in the person of the humanist and knight Ulrich von Hutten. He has been conspicuous to historians because his nationalism and attitude to the Church can be used to illustrate a 'pre-history' of the Reformation. He helped to broadcast the fact that the 'donation of Constantine' was a forgery.[32] He was condemned, along with Luther and Pirckheimer, in the first papal bull against the Reformers.[33] He thought the Church was too Italian, and corrupt. He sided with the emperor against the pope.[34] He is conspicuous for us because he caught the pox, wrote about it and died from it; moreover he was one of the first to introduce the treatment of the pox by guaiacum (or guaiac) wood.

The story begins with the Spanish or Portuguese use of the wood of a tree that grew in the Indies, where it was often thought that the French Disease originated. It was an empirical remedy, to be sure, but it seemed appropriate that it should be found alongside the disease. Rumours of its use reached German-speaking countries between 1506 and 1516 and the Emperor Maximilian and his chancellor, Cardinal Matthew Lang, set up a commission to look into the matter. A group of physicians, including Nicolaus Pol, was dispatched to Spain to gather information on the use of the wood. Pol reported back to Lang at the end of 1517 and after having circulated in manuscript form the report was printed in 1535. Meanwhile other tracts, derived probably in part from Pol's report, and based on the use of guaiacum, were published in Germany. Leonhart Schmaus of Salzburg collected nineteen reports of the wood from the Indies and from Portugal and published a tract on them in 1518.[35] The most important of these works was that of Hutten: *De Guaiaci Medicina et Morbo Gallico*, published in Mainz in 1519. It was a popular book, being translated into a number of vernaculars and going through several editions. It was, for example, translated into English by Thomas Paynel, a canon of Marten Abbey, and so became one of the few books in English on what Paynel called the 'frenche pockes'.[36] The difficulty Paynel found in the elegance of Hutten's prose and the strangeness of the technical terms is a fair indication of the state of medical scholarship in England.

As a reformer Hutten was opposed to the medical establishment. It pleased him that the guaiacum was an empirical remedy. It came, he noted, from a barbarian land where there were no doctors, no aphorisms and no canons of medical theory and practice.[37] Its effectiveness as a cure (on which he insisted) highlighted the inability of orthodox medicine to deal with the disease.[38] Hutten, the pox-stricken patient, attacked the medical men for being more concerned with the discovery of causes than with attempting to treat such a foul disease. (Like several Italian authors whom we shall meet in the final chapter, Hutten says the pox was much more violent when it first appeared than when he was writing.)[39] He reports the doctors' accounts of the astrological and humoral causes of the disease and dwells on the fact that frequent disputations show that no true answer had been found to the questions of the cause and treatment of the disease. For two years, says Hutten, the physicians 'meddled with such disputation', and he is bitter that their treatment of his own case was useless.[40] He implies that the uncertainties of the physicians were seen as ignorance and error over a period in which surgeons and empirics took the opportunity to enlarge their practice and sell their own specifics.

Although he was recommending an empirical remedy and grumbling about the elaborate apparatus of orthodox medicine, Hutten argues not only that the specifics of the surgeons and unlicensed practitioners were often useless or dangerous, but that their single remedy, applied with a single technique and irrespective of the constitution and circumstances of the patient, was bad practice. The learned doctor had indeed long maintained the reputation of his kind by a show of adjusting his practice to the individual requirements of his patient on the Hippocratic and Galenic models. It was clearly a display that worked, for here is Hutten complaining of its absence. The great detail of diet and regimen in some of these early tracts throws interesting light on the eating habits of the time (in places they are like cookery books) and are designed to supply alternative items of diet, out of which the rational, learned doctors could make a show of accommodating the individual requirements of the patient.

The same point is made when Hutten's criticism of the doctors continues with his account of guaiacum. The Spanish nobleman who found guaiacum of use on the island and took it home found that the doctors would not allow it, Hutten observed.[41] No doubt they disliked it because they saw it as a specific, a remedy of empirics, and, as Hutten sharply points out, because it would have taken their business away. When personal use had persuaded them of its benefits, says Hutten, they brought it into practice, but attempted to appropriate it to learned medicine by declaring that without their own directions for use it was valueless. Hutten is quite clear about the market value of learning, as an advertisement, to the doctor who is selling his services, and sees that it is very much bound up with the possession of the medical degree. He is accordingly angry with those who (we are not told how) purchased their medical degrees. In their ignorance of Greek and Latin, says Hutten,[42] such people are dangerous to their patients, who cannot doubt the learning 'once garnysshed with the name of Mayster doctoure' as Paynel expressed it.[43]

So, although opposed to much of orthodox medicine, Hutten did not doubt that real medicine lay in the skill acquired from learning, rationality and experience. These things alone were of use in producing a treatment. Only if the guaiacum were prepared in a suitable way would it be effective. Hutten's own description of how to prepare the wood also shows that he accepted much of the contemporary theory of medicine. He specified that the wood be reduced to very small parts or sawdust and soaked in eight times its weight of water. The water was then to be boiled until only half was left; the foam produced during boiling was removed and dried to provide a powder for the sores, and the decoction was used as a primary medicine. A second boiling provided a weaker potion. Hutten forbade the use of any admixture, which he held would weaken the specific power of the decoction. The associated regimen was that the patient was purged and starved: standard parts of orthodox practice, designed to remove morbific matter and prevent more forming. Moreover, the patient, after drinking his twice-daily half pound of the decoction, was made to sweat copiously in a heated room and with blankets. This was again a standard technique of evacuation and signifies an underlying belief in a morbid matter that had to be removed. Hutten had help from the dean of the Leipzig medical faculty while writing the book, and clearly accepted the professional view of how the body worked and how the doctor should put it right when it went wrong.

Other professional devices were more transparent to Hutten. The ethics of the early-sixteenth-century doctor, where expressed, were strongly in opposition to any over-familiarity or irregular dealing between physician and apothecary. The basis of this was simply that it was the duty of the doctor to maintain the dignity of medicine as a whole, which would be lessened by association with those lower in the medical hierarchy, and almost destroyed if it were discovered that the doctor and the apothecary were conspiring by such a device as the doctor over-subscribing an expensive drug in exchange for a proportion of the apothecary's excessive profit.[44] That this was an articulated item of ethics almost certainly meant that it was in practice widespread. Hutten reports a similar practice. The physicians (he says) saw that guaiacum was so effective that there was a danger that it would render their own receipts useless if it were freely available. Those who sold the wood saw equally that if the doctors stopped prescribing it, and indeed condemned it, they could kill the trade in it. According to Hutten the doctors and the merchants consequently conspired to make it known that guaiacum was indeed effective but only when administered by a physician according to his rational and learned rules.[45] Here Hutten records a conversation with the dean of the Leipzig faculty, Heinrich Stromer (1482–1542), in which Stromer with the physicians' customary 'great gravitie of wordes' told Hutten of his fears that the wood would lose its reputation if administered by the unlearned.[46] Hutten adds that even physicians who at first denied the effectiveness of the guaiacum and thought it merchants' propaganda changed their mind when after experience with rich patients they began to appreciate larger fees.

The merchants mentioned by Hutten here were the Fuggers, who had control of the guaiacum trade.[47] It has been claimed that their arrangement with the physicians included payments to Stromer. And it was Stromer who helped Hutten write the book on the guaiacum, no doubt supplying some of the standard medical theory that we have noticed.[48] Unwittingly, it appears, Hutten the patient was playing his part in advertising the wood for the benefit of the medical profession and the merchants. The merchants' interest in maintaining the price of the wood and the physicians' interest in medicalising it coincided too in the pox-hospital established by the Fuggers in Augsburg. It was called the Poxhouse, or the Woodhouse, because of the extensive use of guaiacum within it.[49] Hutten mentions the Fuggers explicitly later in the tract,[50] where he describes them as dealing in home grown crops in exchange for those of exotic provenance (perhaps guaiacum).

Hutten disliked monopoly, whether of the merchants (in relation to guaiacum) or of the physicians (with their internal practice of medicine). He saw that the medical monopoly was made possible by means of obscure learning, a learning which also tried both to appropriate the use of guaiacum and to reinforce itself, often enough, by claiming that the pox was an old disease, with a place in medical learning. His message – that a simple decoction of the guaiacum is not only the most effective remedy for the pox, but one that every patient can procure for himself without the complex ministrations of a doctor – is the message of a reformer who saw parallels with the Church's sale of privileges, with its claim to learned authority of long standing and the necessity of the priesthood. Hutten believed that remedies like guaiacum were given by God and needed no medical sophistication. In any case, simple remedies were often the best, he said, as witness the Saxon who cured all his ills by drinking hot buttered beer.

We must glance now at a much more radical figure who was directly involved with medicine, if not so personally acquainted with the pox, Paracelsus. Others called him *Luther medicorum*, the Medical Reformer, and in a characteristically bombastic passage he drew attention to the parallel between himself and Luther.[51] He has also been the subject of an extensive literature, and this is not the place to retell the story of his influence in medicine. Paracelsus was opposed to the use of guaiacum in treating the pox. He was, then, opposed to Hutten and the Fuggers. He was opposed to, and was opposed by, the dean of the medical faculty of Leipzig, Heinrich Stromer, who had helped Hutten write his book on guaiacum. Indeed, Paracelsus was opposed to all learned physicians because they relied on Galen and Hippocrates. He seems to have thrown Avicenna's *Canon* on the fire and did a great deal to annoy established physicians. With Stromer it mattered, for Paracelsus wrote eight books on the French Disease while in Nuremberg in 1529, but they were suppressed on a recommendation from Stromer.[52] One of the reasons for all this is that Paracelsus promoted mercury as an internal specific medicine. He believed that metallic mercury was dangerous, and advocated its use in combinations that made it less poisonous; but not content with this he published a tract attacking the use of guaiacum. This could not have pleased the Fuggers or their friend and beneficiary Stromer. Paracelsus quickly left Nuremberg.

Paracelsus thought that the rationalising classical authors were pagan and erroneous. He resented the monopoly of internal medicine claimed by the rational and learned doctors of the universities: he saw through the professional image they cultivated with their syllogisms and Latin learning. He believed that doctors were not made, but born, with a special gift from God for medicine. But it was their duty not to benefit from the practice of medicine as the monopolistic faculty benefited, but to lead people to see the easily available remedies that God had put into the world. These included not only the essences of plants which the alchemists came to believe they could extract from them by distillation, but also chemicals. Mercury had long been used both by the alchemists and by the surgeons, who used it in treating skin conditions. Paracelsus preferred it to guaiacum partly because the wood was imported: he believed that *local* plants were those best suited to the inhabitants and the local expression of disease.[53]

Paracelsus the Medical Reformer called for changes that had parallels with religious Reform. The monopoly of the Latinising physicians of the universities looked like the control exercised by the priests over the word of God, also kept in Latin. The protestants wanted every man to be able to read the scriptures in his own language without the interpretations of a priesthood, and to know about God for himself, even by a study of nature. Medicine should be based on the remedies that God had put into the world and men should take responsibility for their own health. In major ways in the northern, protestant countries, there was dissent from old orthodoxies.

Thus for Paracelsus the identity of the French Disease, its classical name, was of no importance: we only have to know what God intended for its cure. For him the disease had an identity of a different kind. All diseases were entities and the 'anatomy of disease', based on an extensive macro–microcosm parallel, was its distribution among people and places. Diseases had 'bodies' like veins of metal in the earth. The organs of the body corresponded to celestial bodies, and what mattered to Paracelsus was not their physical 'dead' anatomy but their celestial anatomy. Organs, not humours, were the site of diseases. All this was fiercely and consciously radical. Paracelsus' new medicine was pious where the old authors had been pagan. It was to be a God-guided empiricism, devoid of the sterile logic of the schools.

Since diseases were entities they had their own characteristics. The French Disease, said Paracelsus, was a specific poison which was attracted to the bodies of those who are indulgent and luxurious, qualities it attacks.[54] But it rarely comes first, generally settling on another disease already there, changing its symptoms. This was important, for according to Paracelsus the evacuations performed on the patient by traditional physicians acted merely on the symptoms of diseases, not on their essences. For him treatment was to apply a remedy as specific as the disease, to which it was linked by astral correspondence.

It is plain why Paracelsus ran into trouble. All learned and rational physicians sought to avoid specifics, to cultivate learning and logic, to stress the individuality of the patient rather than of the disease, to make the most of the wide acceptance of the notion of the four humours and to display physical anatomy as a mark of learning and the foundation of medicine. Paracelsus found more converts among protestants than catholics but by no means all protestants agreed with him. Leonhart Fuchs (1501–66) thought that physicians were made, not born, and made by their classical – indeed Greek – erudition. He was as hellenist as Leoniceno had been, having learned his Greek at Ingolstadt. Like Leoniceno too he was concerned with precision in anatomy and the naming of simples, those unmixed natural substances, mainly from plants, that were used as medicines.[55] Like him he was busy trying to restore the *prisca medicina* of the Greeks by pointing out the errors of the Arabs and recent writers, who had corrupted the ancient wisdom. But it is also now, in the hands of Fuchs, a very protestant affair. Fuchs dedicates the book to the Duke of Wittenberg – where the university was very protestant[56] – and urges him to continue and complete the Reformation. For Fuchs, this was a religious, political and intellectual reformation: Duke Hildrick (says Fuchs) has been appointed by God to lead his country out of the present calamities and to be 'the great Instaurer of religion itself, of true piety and thus of true studies'.[57] Fuchs makes much of the interdependence of intellectual, academic and political virtue. His advice to the duke on how to choose the best academics from a range from anabaptists to papists is so pointed as to read like an application for a job (it probably was). But, all the same, Fuchs paints a picture of political stability resting on a firm religion, and this in turn on careful education. In restoring the school at Tübingen, Hildrick must recognise that 'no *imperium* or religion can be preserved without a study of letters'. As Fuchs explains, princes and learned men mutually support each other, for the scholar gains (politically useful) wisdom and prudence from a range of disciplines not available to busy princes; and the learned man needs the political protection of the prince.

Fuchs' programme of continued Reform in medicine and other parts of learning was a protestant hellenism, a belief that by excising the scholastics from the fabric of medicine the worth of Greek medicine would be seen more clearly. Catholic hellenists reached the same destination by another route. Like them, Fuchs is scathing about the practice of earlier scholars. Theologians of previous generations, he says, knew little Hebrew or Greek, and so could make little of the sacred page, the true fount of our salvation. In its place (he continues) they had resort to posing sharp and sophistical questions, of little real importance. He is of course, referring to the schoolmen of the middle ages. But the important thing here is that for Fuchs the schoolmen were *unreformed*. Their religion in Fuchs' view was the corrupt Catholicism that the Reformation had tried to correct. Fuchs' programme was to extend and complete the Reformation, not only in theology, but in all learning, especially medicine, and in the political power needed to support it. Medicine, like the study of the sacred page (he says), has been much corrupted by ignorance of languages. Names of drugs, parts of the body, living things, metals, weights and measures are so often confused that part of Fuchs' medical reformation is to generate a *prisca* terminology.

This is why he treats pox as he does: quite unlike Paracelsus, for Fuchs the important thing was to discover the true name of the disease. He deals with it first in his 'Medical Paradoxes', *Paradoxorum Medicinae libri tres*, and is mostly concerned with clearing away erroneous names. He argues that *lepra* and *elephantiasis*, often regarded as names for the pox, mean different things in Greek and Arabic authors. Fuchs calls the pox the 'French Disease', a term he recognises as vulgar: necessarily so, since he believed it had no classical

precedent. No, he argued, it was not *lichen* or *impetigo* and Pliny was very
much to blame in generating confusion here. To attack Pliny was to emulate
Leoniceno; but it was not just a hellenist tactic in their war against the
barbarians, for, as Leoniceno urged, the real problem about misidentifying
diseases and drugs in the old writings was that the wrong remedies would be
used, with dangerous results in medical practice. Fuchs' views on the identity
of the pox had led him into a controversy with Symphorien Champier (1471/
2–c.1539) on this issue. Champier had attacked Leoniceno on the same
question, and Fuchs is obliged to take sides, attacking Champier, defending
Leoniceno and attributing errors to Pliny.[58]

The same message can be read in Fuchs' *Institutiones* of medicine.[59] He is
now established in Tübingen (he seems to have got the job) and he is busily
teaching a reformed and classical medicine that has 'only recently emerged
from barbarity' – partly, he adds, by his own efforts. He is still concerned to
show that Arabic medicine is derivative and corrupt, and is anxious to expose
the young only to the pure medicine of Hippocrates and Galen. He is still
convinced that the ability to govern society rests on true learning. It is an
indication of the novelty that Fuchs feels in his position as a Reformer of
medicine that he begins his Institutes with a little history of medicine. (Such
things are generally justifications of novelty.) Fuchs derives medicine as much
from the divine gift to Hippocrates and Galen as from the Bible. His classical
orientation is such that we learn from him more about Chiron the Centaur
and Podalirius, legendary founders of medicine, than we do about Arabic
medicine, which is dismissed in a sentence. The history of Fuchs' medicine is
essentially over at the death of Galen; the schoolmen are not even mentioned.
Naturally for Fuchs traditional natural philosophy, purified in a classical way,
was the basis of medicine. The elements are fundamental,[60] and he takes the
reader through the Galenic seven 'naturals' that constitute the link between
natural philosophy and the theory of medicine: the elements and qualities; the
qualitative temperaments; the qualitative humours; the solid parts of the body,
the animal, vital and natural faculties; animal and natural actions, and finally
the three spirits of the body. The contra-naturals, that is, those things that
cause disease, are also Galenic for Fuchs and act by their qualitative effect on
the body. So when Fuchs comes to clarify the names of diseases he does so
in an entirely classical way. He argues strongly that the disease 'which today
they commonly call French, Neapolitan or Spanish' is not to be identified
with the *impetigo* or *mentagra* of Pliny.[61] It would have been impossible for a
hellenist like Fuchs to have admitted that the erroneous and unreformed
authors like Avicenna and Pliny had known and named the French Disease
while the Greeks had not.

Classicism of this kind left no room for causes that were outside the
category of manifest elementary qualities, that is, 'occult' causes, which were
so important in the Pollich–Pistoris disputation and to which physicians
increasingly turned to explain the nature of the French Disease. We shall

examine the nature of such explanations in later chapters, and here we need to note that to accept 'occult' causes meant a departure from standard natural philosophy, the agreed and largely Aristotelian view of the nature of the physical world. That was a radical step to take. It was taken by a few who had, perhaps, other reasons also to depart from orthodoxy. One of them was the Italian Girolamo Cardano (1501–76), whose religious orthodoxy was questionable.[62] He was finally accused of heresy, perhaps because he cast the horoscope of Christ, but more likely because of his protestant sympathies.[63]

Cardano faced the question they had faced in the disputation at Leipzig. All agreed that changes in the air were one of the causes of the French Disease. Yet how could the air change? Could an (Aristotelian) element change its nature? Could its qualities become corrupt in some way? Cardano took the radical line that two of the four elementary qualities, cold and dry, had no autonomous existence, simply being a state of privation of their opposites, hot and wet. If accepted, this would destroy the theoretical basis of traditional medicine. The apparatus of logic within medicine rested on a number of natural axioms, like 'opposites cure opposites'. Perhaps the most important of these axioms was the qualitative nature of the elements: fire warmed, water cooled. These simple relationships, involving the action of the humours and of medicines, were axiomatic because self-evident: they could not be questioned on logical grounds, and they enabled the doctor to syllogise about the physical world. They were fundamentally important to the theory of medicine. But Cardano made it thinkable to question them. A number of medical authors accepted that in place of, or in addition to, the action of manifest qualities there were in the physical world natural actions that were more powerful and less understandable and were mostly at work in contagious diseases, of which the French Disease was the most notable. These authors borrowed Cardano's term and called these hidden causes 'subtlety'. We shall meet them in a later chapter.

Astrology

We have seen that the issues raised at the Leipzig disputation were interpreted differently by different groups. One of these issues was astrology and whether it was part of medicine. Both doctors and laymen discussed how it explained the occurrence of the French Disease.

Belief in astrological causes of the pox was very general in both northern and southern Europe, and we have noted how astrological conjunctions were held to cause corruption of the air. Astrology was a very real part of the understanding of, that is, knowledge of, the pox in the fifteenth and sixteenth centuries, and it is important for the historian in discussing the contemporary perception of the disease – its construction. To put it another way, astrology was an intellectual resource that could be used by those, whether doctors or

Plate 5.2 'The planets at the Creation'

laymen, who wanted to explain how the French Disease had arrived. But what determined whether astrology was used in an explanation or was convincing in an explanation were wider cultural matters. Astrology, especially in its mathematical and judicial form, was not classical and did not always appeal to the hellenists and humanists. Its Arabic component could look pagan and the necessary relationship it implied between astral causes and mundane effects could seem to be impious, detracting from God's absolute and arbitrary power. This image had to be corrected: Plate 5.2 shows God very obviously in power through His angels over the Creation. This gave a timetable for the Arabic doctrine in a Christian context. The earth represented by the Church is shown in the centre.

But astrology had its uses, particularly to the medical man. He could use its elaborate theory as part of the learning that characterised the university-trained physician and on which his professional reputation and success was built. In particular astrology related directly to prognostication. Its implied inevitability provided the doctor with a refuge when treatment failed to cure. Part of astrological theory, the doctrine of the Great Conjunctions,[64] was extremely useful in explaining disastrous events separated by long periods of time, like the plague and the pox.

For these reasons many doctors increasingly used astrology in their practice. It had played little part in Western education as it was formalised in the universities in the thirteenth century, but largely because of medical interest in its powers of prediction it became widespread in the fourteenth and fifteenth centuries, appearing in university statutes. So when (as we have seen) Pistoris said that astrology was very useful to medicine, although not actually part of it, he was simply expressing a very common view. Astrology was part of the learned apparatus of medicine, and not to have explained the relationship between it and the French Disease would have been to leave a space in which other kinds of practitioner would exercise their authority and gain advantage. The pope's physicians (whom we shall meet in the next chapter) felt the same.

But astrology had to be handled with care, even by doctors, for the reasons we have noted. In the Christian West it would have been difficult to insist on the necessity of the relationship between astral configuration and events on earth. The Arabic doctrine of the Great Conjunctions had been developed in harness with the belief in the divide between God and man. The Western context was different and conjunctions, whether great or small, had to be seen as merely God's instruments, not as quasi-autonomous principles. The Great Conjunctions were calculated from the moment of Creation (see Plate 5.2).

Accepting or denying that the pox had astrological causes often depended on such attitudes to astrology. Pistoris, for example, adopted a medieval view of astrology from Pietro d'Abano, as we have seen. Perhaps he felt that Pietro, the great scholastic 'Conciliator', was like himself a man of the schools with a good grasp of the technical business of medicine and astrology. His own medicine was humanistic enough to have the historical understanding that the ancient doctors had not practised mathematical predictive astrology, but Pistoris had little of the hellenists' feel for the purity of Greek medicine (which could not therefore be astrological). Let us take as an example the materials used by Grünpeck in constructing his image of the French Disease.[65] In cultural terms his resources were classical literature and Christian doctrine, two fields where a man's training and predilictions might lead to different emphases. Grünpeck does not emphasise one more than another but jumps from one to the other. In the third chapter of the tract we met Grünpeck writing as a classical poet, calling the pox (and the plague) arrows of the gods. Classical allegory was a medieval genre that allowed an author to express things that in literal terms would not be compatible with Christian beliefs, and Grünpeck is using it to give the dignity of age to his astrology. In the following chapter he drops the allegorical mode. The gods of the pantheon become mere planets, the visible secondary causes that ominipotent God uses on earth. The heavens are like the cover of a book, says Grünpeck, whose letters are denied to no one. He now displays an astrology carefully groomed for its role in Christian Europe. He begins by asserting, in the company of theologians and astronomers, that God created the world with the planets standing in the positions of the vernal equinox – the world was in the spring of its existence with the sun in Aries. He gives details of the position of the other planets in each part of the zodiac, and explains God's purpose for each of them. Collectively, they act as a paterfamilias, to govern domestic matters on earth. Mars is Judge, Saturn the executor of Justice. The other planets are mediators, who may intercede to soften the severity of judgement.

It is into this Christian picture that Grünpeck fits the Arabic doctrine of the Great Conjunctions, invoked to give authority to an explanation of the origin of the French Disease. He is concerned with Saturn, which (he says) completes its course in twenty years, and Jupiter, which takes twelve years to move round the zodiac. It follows, he says, that they meet in a 'minor conjunction' every twenty years. But these minor conjunctions occur in a different zodiacal sign three times, occurring again in the same sign after sixty years. This is a 'large' conjunction, a *magna conjunctio*, signifying events in the lives of princes, in the yield of crops and in the birth of prophets. Because the signs of the zodiac were characterised by their elementary qualities, the twelve formed themselves into four groups of three, according to matching qualities. Each group of three was known as a 'triplicity'. The occurrence of the conjunction of Saturn and Jupiter in successive triplicities allows the astrologer to count a 'larger' conjunction, *congressus major*, at 240 years and a Great Conjunction, *congressus maximus*, at 960 years. Such conjunctions, says Grünpeck, signify changes in kingdoms, and natural disasters.

Grünpeck is anxious to make his astrology as pious as possible. The Great Conjunctions are to be used in alliance with revealed knowledge to illuminate the date of Creation and the ages that the earth has passed through to the present. Adapting a view of Augustine, Grünpeck held that the history of the world fell into six periods, corresponding with the six days of Creation. The first of these was from Adam to the Flood, and the last was from Christ to the present. The total period from Adam to Christ was 5,099 years (a very specific contradiction of Aristotle's eternal world). The Great Conjunctions, then, have not been numerous. Grünpeck says that since a full 960 years did not have to elapse from the position of the planets at Creation to the first Great Conjunction, there have been only seven such conjunctions (the eighth being due in 1693).

Grünpeck invokes these fundamental principles in order to explain how and why the French Disease arrived when it did. To take the 'how' first, his explanation is partly the general one that in judicial astrology the critical thing was the aligning of the good or evil forces of planets at conjunctions, oppositions and geometrical 'aspects'. It was partly too that the planets had elementary qualities which had a direct effect on earthly objects sharing their qualities. Mars was hot and dry and protected the hot and dry humour – red bile – within the body and its domicile, the gall bladder. Mars was thus thought to provoke war in society and sharp, acute diseases in the body. As Grünpeck adds, Saturn, cold and dry, encourages the increase of black bile – melancholy – and was responsible for chronic diseases. The pox, concludes

Plate 5.3 'Saturn and Jupiter in their chariots'

Grünpeck, being generated by both planets, had all the acuity of an acute disease and the duration of a chronic disease.

As to the 'why' of Grünpeck's explanation of when the pox arrived, he and the astrologer were in difficulties. Modern planetary tables for the fifteenth century show that the pox occurred at a time rather remote from any significant conjunction, and Grünpeck is hard pressed to find a simple and impressive correlation. Indeed, it is at this point in his tract that he breaks off his account to take his allegorical trip to the Egyptian academy (which we met above). When he returned, mysteriously wiser, he was able to record that the fateful event was a conjunction of Saturn and Jupiter at four minutes past six in the evening of 25 November 1484 (ten years before the arrival of the pox). Mars was at an unfavourable aspect, in his own house, and the combined evil forces of Mars and Saturn overcame the benignity of Jupiter.[66] To this Grünpeck adds an eclipse of the sun in the following year. This was followed by pestilences, wars and famines, and finally the pox. Both the people to be first affected (continues Grünpeck) and the locations where the pox spread were determined by the elementary qualities that characterised them. To continue using Grünpeck's language, each planet had a House in the body and in different countries, where effects were provoked on the basis of shared elementary qualities.[67] Plate 5.3 shows the planets as divinities who are represented here in chariots that are carrying them around the zodiac on a way to a conjunction. The wheels of the chariots indicate the proper houses of the planets in which the planets exert their strongest powers.

Grünpeck's astrological vision and explanation of the pox was published in 1496 and few would have disagreed with it in principle. But the picture changed suddenly when, in the same year, Giovanni Pico della Mirandola published his *Disputationes* against judicial astrology which had a European impact. Neither Christian nor classical, mathematical predictive astrology lost favour among hellenist and humanist scholars of the renaissance. The freedom of the human spirit, Pico argued, was not to be curtailed by the predispositions that stars produced, and owed its range beyond the physical world to supreme providence. Arguments that the relationship between human events and the heavens was *necessary* denied free will on the part of man and hinted at it on the part of God. The learned doctors knew from the actions of their own enemies that it was possible to attack both a discipline and its practitioners, and Leoniceno would have agreed with Pico that astrologers had by a show of learning and mystery secured considerable standing.[68]

After Pico's attack on judicial astrology some doctors, especially of the hellenising kind, thought twice about it, as we have seen in the case of Pistoris and Pollich. It was the same in Rome, as we shall see in the next chapter, where the papal physicians, Gaspar Torrella and Pere Pintor, were engaged in a similar battle about the French Disease and astrology.

Chapter Six

The French Disease and the Papal Court

Introduction

In previous chapters we looked at perceptions of the pox by laymen and at how it related to natural philosophy in university and court circles in Italy and Germany. In this chapter we shall investigate the medical response to the first appearance of the French Disease in the most important court in Christendom, that of Rome.

It was the time of Alexander VI, pope from 1492 to 1503, who had been born Rodrigo Borjia (henceforth Borgia) in Játiva, Valencia, in 1431.[1] He comes into our story only indirectly, as the centre of the court, for he did not contract the disease himself. But many at the papal court did. Several members of the papal *familia* were early affected: the cardinals Joan Borjia, Bertomeu Martí, Joan Borjia-Llançol and Rodrigo's own son Cesare, cardinal of Valencia. Other cardinals were also stricken: Ascanio Sforza, Jean Villiers de la Groslaye, Ippolito d'Este and Giuliano della Rovere (who became Pope Julius II in 1503).[2] Alexander VI and his *familia* had seven physicians in their retinue; we are concerned with the two Spaniards, Gaspar Torrella (c.1452–c.1520) and Pere Pintor (c.1423/4–1503), who published on the French Disease.[3]

The Problem with the Pox

Torrella and Pintor shared to an extreme degree the problems of all physicians facing *Morbus Gallicus*. The disease was apparently new, or at least had no ancient name by which it could be understood within learned medicine. It was very widespread and was known to be a particularly intractable disease. But the problem was not primarily that the doctors were unsuccessful in curing it, and were therefore forfeiting the confidence of the public. While it is true that patients like Hutten berated the doctors, this was because they were as much radical Reformers as unrelieved patients. The main problem was that the disease was seen as divine punishment or as having been generated by conjunctions of the planets, and that therefore the scope for any human endeavour to alleviate it was seen as very limited. The physicians' problems were more professional. The learned, university-trained physicians were under great pressure to act – to bring relief to the suffering, to prevent the spread of the disease and to give advice. There was pressure not only from their patients, but also from civil authorities who were concerned with the health of populations. Lastly they were under pressure to preserve the professional status quo, for inaction or admitted failure would give an opportunity to unlicensed practitioners to take the initiative. That is, because the disease did not have an ancient name, it could not be handled by the theoretical apparatus of learned and rational medicine, on which the reputation and advantages of the university-trained physician rested. He was in no better position than the empirical practitioner who claimed to have a specific, that is, a remedy proven by experience rather than reason (and probably kept secret).

These pressures must have been more extreme in the papal court than in very many other situations. Clearly the publications of Torrella and Pintor were strategies towards a solution. Much of what we see at the papal court can be recognised as actions prompted by the pressures generated by this new and disastrous scourge. We shall look mainly at two areas where the papal physicians were active. We shall examine first their resources, whether intellectual or material, and second the strategies they adopted. We shall see that part of the story is the competition between different classes of practitioner, from the unlicensed empiric to the university doctor, and also between different types of university doctor, especially between Torrella and Pintor.

It is clear that to maintain his position and to solve the problem of the pox, the learned and rational doctor had to bring it into the medical system. It had to be identified with something that the medical literature contained, for only then could he talk of causes, remedies and prevention and in this way be learned and rational about it. It was his knowledge of the medical literature that quickened his eye when looking at poxed patients and what his fellows had written about them. What was significant in the disease was what was in the literature, and therefore in this sense the learned physician constructed a picture of the pox.

Resources

It is not surprising that two learned medical men should see rather different things as significant. Partly this had to do with their training. Torrella and Pintor both came from Valencia, the home too of Alexander VI, who perhaps showed them special favour on that account. Both men belonged to families of Jews who had converted to Christianity, and who later suffered persecution by the Inquisition in Valencia.[4] Pintor's family was destroyed and he found protection with the cardinal, Rodrigo Borgia. Of Torrella, as of many other fellow countrymen who decided to stay in Italy after completing their university studies there, we can only presume that his choice of Rome as a place to settle was related to the situation created by the Inquisition in Valencia. The social climate resulting from the inquisitional offensive in Valencia was unfavourable to the return of those who had reached elsewhere some professional level and where they could enjoy a greater degree of intellectual and religious freedom.[5] It was therefore natural that both of them should settle in Italy. But there were differences as well as similarities between the two men. Torrella was a priest and had studied medicine in Siena and Pisa; Pintor, a generation older, did not leave Spain for his medical training and studied the subject in Lérida, the *studium generale* of the Crown of Aragon.

The differences between Torrella and Pintor derive mostly from their different universities. While both accepted the Avicennan Galenism that was the common property of the learned physicians as a group, Torrella shows evident traces of the Italian intellectual world of his time. He was at his Tuscan universities at the time – the 1470s – when the Neoplatonist circle of Marsilio Ficino was active in Florence, and one of his teachers, Pierleone da Spoleto, was an outstanding member of the circle. Torrella adopted some humanist values from Italy, although we should not, for reasons given earlier, regard him strictly as a humanist.[6] In all this he was different from Pintor, who was thirty years older and without an Italian training.[7] It is clear from what they wrote that there was an intense rivalry between them. Perhaps it was intellectual, the result of their different training, or perhaps it was because they had to compete for the favour of the same patron; at all events their rivalry is not only revealed in their work on the French Disease but was a factor in encouraging them to write.

Publication indeed was one of the main resources available for these two physicians when faced with the general problem of the pox and with the problems of their own personal situation. But publication now meant something different: the printing press had not existed when Pintor was born, and not all medical men were sure that it was a good thing. To us the press means an invariant text, more copies and a consequent more rapid spread of knowledge. We have seen in the case of Leipzig how a personal dispute could be followed by a wide audience through a printed pamphlet war, and something similar happened in Rome, an important centre of printing. The close connection of the two men with the pope[8] and Torrella's personal position as physician to Alexander's son Cesare must have ensured them a wide audience, demonstrating the power of the press as a resource.[9] No wonder that Torrella decided to resort to the press for the first time two years before Pintor. Books formed a related resource. Torrella was appointed librarian of the Vatican library by Alexander in May 1498. He was there for two years at least, and he probably took advantage of the manuscripts and printed works in producing his own written material.[10]

Pintor's education was also a resource for him. His training in medicine in Lérida began in the late 1430s and he was practising medicine by 1445. He was much more a practical physician than Torrella, whose medical degree was secured only with the help of Alexander VI, some years after Torrella had finished his studies. Pintor was the city's examiner of physicians in Valencia four times between 1455 and 1481, and lectured in the Valencia school of surgery for periods between 1468 and 1485.[11] Indeed, he was instrumental in setting up the school in 1462 and in reorganising it in 1480; it was the core of the new medical faculty when the *university* of Valencia was established in 1499.[12] Clearly the surgical component of medicine was important for Pintor, which must have been significant when he came to write on the pox, which was often seen as a skin condition and therefore surgical. He had, moreover, been practising medicine for about forty years when he ran up against the Inquisition and left Valencia by 1484[13] to become personal physician to Rodrigo Borgia in Rome.

Given that the two men had very different backgrounds and different resources on which to draw, it is not surprising that they differed in their reactions to the pox and its problems. There is a strong sense in which they were both successful. That is not to say that either found a cure or a preventive regimen, but that both were perceived to be successful. That is, the strategies they developed from their resources worked. Both remained as papal physicians and Torrella survived the purge of the Borgias instituted by Julius II, Alexander's successor. We have already seen that Julius suffered from the French Disease and he chose to keep Torrella in his position as papal physician, despite his connection with the Borgias. Clearly Torrella's strategies had worked, and he had a reputation as a pox-doctor. Both popes showered him with benefices.

Strategies

The writings of both men enable one to examine their strategies at work. Of Torrella's output, five medical works and an astrological prediction survive from the period 1497–1506. The prediction was actually a letter addressed to Cesare Borgia in 1502 and was published in 1506 at the request of the apostolic *datarius*, Giovanni Gozzadini, who was interested in the astrological effects of a comet that appeared over Rome in that year.[14] It is interesting that even if at this time astrology was beginning to come under attack, both Torrella and Pintor used it, albeit in rather different ways.

Torrella's more strictly medical works are mostly directed at infectious diseases. His *Consilium* on the pestilence known as 'modorrilla', which broke out in the Castilian fleet at Flanders and spread over the Iberian kingdoms, was published twice, in Rome and Salamanca, in 1505.[15] Another *Consilium* was directed against a pestilence that occurred in Rome in 1504.[16] Then there was his *Regimen Sanitatis*, a preventive regimen presented as a dialogue addressed to Julius II in 1506.[17] All these followed his *Tractatus cum Consiliis* on the pox of 1497 (republished in about 1498) and his *Dialogus* on the same subject in 1500.[18] Clearly Torrella saw publishing on infectious diseases, both pestilential and not, as a strategy to deal with the problems that faced him.

The same can be said of Pintor,[19] although only two of his works are known, on pestilence and pox, published respectively in 1499 and 1500.[20] He addressed them to his patron – Alexander VI which, as in all patron–client relationships, had advantages to both parties. The patron was flattered and furthered his reputation[21] and the client strengthened his security of employment.[22] Like Torrella, Pintor found that to publish on infectious diseases during the first years of a disastrous new scourge was to become an authority. A further similarity is that both men found a proper medical name for the pox. Torrella called it *pudendagra*,[23] because often it first appeared in the genital organs, *pudenda* (*-agra* was a common ending for a disease name, as *podagra* was 'disease of the feet').[24] After searching the literature, Pintor came up with the term *aluhumata*.

That Torrella should invent a neologism and Pintor should find a term from the medical literature is characteristic of the two men. Pintor's long medical practice, his greater age, his Spanish training all made him want to find a solution from within available sources. His first work, on pestilence, reveals the same tendencies. He called it an *Agregator Sentenciarum*, a collection of opinions of the learned. This was a medieval technique, even a genre of literature, and renaissance authors sometimes looked down their noses at it.[25] Pintor collected summaries of opinions of people like Pietro d'Abano. The surgeon Guy de Chauliac had expressed the principle of 'aggregation' as the cumulative addition of work by means of which knowledge grows and the art progresses.[26] Guy was doubtless one of Pintor's major intellectual mentors, particularly since, unlike Torrella's, Pintor's medicine included a large and practical interest in surgery.

These then are some of the differences between the two physicians who were facing the problem of the pox at the Roman court. Their first step towards a solution was the epistemological one of identifying the disease. We have seen that some doctors, like the Bolognese teacher Natale Montesauro,[27] accounted for the apparent newness and strangeness of the disease by assuming that it was a compound entity, combining features of more than a single disease. But Torrella and Pintor followed the simpler course of taking it as a single disease. It had then a single cause for the pains and the sores which made their task in explaining the nature of the disease much more straightforward.

It is necessary to underline here their difficulty in dealing with a very real phenomenon that had only a vernacular name. It was partly that the professional knowledge of the learned physician was so structured that it could not deal with an unnamed disease. It was also partly that it was a common medieval belief that names *meant* something about the essence of the things they signified. The laboured etymologies of the middle ages from Isidore onwards were expressions of this. But this system worked only in Latin and, in an age when Latin was the language of medicine and philosophy, for something to have only a vernacular name was to devalue it.

Thus, in seeking a Latin name for the new disease, Torrella and Pintor had to grasp its essential nature. This meant also discovering how it had arisen. This was more than discovering historically whether or not it was indeed a new disease, and meant learning about its nature from the causes that produced it. Torrella held that the disease had originated in the French Auvergne in 1493 and had subsequently spread by contagion to the rest of Europe and indeed the world.[28] He was expressing the devalued worth of a vernacular name when he said in 1500 that the French Disease was first seen among the French troops in Naples, and that the Italians thought that it was 'connate to the French people'; correspondingly, when Charles took his diseased troops back to France, the French thought that the pox had originated in Naples and gave it an appropriate name, the 'Neapolitan disease'.[29] The variety of vernacular names also lessened their authority. Torrella reports that the French also called it the *grosse vérole*, the Valencians, Catalans and Aragonese the *mal de siment*, and the Castilians the 'curial disease' because it 'followed the court'.[30] Pintor agreed that the disease was commonly known as the French Disease, *Morbus Gallicus*, and, like Torrella, felt the difficulty of the range of vernacular names (but he does not particularise).

Another reason why vernacular names devalued medical things was that they were used by vernacular people. The unlicensed, the empiric, the apothecary and the common surgeon would not have used Latin, and it was for professional reasons that the physicians insisted on Latin. They identified the use of the vernacular with groups of practitioners with whom they were in competition. The French Disease had to have a Latin name so that the physicians could draw it into the apparatus that distinguished them from other groups and justified their claims to superiority.

Part of this apparatus was that diseases fell into categories. There were *kinds* of disease, species within genera. They made a point of entry for the pox. If it could be shown that the disease resembled another then it might be a new species of some genus. Torrella, for example, was prepared to accept that the French Disease was a nameless species of a kind of disease called *scabies* in the Latin version of Avicenna.[31] He could not allow it a vernacular name, of course, and in inventing a name for it he was extending the subdivision in Avicenna's classification of disease.

Pintor was in a similar position. As a learned and rational doctor he saw that to allow the disease to be new, with only a vernacular name, was to allow competing medical groups a double advantage. He too made it partly new, so to speak, by claiming that it was to be identified with a third and obscure species of the *variola* kind of disease, a species which he found in Avicenna and Rhazes, called *aluhumata*.[32] So his strategy, to pick up and expand an obscure part of the learned apparatus, differed from Torrella's, which was to insert a new subcategory into the apparatus. The 'part newness' of the disease according to Pintor was also due to the fact that it had an astrological cause. Such things of their nature were infrequent, and the pox was, says Pintor, unknown before its recent irruption. Both authors are giving their topic a history, in two senses. First, as we have seen, to enquire into the causes of the disease, whether or not astrological, was to learn about its essence. Secondly, in general terms, to give a new thing a history was to give it the dignity and authority of age. To show that some new scheme of things had been perhaps adumbrated but not systematised by the ancients made it more credible. Torrella and Pintor were achieving that credibility by fitting the pox into the apparatus of the ancients and the Arabs.

Pintor thought that he had been particularly successful in this strategy, and while ignoring what had been published by others he made great claims for his own intellectual understanding of *aluhumata* − systematised from Avicenna and Rhazes − and for his ability to treat it. Pintor too was rewarded by his patron, and his strategy was in that sense successful. The essential thing about a strategy was that it had to be intelligible and convincing to the patient or patron. The specialist knowledge of the doctor was of the same kind as that of most learned men and was simply more extensive in a way that they recognised. So in returning to his resources, the medical literature, and modifying it by accommodating the French Disease, Pintor looked as though he was refining medical knowledge.

Astrology

As we saw in Leipzig, opinion could be divided on the question of whether astrology was part of medicine. In the popular mind there was perhaps no doubt that it was, but the learned doctors, especially the hellenising kind, were aware that the Greek physicians had not used astrology, certainly not the mathematical and judicial sort. Yet it remained the case that medical prognosis was closely linked to astrological prediction. It was part of the apparatus, and both Torrella and Pintor had to explain the relationship of the French Disease to it, or once more they would have left a space in which other kinds of practitioner would exercise their authority and gain advantage.

Let us first take the case of Pintor. We have seen that in explaining how the disease arose he was in a sense explaining its nature. Yet he allowed another strategy to remain open for development. He frequently calls the pox a *morbus foedus et occultus*. He meant in the first place a loathsome and perhaps shameful disease. *Occultus* is 'hidden', whether by ignorance or by incapacity of the senses or reason to grasp it. Pintor is saying that part of the causality lying behind the appearances of pox was unknown, perhaps necessarily so. On the medical front this meant that the job was partly to fit the French Disease into the apparatus by reason of its effects and appearances. But by the same token the astrological apparatus was opened up because often the conjunctions, oppositions and 'aspects' of the planets were seen to be causes of lower events, but the mode of action of the causes was unknown or 'occult'. The contrast was with Aristotle's system of physical causality, as taught in the schools, which was universally held to be intelligible in all its stages. Pintor held that the French Disease arose from a planetary conjunction in 1483, but that its manifestation had been delayed in Italy, France and Spain until 1494 and that it would end in 1500.[33]

In a similar way Torrella saw that astrological explanations had to be faced. There was good reason to think that a disease so widespread as almost to be universal should have universal causes: that is, major conjunctions that affected everyone. In 1498 he quoted from Pietro d'Abano the baneful effects of the presence of Saturn in Aries and related this to the appearance of the pox.[34] But by 1500 he was doubtful of predictive ('judicial') astrology. In the dialogue of this date he has a layman expressing doubts to a physician about astrology because the astrologers in practice were working from effects – the pox itself – back to causes – the conjunctions – when they should have predicted the effect before it happened. 'Formerly I firmly believed in astrology, but my early credulity has cooled on seeing that Jews who claim to be first-class astrologers had predicted nothing about this disease, or indeed anything about their own persecution.'[35]

Torrella is essentially separating his own group, that of the rational and learned doctor, from that of 'astrologers' as a non-medical group. He achieves the same end by also pinning the astrology label on to the Jews, the despised and persecuted minority, but ironically his own ethnic group. He also hints at 'forbidden practices' among astrologers who fail to predict the future.[36] Torrella is really inventing a little history of astrology to justify his present beliefs. He praises Ptolemy's work, and allows that the heavenly bodies *do* predispose man to act in certain ways and that there are specific relationships between the stars and natural objects on earth.[37] This for Torrella defines the central and sound essence of astrology and what is proper for a rational and learned doctor to know. This is as far as his strategy of occupying astrological ground will go. It is, of course, *other* people who go to improper excess. It is, first, the people who have not the moral fibre to resist their passions who follow the predispositions induced by the stars. Nor, says Torrella the rational doctor, do these people have the *reason* to overcome the predispositions. Torrella derives from Ptolemy the aphorism that only the wise will be master of the effects of the stars. Secondly, Torrella notes some conspicious examples of astrological failure in the past, such as the illustrious death promised by the Chaldean mathematicians to Pompey and Caesar; the favourable prospects offered to the Neapolitan barons in their quarrel with Ferdinand I in 1484; and the sad fate of Lodovico Sforza, Duke of Milan, and his brother the Cardinal Ascanio, neither of whom ever acted without the advice of astrologers.[38]

The intellectual resource that made this strategy possible was Giovanni Pico della Mirandola's *Disputationes*, directed against judicial astrology, which appeared in 1496. This work had a big impact across Europe,[39] and we have seen something of its effect in Leipzig. Judicial astrology began to go out of favour because it was neither classical nor Christian to hellenising and human-ising scholars of the renaissance. To argue for a necessary causal relationship between the heavens and human events denied human and even divine free will. Pico argued that the human spirit was not constrained by the (admitted) predispositions engendered by the stars and ranged beyond the limits of the physical world, obeying only supreme providence.[40] He agreed with Leoniceno in seeing astrologers as insinuating themselves into powerful posi-tions by astrological tricks.[41]

Thus Torrella's strategy was to occupy the centre of the astrological business and purge it of things that he thought the rational, learned and pious doctor would be best rid of. Make these the characteristics of groups that differed politically, ethnically, professionally and religiously and they become unethical for one's own group to hold.

Causes and Contagion

It is arguable that both the Black Death and the French Disease had an important effect on Western medical thinking. Greek medicine centred on diseased people rather than on disease. A diseased person had his or her humours in imbalance. This was caused by, among other things, poor regimen or diet or congenital weakness and was affected by age, sex, habits, seasons. The doctor's assessment took all these things into account and was essentially an estimate of how far that person departed from a normality that would have been proper for that person at that time. It was almost entirely personal, despite the fact that Greek medicine included named diseases, which had similar symptoms in different people. But the plague and the pox were *things*, disasters that affected huge numbers of people at the same time. Whether they were the effects of a conjunction of planets or the punishment of God, it was something imposed, not an internal and fortuitous imbalance.

This made the medical men look for external causes. In particular they asked whether the original causes of the disease continued to operate as the disease continued. As the planets entered new conjunctions or as God's anger waned, would the disease disappear, or had some secondary cause persisted? Experience showed that in both plague and pox proximity to diseased persons often resulted in the new appearance of the disease in another person. With the feeling that the disease was a thing, it seemed to contemporaries that some matter or influence was passing from one person to another. This was *contagio*, whether by touch or at a little distance: little distinction was made between *contagio* and *infectio*.[42]

It is within the context of these ideas that we must examine reactions to the pox in general and those of Torrella and Pintor at the Roman court in particular. Torrella insisted, at least after its first appearance, that the French Disease was merely contagious.[43] He denied that there was a general change of the air (which Leoniceno believed) like the corruption thought to cause 'phthisis' and 'pestilential fever'. *Something* was transmitted from skin to skin. Torrella described it as 'something thick that adheres to the surface and quickly evaporates'.[44] This substance not only began the irritation of the skin but created a sort of infective halo round the diseased person, which could by its own action spread the disease to another person without skin contact. Three of Torrella's *consilia* illustrate this. The first is a case of direct sexual transmission, where it is said that the agent of transmission were corrupt vapours from the uterus entering pores in the male member of 'Nicholas the Young'.[45] Another case is of indirect contagion, in which an older man caught the pox by sleeping in the same bed as his brother, who was already infected. In the third, Torrella simply speaks of 'contagion'.[46] By 1500 he thought that the disease could also be spread contagiously to infants from the breasts or mouth of their wet nurses and indeed that an infected infant could then pass the disease to another nurse.[47] Nevertheless, Torrella maintained that in the majority of cases it was the genital organs that first became infected with the *pudendagra*, by contagion.

By offering a model of a merely contagious disease, and especially one transmitted sexually, Torrella was making possible some concerted civic response, such as control of prostitution. But it was not part of his strategy, by emphasising contagion, to deny himself access to the part of medical theory which said that disease was a *dyscrasia* of the humours. Indeed, he allowed that an improper regimen of life could cause the pox. The regimen involved the six non-naturals, especially diet, exercise and cleanliness. Those are liable to the pox who indulge in anger or melancholy or those who 'make use of salted, sharp and bitter foods or drink . . . who do not take baths as they used to do; who do not change their clothes; who do not take exercise or massage; who take meals or medicine that brings matter to the skin; who drink sharp and old wines or those sweet and heated too long'.[48]

Here Torrella was offering a model of the pox that was of use to the individual rather than the state and so was widening the market for his medicine. He reinforced his message with other *consilia*, providing examples of what could happen to any individual in the absence of his advice. The first is chosen to make his point because the patient, the Catalan Antoni Marc, was himself a university-trained physician. He had been on a voyage on which only the wrong food and drink (as in the quotation above) had been available.

Torrella can thus portray himself as the physician of physicians. A sea-voyage and excessive exposure to the sun during the course of it also featured in the second of the two *consilia* that he uses. Also to blame in this case was a disordered regimen, by which he may mean either a dietary or a sexual one. Like others Torrella thought that excessive sexual activity could produce a *dyscrasia* in the body that encouraged the appearance of the pox, so in this case he may not mean transmission by contagion.

To a certain extent Torrella and Pintor found a bigger market for their medicine by offering different emphases from different parts of the theoretical apparatus to different parts of their clientele, whether it was a case of the individual's regimen or the city's control of infected groups. Their audience was also largely male and their medicine was adapted to this fact too. For example, all Torrella's patients were male. It was a male-centred account of the disease that Torrella gave when he asserted that the men suffered more from the disease than did women. This (he explains) was because men had a hotter complexion than women and that the uterus encouraged the corruption of vapours in infected women. It was of first importance, accordingly, that men should avoid infected women. But the reverse was not true. Since the uterus was cold, dry and dense, it did not, according to Torrella, suffer damage very easily, and it was only after repeated sexual contact with infected males that women became infected.[49]

Torrella's medical language was also directed towards fee-paying males. Most of them would have been educated and so would have understood the language of causality used in the natural philosophy of the arts course. Medicine had its own additional language of causality perceptible to if not fully comprehended by the educated male patient. Torrella, as any Galenist might, spoke of an antecedent cause, a localised or general humoral *dyscrasia*, and a conjoint cause. This was the thick matter we have met, which was responsible not only for the contagious spread of the pox but for its principal symptoms, the pain and the skin lesions.

Another cause of the French Disease was its astrological origin, and we have seen how Torrella differed from Pintor in giving it less attention. Without leaving the topic of causes we can now look at how Pintor handled the question of pestilential or merely contagious diseases, a question that we have seen was of great practical importance for the individual and the city faced with the French Disease. Pintor's strategy was, like Torrella's, to exploit his resources to formulate a strategy. He too would have wanted to reach as many people as possible, if only because he thought his was the best medicine. He too had to address men who understood what kind of thing a medical explanation and a medical cause were. No more than Torrella could he neglect a poor regimen as a cause of a *dyscrasia*. A *dyscrasia* was not only an imbalance of humours but the presence of a 'peccant' humour, of which the qualities had become distorted. For Pintor the remains of the menstrual blood from which the body had originally been formed could also form a peccant humour and both these causes were 'antecedent'. The 'conjoint' cause was more immediate to the symptoms, and was a thick and heavy melancholic blood, too cold for proper concoction and nourishment. Pintor's hierarchy of causes next included particular causes, both internal and external, which generated a pathological concoction in this intractable blood. Such were excessive exposure to the sun (compare Torrella), an unseasonably hot and humid spring (compare Leoniceno) and nature's attempt to expel from the body melancholic matter generated by a poor regimen.[50] All produced *aluhumata* by disturbing the blood.

Although such theoretical apparatus was flexible enough to give different explanations to different physicians, it was not infinitely adaptable. In particular, a thoroughgoing astrological explanation of the continuation of a disease was not compatible with an equally thoroughgoing theory of contagion. Pintor was in the same difficulty as Torrella in that his patients and the civic authorities wanted to know whether the pox was contagious, which experience suggested it was. Empirical experience was an area where the empiric had the same standing as the learned and rational physician. Torrella solved the problem by applying to the French Disease the transmission pattern of *scabies* and other merely contagious diseases. Pintor solved it by emphasising the value of the astrological theory of epidemics over empirical knowledge of contagion; but he took care not to ignore contagion and so leave it an uncontested field for the empirics.

To understand Pintor's strategy here we must go back to his astrology, as we looked at Torrella's. As an explanation of why so many people were ill with the same disease at the same time, Pintor invoked the universality of astrological causes. The effect of those causes was an epidemic. Now, both the planets and the 'houses' (zodiacal signs) through which they passed had characteristics which related directly to things on earth, including named countries. Over-sophistication of the theory of astrology could therefore explain why the pox affected some places rather than others. Where the qualities of the heavenly bodies and places were elementary (Mars for example was hot and dry), an intelligible explanation existed for why they should exert influence upon earthly things, which were made up of the four elements. Elements and qualities were the fundamentals of the Aristotelian world picture, and every educated man accepted them. But astrology was older than school natural philosophy and had been fully articulated as a predictive art in the West before the universities gained recognition, and part of its mode of action could not be explained in Aristotelian terms. When a planet 'rejoiced' in a particular house and was accordingly more powerful in its effects, no intelligible Aristotelian explanation was offered. The mathematics which predicted the effects of planets at certain aspects to each other was not an Aristotelian doctrine, nor did it offer any explanation of the effects on earth of the aspects. There was good reason to call these unknown influences 'occult', because they were hidden from the standard late medieval rationality.

Pintor found additional and medical authority for the term in Avicenna's standard explanation of the causes of pestilence and believed that there was 'a certain occult influence or property' directly linked in a causal way to his *morbus foedus et occultus*.[51]

Pintor systematically examined the planetary 'aspects' (especially conjunction, opposition and lunar eclipses) from 1483 to 1494, that is, from the date he believed the disease was formed to its actual appearance in different countries (governed by their different signs). The technical details of astrological prediction are too complex to discuss here, but two points need to be made. The first is that it was elaborate enough to account for all appearances. That Saturn, a baleful planet, should have conjunctions with other planets in Scorpio, was enough to explain why the pox began in the genital organs, which were under the influence of Scorpio. Its spread through the body was likewise affected by the other signs as they entered new relationships; and its spread through different regions of the earth was likewise a planetary and zodiacal matter. Secondly, it was elaborate enough for there always to be good reasons why its predictions often did not work. Here astrology was a natural partner of medical prognosis. A prognosis or prediction that turned out right acted more powerfully on the mind of the observer than two that did not, even while explanations were similar in all. The medical men were taught how to qualify their predictions by following Galen in saying something like 'if the patient faithfully takes his medicine, the assistants follow their rules and there are no external accidents, then . . .'[52] The astrologers had many similar qualifications that explained how the certain predisposing powers of the heavens were often frustrated by the imperfect nature of material events on earth.[53]

Pintor also invoked the astrological doctrine of nativities to explain the distribution of the pox. That is, the position of the planets and signs at the moment of a person's birth determined his constitution and vulnerability to external causes, including the astrological. Whether an individual developed the French Disease was thus doubly astrological, and Pintor is exploiting his resource in another way. Furthermore, he held that the astrological cause of the pox in the years after birth was complex enough to be very rare or even unique, so that the disposition of the planets was a one-to-one cause of the disease. It was in this that the *occultness* of the disease consisted. Pintor says that the planets in that position have a 'whole property or specific power', *tota proprietas seu virtus specifica*, which generates the pox.[54] These words recall the medical doctrine of the 'whole substance' by which Galen explained how some drugs acted in a way 'hidden' from Aristotelian causality.

This system enabled Pintor to explain the variations in the distribution of the French Disease. While it could affect anyone, it most often appeared in those whose constitution inclined towards the melancholic, which as we have seen was the nature of the *aluhumata*.[55] This disposition was determined either by the individual's astrological nativity or by his regimen, a strictly medical category: Pintor's strategy is here to keep the astrological and medical systems together. This is clear also when he goes on directly to assert that, whatever its origin, the *aluhumata* is contagious. His argument is drawn not from experience but from authority, for having defined the disease as a species of Avicenna *variola* he claims that it must have the contagious nature of the genus to which it belongs. Here too Pintor binds the medicine to the astrology, for he says that the astrological causes produce the disease by corrupting the air and that an infected individual does just the same, so that the chances are doubled of a second individual developing the disease in proximity to the first.[56]

So finally Pintor comes to the point where he can give practical advice. It is very practical: 'Go away quickly, stay there a long time, and come back slowly.'[57] This is pestilence-advice and reflects Pintor's belief that the pox was a pestilence. How it was to be put into practice also reflected his theoretical position. Some were to escape by going down to low-lying places where the air was thicker and more resistant to changes issuing from the heavenly bodies. This was justified also by experience, for Pintor points to the absence of the pox from communities living in marshy places with thick air, and also from gaols (presumably in low-lying areas) and enclosed religious communities. On the other hand if the prevailing causes were coarse and material, leading to melancholy, high places were to be recommended. Thirdly, those who had remained untouched in an infected place (so demonstrating their immunity) need not go anywhere. Like the predicting astrologer and the prognosticating physician, Pintor is playing fairly safe: leaving options open, but occupying a central medical territory and claiming it for the learned and rational physician. In contrast, it must have been direct experience that made Pintor agree with Torrella that contagion took place most often sexually. He even largely agreed with Torrella why this should be so.

Diseases, Signs and Symptoms

We have argued that the historian is wrong in trying to identify a modern category, such as a named disease, in the past. The problem is compounded because the people of the past were using different procedures of identification – in the case of the French Disease, two procedures. First, the early authors recognised when someone had the pox. In the first decade or so there was no recorded discussion of how to identify the disease, no critical list of symptoms or procedures of examination. Most of the extant early publications give only brief descriptive phrases and these were not meant as an aid to identifying the disease. At this level everybody knew what the French Disease was. There was common consent that some set of appearances and circumstances which we cannot now properly reconstruct constituted the 'French Disease'.

Second, to identify properly the disease the doctors had to find its real name and essence. These were basic preliminaries to the way in which the rational and learned physicians handled it. Signs and symptoms were important in this process. While all agreed what the pox was, the physician had to show his mastery of theory by explaining how the signs and symptoms related to the causes of the disease and helped the doctor in his treatment. Again we may suppose that a reasoned and learned account of symptoms had the power to impress, even though the physician used the same remedies as the empiric, from whom indeed they were often borrowed. As a learned and rational practitioner he had to defend his own kind of medicine.

For the learned doctor the physical appearances associated with the disease were either, in Aristotelian terms, effects or properties of a cause – the disease – or 'accidents', things that might happen in this or that kind of matter, but which were not part of the formal causal system. It was possible for the physicians to distinguish, within this framework between *signs* which perhaps fortuitously helped the physician decide on the essence of the disease, and *symptoms*, which were related in their nature to the essence. In other words, this is another part of the medical apparatus that could be employed by the learned physician in his slow approach to practice. With signs and symptoms he is at least dealing with matters of observation that precede the selection and application of a remedy. Necessarily his discussion of signs and symptoms had to agree with and indeed appear to be derived from his theoretical understanding of the causes and essence of the disease.

It is therefore useful to compare what Torrella and Pintor had to say on this matter since their theories were different. Torrella believed that the *pudendagra* had a material cause – the 'thick matter' – which was instrumental in making the disease contagious, and therefore gave attention to the first appearance of a physical symptom. It fitted his theory that this should first appear in the *pudenda*, as he makes clear in the first *consilium*. He clearly refers to an ulcer on the penis 'with a certain long hardness tending towards the groin like a *radius*', together with dirtiness from the ulcer.[58] By 1500 he was prepared to acccept transmission and first signs appearing elsewhere on the body, although less frequently.[59]

Pintor, in contrast, thought of the *aluhumata* as an occult disease, without an ultimate material cause. He did not therefore look for a manifestation of this matter, but gave his attention to the symptoms as the only means by which the nature of the disease could be grasped. Both agreed that skin lesions and pain were the principal manifestations of the disease. But because of the different way they had used the resources of medical theory, their treatment of the pain and lesions was correspondingly different. To reconstruct in detail each man's scheme would be tedious, but we can see again that each is using medical theory to put together a coherent scheme for his own purposes. 'Pain' and 'sores' are fairly simple medical categories, and it was good for Torrella and Pintor to be seen to be employing sophistication on them. Torrella distinguished 'essential pain' from that felt 'by contiguity', *per essentiam* and *per communitatem*. These two catagories represent Galen's distinction between a part that suffers on its own account (idiopathically) and others that suffer with it by reason of communicating structures (that is, sympathetically). This is why, for Torrella, the parts involved are long, joining one place to another: muscles, tendons, joints (between long bones) and nerves. The different kinds of 'essential pain' Torrella found in the disease were also grouped into the four humoral kinds that also characterised the four species of *pudendagra*: sanguine, choleric, melancholic and phlegmatic.[60] By 1500 he had distinguished some fifteen different kinds of pain associated with the French Disease by making sophistications upon schemes suggested by Galen and Avicenna.

Pintor chose a different part of the apparatus on which to practise sophistications. Since he had decided that the pox was a species of *variola* there was a ready-made species–genus relationship in Galenic theory. He could distinguish between the signs common to all species of *variola* and those proper to the *aluhumata* itself. The most important of the common signs were back-pain and tiredness of the whole body. He was able to elaborate on this by exploiting Avicenna and Rhazes as resources, adding that other common signs included itching of the nose, fearful dreams, general heaviness, especially of the head, redness of face, tears, palpitations with difficulty of breathing, pain in the throat, dryness of the throat and so on.[61] As a use of resources this is similar in its degree of elaboration to Torrella's analysis of the fifteen types of pain. But Pintor has a second strategy, to perform a similar exercise on the proper signs of the *aluhumata* itself.

The early signs of the third species (of *variola*), that is, the early signs of *aluhumata*, are small pustules like needle-pricks in the external skin of the parts, mainly in the chin, the tip of the penis in the male and the small skin of the vulva in the female; sometimes also in the skin of the forehead and head, sometimes in other parts but very rarely in all of them at the same time. These needle-pricks later extend to the size of small or even large lentils, and in some patients to the size of a carlino. In time they can grow to the size of a hand. They are mostly dry with little moist pus: some as dry as scales, others moister.[62]

Here, because he believed that the disease was astrologically determined, Pintor was not concerned, as Torrella was, with the chronology of the appearance of the sores, but simply in which parts of the body they could appear. As we have seen, Torrella in contrast *was* concerned with the sequence of appearance of the pustules because of his belief in material contagion.

Like Torrella, Pintor took pain to be a mark of the pox. For him it was a proper sign and like Torrella he saw many varieties of it. But he did not attempt to subdivide it into different categories; rather to explain how it varied within the individual. Thus the very acute pain in the lower arms and lower legs, he said, was sometimes intolerable and sometimes less severe, but it never ceased. He was obliged to give a material basis for these changes and claimed that some matter had been absorbed by the nerves and the membranes of the bones and muscles.[63] By its nature this matter did not easily escape through the pores of the skin and when agitated by internal or external heat it emitted vapours: it was these that caused the pain when trapped and eased it when escaping from the body. The matter itself remained lodged in the nerves and was the cause of the pain's durability. Pintor recorded that the pain was often associated with movement and that it was sometimes so severe that the patient could not move his legs.

Practice

Prevention

Thus far we have seen how physicians of the late fifteenth and early sixteenth centuries approached medical and professional problems with the pox and how they used resources and strategies to overcome them. We have seen how they used the apparatus of their medicine to identify the disease, its symptoms and its causes in order to *understand* it in the context of their medical learning. Only then, in the same context, were they able to begin the practical part of medicine and think about prevention and cure in a way that marked them off from the nostrum-mongers and specific medicines of the unqualified practitioner. While Torrella and Pintor shared the general intellectual position of late medieval Galenism, with its canonical progression within therapy of regimen, pharmacy and surgery – each adapted to the needs of the individual – their differences again tell us about their different resources and strategies.

Torrella believed in material contagion as the main means whereby the French Disease was transmitted, so that his main strategy for prevention was avoidance of contagion. In 1497 this was his only advice, namely urging men to avoid sexual contact with infected women, because, as we saw, he thought that men contracted the disease by contagion much more readily than women. Three years later his advice had radically extended from what the individual should do to what the city or state should do. The argument about contagion was still the same, but now Torrella was acting as a public health adviser, as doctors had done for several centuries.[64] As we have seen in our discussion in Chapter Two, Torrella proclaimed that the definitive and only sure prevention of the pox was for the authorities to round up, isolate and medically treat all infected prostitutes. With the help of God this would eradicate the disease entirely: 'In this way this horrendous and contagious disease will be infallibly extirpated.'[65]

Perhaps it was too radical a proposal, and at the end of this *Dialogus* Torrella regretted that none of the leaders he had addressed had done anything about it. He now urged that in the cities especially matrons should be given powers, with the support of the secular arm, to examine prostitutes and commit those who were infected to a special institution with its own doctor.[66]

Torrella clearly expected that his views were known to the potentates he had addressed. He might well also have thought that his views were spread wider: as papal protophysician he had a reputation that would have made for easy access to European princes, and in 1498 and 1499 he went with Cesare Borgia on a diplomatic mission to the court of Louis XII of France; he had professional prestige as an author on the topic of the pox, and many political leaders visiting Rome – often poxed themselves – must have sought out his advice.

Notwithstanding how widely his message was spread and how conspicuous his own status, nothing was done at this time, although there is evidence that later in the century his advice was put into practice in his own home town of Valencia.[67] But Torrella's case was part of an important broader question. Cities often paid a physician for medical advice and action on matters of public health, particularly at times of epidemics. But locking up the prostitutes was not a medical business. Had his advice been taken, Torrella would have extended the power of medicine over other aspects of civil life. It was no doubt tempting for the authorities, for Torrella had identified a social scapegoat for a social anxiety and had targeted a marginal and easily controlled group, public prostitutes, who worked at the city brothel (the *publicas mulieres* at the *prostibulum publicum*). But there were others, not so easily controlled: those at the public baths and the private *bordelages*, and those working on their own as residents and visitors.[68] We cannot now tell whether Torrella's public health proposal was simply too difficult to implement, or not convincing.

Pintor, in contrast, attempted no 'medicalisation' of civic arrangements. Without Torrella's emphasis on material contagion of the pox through society, Pintor used his resources as best he could in a fairly traditional way. While both authors call for the help of God, it is in Pintor's case a medical prayer, for he believed that God's anger was a continuing cause of the disease.[69] For the rest, it was a question of the proper regimen to be followed by those who were predisposed to the disease, or who had it in its early stages, for once established it was difficult or even impossible, said Pintor, to cure.[70] This regimen followed the six non-naturals, air, exercise and rest, eating and drinking, sleeping and waking, inanition and repletion, and accidents of the soul. All these gave an indication of what was to be sought and avoided in view of their action of the 'primitive' cause, the morbid matter, and the 'antecedent' cause, the individual's predisposition. Pintor used the regimen in line with his belief that the pox was pestilential. All this is fairly standard within the medical theory of the time, and Pintor is building upon what he had published a year earlier in his *Agregator*.[71]

We can see what Pintor meant by regimen in his detailed instructions.

Because he thought that the pox was an epidemic arising from an upper cause in the heavenly bodies, it was an important part of his advice to avoid air at any altitude. Air was the first of the non-naturals and what is in Pintor's mind is that it is in some way disordered or corrupt in causing the pox. His advice was therefore to remain indoors, or in low, even underground, places. Air entered the body not only in breathing, but, the doctors believed, through the pores of the skin. It was therefore important that the regimen did not allow excessively deep respiration or states of the body that opened the pores too much. Here exercise, the second of the non-naturals, was implicated, and Pintor advises moderation: a certain amount of exercise was necessary to maintain health.[72] The rest of his regimen follows similar lines and is not very different from much other medical advice founded on regimens. Moderation was the key because health was a balance between extremes, including those connected with the non-naturals. Food was necessary to maintain health, but hot foods were to be avoided because they were drying and cold and because they encouraged the cold, dry morbid matter to settle on the 'fibrous' parts (nerves, spinal cord, brain, bones and teeth).

Moderation was also the key to the evacuative procedures central to medicine and to a preventive regimen. Since the *aluhumata* had a material cause, it was to be removed or avoided by appropriate evacuation. Pintor suggested blood-letting to get rid of excess blood in plethoric cases where the morbid matter was carried by or related to blood. Where the morbid matter was not related to blood, medicines had to be chosen in the light of the individual's condition, to dissolve the matter and purge it. Excessive purging would lead to loss of essential humidity and the occurrence of other diseases; too little, especially of the *aluhumata*-related melancholic humours, would not move the morbific matter. This is perfectly standard: in steering a middle course with arguments for and against on either side, Pintor and the physicians could be seen to be taking action based on the whole theory of medicine, yet in practice not exposing themselves to the practical test of heroic remedies.

Treatment

It was consistent with their standing as university-trained rational and learned physicians that both Torrella and Pintor claimed to use for the pox a treatment that was 'rational', 'regular' and 'canonical'. Not to have done so would have been to rely solely on experience. The learned doctor did not indeed deny experience and valued it as something that could be made more meaningful than mere empiricism by the use of reason. But within this formula, as we would expect, Torrella and Pintor, with their different notions on the identity and cause of the pox, differed considerably in their practical treatment of the disease.

The most striking feature of Torrella's view of *Morbus Gallicus* was his

optimistic opinion that it was both known and curable. He claimed that he
had treated successfully seventeen cases in just the two months of September
and October 1497. To emphasise the point in his earliest work (of the same
year) he included the medical reports – consilia – of five of his allegedly cured
patients, which also allowed him to illustrate several species of the disease.[73]
Consilia constituted a well-known form of medical literature in the middle
ages,[74] but Torrella was the only one of the early physicians writing on the
pox to use the form. He probably did so as part of his confident, even
aggressive rhetoric of success. Clearly, one strategy open to a man at the top
of his profession, who had by now fitted an apparently new disease into the
extant medical apparatus, was the bold one of announcing his mastery of it.
Since it was seen as a new disease, there were no common expectations about
its durability or curability. Torrella seems to have decided to fill that space,
with the help of the printing press, with claims about his own insights into
the disease and his practical ability to cure it. He accordingly seized on the
differences between his own claims and those of others who saw the disease
as unknown and incurable. Whether these others were merely straw-men,
Torrella used this pessimistic approach as a rhetorical mirror to reflect his
own views.

> many modern people have believed that this disease arose from an upper cause,
> so that it missed no region or time and did not respect the age, sex or
> complexion [of its victims] and did not follow a regular sequence of invasion,
> by reason of the diversity of its peccant matter. . . . Thus they did not give
> attention to its cure and decided to do nothing but wait until nature had
> eliminated it, because some of their attempted cures of people ill with the
> disease did more harm than good. For this reason they claimed that the disease
> corresponded to no specific and adequate category [of the medical apparatus]
> and was irregular and incurable.[75]

Torrella attacked such passive pessimism with a charge of impiety. Medieval physicians not uncommonly used, to justify their profession, an argument
taken from Ecclesiasticus: God created medicine and He is the only one able
to cure us; but He has not forgotten to teach God-fearing people the art of
curing.[76] Torrella uses the argument too, claiming that it would be a sin not
to intervene as a physician in these cases of pox. He accordingly advised
'everyone to remember that they are mortal and sinners, and first of all to
praise God's help as is proper, and afterwards to consult physicians, since God
Himself . . . allows both physicians to understand this disease and medicines to
act according to the properties given to them by Him.'[77] In other words, here
is a university-trained, rational and learned physician claiming for his kind no
less than a uniquely God-given ability to understand the disease, that is, to fit
it into his professional learning and rationality. It is also a personal claim for
Torrella because not all university physicians were so optimistic about the

disease: they had not adopted Torrella's strategy. Torrella added this personal claim to the evidence provided by the *consilia* for the value of the medical 'product' he was offering, in order to emphasise his own professional worth. In addition, in dedicating the *Tractatus* to Cesare Borgia and claiming to have cured him of the pox, Torrella is also using his patron's name as authority for his own virtues:

> No one can question the degree to which humanity is indebted to you [Cesare Borgia] since in your time and because of you we now know not only the essence of the disease, which everyone considered incurable, but also the method of cure. It is thanks to precisely this knowledge that those infected will be optimistic and confident. . . . this confidence will enable them to regain and maintain their health. . . . From this it is obvious that your most Reverend Lordship has cured the infected and kept others healthy as the result of their expectation of health.[78]

So what was there in Torrella's treatment of the pox to justify this optimism? The starting point of his cure was the standard regimen, based on manipulating the six non-naturals, with an eye on the individuality of the patient, and with the view of digesting and evacuating the peccant matter. In other words it was just the same as Pintor's preventive regimen and hundreds of others. Torrella's difference lies in the emphasis he gave to the sixth non-natural, the 'accidents of the soul', that is, the mutual effects of the soul and the body. He treats it first and devotes a large amount of space in the *Tractatus* to it. In fact the quotation above is part of it, and its message is that confidence itself in the treatment and cure is the most important therapeutic device available to Torrella. He linked the patient's confidence to his faculty of imagination, *virtus imaginativa*. This was not simply the patient's 'imagination' in our sense, but was more literally the power to conjure *images*, whether directly from the senses or indirectly from the memory. It was part of the medieval apparatus that linked the internal senses with the external. These links made it possible for Torrella to discuss the matter theoretically, and so to justify it in practice. They also provided him with the avenues of approach to the patient in whom he in practical terms wanted to generate confidence. Torrella used the same linkages to provide an apparatus for (to 'understand') other therapeutic practices like exorcism and charms. What is notable in this side of Torrella's medical thought is the extent of his Platonism, which he may have been cultivating since his days as a medical student and which was anyway in line with the tastes of contemporary courtly culture, including Borgia's Roman court.[79]

Next Torrella turned to some standard pharmaceutical practice. The purpose of giving medicine to the patient was ultimately to remove the morbific matter of the *pudendagra*. The physician's objective in many diseases was the removal of morbific matter or peccant humours, and there were a number of ways of doing it, often called 'intentions'. Torrella's three intentions were evacuation, resolution and desiccation, and consumption (or destruction). His first 'intention' was to let blood when he thought that this humour partook in the morbific matter. This too was standard practice and we have seen that Pintor's preventive regimen included it. With other morbific matter, Torrella first used 'digestive' or 'alterative' medicines that prepared the matter for evacuation, perhaps by changing its nature, and secondly purges to eliminate it. When he considered that enough of the morbific matter had been evacuated Torrella employed his second intention, which was to move the largely vaporous remainder of the peccant matter from its interior location to the skin, whence it could be expelled. This needed resolutive techniques to break down and mobilise the matter and drying techniques to draw it to the skin. In practical terms this meant making the patient sweat by fumigations, baths and especially the 'dry stove', a device big enough to contain the patient wholly.[80]

Torrella's third 'intention' followed, to remove the skin lesions. These were generally taken to be the appearance and actions of the morbific matter at the skin, and so their appearance during treatment could be taken as a sign that the first two intentions had been successful in drawing the matter to the skin. It was also the point at which the arguments and learning of the university doctor in his traditional practice of internal medicine met the practical, external and experiential learning and practice of the surgeon. Torrella, like most university physicians of the time, then used ointments, liniments and lotions. Like the surgeons too he used a range of corrosive and abrasive substances: mercury, yellow litharge, sulphur, ceruse, watered calx, ammonia and verdigris. By 1500 he was also using 'live' calx, alum, rock salt, tartar emetic, ink, vitriol and aqua fortis. To these minerals he added vegetable substances like turpentine, mastic, incense, myrrh, galbanum and opopanax. Many of these must have been not only extremely painful but also dangerous. The most notorious of them was mercury, and we shall later meet the troubles it caused to our two courtly physicians (and their different explanations of them).[81]

For the rest of Torrella's treatment of the pox, he has some simples common to European materia medica before the arrival of new materials from the New World. Most of the traditional substances that he used were those named on Avicenna's Canon in the chapter on scabies, to which Torrella had related his pudendagra.[82] In the second edition (about 1498) of his first work on the pox Torrella added some remedies for certain symptoms of the disease (the sores and nodosities in the parts and alcola in the mouth),[83] but it was not until 1500 that he rationalised these 'accidents' of the pox into a formal medical treatment; he now considered that he had completed his treatment of the pudendagra.

Pintor's practice in the case of the pox was formed by the same kind of constraints as Torrella's. Like Torrella, he had related the apparently new disease to another well known in the medical apparatus, so that he was bound to be partly guided by the therapeutic indications offered by the apparatus (which was the point of so relating the disease to it in the first place). The details of Pintor's recommended course of action were somewhat different to Torrella's because he had chosen a different part of the apparatus in which to 'understand' the pox. It was still a question of attacking the morbific matter, changing or digesting it and expelling it, whether by phlebotomy or purges or by encouraging it to come to the skin. It was still a matter of the learned and rational physician's personal skill to decide on the timing of these measures in view of the success of the intentions, the severity of the symptoms and the individual characteristics of each patient.

In other words, most of Pintor's practice derived from the fact that he had made the pox, his *aluhumata*, a kind of *variola*. But Pintor had made pain the distinguishing feature of the pox, which distinguished it from other kinds of *variolae*. It was pain that could itself kill the patient, and was therefore more than a symptom or sign.[84] One means of attacking the pain was the usual technique of applying alterative and evacuative remedies to the matter that caused it, but Pintor was unusual in believing that because it was so important to limit the pain it was permissible to use narcotic or sedative remedies. While such things were always harmful, the localised and minor damage they caused was justified by their control of the dangerous pain. In practice all of these remedies were ointments containing mercury, generally in what we would call chemical combination. Pintor, like Torrella and others, had techniques which he believed would modify the known danger of mercury without limiting its effectiveness. When he says it was to be 'extinguished with the saliva of a fasting person' he seems to have had in mind some combustive process upon metallic mercury.[85] He also used medical simples for the same purpose, to lessen the danger but not the effect of mercury. He drew authority not so much from the great classical authors as from the Arabs and medieval Westerners, including Rhazes, Avicenna, Bernard de Gordon and Guy de Chauliac, all of whom had used ointments of this kind to treat disease like *scabies*, *malum mortuum*, *impetigo*, *serpigo* and *pruritum*, most of them skin diseases, like the sores of the pox.[86]

Treatment with Heat

Our two authors disagreed in a major way about the use of heat in treating the pox. In order to understand this we must recall that even at this direct and practical therapeutical level actions were generated by theory. The fundamental conception of heat, or the Hot, at the natural-philosophical level was that it was one of the four elementary qualities (along with Cold, Wet and Dry) which in pairs characterised the elements (so that water for example was Cold and Wet). The Aristotelianism of the university arts course taught that these qualities were not necessarily directly perceptible to the senses, and Aristotle for instance had thought that ash was hot (because a great deal of heat had gone into its production), but was not warm to the touch. The same theory of elementary qualities structured the theory of medicine, for the four humours had the same pairs of qualities and the humoral balance – complexion and temperament – of the body was affected by the same qualities in medicines. 'Heating' medicines were, like ash, not necessarily hot to the senses (although things like pepper were). Lastly, the living body had 'innate heat'. Although this manifested itself as tangible heat, it was not the same, and was related more to the generative and celestial heat of the sun.

Thus when a medieval doctor talked about the hot in the body it was not simple physical heat. Pintor believed that a deficiency of innate heat in the part was one of the causes of pain in cases of the *aluhumata*. He believed he could help in these cases by applying temperate medicines equivalent to or a little greater than innate heat in the degree of hotness. Earlier in the middle ages the doctors had refined Galen's qualitative classification of medicines by dividing each quality into a number of degrees and, as Pintor's choice shows, innate heat was thought to be in the middle of the range. In applying temperate medicines Pintor thought that he was strengthening the innate heat of the pained part and enabling it to resolve and expel the morbific humour.

Because innate heat *manifested* itself as physical heat in the body, just as physically cold 'heating' medicine generated heat within the body, so external physical heat was a tool the physician could use to intervene in the processes connected with the innate heat of the body. Pintor discusses baths, ointments, fire, poultices and cauteries. He was generally against the use of baths in cases of the pox except where the particular quality of the water (such as that of a spring near Viterbo) was therapeutic.[87] His argument was that since the pains were localised the baths should be 'partial', that is, applied only to the part in pain. Thus wine, thought of as heating medicine, was to be used (says Pintor) mixed with boiled water as a partial bath for a limb painful because of a weakness of innate heat. Common (olive) oil was not only qualitatively heating but could be used physically hot in a partial bath for the fibrous parts. Pintor's recommendations for procedure are as follows:

> the painful part should be immersed in a half barrel [*semicupo*] full of warm oil for as long as necessary to make the patient's soul free of anxiety and sadness and full of pleasure and joy. Then the part should be dried with linen that is hot and well drained after being soaked with an infusion of mallows, roses and camomile. Thus the stickiness of the oil will be removed from the part in order to keep its pores open. This bath can be taken twice a day, in the morning before breakfast and in the evening before dinner. It will be a singular remedy for pains in those parts suffering from *aluhumata*. Such baths will be taken on as many days as is judged sufficient by a wise medical practitioner.[88]

Partial baths were not always possible, and Pintor suggested that instead fomentations should be applied. He took some of his receipts for these from the surgeon Guy de Chauliac, a natural resource for a man like Pintor with a surgical background. The emphasis on cleanliness both before and after the baths and fomentations was to keep the pores of the skin open for the evacuation of the morbific matter. If the matter remained obstinately constricted within the pores, as a last resort and as a result of his own experience, Pintor advised cautery. This was to be used where the pain was intense and enduring and where the characteristic tumours appeared, which were hard and not very sensitive to the touch. There were two kinds of cautery, 'actual' – fire – and 'potential' – caustic medicine. The aim now was to destroy the morbific matter directly, rather than help the innate heat to dissolve it. Actual cautery did this more quickly, and Pintor, as would anyone with a surgical background, detailed the points at which the cautery should be applied.[89]

We saw above that at the level of both theory and practice Torrella and Pintor disagreed profoundly on two major issues in the treatment of the pox, the dry stove and the use of mercury. Their views of the dry stove were most opposed, for Torrella's second therapeutic 'intention' turned on the use of this remedy while Pintor completely rejected it. As for mercury, they both accepted its use in principle but disagreed over the form in which it was to be applied. In conclusion we shall examine the views of both practitioners about each type of treatment.

Two Controversial Remedies

The 'dry stove'

The use of the *stufa sicca* (see Plate 6.1) in the treatment of the French Disease was very popular in early modern Europe, especially after the introduction of guaiacum.[90] Torrella used it from 1497, which means that he was one of the first doctors, if not the first, to do so. He claimed in that year that one of the best therapies he had tried in treating the pains and sores of the *pudendagra* was to make the patient sweat 'into a hot furnace [*furno calido*] or at least a stove [*stufam*] for five days without any breakfast'.[91]

By 1500 he was arguing that the 'dry stove' should be purpose-built and, although his description is not entirely clear, its basis was a wine-barrel big enough for the patient to sit in. Heated stones were placed on a bed of sand at the bottom of the vessel and a large, perforated seat was provided for the patient. The device also contained two *solaria*, literally 'sun terraces', but whether they received or provided heat is not clear. The whole was perforated and enclosed within a framework carrying a cloth.[92] The purpose was to provide an enclosed space that could be heated so that the patient sweated

Plate 6.1 'Dry-stove treatment', from *L'Espagnol affligé du Mal de Naples*, a satirical illustration that appeared after the 1647 Neapolitan revolt against Spanish domination

copiously. Any small space would do, and Pintor said that a *stupha* was simply a walled space, the air and walls of which were heated either by fire or by water, perhaps with an admixture of minerals or other things.[93]

For Torrella the use of the dry stove was the final part of the treatment, designed to remove the last vestiges of the morbid matter that had resisted conventional alteration and evacuation. The patient was denied food (presumably to prevent the formation of noxious humours) and ordered to sit in the apparatus as long as he could stand the heat. Torrella's patients did so for an hour or two at a time, sometimes twice a day, and continuing for anything from three days to a week.[94] They suffered heroically for Torrella's theory that the dry stoves 'make the patient sweat, opening his pores and drawing out his humidities', including the antecedent and conjoint causes.

Pintor's patients, on the contrary, were not exposed to such rigours, for he warned against the use of the stove 'in any stage of this disease, whether accompanied by symptoms or not'. It was again of course a matter of theory, for Pintor thought that the heat of the stove would dry out the cold, dry and thick melancholic matter of the *aluhumata* and accordingly make it even more difficult to remove: exactly the opposite of what Torrella claimed.[95]

When the different theories of the two men produced different practice, it was warfare. They were competing for patients, reputation and patronage.

Torrella's strategy was to persuade his patients that nasty diseases required nasty treatments. Pintor in reaction offered a far less rigorous regimen that must have offered hope to the faint-hearted. Torrella replied, a few months after Pintor's rejection of the dry stove, with an angry attack on those who relied simply and stubbornly on medicines and denied the stove. Pintor's name is not mentioned, but it can be no one else. Torrella's rhetoric is that since it was universally agreed that the main canonical intention was to remove the morbid matter in all diseases, and since it was evident both to the senses and to reason that the dry stove did this, then his opponent was deficient both in reason and in the senses. To this almost syllogistic argument Torrella adds another from the 'jury principle': ask the patients he had cured.[96]

Mercury

The practice of making the patient sweat was well known to Galenist physicians, and they used sudorific medicines for the purpose. The use of external heat in an apparatus so elaborate as Torrella's purpose-built dry stove may have been new. It is again a question of resources and strategies, whether sudorifics and converted wine barrels or to sweat or not to sweat. Another strategy was the use of mercury, and here too our two authors differed. Mercury had been a resource in the treatment of skin disorders, including *scabies* and lice (*pediculi*),[97] since the time of Avicenna and Rhazes. Although as an external and practical treatment it fell within the province of surgery, these Arabic authors gave the method respectability in the physicians' eyes. From twelfth-century Salerno onwards its therapeutic effectiveness in skin complaints was endorsed by such university-educated physicians and surgeons as Petrus Hispanus, Guglielmo da Varignana, Arnau de Vilanova, Bernard de Gordon, Guy de Chauliac and Valescus de Taranta.[98] These were among the authors from whom Torrella and Pintor sought authority for their use of mercury, which seemed an obvious choice for the skin lesions of the pox.

The treatment of the pox with ointments or lotions containing mercury lasted from five to thirty days or more. During this period the mercury would be applied at least once a day and in a closed room near a fire, as in the stove, to help the patient sweat. University physicians believed that this evacuated the moisture of the morbid matter and so relieved the pain and reduced the pustules. When the patient relapsed, the treatment was repeated.[99] Torrella commonly used the method for a period of three to six days, Pintor for about eight. Pintor made a point of anointing the parts where the pain was most severe twice a day, making sure that, as in Torrella's treatment with the stove, the patient had not eaten before the treatment. The hand that applied the ointment – presumably Pintor's own – was first warmed before the fire, to ensure that the warmed ointment entered the pores of the flesh more easily; Pintor believed that it reached the membranes surrounding the bones and nerves. He claimed that the pustules disappeared after four to six days of the treatment, while the pains, although at first growing stronger, vanished by the eighth day.

There were two principal disadvantages with mercurial applications used by university-trained physicians. First, they caused serious side effects. Second, they were tainted by a history among the surgeons and unqualified practitioners, as we saw in Chapter Two. For professional reasons it was essential that the rational and learned physician should draw mercury into *his* realm and show that its correct use belonged to his kind of doctor. One of the ways in which he did this was by claiming that the side effects of mercury treatment were the result of its wrong use at the hands of the *unqualified* practitioner, a strategy which also served for the specific and empirical remedy for pox, guaiac wood. Another way of drawing mercury into learned medicine was to argue that although administered externally as an ointment its effect was internal and thus part of the physician's business.

We can see these forces at play in Pintor's long discussion of mercury-containing 'narcotic' medicines, which takes up as much as a tenth of the whole work.[100] He was clearly concerned about their use in treating the pains and sores of the *aluhumata* and like Torrella had to balance their effectiveness against their side effects. His conclusion was that the advantages outweighed the disadvantages *only if used* by a physician who was 'rational', 'learned' and 'very prudent', especially in relation to those taken by the mouth. Then, he claimed, a complete cure would be effected (provided that the amount of morbid matter was not large) by the help that was given to the native heat in dissolving the matter. We can see the force of his words, for these were mercury compounds and very poisonous. The prudence he advised consisted in deciding the dose, the moment of taking the medicine, the duration of treatment, the nature of the patient and the prognosis. These were parts of a learned practice that the university physician jealously guarded and for which there were rules in the learned literature. Indeed, the prescription of internal medicines was claimed by the university physicians as their monopoly; it was no accident when Pintor said that internal application of narcotics was a final resort, after the failure of the partly surgical ointments, and when the patient began to weaken. This by implication is when the learned and rational physician is most needed, for he understands the body, the disease and how medicines have their effects.

Pintor expressly contrasts the practice of the 'rational, learned and prudent' physicians with the 'inexperienced and ignorant' people who recklessly applied narcotic ointments, anointing not only the painful parts but the groin and armpits, which, the learned doctor believed, gave direct access to the vital parts of the body. The result of this, claimed Pintor, was that the patients suffered pustules and sores, even in the windpipe and lungs, threatening 'the greatest constriction and suffocation' of the throat, 'which is a pernicious thing increasing the danger of death'.[101] But these undesirable side effects, he says elsewhere, are almost exactly the same as the common symptoms of *aluhumata*. Clearly, the difference between a side effect and a symptom depended on the position from which it was viewed.

For the benefit of university physicians and educated people, Pintor discusses seven narcotic ointments, all containing mercury 'extinguished with the saliva of a fasting person', as we have noted.[102] He advised against one of them, which he believed had caused the death of a cardinal, as we shall see. One other ointment was for use in certain cases only, but the remaining five, less harmful, were recommended by him for patients of different complexions. He was, therefore, claiming for his own type of practitioner and its patrons the most effective type of medicine, that which was accommodated to the individual. It is another opportunity to pour scorn on the 'vulgar and inexperienced' who were producing an increasing number and variety of what he saw as very dangerous remedies. He directs his peers to places in the learned literature where they can find remedies that will enable them to outshine the vulgar and inexperienced practitioners.[103]

Since this is all he wrote on mercurial remedies, we cannot tell whether Pintor continued to give them his confidence. The case is different with Torrella. In 1497 he preferred quicksilver – *argentum vivum*, metallic mercury – to its corrosive sublimate, *argentum vivum sublimatum*. He accordingly recommended five local ointments containing metallic mercury and only one general lotion containing the sublimate.[104] But by 1500 he had dropped metallic mercury entirely and recommended the sublimate for his five local ointments and lotions.[105]

The same factors governed Torrella's choice of remedies as Pintor's. In the first place he believed that he was prescribing the most effective medicine for the pox. But it had also to be seen to be better than the prescriptions of the unqualified practitioners and so had to have some learned and rational authority. He was also in competition with other learned and rational physicians, most notably Pintor, and his remedies had to be distinctive if he was going to enhance his reputation as a pox doctor. It was probably for this reason that he recommended none of the ointments prescribed by Pintor. Moreover, in 1500 he singled out for condemnation four 'pernicious ointments', all containing quicksilver, and urged that people should 'flee from these ointments as from the plague'. Two of them were the two that Pintor had also warned against, and in this case we see Torrella and Pintor as learned physicians attacking those who were unqualified. But two of them had been recommended by Pintor; and when Torrella called upon the *protomedici* to take action against 'the ignorant, the impostors and swindlers', who made a great deal of money from and did much damage with such remedies, it was a charge not only against the quacks outside his own professional group but almost certainly against Pintor.[106]

In other words, one of the reasons why Torrella abandoned the use of metallic mercury was because Pintor persisted with it. In his tract on the pox

Pintor revealed that he had been attacked by 'someone' – almost certainly Torrella – for his use of quicksilver in remedies. His answer was the argument we met above, that it was better to use even a dangerous remedy than allow the pain to kill the patient by overcoming his vital powers.[107] Both Torrella and Pintor knew how dangerous mercury could be, and that mercury was implicated in the death of the cardinal of Segorbe. It was important then that its use was tightly disciplined. Pintor clearly thought such discipline could be achieved, Torrella evidently thought not. Containing the danger and exercising discipline were areas which gave opportunity for medicalising and empirical remedy so that it could be seen to be used in an elaborate and rational way. For the rational doctor mercury was given in doses that were calculated, not empirical.

How much mercury was to be given depended on where it stood on the scale of degrees of the qualities; we saw above that this was a part of the apparatus of learned medicine that was available to the rationalising physician. The qualitative nature of mercury was much discussed in the sixteenth century, largely because of the therapeutic implications for the pox, and Pintor's is a very early discussion. Was it true, he asked, that mercury was hot and humid in the fourth degree? Or cold and humid in the second degree? He did not want it to be cold, for then it would not seem capable of expelling the morbid matter. He pushed the argument in the direction he wanted, as medieval scholars so often did, by making a *distinctio*, that is, by drawing two different meanings out of a term and using one preferentially. Pintor 'distinguished' between natural or mineral quicksilver – that found in mines – and 'artificial' quicksilver, formed by burning mercury ore. He could then maintain that mineral quicksilver was cold in the second degree, but that the artificial sort was hot (because it had been burned) in the fourth degree. The same kind of reasoning might also lie behind his claim that mercury sublimate, having being sublimed, was hotter still. This was an argument against his opponent, whom we have with some caution identified as Torrella. Certainly Torrella was using the sublimate,[108] which Pintor now argued, from Avicenna, was often fatal.[109]

The Cardinal of Segorbe: a case study

We have already noted that Torrella gave five clinical accounts of cases of the pox in his first work on the disease, but we have not yet examined Pintor's long and interesting patho-biographical account of the cardinal of Segorbe. It is clear that Torrella and Pintor had different ideas about the cause of the cardinal's death.

Pintor's cardinal was Bertomeu Martí, born at Játiva, the same Valencian town as Rodrigo Borgia, his close friend and probable relative. Bertomeu moved to Rome and became a bishop; but he later renounced the bishopric and became head of the palace household to Rodrigo Borgia, then a cardinal. In 1496 Borgia, now Alexander VI, invested him as cardinal. By March 1499 he was ill with the pox and he died a year later, four and a half months before Pintor published on the disease.[110]

It is likely that the case of the cardinal influenced what Pintor wrote on the pox. His particular emphasis on pain and on the danger it posed to the vital faculty may have derived from the case of the cardinal, who, said Pintor, was racked by the most terrible pain, especially at night, so that he could not keep still or sleep, and often fainted – a sign that his vital faculty was threatened. A Portuguese visitor offered him an ointment consisting of litharge, ceruse, incense, mastic, pine resin, pig's fat, roseate oil and quicksilver, which he claimed had cured many of the disease.[111] Whether the visitor was a qualified medical man is not clear. Perhaps he was not, for he was highly secretive about his remedy, and the cardinal took the precaution of asking a number of physicians, including Pintor, their opinion of it. They agreed, says Pintor, that the remedy was appropriate except for the large amount of quicksilver it contained. This, they believed, by its coldness, humidity and poisonous quality, would block rather than open the pores of the body where the morbid matter was lodged.[112]

Pintor's own opinion, as we have seen, was that mercury was particularly useful when the morbid matter was not yet abundant, for it helped the body's natural heat to expel the matter. But when the matter was present in great quantity, as in the cardinal's case, the mercury simply had an initial narcotic effect, after which the pains returned stronger than ever, with anxiety, melancholy and sleeplessness, because nature was unable to expel the morbific matter. In his constant attempt to lessen the pain (says Pintor) the cardinal continually rubbed the ointment on to himself, damaging his radical moisture and faculties. What actually killed him according to Pintor was a new ointment containing pig's fat, ashes of white-grape vine, juice of lemon balm and, once more, quicksilver. But rather than the quicksilver, it was where the cardinal applied it that was dangerous: he rubbed it into his armpits and groin, regarded by Galenic doctors as the places where the heart and liver discharged some of their superfluities. The ointment and its mercury thus had access to these important organs and their powers, the vital and nutritive faculties. The result was the collection of symptoms that Pintor considered either as the natural signs of *aluhumata* or the pernicious side effects of misused ointments, depending on whether the practitioner was a physician or quack – they included suffocation of the windpipe and throat. Shortly before he died some pustules appeared on the cardinal's thighs. Pintor thought that this was a good sign, that the morbid matter was beginning to be expelled. But the cardinal's excessive pain before these eruptions was an indication of the abundance and tenacity of the morbid matter.

Torrella was much more direct. It was, he said, the Portuguese ointment that had killed the cardinal. It was one of the four pernicious remedies that he condemned in 1500. He vigorously attacked the secret manner in which the ointment had been offered to the cardinal and the false claims made by its profferer about its effectiveness.[113] According to Torrella, despite the secrecy, the ointment was in fact widespread, being made and used in homes and even hospitals. Unlike Pintor, Torrella did not think that the second ointment, which the cardinal applied himself, was a cause of death but he thought that it caused much mischief to other members of the Borgia family. He also thought that it had the same Portuguese source; his receipt for it contained six times as much quicksilver as Pintor's.[114]

Death from the French Disease could, then, be interpreted as widely as the disease's origins, transmission, prevention and treatment. Like those events, too, it reveals how different men used resources and strategies in promoting or defending themselves or their group. It shows that for the learned and rational physician no level of practice was unrelated to theory and that death itself was part of their battleground.

In the following two chapters we shall broaden our approach from examining the French Disease as an exclusively medical problem to a social and religious problem. We shall, in short, look at strategies evolved by Italian city-states to cope with this new threat to public health. Clearly, though, the medical themes with which we have dealt in the last three chapters are far from irrelevant to our story. As we saw in Chapters Two and Three, medical theory concerning the nature of the French Disease informed the reactions and understanding of the laity who ran governments. Indeed the following chapters will show that the Incurabili hospitals established to treat, among others, those suffering from Mal Francese provide an ideal context within which to examine the relationship between the medical theory of practitioners, such as Torrella and Pintor, and its implementation on a grand scale in hospitals. But, just as those sick from the pox cannot be examined in isolation, as a 'medical' problem, so it is also necessary to consider the development of the Incurabili hospitals within the wider context of the society in which they were established.

Chapter Seven

The French Disease and the Hospitals for Incurables in Italy until 1530

Introduction

Most of the preceding chapters have concentrated on the medical response to Mal Francese and the impact that this new disease had on both how physicians perceived themselves and how they were perceived by their patients. Where the practical implications of the disease have impinged on our story it has been in relation to the treatment of temporal and ecclesiastical lords. The following two chapters will instead turn to focus on what was provided for those classes of society who were unable to afford to pay for expensive courses of treatment, especially after the introduction of guaiacum, the new 'wonder drug' from the New World.

Phase One: the Company of Divine Love and Mal Francese in Genoa, 1496–1504

The earliest initiative to deal with those suffering from this new disease in Italy appears to have been taken in Genoa. It derived from within a circle of pious laity and in particular came about as a result of a fruitful collaboration between two prominent Genoese. The first was a lady renowned for her good works, Caterina Fieschi Adorno, who came from a prominent local family and was later sanctified. The second was Ettore Vernazza, an important local notary, who fell under Caterina's influence and came to form the spearhead of this initiative as it later spread outside Genoa.[1]

Vernazza established a confraternity called the Compagnia del Divino Amore. It later became a model for similar fraternities in other parts of Italy, so it is worth examining in some detail how this and its related hospital functioned. The original statutes of 1497 explain its title: 'Brothers, this our fraternity is not instituted for any other purpose than to sow and plant in our hearts the divine love, that is charity.'[2] A fraternity provided the natural environment within which a member could develop the two main aspects of the Virtue of Charity: the first was the love of the divine, for charity was the bond which linked God to man by creating love of God within man. The second was to obey Christ's command to His Apostles to love their neighbours as themselves. These ideas were certainly not new. They had in the broadest sense provided the moral underpinning for the government of medieval communes, and in a more restricted context for lay fraternities which formed such a characteristic aspect of late medieval European religious and social life.[3] However, what appears to have been new was the statutes' repeated and explicit insistence on divine love as the *raison d'être* for the fraternity's existence. It has been suggested, moreover, that the novelty of this insistence may have derived from the influence of Neoplatonism, especially as defined by Marsilio Ficino in his Neoplatonic circle in Florence.[4]

Whatever were the actual connections between the Company of Divine Love in Genoa and the Neoplatonic circle in Florence, this group, in common with many medieval confraternities, put into practice the two strands of charity: spiritual exercises and charitable works. The former involved members in saying a series of prescribed prayers every day as well as attending Mass, meeting in their oratory every week and on all feastdays ordained by the Church to join in the recitation of more prayers and orations and to practise voluntary flagellation in penance for their sins.[5] These devotional practices cannot be described as new for they were based firmly on past confraternal practices in medieval Italy. This is underlined, moreover, by their devotion to St Jerome, who was their especial patron saint and whose penitential exercises in the desert had formed the inspiration for a series of fraternities in fifteenth-century Italy. Even more specifically this pointed to the influence of the Observant Franciscan Bernardino da Feltre. In 1494 he had founded a fraternity in Vicenza, the Compagnia di S. Girolamo, which combined devotional and penitential exercises with important charitable work, the collection of alms which its members distributed to the sick poor.[6]

It is more than probable that Bernardino helped to inspire Caterina Fieschi and her circle to found a charitable fraternity when he became her spiritual adviser during his stay in the city in summer 1492, an idea kept alive during their subsequent correspondence.[7] This would have been given extra impetus by the arrival of Mal Francese in Genoa four years later. But Caterina was no stranger to the sufferings of the sick poor. She had for some time seen it as her special responsibility to tend to the sick, helping them in the streets and then in 1478 taking up residence in the city's main general hospital, the Pammatone, where she was appointed rector in 1489, an extremely unusual role for a woman, even one as saintly as Caterina Fieschi. Her desire to help the sick poor can be seen in a contemporary biography written by her confessor, Marabotto, and Ettore Vernazza:

And when her stomach was disturbed by the filth, and she was about to vomit, immediately she put it [not specified] in her mouth to conquer the rebellion of her feelings. She took the clothes of those sick, that were full of fleas and other nastinesses, and carried them home, and then having cleaned them returned them to them [the patients]. . . . She tended to the sick with the most fervent love . . . not being disgusted ever by any sick person of any kind, whatever horrible sickness he had or [however horrible his] stinking breath.[8]

Charitable works thus formed the second aspect of the mission of the Compagnia del Divino Amore in Genoa. The first set of statutes prescribed that members should help each other when in distress and sickness.[9] In time they also developed other charitable functions: providing dowries to poor girls who wished to follow a religious life in the monastery of S. Andrea and also giving spiritual comfort to prisoners condemned to death.[10] These activities were also features of late medieval fraternities, as was also true of what in time became their major function, the establishment of a hospital. In 1497 the Company of Divine Love set up another confraternity, the 'Societatis Reductus Infirmorum Incurabilium, sub titulo Beate Marie', in order to raise the funds to pay for the new hospital, the Ridotto or refuge. Subsequently the officials were responsible for making sure that the institution ran efficiently and that the sick were cared for properly.[11]

It is not entirely surprising that the confraternity founded a hospital, given Caterina Fieschi's predilection for wandering the streets in search of the sick poor and her directorship of the Spedale di Pammatone. But, despite the fact that it was based inevitably on medieval precedents, the hospital which was established by the fraternity was distinguished by its clientele from the majority which had preceded it in Italy. In the first place it specialised in those categories of sick poor who were excluded from all general hospitals like the Pammatone. This complementary arrangement emerged out of Caterina's experience. The Pammatone admitted only those with acute conditions.[12] Yet she would have been persuaded of the necessity to provide help for those whom she encountered in the street with 'horrible infirmities', especially in this decade of scarcity and unemployment. Neither of the two alternatives to the general hospital would have been suitable for the 'incurables': the isolation hospitals (or Lazzaretti) for plague, which would have been in use in this period, and the old leper houses, which were now too small for the problems of the new epidemic.[13]

The 1499 statutes of the Ridotto explained its role as specifically to treat the 'incurable poor'. The confraternity saw the hospital's clientele as distinguished from most other categories of the poor, for, as the statutes argued, these people were unable to earn a living, and, furthermore, 'on account of having the gravest and longest-lasting infirmities are abandoned by everyone'.[14] Concern for the 'incurable sick' in the late 1490s suggests that the hospital of the Ridotto was a response to the advent of Mal Francese. It is interesting, though, that the statutes themselves do not actually mention this disease. The omission of *Morbus Gallicus* in the list of those accepted by the

Ridotto may not be particularly significant since no other disease is specified either. However, even if some chroniclers in the 1490s did not always regard the *mal franciosati* as being incurable, it is probable that they were included in the broad definition of the patients accepted by the Ridotto: those who had been rejected by the Pammatone on account of being 'the wretched poor and with an incurable disease'.[15]

There were other ways, moreover, to make sure that only certain categories of people were admitted. Thus, to ensure that an applicant did not attempt to enter on spurious grounds, he (though it could be she) had to prove his case by supplying a ticket from the Pammatone stating that he had been barred from admission.[16] Then when he arrived he was examined by a board, made up of a series of administrators together with a physician. Although no further details were provided concerning how thoroughly the applicant was examined, either through questioning or through physical observation, it is probable that, as later on, much reliance was placed on outward appearance and the presence of incurable ulcers and sores. The only further qualification a potential applicant was required to possess was to be a local resident rather than a stranger; he had to have been living '[in] the city, [in] streets outside the city walls and [in] the suburbs', although the statute does not specify what residence meant in time.[17]

Even though the quite stringent terms of admission may seem to suggest that the space available in the Ridotto was not sufficient to match demand, the administrators did not rely on personal applicants alone to fill their beds. Two officials called 'searchers' (*inquisitores*) were appointed 'to search for the sick through the alleys and [under the] vaults and in other places'.[18]

When an individual was found he was taken to the hospital, where he was subjected to the same procedure as outlined above.[19] But, after only a year in existence, the administrators of the hospital evidently found that they had unearthed a much more severe problem than they had at first imagined. In asking for official approbation for their statutes, they petitioned the governor of the city in 1500 for a subvention to help underwrite their expenses, which were caused by the discovery that:

> many who are ill, labouring with incurable diseases, crushed by extreme poverty and misery and lying on the ground are to be found in almost all parts of the city. Of these, some are abandoned by their neighbours and sons and wives because of the great violence of the disease and depth of poverty; others by their own parents; others by their friends and relatives, so that they finally lose not only their bodies but their souls.[20]

It now becomes clearer that the Ridotto had a dual motivation which would have appealed to the city's administration. In the first place the hospital was anxious to make sure that these poor 'incurables' were treated for their physical and spiritual sufferings in order to help save their souls from damnation. Indeed the hospital had an important religious role. When a patient entered he was required to confess, and the priest, who actually lived in the hospital, celebrated Mass every day for the sick and heard their confessions regularly.[21] In the second place the Ridotto's *inquisitores* helped to clear the streets of the undoubtedly unpleasant sight of these 'incurables', who, as we have seen, contemporary chroniclers suggest were increasing as a result of the onset of Mal Francese. This problem must have been especially grave in a port such as Genoa, where the large numbers of people arriving inevitably brought not just their merchandise, but also their diseases, as had been seen over and over again in the case of epidemics of plague.[22]

Despite the fact that few detailed records survive concerning the treatment of the patients of the Ridotto in the sixteenth century,[23] this discussion of the Company of Divine Love and the Ridotto in Genoa provides a useful framework within which to examine the other related fraternities and their 'incurable' hospitals established on this model. However, we must beware of offering too uniform a picture. Most writers who have discussed the treatment of 'incurables' in sixteenth-century Italy have tended to make the assumption that all initiatives stemmed from what has been viewed as the 'movement' of the Companies of Divine Love. This has been particularly true of the strongly hagiographical accounts which have stressed the close association between these companies and the origins of the Catholic reform movement.[24] Before discussing this phenomenon in more detail, we should look briefly at the circumstances surrounding the origins of two other 'Incurabili' hospitals, in Bologna and Ferrara. The initiative which led to their foundation appears to have been unrelated to the Companies of Divine Love and yet can be dated to the same period as the Ridotto in Genoa.

Bologna and Ferrara

Since Bologna and Ferrara were the sites for the debates within the medical world over the nature of Mal Francese in the late 1490s, the authorities in these two cities were possibly more aware than most of the need to find an institutional solution to the problem. As we have seen, the chroniclers of Bologna and Ferrara provided what were among the earliest and most detailed descriptions of the impact of the disease on their cities. In addition two of the Bolognese chroniclers, in stark contrast to other early accounts elsewhere, mentioned the setting up of a hospital for the treatment of the *mal franciosati*. Friano degli Ubaldini wrote:[25]

the [existing] hospitals did not want to receive or give shelter to anyone who had such a sickness for which reason a large number of poor people, both men and women, did not have anywhere to go. [Therefore] certain good men from Bologna began a hospital for such a sickness and began to put there beds and

Plate 7.1 'Mary, St Job and members of the flagellant confraternity of S. Giobbe in Bologna', from an indulgence to the Hospital dei Guarini e di S. Giobbe, 1525

other furnishings in the hospital of San Lorenzo dei Guarini and it was called the hospital of St Job, which was given many alms and it was full of the said poor people, men and women, and they were looked after well.

The Bolognese story is similar to the one at Genoa, without, however, the influence of the Compagnia del Divino Amore. Apparently moved by compassion, a group of leading citizens refounded a fraternity in about 1500, which then rededicated the hospital they administered as a centre specialising in the treatment of those rejected by the general hospitals in the city.[26] Here, though, there is a direct association between establishing the hospital and the impact of Mal Francese. Indeed the *Cronica Bianchina* says that the Spedale de' Guarini was specifically for 'those sick poor people and not [for those sick] from any other disease'.[27] This suggests that from the beginning the Guarini provided a more specialised service than the Ridotto in Genoa. However, given the difference between the sources in each city (chronicle and hospital statutes), this discrepancy may be more apparent than real. It is probable that both hospitals would have treated a range of 'incurable' diseases, which included Mal Francese. Unfortunately no further information survives about the activities of the hospital at this stage to throw light on this question. Only a quarter of a century later in the fragment of the 1524 statutes of the Guarini outlining the role of the surgeon does one get some idea that one of the distinguishing marks of patients admitted was their 'sores', which, as we shall see later in relation to Rome, often covered a wide range of diseases.[28] This is clearly shown in Plate 7.1, an illuminated initial of an episcopal indulgence

Plate 7.2 *San Giobbe*, by Domenico Panetti

to the hospital from 1535. There two images of Job show the saint covered with red marks all over his semi-naked body, reflecting the *bolle*, *varole* and *pustole* recorded by chroniclers as among the main symptoms of Mal Francese. The hooded figures in the centre represent the members of the flagellant company.[29]

The hospital in Bologna was also distinguished from that in Genoa through its dedication to St Job. He became the main patron saint for those suffering from Mal Francese, as was noted by Francesco Matarazzo in his chronicle of Perugia.[30] Indeed in Perugia, as elsewhere, he became the centre of a cult around an altarpiece set up in a chapel dedicated to his name.[31] Plate 7.1 also shows the Virgin Mary, who was patron of both this and the Genoese Ridotto. Mary is represented here as the Madonna of Mercy; sheltering within her cloak are the members of her flagellant confraternity who ran the hospital.

In Ferrara, too, a confraternity dedicated to St Job, the Compagnia e Fraternità di Santo Giobbe, was founded in 1499, and here also the members promoted his cult by commissioning images to adorn their church. Thus within four years the local artist Zohaine dall' Agnolo frescoed the inside of their chapel with *Istorie de' S. Job*. In the same year a better-known artist, Domenico Panetti, also produced an altarpiece for the oratory, his *Virgin*

Enthroned with Saints. It is also very probable that Panetti painted his splendid *San Giobbe* for the confraternity (see Plate 7.2). This small panel, now in the Indianapolis Museum of Art, shows St Job covered with bloody sores praying to God to intervene on behalf of the city of Ferrara.[32]

The initial aims of the confraternity were generic: to pray to God, the Madonna and St Job 'to liberate this illustrious city of Ferrara from each and every persecution, controversy and sickness'.[33] Then within three years the meaning of the term 'sickness' became clearer. Ercole d'Este granted a licence to the company to beg for alms throughout his dukedom in order to raise the cash to underwrite the building of a hospital 'in which to receive those sick from that sickness [*Morbo Gallico*]'.[34] In the event there is little evidence that the hospital was actually functioning before 1525, and this was despite the very personal involvement of the Este dukes and their own experience of *Morbo Gallico*.[35]

We have seen, then, that the hospitals in Bologna and Ferrara were established by confraternities which were independent from the Companies of Divine Love. This is contrary to the assertions of many historians, who have assumed that any such initiative derived from the Compagnie del Divino Amore.[36] The underlying aim of these historians has been to glorify the lives of a series of saintly figures who were associated closely with these companies and the origins of the Catholic reform movement. However, it should be emphasised that none of these initiatives would have been successful without the intervention and support of leading figures in the city. This has already been seen in the case of Genoa, but was equally true in Bologna and Ferrara, where the initiative was taken by private citizens. Yet we must beware of making too sharp a distinction between public and private charitable initiatives. All these enterprises received the support and privileges of both Church and states, and frequently members of these new associations were also leading members of the governing elite.[37] This remained true not just in these cities, but also in all those others which gained an Incurabili hospital in the second and major phase of expansion.

Phase Two: Incurabili hospitals and Mal Francese, 1515–1530

Following the first phase in the foundation of Incurabili hospitals, nearly fifteen years elapsed before another appeared in an Italian city. Why this should have been the case has never been explained very satisfactorily, but it may simply have been that Vernazza was too busy with other charitable missions in Genoa to think about the problems of the sick poor elsewhere. After the death of his wife in 1508 he went to live in the Genoese Ridotto, which became the headquarters of his operations; these included providing alms to the 'shame-faced sick', establishing two monasteries, one for Convertite or reformed prostitutes and the other to provide accommodation for poor young girls to prevent them from falling into sin, and in the 1520s a Lazzaretto for those sick from plague.[38] All these initiatives were important because they came to be associated closely with the activities of many of the Companies of Divine Love. More generally, these types of activity were characteristic of what has been called the 'new philanthropy' of the sixteenth century. This led charitable institutions and the new religious Orders to extend their redemptive arms to include those groups marginalised by society, whether they were prostitutes or those reduced to extreme poverty through a sickness which disfigured their bodies.[39]

Vernazza's varied charitable activities in Genoa can represent only part of the explanation for the lack of further foundations after 1499. As has been seen in Bologna and later Ferrara, Incurabili hospitals were established without the involvement of Vernazza. Furthermore, there was a range of institutional responses to the incurably sick from hospitals labelled as 'incurable' to others which fulfilled this function but which were not given this name either at the time or by historians, to others which included wards for the treatment of the chronically sick. Milan is a case in point. By 1500 a section of the Spedale Maggiore had been dedicated to 'la egretudine de bosole, nuovamente scoperta de la natura humana'. At the same time another hospital, the Brolo, was developed as a specialist centre for 'these *brossolosi*'. Evidently it had been found necessary to designate a larger area for what was perceived as an increasing problem.[40]

The Milanese example may also help to explain the apparent lack of institutional response to the problem of Mal Francese between 1500 and c. 1515. It may very well be that initially in other cities, as in Milan, a section of an existing hospital was put aside to treat Mal Francese. This can be seen, for example, in Orvieto where Ser Tommaso di Silvestro recorded that in 1498 a man called Passarocto died in the Spedale de S. Maria, where he was buried the next day.[41] It would appear, then, that we should suggest another explanation for this apparent lack of an institutional response to Mal Francese. Initially the existing sanitary structure was believed to have been capable of absorbing those sick from this 'new disease'. Also hospitals may have chosen just to ignore the problem given that they specialised in the acute rather than the chronically sick. It may be instead that only with increasing mortality from Mal Francese did the authorities realise that the problem would not disappear, especially with the re-emergence of even worse symptoms as patients entered the later phases of the disease.

The subsequent decade saw considerable expansion, when the rest of the major Incurabili hospitals were founded in Italy. In addition to those at Genoa and Bologna, between 1515 and 1526 were added another seven full-blown Incurabili hospitals as well as at least another three specialised wards within existing general hospitals.[42] The first was the refoundation in Rome of the hospital of San Giacomo in Augusta in 1515. Four years later another initiative was taken in Naples, followed by Florence and Brescia in 1521,

Venice the following year, and, as we have seen, Ferrara by 1525 and then Padua in 1526.[43]

With these hospitals, therefore, specialised institutions to deal with a range of 'incurable' diseases were to be found in the north, south and centre of the peninsula. Even so, there appears to have been a concentration in northern and central Italy, with few of these institutions south of Rome in the Kingdom of Naples (apart from the capital city) and Sicily. Although we shall be concentrating here on the better-documented specialist Incurabili hospitals, we should also not forget that this probably distorts the picture of institutional responses to Mal Francese for it ignores those wards or sections of hospitals which were set aside for treating 'incurables'. The best-known examples in this early period, 1518 to 1526, include Vicenza and Verona.[44] When further research has been done to ascertain exactly how many of these wards were established, a different topographical distribution may emerge, although by the very nature of hospital foundations this will remain an urban phenomenon.

In order to understand properly this distribution of the large Incurabili hospitals in time and space we need to examine the evolution of the Companies of Divine Love, in southern–central Italy and the north, and their links to the evolution of the Catholic reform movement. The close links between these two movements guaranteed the requisite support which led to the success of these confraternities and made possible the establishment and subsequent financing of the Incurabili hospitals.

Incurabili Hospitals in South and Central Italy

Rome

The links between the origins of the Catholic reform movement and the Divine Love company in Rome make it difficult to distinguish what really happened from the accreted traditions of Catholic historiography. For example, the confraternity has been characterised as the 'first cradle of Catholic reform . . . the heart and soul of the saints that renew the Church'.[45] Then after the Sack of Rome in 1527 the hospital of San Giacomo is supposed to have been the 'one spot in the deserted city where the mystic fire still burned'.[46]

In fact, the establishment of the Company of Divine Love in Rome between 1512 and 1515 in the church of S. Dorotea in Trastevere and the subsequent rededication of the existing hospital of San Giacomo in Augusta marks an important step in the movement to deal with 'incurables' in Italian cities.[47] The history of San Giacomo is central to our understanding of the subsequent evolution and development of both the Companies of Divine

Love and their related Incurabili hospitals. In time San Giacomo became both the largest such institution in Italy and the head of a network of these confraternities and their associated hospitals.

The hospital of San Giacomo in Augusta had been founded in 1339 to the north of the city centre and just south of Piazza del Popolo. It occupied a wedge-shaped site between Via Lato (later Via del Corso) and Via Ripetta. Combining with the Compagnia di S. Maria del Popolo, which had administered the hospital since 1451, the Company of Divine Love set about rededicating its activities to the service of 'incurables'.[48]

The exact link between Ettore Vernazza and the foundation of the Company of Divine Love in Rome remains unclear, although his involvement seems certain given that the whole initiative was based closely on the Genoese model.[49] It was founded in the first instance in the church of S. Dorotea in Trastevere, but soon united with the Compagnia di S. Maria del Popolo which administered the Spedale di San Giacomo in Augusta. It was the influence of the pope, Leo X, which was central to the development of San Giacomo; his adoption of the hospital gave the enterprise a much higher public profile in Rome and thereby helped to secure financial support for its expansion. Indeed the importance of papal backing cannot be under-estimated not only for San Giacomo in Rome, but also, as we shall see, for the spread of the whole Incurabili hospital movement throughout Italy. Leo's commitment to this cause is evident in the bull *Salvatoris Nostri Domini Jesu Christi*, published in Rome in 1515, in which he sanctioned the change of use of San Giacomo into a hospital specialising in *incurabili* and essentially provided the hospital with its first statutes. The bull began by outlining the problem for both the sick and the public, as witnessed by the members of the confraternity:

> We have learned, as testified by the new and old honourable brothers of the confraternity of the Hospital of S. Maria del Popolo and of San Giacomo in Augusta in the city, that for a number of years a large number of the sick poor all infected with various kinds of incurable diseases have come together from many parts of the world in this city, the motherland common to all the faithful. [They have come] in such great numbers that they cannot gain entrance without difficulty to the hospitals of the city because of the multitude of such people and they give offence to the sight and sense of smell. Thus the said poor people, who are afflicted with an incurable disease, are obliged for the whole day to look for food through the city, sometimes dragging themselves along on little trolleys and vehicles, giving offence to themselves and blocking the way of those whom they encounter.

Here, as we have seen in many of the chroniclers of the late fifteenth and early sixteenth century, concern was evidently aroused by a whole range of diseases which contemporaries regarded as 'incurable'. However, when the

ELEMOSINA
PER LI POVERI IMPIAGA TI
DELL·INCVRABILI

Plate 7.3 Incised marble plaque showing a beggar with Mal Francese seated on a cart, from outside the Church of S. Maria in Porta Paradisi, Spedale di S. Giacomo, Rome

bull went on to specify more clearly who was regarded as suitable for admission only one condition was mentioned by name: 'all and every person of either sex affected by any incurable sickness, including Morbo Gallico, but excluding epidemic [diseases] and leprosy'.[51] Evidently San Giacomo was now seen as having being founded to cater mainly for those suffering from the French Disease. Although plague victims and lepers were also considered to be a problem, they were clearly not to be admitted here, as elsewhere, because they already had their own specialised hospitals in other cities.

The problem of the 'incurables' was therefore principally regarded as one of public order, relating above all to the poor, one of whom is represented graphically in the incised marble plaque covering the collecting box still in place in the façade of the church of S. Maria in Porta Paradisi in Via Ripetta (see Plate 7.3). The *franciosato* is represented with what looks like only one foot, hence his need to wheel himself around on a cart. He is scantily clad with a turban on his head, presumably to cover up his bald head, one of the symptoms of the more advanced forms of Mal Francese.[52] He is reclining in his *carello* with his hands joined together in supplication towards anybody entering the hospital.

Clearly this problem was exacerbated for Rome, which had long had the dubious reputation as the capital of Christendom for beggars, attracted by the many religious houses and pious institutions providing alms to the poor.[53] In Rome, as well as in other cities, the hospitals were not keen to admit the large number of unpleasant and smelly invalids, who because they were regarded as 'incurable' were thought to be unlikely to recover, compared with the majority of their normal patients who suffered from acute conditions.[54] As in other cities, these wretched diseased paupers came to offend the more affluent, who would have made up the membership of the confraternities at San Giacomo. It was they, fired both with religious enthusiasm and no doubt with disgust, who would have petitioned the pope for official recognition and support for their charitable project. This dual motivation was indeed reflected in the bull, which, as noted in the passage above, talked of 'giving offence to the sight and sense of smell'. But side by side with this sentiment was genuine pity, for 'many of them, not helped by anyone to feed themselves, developed worse diseases and, deprived of any Christian support, met a premature death'.[55]

It was the fear that the capital of Christianity would become overrun by the incurably sick that led Leo X to strengthen the powers of the hospital's officials in their dealings with the poor sick. The syndics were given authority to search Rome for those who were 'afflicted by any illness [and] begging throughout the city'. It was then up to them to decide whether these people were curable or incurable, taking the former to the city's more general hospitals for the acute sick, such as S. Spirito in Sassia, and the latter to San Giacomo.[56] The initial diagnosis of whether a sick beggar was curable or incurable was thus provided by a layman, although here, as in the case of Genoa, the final decision about whom to admit to the hospital was presumably taken by the surgeon and physician when they arrived at the hospital.[57] But even to the untrained eye the ulcerated limbs and physical decay of the *mal franciosati* must have been fairly distinct, as non-medical contemporary chroniclers recorded.

Furthermore, since the aim of the syndics' tours of the city was to clear up the streets, they were given powers to hospitalise the *incurabili*, even against their own wishes.[58] This had a dual purpose. On the one hand, as Leo's bull indicates, the sick needed help in order to avoid a premature death. Even if this sentiment did derive from genuine Christian concern for the poor, the second reason was equally pressing, the improvement of the health of the city. As we have seen, contemporaries held a variety of ideas about how Mal Francese was transmitted; the term 'contagion' could mean both physical contact and infection through the air.[59] Both of these could have been achieved in contemporary eyes by the *mal franciosati* as they begged in the streets and implored attention by seizing hold of the clothes of passers-by or simply by polluting the atmosphere through their smell and breath.

The awareness of the members of the Company of Divine Love and their sensitisation of the pope to the urgency of the problem led him to give substance to his words. Leo was also concerned for San Giacomo's future finances and therefore granted the hospital exemption from gabelles on the goods they consumed,[60] and encouraged both laity and clergy alike to give generously so that the hospital would become self-sufficient. The bull offered a plenary indulgence to all those who provided financial support of at least 5 ducats and the secular clergy were encouraged to nominate the hospital as universal heir. In addition further indulgences were offered to the faithful when they visited the hospital on certain feastdays throughout the year and, just to underline the importance of San Giacomo, it was granted the same spiritual privileges as had already been given to the largest hospitals of Rome, S. Spirito and S. Salvatore.[61] To crown these privileges, in the following year the pope declared that San Giacomo was subject to no authority lower than the papacy.[62]

Initiatives over the following ten years to establish either Incurabili hospitals or specialised wards within existing medical institutions were, as we have seen, scattered throughout Italy, although the vast majority were in the north. Not only were they geographically distinct, but so were their patronage networks. This is not to deny the importance of the links between many of these initiatives provided by the Companies of Divine Love, but while Vernazza and Leo X were the prime movers in Naples and Florence, further north the main impetus appears to have been members of the Catholic reform movement, in particular Gaetano Thiene and Gian Pietro Carafa. These last two were also founders of the new Theatine Order of Clerks Regular, one of whose main emphases was pastoral care of the poor sick.[63]

Naples and Florence

'While the French found themselves in Naples, a terrible illness exploded in Italy . . . and this illness, although it has been called Gallic from the French, did not derive from them but from the Jews, who had been driven out of Spain by Ferdinando "il Vecchio" and gathered together in Naples.'[64] This passage by the papal secretary Sigismondo dei Conti da Foligno, mentioned above in relation to the alleged origins of Mal Francese, reminds us that most contemporaries linked the origins of Mal Francese not just with the French, but also with Naples and through that city with Spain under King Ferdinand the Catholic. It is therefore perhaps surprising that an Incurabili hospital was not established in the city until 1519. Historians who have written about the foundation of the hospital of S. Maria del Popolo have tended to take sides when discussing who was responsible for taking the initiative. The two main candidates are a local noblewoman, Maria Lorenzo Longo, and Ettore Vernazza. Traditional Neapolitan historians have tended to claim Maria

Lorenzo as the sole originator, while historians of the Catholic reform movement have emphasised the role of Vernazza.[65]

The meeting of these two pious laypeople at this time was clearly fortuitous. Maria Lorenzo Longo had allegedly been miraculously cured of an incurable paralysis at Loretto in 1509–10 and on returning to Naples had become a tertiary, subsequently devoting herself to tending to the sick poor, especially those in the Spedale di S. Nicola al Molo. It is hardly surprising, therefore, that when Vernazza arrived in Naples in December 1517 and encountered a pious woman following a similar way of life to his friend Caterina Fieschi Adorno he should have persuaded her to help him to institute a hospital for *incurabili* on the Genoese model. However, according to the *Life* of Vernazza written by his daughter, the Neapolitans were initially against a foreigner telling them how to look after their city, even when his close associate, the Augustinian canon regular Don Callisto da Piacenza, had preached to them on the necessity to found a hospital for 'incurables'. The strength of their *campanilismo*[66] can be judged by their initial reaction to Vernazza's solution to the problem. When Don Callisto suggested establishing a charitable confraternity, which would in the first instance provide spiritual comfort to condemned criminals, they responded: 'Perhaps you believe that you are in your Lombardy? We are lords and we do not want to accompany the condemned.' However, as in all good stories, they relented; they were persuaded eventually to establish the confraternity, which in time became responsible for administering the incurable hospital.[67]

Vernazza stayed in Naples until November 1519, long enough to see his initiative bear fruit. The hospital was first established in the summer of 1518 in two *magazzeni* close to Longo's hospital of S. Nicola, but after a joint fund-raising campaign with the Compagnia dei Bianchi they managed to raise enough money to establish the Spedale di S. Maria del Popolo in March 1522. A public ceremony marked the occasion; all the sick incurables who had been housed at S. Nicola processed through the streets to the new premises. This was a symbolically important ceremony. It signified public acceptance of the institution and also helped to awaken the pity and charity of the onlookers.[68]

An event crucial to the continued acceptance and development of the project had taken place between the beginnings of the enterprise in 1518 and the foundation of the hospital proper in 1522. This was the papal authorisation for 'the foundation of a hospital for poor incurables in the city or district of Naples' contained in the bull *Nuper pro parte vestra* of 11 March 1519.[69] Clearly Vernazza's influence had been crucial and, given his and Leo X's involvement with the Incurabili in Rome, it is significant that the bull stipulated specifically that it 'should be established on the model of the Archhospital for poor incurables of S. Jacopo in Augusta'.[70]

The emphasis was, therefore, once again on the poor and the problems

created by their diseases for themselves. What remains unclear is whether the
inmates were seen as a threat more to public order or public health:

> We therefore desire the best possible results so that provision shall be made for
> the said poor people [who], on account of their contagion and horrible disease,
> are despised by men and rejected from the house in which they were received
> and given hospitality and we are therefore minded to grant your petition.[71]

The abandonment of the poor with a 'horrid disease' reflects the language of
Leo's bull of 1515 in favour of San Giacomo in Rome. And while the
reference to their *contagiosum* may simply be another synonym for 'disease',
the underlying implication may be that the sick could pass on disease. But
evidently this was not the same infectiousness which characterised victims of
an epidemic like plague, as can be observed from a letter written a year later
by the Neapolitan Ufficiali di Sanità (Health Board). Although they were
responding to an enquiry about an unspecified epidemic disease, probably
plague, they said that they had taken the precaution of locking up the
Incurabili hospital and having a wall built around it, 'not so much because it
was infected, but rather through caution'. It was, therefore, the plague which
was regarded as infectious rather then the diseased inmates. Indeed the Sanità
officers reassured their correspondents that the patients in the Incurabili
hospital were only those 'sick from Mal Francese, cancers and other incurable
sicknesses'.[72] The fact that the hospital was seen as a general refuge for all
'incurables' was also recognised by the next Medici pope, Clement VII, in a
papal brief of 1525, which specified that it catered for 'almost innumerable
poor people weak from sicknesses . . . and they are oppressed with the misery
of sores and ulcers and diverse illnesses'.[73]

The foundation of the hospital of S. Maria del Popolo in Naples, therefore,
has significant parallels with the pattern established in setting up Incurabili
hospitals in other Italian cities. Each case began with a confraternity, which
had the task of raising public awareness of the need to tackle the problem
of the incurably sick and then collecting the funds to finance a hospital.
Although Vernazza may have been involved in the majority of these initiatives, this was not a prerequisite. Nor was each confraternity a Divine Love
company, as was even more true of the Incurabili founded in northern Italy.
The success of all these hospitals did, however, depend on the support of the
secular and ecclesiastical authorities, usually guaranteed by members of prominent local families taking a leading role in their administration. The backing
of the pope was also particularly important in the case of Rome and Naples,
where he appears to have shared the concern about the implications for public
order. However, at this stage none of these hospitals appears to have been
exclusively designed for the *mal franciosati*, even if the outbreak of the pox
seems to have been the incentive to establish these institutions.

Florence, however, was unique in this period as a city in which the highest secular and ecclesiastical powers met in the same family. Here Leo's nephew, the Cardinal Archbishop Giulio de' Medici, provided his backing for the foundation of an Incurabili hospital in March 1520. The early history of this institution also offers clear evidence of how local and national influences combined to establish an institution, which is often represented as owing its origins simply to an act of spontaneous piety.[74]

Although it is difficult to disentangle the precise set of influences which led to the establishment of the Spedale della SS. Trinità, it is clear that Giulio de' Medici must have helped to orchestrate events. Historians have recounted that Don Callisto da Piacenza, the Augustinian canon regular we encountered in Naples, preached the Lenten sermon cycle in the cathedral in 1520. Apparently his main theme (the sermons are lost) was the sufferings of the victims of Mal Francese. Following the example of Rome and Naples, he proposed that members of his congregation should form a society to cleanse the streets of these poor creatures and to provide treatment in a specialised institution. The same day a group of 150 citizens met in the church belonging to the canons regular in Via San Gallo, S. Maria della Neve. Then, under Don Callisto's inspiration, they founded the company of SS. Trinità, which established a hospital dedicated to the Trinity.[75]

It should be emphasised that, although this has been dressed up as a spontaneous exercise of noble-minded citizens, Don Callisto would not have been able to deliver one of the most prestigious sermon cycles in the cathedral without the knowledge and invitation of the archbishop. Giulio himself would furthermore have known that Don Callisto was a prominent member of Vernazza's circle and would therefore have known the probable theme and message of his sermon. Indeed the foundation of the confraternity and hospital is yet another example of the extent of Leo's influence on events in Florence.[76]

The confraternity continued to meet in S. Maria della Neve and in the first instance the *incurabili* were placed in two small hospitals also in Via San Gallo, S. Caterina dei Talani and S. Rocco. It was not long, however, before funds were attracted from among leading citizens. The archbishop provided an example. He gave 200 gold florins and the communal treasury another 330 florins, and soon work was begun on the new hospital in Via San Gallo to the south of the Spedale di Messer Bonifazio.[77]

The whole process bears the stamp of Leo's influence. The bull of 25 March 1520, in which Giulio as archbishop of Florence approved the company's statutes, was based closely on at least part of Leo's *Salvatoris Nostri* of 1515; it contains exactly the same passage describing the plight of the *mal franciosati* and their threat to public order.[78] The following year Leo also passed a bull in which he confirmed the foundation and granted full participation in all the privileges and exemptions and spiritual and temporal indulgences enjoyed by the major hospitals of Rome, including San Giacomo in Augusta.[79] And this, as we have seen, was not simply spiritual window-dressing, but guaranteed that these institutions would attract the attention of the public, who would consequently be persuaded to provide financial support. Indeed the statutes underline that in Florence, as elsewhere, the hospital would provide a much needed service to the public. They stipulated that four 'custodians' should be appointed each year who 'had to search diligently through the city for those sick poor people whom they regarded as oppressed by any infirmity or from *Morbo Gallico* or any other incurable sickness, except for leprosy or plague'.[80]

Thus Florence shared with the other cities we have examined their desire to hospitalise 'incurables' who were poor, could not look after themselves and were not admitted to other more general hospitals. Evidently here, as in Naples, those sick from Mal Francese were the incentive behind the establishment of the Incurabili hospital, which also admitted other types of 'incurables'. This too was the motivation behind the foundation of similar institutions in northern Italy.

Incurabili Hospitals in Northern Italy and the Catholic Reform Movement

Catholic historians have linked the origins of the Catholic reform movement to the evolution of the Companies of Divine Love. The great historian of the papacy, Ludwig von Pastor, for example, described them in glowing terms: 'they, in the fulness of their holy enthusiasm, laid the foundations of a citadel for the observance of the means of grace, for the contest against vice and abuses, and for the exercise of works and charity'.[81] Conversely, the Divine Love companies would not have flourished had it not been for their connection with the leading members of what became the Catholic reform movement. Indeed it was this association which helps to explain why these confraternities and their related Incurabili hospitals spread so rapidly in the period between 1515 and 1526. It was only when the Genoese circle associated with the Ridotto, and in particular Ettore Vernazza, had made contact with some of the leading members of the reformist circle in Rome that the confraternity became a truly national movement. The geographical origins of these individuals also helps to explain the location of these companies and their related hospitals.

The foundation of the Company of Divine Love in Rome came at a particularly significant period. In 1515 Leo X was under severe attack from Luther for the luxury and corruption of the papal court. Little wonder that Catholic historians have seized on the Companies of Divine Love as an example of incipient renewal within the Church. Little wonder, too, that Pastor emphasised the importance of the role of 'works of charity', especially as hospitals were one of the few features praised by Luther in his journey through Italy in 1511.[82]

It was the association of a small group of reformers with the early history of the Roman Company of Divine Love which gave the confraternity such an important influence in Rome and beyond. The principal members were Ettore Vernazza and Gaetano Thiene and later Gian Pietro Carafa in 1520, although, as we have seen, it was the support of Leo X which was crucial to the real establishment and subsequent spread of the confraternity. A mid-sixteenth-century record of the Roman company at San Giacomo in Augusta dwelt on the glorious composition of the early membership, which included 'Pope Leo with all the College of Cardinals and a great number of prelates and gentlemen'. Of course, many of these people were probably honorary rather than active members. But the important point, stressed by the company historian, was that this association led the company to receive many gifts which then paid for the charitable work of the hospital.[83]

Gaetano Thiene apparently joined the Company of Divine Love in Rome in 1516, a year of particular significance for him because contemporaneously he received minor orders. Both acts would have expressed the rededication of his life to the 'divine love, which is charity': concern with both deepening his spirituality symbolised by an outward concern for the poor sick. This association was also significant for the company since it opened up another avenue to the papacy, Thiene being a papal proto-notary.[84] Another important event for the development of the company was when Carafa, bishop of Chieti (later Pope Paul III), became a member in 1520. He was an important curial official and reformer, who had returned in that year from England, where he had headed a diplomatic mission for the pope.[85] Although Thiene was absent from Rome in this period, following his return in 1523 these two men joined forces to establish a new Order of Clerks Regular or Theatines, a society of priests who engaged in pastoral work. Their aim was to raise the standard of clerical life through the establishment of a small exclusive Order which would include trained reformers, who would then take a leading role in the reform of the Church. The Theatines came to number many bishops among their members and through the support of influential churchmen were an important inspiration for the subsequent implementation of the Counter-Reformation.[86]

The significance of this new Order for our purposes was that the Theatines grew out of the ideals of the Company of Divine Love, and therefore as the influence of the new Order grew so did the importance of the confraternity. Even though by 1523–4 Thiene had apparently decided that the company was an insufficiently powerful instrument through which to achieve his aims, the Order itself retained much of the exclusive character of the confraternity.[87] Furthermore, Thiene, Carafa and their associates retained close connections with the whole Divine Love movement. When Thiene went back to Rome in 1523 he returned to the company and became first its administrator and then helped in the Spedale di San Giacomo, as did Carafa.[88]

It is against this background that one can best understand the spread and then the growth of the companies of Divine Love and their associated Incurabili hospitals in northern Italy. For before 1524 Thiene still believed that the best way to achieve his aims was to remain in minor orders and minister to the laity through confraternities, encouraging their members to deepen their own piety and above all to help the sick poor.

In 1518 Thiene left Rome and went to Vicenza, where within a year he had joined the Compagnia di S. Girolamo della Carità.[89] This company had been established in 1494 by the Franciscan Observant Bernardino da Feltre, who had done so much to encourage and inspire Caterina Fieschi Adorno in her work among the poor and sick in Genoa. Following Bernardino's lead, members of the Compagnia di S. Girolamo also tended to the poor sick, first in their homes and then from 1506 in the major general hospital of Vicenza, the Misericordia di Pusterla. Once Thiene joined the company his association with the Misericordia grew closer. First he decided, like Caterina Adorno and many of his reformist colleagues, to live in the hospital. Secondly, he organised the confraternity and the Misericordia to tend to the incurably sick of Vicenza: members of the former collected them up from the streets of the city, from where they were taken to a specially designated ward within the hospital.[90] Then, to ensure that this work would continue after his departure, Thiene made use of his contacts in Rome, and the company and hospital were united to San Giacomo in Augusta. This connection obviously imparted prestige to the Vicentine institutions and through subsequent papal privileges and indulgences helped to guarantee their future income.[91]

Apparently during his stay in Vicenza, Thiene visited Verona at the invitation of the Compagnia del SS. Corpo di Cristo. In common with the company of S. Girolamo in Vicenza and the Divine Love companies, one of the main aims of this Veronese company was to promote more frequent communion. But it was apparently under Thiene's influence that it developed a new role, tending to the incurably sick. It remains unclear at the present state of research when the Spedale della Misericordia was established for the *incurabili*. Certainly by 1580 the Spedale came to admit only 'those who have sores, the consumptives [*ethici*], and those with dropsy, and similarly those with the French Disease'.[92]

The cases of Vicenza and Verona show not only how much influence one man could have in instigating a charitable institution, but also how close were the connections between many of these new sacramental companies.[93] Furthermore, it demonstrates how many confraternities were established on virtually the same model, becoming Companies of Divine Love in all but name. There are also examples of other Incurabili hospitals or specialised wards being established under the influence of the Divine Love circle in the Venetian territory. In Brescia, for example, Thiene's colleague Bartolomeo Stella established an Incurabili hospital in 1521, and by 1526 Padua had another, dedicated to S. Francesco, which was granted indulgences by the pope.[94]

A particularly significant event had taken place between the foundations of the Brescian and Paduan hospitals: the establishment of the Incurabili hospital in Venice in 1522.[95] This was significant because it symbolised the acceptance by the Venetian government of the necessity and utility of these hospitals not just in the territory, but also in the capital itself. The case of the Spedale degli Incurabili in Venice is especially interesting because, unlike many of the hospitals in the territory, comments survive about the early history of the institution which derive not only from the circle which established it, but also from people on the outside who were involved only indirectly in its foundation, such as the contemporary diarist Marin Sanudo. The Venetian Sanità, on the other hand, appears to have been the only Health Board in Italy to have left records of its involvement with the problem of the *mal franciosati*. These records provide a more balanced account of the pious legends which have tended to dominate so much of the literature about the early history of these hospitals.

According to Marin Sanudo, the Incurabili hospital was begun in Lent 1522 by two noblewomen, Maria Malipiera Malipiero and Marina Grimani. They led three poor women covered with the sores of the Mal Francese whom they had found near the Scuola di S. Rocco to a house near the church of S. Spirito. Whether they were already in contact with Gaetano Thiene is not recorded, but according to Sanudo he was involved closely in the prosecution of the project. Clearly Sanudo was impressed by the rapid expansion of the Incurabili. Writing only two years after its foundation, he recorded that the administrators had bought extra houses on the Zattere and the hospital complex already housed eighty people, including a physician and apothecary and the nursing staff and both male and female patients.[96]

The example of Venice in many ways summarises some of the major themes we have been examining in relation to the foundation and development of Incurabili hospitals in Italy: the prominent role of women, the institutional underpinning of the Company of Divine Love, the support of the patriciate and in time of the government and the papacy, and finally the mixture of charitable and intolerant attitudes which underlay contemporary responses.

In the first place the initiative in Venice was taken by two upper-class women with particular sympathy for the sick poor. The close involvement of charitable ladies remains a feature of many of these initiatives, including, as we have seen those of Genoa and Naples, where they took a leading role in raising public awareness of the problem of the incurably sick and tended to the inmates of the hospitals. Indeed the prominence of women distinguished the Incurabili movement from many of the charitable initiatives of the previous 100 years, which had on the whole been started by male-dominated fraternities.

The role of women should not, however, be exaggerated. Their success was predicated on the support of men with influence in both the Church and state. There seems little doubt that in Venice Gateano Thiene was initially involved in the hospital. Although he returned to Rome in 1523,[97] he had already established a Company of Divine Love, which ensured the successful prosecution of his project and included a whole series of men and women from prominent families. Clearly the Venetian patriciate had committed themselves to the project. Sanudo recounts that in June 1522 the doge himself, Antonio Grimani, visited the hospital 'of the incurable sick'. The diarist was struck by the fact that the sick were 'served by gentlemen', which Grimani would have known in advance since his son Vincenzo was one of them, and 'many important ladies'.[98] Two months later the patriciate were further incited to provide generously of their time and purses by the bishop of Scardano, who said Mass at the hospital and preached a sermon 'which made all [who heard it] weep and want to help these sick people'.[99] Here again we see the influence of Rome, for the bishop, Tommaso de' Negri da Spalato, was a papal legate on his way to Croatia.

This pious picture, then, of weeping congregations and beneficent patricians created the necessary atmosphere to help stimulate financial support through donations and bequests.[100] While not denying the very genuine Christian impulse behind this initiative, we must also not forget the fear and disgust engendered by the appearance of the *mal franciosati* on the streets of Venice. The decree by the Health Board on 22 February 1522 was directed towards the problems created by 'any people who are sick and with the sores of Mal Francese and other illnesses'. Here, as in the case of contemporary commentators, Mal Francese is singled out as the main but not the exclusive concern of the authorities. Once again it is the poor sick who are seen as creating the problem and, in language reminiscent of Leo X's bull *Salvatoris Nostri*, the Sanità attributed much of the problem to beggars, that group of society who traditionally took the blame for disturbances of public order:

> Some of these persons in their bodily weakness languish in the streets and the doorways of churches and public places both at San Marco and the Rialto to beg for a living, and some, being inured to their profession of begging, have no wish to seek a cure and loiter in these same places, giving forth a terrible stench and infecting their neighbours and those with whom they live.[101]

As during epidemics of plague, it was convenient to find a scapegoat to blame for the epidemic.[102] The beggars here are represented as wilfully increasing disease by refusing to be treated and in that way jeopardising the health of the community. The Sanità believed that this could be done because 'the stink [*fetor*] may breed infection [*contagion*] and disease [*morbo*]'. Here, as elsewhere, we see that the way the term 'contagion' was used allows for a much wider interpretation than merely transmission by touch. It was the *fetor* which led to infection through the diseased air given off by the bodies and exhaled by the sick.[103] The 'contagion' was then both a synonym for the sickness and the method of transmission. Therefore those sick people who ignored the requests of the hospital's officers and refused to receive treatment were seen as a threat to the health of the community and therefore became the responsibility of the Sanità. Their officers were authorised to put the beggars in a boat immediately and 'send them outside our territory at the expense of our magistracy'.[104]

The mixture of Christian charity and intolerance remained, as elsewhere, a feature of the development of the Venetian Incurabili hospital. This helped to convince the citizenry both that the problem was being dealt with and that it was a cause worthy of their financial support. Further public displays of piety helped to promote the cause, and during the ceremony at Easter 1524 a series of ladies and gentlemen, including the procurators of the hospital, 'with great humility washed the feet of the poor who were sick from Mal Francese'.[105] In imitating Christ's action in washing the feet of the leper, the patricians were indeed demonstrating their humility. Yet at the same time they must have believed that their Christian motivation afforded them some protection from the 'contagion' of the sickness, or that once removed from their fetid surroundings, washed and clothed anew, the patients would be less likely to infect their patrons.

The support of the Church remained important for exciting charity within Venetian patrons. The Incurabili became a centre for sermon cycles, encouraged by a series of privileges from the papacy, especially in the Jubilee year of 1525. The pope granted a plenary indulgence to anybody who visited the hospital to hear Mass, especially pilgrims before their embarkation for Jerusalem.[106] The papacy's involvement in hospitals Incurabili did not just derive from personal interest, especially in the case of the Medici popes Leo X and Clement VII, but also reflected the pressure of the prestigious group of Clerks Regular established in Rome under the inspiration of Thiene and Carafa. In February 1527 they had been appointed by the governors of the Incurabili hospital as representatives of their interests at the papal court.[107] These links were underlined further in 1527 when the Venetian hospital became for a number of years the centre for the early Catholic reform movement. Having fled Rome during the Sack, the group arrived in Venice where they were met by the procurators of the hospital, who arranged their lodgings and invited them to dine at the Incurabili.[108]

Over the following decade the Theatines remained associated closely with the Incurabili, assisting with the patients in the hospital and helping the governors to raise cash. Carafa in fact stayed in Venice until his elevation to the papacy as Paul III in 1536. The Theatines' influence among the patricians ensured continued support not only for the *mal franciosati*, but also for other charitable enterprises associated with many of these reforming Orders founded in the first half of the sixteenth century. Thus a centre for the moral rehabilitation of prostitutes was established in one of the wings of the hospital, while during the famine of 1527–9 the Incurabili also opened its doors to orphans.[109] This represents one of the main traits of what has been called the 'new philanthropy' of the sixteenth century and was already present, as we have seen, in Ettore Vernazza's charitable programme in Genoa.[110] The aim was both to reclaim the fallen from further sin and to prevent the weak and powerless – children and unmarried women – from being exploited by the wicked. Clearly this was also considered to be for the good of society, since in this way the moral corruption associated with physical corruption would not spread its degenerative power more widely.

It is within this broader context that one can best understand the connection between Mal Francese and prostitution. Although contemporary writers of sonnets and satirical literature adopted a moral tone when discussing these matters,[111] this was far from being the only theme which informed institutional and governmental reactions. The close association of at least some of the major Incurabili hospitals – Genoa, Naples, Rome and Venice – with the convents for Convertite indicates that the treatment of the *mal franciosati* has to be seen within the context of this concern for the moral rehabilitation of prostitutes and later on for preventing young unprotected girls from falling into a life of sin. This concern, then, demonstrates a much more subtle association between morality and sexuality than is usually presented by the more traditional medical historian, whose main aim was to stress that prostitutes were the main transmitters of Mal Francese.[112]

Conclusion

This chapter has traced the initial reactions of non-medical men and women to what they perceived as the threat of a new disease in early sixteenth-century Italy. What still remains unclear is the nature of governmental reactions to Mal Francese. This partly stems from the nature of the sources which have been consulted for, as we have seen, chroniclers rapidly lost interest in the disease. It may very well be that research in local archives will lead to the discovery of new features of local policies in the early sixteenth century.

It is equally possible that the very nature of Mal Francese meant that no consistent policy at the level of government emerged in the short term. It took time for both medical and non-medical men to achieve a reasonable consensus about the disease and its causes and most importantly about whether it was just a temporary phenomenon. After all, it had taken a number of decades for even the most centralised city-states such as Milan to establish any consistent policy after the appearance of plague in 1348.[113] But the pox differed from plague in that it was a chronic disease which gradually ate away its victims rather than a short-term emergency which disappeared as quickly and as inexplicably as it had appeared. The authorities only gradually realised that the problem was not going to go away and this may help to explain why few chroniclers recorded measures taken to deal with Mal Francese.

The initiative was taken instead, as we have seen, by independent fraternities and hospitals founded by charitably minded lay men and women. But it is a mistake to assume a rigid division between public and private initiatives in this period, any more than between lay and religious inspiration. Although the Companies of Divine Love, which were a leading force in establishing Incurabili hospitals, have been viewed as an independent movement of confraternities, many of their members were from prominent local families who were frequently responsible for the government of the state.[114] Little wonder, therefore, that local governments very rapidly granted privileges and exemptions to the companies and their associated hospitals.[115]

Official acceptance of this movement was doubtless facilitated by the strong backing of the Church, both at the local level and through the connection with the new religious Orders and in particular with the Theatines. But there was also the enthusiasm of the papacy for Incurabili hospitals, especially from 1515, when Leo X's bull created a federation based on San Giacomo in Augusta. In future connections were strong between Rome and new foundations for the *mal franciosati*.[116]

Attempting to force any movement into a national pattern is hazardous in a country such as Italy characterised by strong local particularism. As we have seen, the Incurabili hospital movement was in the first place an urban phenomenon and also heavily biased towards northern and central Italy. There were, moreover, foundations which were unconnected with the Divine Love companies, as in Bologna, Ferrara and Milan. Furthermore, we should also not forget that other initiatives resulted in the establishment of a variety of options for the treatment of the pox from general wards to specialised sections within existing hospitals. In the 1490s *mal franciosati* were being taken to the local general hospital in Orvieto along with patients with other ailments. In Milan a separate ward was first established in the Spedale Maggiore before the Brolo was converted for the provision of specialised treatment for pox. In Padua, on the other hand, the Spedale di S. Francesco, although set up as an Incurabili hospital, apparently came to treat a wide variety of the poor sick.[117]

We have stressed in this chapter the need to move away from the hagiographical character of much traditional historiography of the subject and to recognise how personal disgust at the sight of the sick poor in the streets also acted as a strong motivating force behind the measures taken to deal with Mal Francese. The case of the Venetian Sanità in 1522 is a good illustration of this point and underlines the need to examine reactions to Mal Francese in relation to official policies towards the poor in general and the sick poor in particular.

This raises the wider point to which we shall return in the next chapter, as to how far the appearance of Mal Francese might have helped to shape the greater intolerance, which has been seen as characteristic of early modern attitudes towards the poor. Certainly Mal Francese appears to have heightened public awareness of the plight of those sick from what they saw as 'incurable' diseases, especially in the early sixteenth century when it was linked together with other conditions which were difficult to treat successfully. Indeed the sources we have examined appear to reflect a growing awareness among non-medical men of the gravity of the problem caused by the pox in particular. The early statutes of the Incurabili hospitals described their potential clientele only in general terms. The Ridotto in Genoa, for example, defined them as 'the wretched poor and incurably sick', as those who 'because they have the most grave and long-lasting sickness are abandoned by everybody'.[118] But by 1515 when Leo X published his bull *Salvatoris Nostri* he mentions not only the sick who were 'consumed by sores' and 'disturbing to the sight and sense of smell', but also those suffering from the French Disease.[119] Not surprisingly, given the close links between Florence and Rome, the 1521–2 statutes of the Florentine hospital were also more specific: the 'poor sick who are understood to be oppressed by some sickness or by the French Disease or another incurable illness, except for leprosy, plague and those people who are found to be sick from a curable ailment'.[120]

The non-medical men therefore reflect a growing association between Mal Francese and incurability; indeed the French pox, after the traditional scourge of leprosy, came to be seen as *the* incurable disease. This stemmed partly from the fact that it was now so widely spread in Italy and partly from the establishment of the Incurabili hospitals. The very founding of these institutions to deal with this specific threat led to growing public awareness and to a sharper definition of the problem. Now the threat of Mal Francese, in common with leprosy, and even with plague, had come to be institutionalised its victims could be isolated temporarily from society. Furthermore, because this period saw repeated outbreaks of plague, the general association between poverty and epidemic disease came to be further emphasised in relation to the pox.

Chapter Eight

The French Disease and the Incurabili Hospitals, 1530–1600: the case of Rome

Introduction: developing reactions to Mal Francese and the poor

The period from 1530 to the end of the sixteenth century saw the continued expansion in Italy of specialised services for those categorised as 'incurable'. This was a recognition both of the seriousness of the problem of Mal Francese and also that the Incurabili hospital was the most suitable institutional response. Local governments therefore continued to provide their support to these institutions through financial grants and privileges. But, as in the case of the initial period of foundation, the Incurabili hospital was less a product of direct state intervention than an alliance between the Church and a series of independent lay initiatives. With one notable exception, the Spedale di S. Matteo in Pavia, there was an expansion of existing facilities in this period rather than the foundation of new Incurabili hospitals.

This continued expansion of the facilities provided by Incurabili hospitals should also be seen within the social and economic context. In many major Italian cities, such as Naples, Rome and Venice, population levels continued to grow in the second half of the century, despite the recurrent outbreaks of more acute epidemic diseases such as plague and petechial fever.[1] Even if economic historians now no longer depict the Italian economy in this period as suffering from a uniform decline, towards the end of the century there was a fall in standards of living and a growth of poverty among the lower strata of society. This was especially true of the years 1589 until the late 1590s, which saw severe dearth and very high prices. Inevitably those who were most at risk were the poor, and the worst affected were those suffering from incurable diseases such as Mal Francese.[2]

The New Orders and the Incurabili Hospitals

The association between upper-class support, recently founded religious Orders and the 'new philanthropy' which we have seen in the period up to

1530 remained a feature of many subsequent charitable endeavours. This can
be observed in the case of the Incurabili hospital which was founded unusually late in Pavia. It was established in 1566 by the nobleman Marco dei Conti
Gambarana. He had decided to dedicate his life to looking after the sick poor,
having been inspired to do so by Girolamo Miani's new Congregazione
of the Somaschi, which by the mid-sixteenth century was linked to the
Theatines.[3]

The three main Orders which became involved in the Incurabili hospital
movement derived from the circle surrounding the early reformers of the
Church. Many of these were, moreover, as we have seen, connected through
the Companies of Divine Love and in particular through the circle in Rome
around the Spedale di San Giacomo. Ignatius Loyola had since 1516 attended
various Companies of Divine Love and, from the mid-1520s, the Venetian
Incurabili hospital became his headquarters.[4] The works of mercy became for
the Jesuits, once the order was founded, one of their main missions, and, in
common with many of the new Orders, one of the hallmarks which served
to distinguish them from their predecessors was their service to the institutionalised sick poor. Ignatius Loyola himself provided an example by serving
in the Incurabili hospital when he was in Venice in 1537.[5] Later the Jesuit
Constitutions provided that each novice, as part of his training, should spend
a month serving in a hospital.[6] Inevitably this meant that it was the Roman
hospitals which were most favoured by this service and above all the Spedale
di San Giacomo. As individual fathers later recorded, this experience made an
indelible impression on these young Jesuits, an impression which they carried
with them and which reinforced the association between the Order and the
Incurabili hospitals.[7]

The second new Order to become involved intimately in tending to the
sick were the Capuchins, the Frati Cappuccini.[8] In fact when they began in
Rome in 1528 the Order was founded in a small house in the neighbourhood
of the Spedale di San Giacomo. Particularly in their early days they provided
an important service as nursing staff to 'incurables' here as in Incurabili
hospitals elsewhere in Italy, including Naples and Genoa.[9] They cleaned the
hospital wards and, according to their chroniclers, helped the sick with little
regard for their own health. A later account, based on contemporary records,
relates that: 'They did not feel any repugnance to any stench of a patient or
anything else, nor was there anything exhausting, harsh, hard or bitter that
they did not embrace with great alacrity of spirit. . . .'[10]

According to the Jesuit historian Tacchi Venturi, the nursing role of the
Frati Cappuccini at San Giacomo in time became a less important part of their
mission.[11] If this was the case, it may have been due to their involvement with
helping plague victims, although other types of evidence suggest that, on the
contrary, the friars did retain a close connection with the hospital.[12] In 1612
the confraternity which ran San Giacomo decreed that they 'should not take
any preacher who is not a Capuchin, either for Advent or Lent, knowing

through experience that it has been seen in our church that when other preachers have preached who are not Capuchins we had a small congregation'.[13] This association also remained important elsewhere, as can be seen in Naples through the noblewoman Maria Lorenza Longo, who had played such an important role in setting up the hospital of S. Maria del Popolo degli Incurabili. In 1535 Longo joined the enclosed female Order of the Cappuccini and with her colleague Maria Ayerbe, Duchess of Termoli, remained involved intimately in running the hospital and looking after patients.[14]

In time apparently the place of the Cappuccini at San Giacomo in Rome was taken by yet another Order, the Ministri degli Infirmi, who, as their title suggests, dedicated themselves almost exclusively to the service of the sick. It was founded by Camillo de Lellis, and the story of his involvement with this mission has all the propaganda value of a Pauline conversion. Returning from a military campaign with an incurable sore, Camillo ended up in San Giacomo, where after being treated he served as a nurse and then administrator. It was this experience which convinced him of the need for a nursing Order dedicated exclusively to serving the sick in hospitals; the Ministri began in San Giacomo and spread gradually throughout Italy.[15]

The close involvement of the Orders in the establishment of the Incurabili hospitals also had an important effect on the moral character of these initiatives. As has been seen, this was clear from the very first in public documents such as Leo X's bull *Salvatoris Nostri*, with its evident desire to rid the streets of the chronically sick.[16] And yet, despite the provision in the bull and other early Incurabili statutes that officials had the power to force the sick poor into their hospitals for treatment,[17] within two decades there is evidence that these expanding hospitals no long wanted to cater for unruly beggars. The 1539 statutes of the Incurabili hospital in Naples, for example, declared in no uncertain terms:

> Item it is ordained that the sick who are received into the said hospital cannot leave and go begging through the city, and when they are discovered they are thrown out of the hospital and punished by the governors in such a way as to provide an example to the others, in order to maintain the hospital as a house of piety and not a centre for rascals and the indolent.[18]

In Naples, as in other Italian cities, the founders of Incurabili hospitals were sometimes also associated closely with another moral mission typical of the reform movement in the sixteenth century, the preservation of female honour and the rescue of either fallen women or vulnerable girls from the perils of prostitution.[19] This led to the establishment of convents for Convertite, homes for unmarried women and refuges for battered wives.[20] If the general aim was to make sure that women were not led astray into a life of wickedness, the fact that some of these institutions were associated with the

Plate 8.1 'The history of a Prostitute'

Incurabili hospitals underlines a widespread assumption that there was a connection between prostitution and venereal disease. This association can be seen reflected vividly at the popular level by the moralistic themes underlying contemporary broadsheets, as in Plate 8.1. Here we see the sad story of a prostitute who in the 'flower of her life' had been courted by gentlemen on bended knees. She was reduced to misery and death in hospital (*Ospeal*) surrounded by chamber-pots and urinals. Then as if the pain of Mal Francese was not bad enough, after her death she was condemned to go to the burning fires of hell for eternity.

If in fact the close association between prostitutes, the spread of Mal Francese and their subsequent hospitalisation is difficult to document – here she was after all given the disease by her lovers – the aim of these popular broadsheets and satirical poems was certainly to point a simple but moralistic message which became one of the themes of the Counter-Reformation. There is, however, no evidence to suggest that Italian city-states enacted a measure which was enforced in Valencia, where prostitutes from the *bordello*

Plate 8.2 *Ordini del dare acqua del legno*, from the Spedale di San Giacomo, Rome

were obliged to enter the hospital for treatment if they were discovered to have Mal Francese.[21]

When the prostitute entered the 'Ospeal' she would not have escaped the moralistic atmosphere. This is reflected in the way in which, for example, San Giacomo in Rome was run, as can be seen in their 'Orders to be observed by those who take the Acqua del Legno' (see Plate 8.2). The 'Ordini' list a series of prohibited activities, which presumably were common enough to need to be the subject of these rules. Patients were forbidden, for example, to swear, play games, joke and make a noise, and display the 'dishonest parts of the body'. On the left-hand side of the panel at the bottom of the sheet disobedient patients are shown playing cards; hospital staff are seated on the right; and a wrongdoer is beaten and carried out struggling towards the door of the hospital on the left for handing over to the proper judicial authorities.[22] A well-known example of somebody who was thrown out after card-playing was Camillo de Lellis when he was at San Giacomo both as patient and as nurse. Such was his apparent addiction to this pastime that he used to pursue it outside the hospital premises, even at the expense of the patients. Despite repeated warnings he continued to play and was finally ejected after a pack of cards had been discovered under the bolster of his bed.[23]

The process through which an individual was punished can be seen in the less well-known case of Giovanmaria da Parma, who had been thrown out of the hospital on 6 September 1562 for having stolen from Giovanmaria da Siena a series of items of clothing and for having:

> broken the hedge of the garden [when he] jumped outside the hospital at night with the said goods [and] was taken by the servants of the house and was put in the stocks for four days through the orders of the Lord Guardians, then the Lord Guardians not wanting to punish him any more sent him away without any hope of being able to return again and thus it was concluded in full congregation.[24]

Evidently, then, the Guardians did have some power to punish infractions of the hospital's rules and presumably the 'full congregation' of the governors is represented in the scene in the right-hand section of the bottom panel. The punishments which could be inflicted were, then, either to put the miscreants into the stocks or to send them away, and then in the more extreme cases actually to hand them over to the Roman courts.

San Giacomo, therefore, in common with other Incurabili hospitals, came to combine all the main characteristics of Counter-Reformation charity: a desire to reform the morals of the poor, to serve the sick poor in their role as the image of the suffering Christ, and to help to solve the problem of public order.[25] It was this mixture of reasons which motivated the highest prelates of the Church in offering their protection to San Giacomo, which consequently became in time one of the largest Incurabili hospitals in Italy, treating thousands of patients each year.

The story of the initial involvement of the new Orders with the Incurabili hospitals has remained inevitably orientated towards Rome. It was here that many of these Orders had their headquarters and training grounds. Furthermore, as has been seen in the period before 1530, the proximity to the centre of papal power meant that, once a series of popes became involved, Incurabili hospitals were guaranteed Church support in their expansion into other parts of Italy. The status of San Giacomo in Rome as the Arcispedale would moreover have underlined the Roman connection and have led to the granting of both ecclesiastical and secular privileges for new local initiatives. The papacy and local bishops provided privileges and indulgences to encourage the donation of alms and also regular sources of income from ecclesiastical revenues.[26]

The role of the religious Orders was therefore two-fold. First, they were indispensable initially in raising consciousness of the virtues of this type of institutional solution to the problem of the incurably sick, and secondly they served the sick once hospitalised. There remained, however, the continuous problem of funding these institutions, which became increasingly expensive to maintain as they expanded in response to growing demand.

The Construction Programmes

As we have seen in the previous chapter, the Incurabili hospitals were financed principally by private donations raised by the members of the confraternity which had been responsible for establishing the hospital. Appeals were made to the local population through collection boxes and charitable missions, and to powerful local figures.[27]

Well-orchestrated public ceremonies were also mounted, as in the case of the washing of the feet of the poor *mal franciosati* in Venice in 1524. Indeed Incurabili hospitals often became the centre of attention on feastdays when the public was drawn to their churches by ceremonies. This was the case in 1575 when the English Catholic Gregory Martin visited Rome for the Jubilee:

> The Hospital of St. James d'Incurabili . . . very fitly to resemble the miserable persons here releved, upon St. James day in Julie, when al the citie visiteth this Hospital, there are set forth in lively purtraicts Job with his sores upon the dunghill, his wife holding her nose for niceness not abiding her husband's stinche, his three frendes weeping and lamenting his case.[28]

Like the Roman San Giacomo, Incurabili hospitals in other Italian cities all excited the charitable instincts of both visiting and local notables. As at the time of their foundation, many of the people later involved in both the administering confraternities and their hospitals were members of local patrician families who had close links with the government.[29] Furthermore, just as in the 1520s Venetian noble men and women washed the feet of the *poveri infermi infranzosati* outside the Incurabili hospital in Venice, so in Rome both were involved in tending to the sick. When Carlo Bartolomeo Piazza published his *Opere pie di Roma* in 1679 it had become the fashion for 'many princesses and leading ladies of the city' to visit regularly the women's ward of San Giacomo in Rome, 'supplying also various kinds of refreshments and delicacies to strengthen the same [female patients]'.[30] The statutes of twenty years earlier record that gentlemen also gave of their time voluntarily as 'visitors', whose role it was to go round to all the patients twice a week 'in order to ascertain how each one is treated through remedies, both physically and spiritually, and in feeding and in the rest of the service that they should have. . . . They must also in the presence of the said patients, or elsewhere, taste the wines they are given . . . and also console them with good memories and advice, encouraging them to have patience. . . .'[31]

Even if the close involvement of ladies and gentlemen in the running of the hospital means that it can be difficult to separate public from private initiatives, there was in fact a clear division of responsibility. In their public role local patricians provided privileges, tax exemptions and small grants of grain and salt,[32] while in their private guise they gave substantial sums of money. In Naples, for example, the viceroy was the first governor of the hospital and it later received the support of the duchess. In Florence, Elenora of Toledo provided money in 1541 and later in the century Senator Capponi paid for the restoration of the fabric of the hospital.[33] In Rome the unusual position of each of the city's hospitals having a 'cardinal protector' meant that affluent prelates promoted their institution's interests at the papal court and sometimes also provided substantial subsidies from their own pockets. This happened in the case of San Giacomo when Cardinal Antonio Maria Salviati paid almost single-handed for the enlargement of the church and hospital in the last decades of the sixteenth century.[34] Indeed in this case the temporal and ecclesiastical powers met in the same person. But this was not unique to Rome; in Florence in 1521, Giulio de' Medici, who was behind the establishment of the Incurabili hospital, was both the leader of the Medici family and archbishop of the city.[35] The alliance between bishop and the ruling family in support of these hospitals was also evident in Ferrara in 1586, when the bishop joined forces with Cesare d'Este to open the new hospital.[36]

These alliances were necessary when it came to raising the cash to construct substantial new hospitals, as was true of San Giacomo in Rome.

Rome

Based between Via Lata (later Via del Corso) and Via Ripetta, the hospital complex, including two churches, passed through three main periods of expansion. The development of this site, which came to include not just the hospital but the famous chapel of S. Maria in Porta Paradisi, has become well known through association with a series of important architects: Antonio da Sangallo and Baldassare Peruzzi in the earlier phases and Bartolomeo Gritti, Francesco da Volterra and Carlo da Maderno from the middle of the sixteenth century to the early seventeenth.[37]

The first phase (1519 to 1526) consisted of building a new ward which incorporated the earlier medieval sections, and also constructing the chapel of S. Maria in Porta Paradisi to the plans of Giorgio de Coltre. The second phase, begun in 1537 and lasting until 1549, further increased the building to expand the women's ward, and at the same time the older church of San Giacomo was restored. This phase of construction can be seen in the map of Rome made by Pérac–Lafréry in 1577 (see Plate 8.3). The map shows the site from the more unusual perspective of Via del Corso. The chapel of S. Maria in Porta Paradisi is readily apparent at the top on the corner of Via Ripetta. The ward runs behind it and parallel to what was then called Via delle Tre Colonne (now Via Canova) and housed both male and female patients; the former occupied three-quarters of the area and were divided from the latter by a tall screen. The small medieval church of San Giacomo is shown fronting Via Lata, parallel to Via Ripetta, just above 'T. S. Jacobi'. The third and most ambitious phase from 1579 to the end of the century was commissioned by Cardinal Antonio Maria Salviati. A completely new male ward was constructed, measuring 100 metres in length and 10 metres in width. Finally, a large new church was begun in mid-1592 with Volterra as architect, although on his death in 1594/5 he was succeeded by Maderno.[38] Volterra, taking into account the available space on the site between the two wards, opted for building the church to an oval plan, only the second such in Italy.[39]

The last two phases of construction are well caught in the plan of Rome by Antonio Tempesta, which shows the hospital from the perspective of Via Ripetta. Here one sees the site in 1593 with the completed Corsia Salviati – the new ward financed by the cardinal – on the left-hand side behind an imposing Neoclassical façade. The church was, however, still being constructed; the site is shown at the top of the print between the two wards (Plate 8.4). The whole area with the completed church inserted into the first courtyard is clearly shown in Giovanni Battista Falda's map of 1676, once again looking from Via Ripetta towards Via del Corso (Plate 8.5). A good idea of what the façade on Via del Corso would have looked like to a contemporary can be obtained from Falda's print produced at about the same time as his map (Plate 8.6). This shows clearly the splendid façade of the new church with the small entrance to the original San Giacomo to the left. On the right is the Corsia Salviati, constructed on two floors. A clear impression of the scale of the hospital can be gained from two views of the top floor of the new ward, one a print from the nineteenth century and the other a photograph taken in the early part of this century when it was still in use (Plates 8.7 and 8.8). In both the beds are lined along the walls and stoves placed down the central aisle, but the later view shows the addition of a walkway with balustrade to facilitate observation of the patients. The later view also shows the removal of an integral part of the earlier hospital, frescoes showing religious scenes painted to inspire and comfort the patients.

These large airy wards were built, then, to meet the increasing demand for Holy Wood (guaiacum) treatment. In the late sixteenth century the upper storey of the Corsia Salviati contained 170 beds, with 19 on the ground floor. This whole wing was designated for the treatment of men, while in the separate female ward there were another 102 beds. Then when the Holy Wood was administered this number was doubled to a total of 730 beds with the addition of extra rows of temporary beds on wheels, *cariole*, in the wide aisle visible in both prints.[40]

Venice

The same period also saw the physical expansion of Incurabili hospitals in other parts of Italy, though few were on the scale of Rome. The Venetian

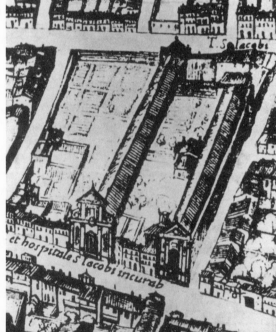

Plate 8.3 'The Spedale di San Giacomo', detail from a map of Rome by Stefano de Pérac, printed by Antonio Lafréry, 1577

Plate 8.4 'The Spedale di San Giacomo', detail from a map of Rome by Antonio Tempesta, 1593

Plate 8.5 'The Spedale di San Giacomo', detail from a map of Rome by Giovanni Battista Falda, 1676

Plate 8.6 *View of the Spedale di San Giacomo along Via del Corso*, by Giovanni Battista Falda, 1676

Plate 8.7   The upper male ward of San Giacomo, from a late nineteenth-century print

example is perhaps closest because, according to Ettore Vernazza's daughter Suor Battista, it was created 'according to the fashion of that of Rome'.[41] This hospital is also among the best studied from the architectural point of view, particularly because of the involvement of two distinguished architects, Jacopo Sansovino and later Antonio da Ponte, in the design of the church between 1566 and 1600. As in Rome, the physical expansion of the hospital itself was necessitated by demand, as was made clear by the Venetian Senate in 1588: 'And the hospital of the poor incurables of this city has a great need for expansion because of the large number of various kinds of sick poor who collect there, especially when it is the time to provide the waters [of the Holy Wood] and the general purges.'[42]

The scale of the new hospital can be appreciated from a contemporary view of the front elevation on the Zattere (Plate 8.9). This impressive edifice was a symbol of the Venetian commitment to coping with what was viewed as a grave and continuing problem, the incurably sick in their city. Recent historians have suggested, moreover, that Suor Battista's comment refers not just to the way the hospital was run, but also to the actual design.[43]

Plate 8.10, an eighteenth-century ground plan of the completed site, clearly shows the elliptical shape of the church in the centre of the courtyard, a design which was unique at that time in Venice. The hospital surrounds the church, and indeed, contrary to accepted opinion, it has been suggested

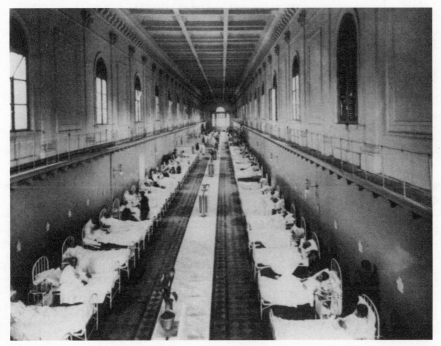

Plate 8.8 The upper male ward of San Giacomo, from an early twentieth-century photograph

recently that the former was built first and the church afterwards. The plan shows that, as at San Giacomo, there were two long lateral wards, one for the males and the other for females. They were built between 1572 and 1591.[44] A photograph of the ground floor of the left-hand ward in about 1930 (Plate 8.11) shows another light and airy space, which was, however, on a much more modest scale than San Giacomo in Rome.

Florence

We have seen, then, that just as the Divine Love companies provided an example for the devotional and charitable activities of confraternities in other cities, so San Giacomo inspired the organisational and architectural models of the Incurabili hospitals themselves. However, we should not assume what would appear to be the obvious corollary, that all Incurabili hospitals derived from the same model. Just as the hospitals in Bologna and Milan were established outside the Divine Love circle, so San Giacomo cannot be claimed as a national architectural prototype. This can be seen from the plan of the Florentine Spedale della SS. Trinità (Plate 8.12).

Built between 1525 and 1534 it was extended in the 1590s by Giovanni Battista Pieratti.[45] Its designs owed more to the local tradition of hospital architecture, which was close at hand given that the hospital was constructed in Via San Gallo, one of the major concentrations of charitable and religious

Plate 8.9 Spedale degli Incurabili, Venice: façade on the Zattere. From Luca Carlevaris

Plate 8.10 Eighteenth-century ground plan of Spedale degli Incurabili, Venice, by Cesare Fustinelli

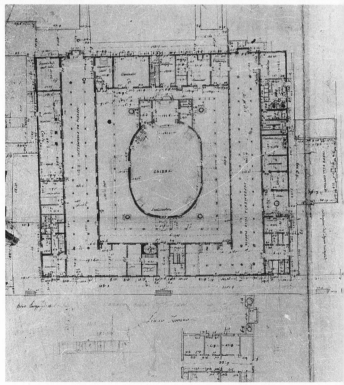

institutions in the city.[46] Instead of two parallel wards, as at Rome and Venice, the Spedale degli Uomini was on the ground floor and the Spedale per le Donne on the first floor. In common with other Florentine hospitals, the Incurabili had a loggia on the front elevation and the building gave directly on to the street. While each long nave-like ward had a small chapel at its west end, there was also a church with an entrance on to Via San Gallo. All the other main activities were also represented by separate architectural spaces, from the medical role of the pharmacy (*spezieria*) to the kitchens and separate eating and sleeping areas for the nuns who served the sick. Perhaps, however, one of the most striking features of the plan is the very substantial garden, which was almost equivalent in area to the rest of the site.

Size and Treatment

The expansion of these hospitals was justified on the ground that demand for their services was outstripping supply. Figures for the number of beds or number of patients treated each year are, however, often difficult to estimate from existing records, except in the case of the largest Incurabili hospitals, especially in Rome, where the patient registers survive. Appeals made by the governors of these hospitals for funds refer, as Bologna's did in 1597, to the 'great multitude of poor people' who frequent their institutions, rather than providing exact numbers.[47] There was, though, great variety in the size of these hospitals. Thus the new foundation at Pavia was very small compared with the larger-scale operations of the older establishments; it had only twenty-four inmates in 1584–5.[48] The Neapolitan Incurabili, in contrast, already had 600 patients by 1535, only fifteen years after its foundation, while at Venice in the period 1565 to 1588 there were between 350 and 450 inmates.[49]

Obviously there was a close correlation between the capacity of a hospital and the size of the city; at two extremes, Pavia c. 1550 had a population of about 13,000 compared with Naples' 210,000. Furthermore, populations in some Italian cities, especially in the south, increased considerably in the second half of the sixteenth century: Naples from 210,000 to 250,000 and Rome from 45,000 to 110,000.[50] This demographic growth led to increased demand for charities in general and hospitals in particular as people from surrounding areas came into cities in search of work, resulting in more crowded housing conditions and increased disease among the economically and socially marginalised. This relationship can be illustrated clearly from the records of San Giacomo in Rome, a city which, as has been noted, experienced an extraordinarily rapid demographic growth in this period. Patient figures before the mid-sixteenth century are rare, but during the ten months preceding the Sack of Rome in May 1527, 123 women were admitted, and 82 males during the first nine months of 1530.[51]

Plate 8.11   Spedale degli Incurabili, Venice: ground-floor ward from a photograph of c. 1930

Plate 8.12   Early eighteenth-century ground plan of Spedale di S. Trinità, Florence

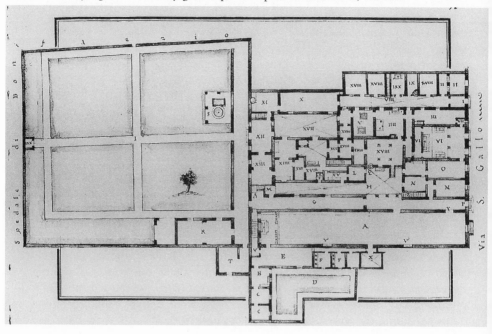

Only forty years after San Giacomo's refoundation in 1515 the admission books become sufficiently complete to analyse consecutive years. The scale of the operation had expanded enormously by the middle of the century; during the five years to 1559 the average annual intake of males was 620.[52] The number of patients continued to increase especially during Holy Wood years. By 1569, a year for which records for women also survive, a total of 1,442 males and 335 females entered.[53] This process continued unabated over the next few decades; in 1581 a total of 2,208 patients entered San Giacomo.[54]

The reason given in the records of these hospitals for their expansion and the growth in the number of admissions was often phrased in terms of the popularity of the new drug, guaiacum, and before turning to examine in detail the patient records of San Giacomo in Rome we should consider the nature of the main treatment offered by the Spedali degli Incurabili.

As we have seen in the previous chapter, during the first decades following the appearance of *Morbus Gallicus* the main treatment prescribed by physicians involved the application of various kinds of mercury ointment, which throughout the middle ages had been the traditional way of treating skin diseases. Since the aim was to expel corrupt matter from the body, doctors combined the application of mercury with other ingredients and promoted sweating through proximity to hot stoves.[55]

The application of mercury was, however, extremely painful for, as Francesco Guicciardini later remarked, when the doctors applied this remedy the effects were often worse than the illness itself.[56] As we have seen in Chapter Six, doctors defended themselves by claiming that it was the empirics who gave mercury a bad name because they prescribed excessively high doses. Although mercury did continue in use, its place as the primary remedy was soon taken by the new 'wonder drug', guaiacum or Holy Wood.[57] The Spanish priest Francesco Delicado, who wrote a treatise praising guaiacum, claimed that it was already in use by 1508, when because of the 'wonderful experience' it was 'distributed through all the hospitals' of Spain. However, according to Delicado it was not employed in Italy until 1517.[58] But once it was introduced, ever increasing amounts were imported from the New World in the second decade of the sixteenth century, helping to increase the wealth of the German banking house of the Fugger family, who achieved an almost complete monopoly of the trade in Europe.[59] One of the biggest customers for guaiacum would have been the Incurabili hospitals. Even though early records are not always sufficiently complete to determine exactly when they adopted the treatment,[60] it is probable that their popularity and expansion were linked closely to the perceived good results of the treatment provided in these institutions. In Rome, for example, although the treatment was already available by the 1520s, the first patient records to survive which enable one to examine how many were treated date from 1549–50 and reveal a large patient population.[61]

The way in which guaiacum was prepared was outlined in some detail and with little variation by a series of writers from the early sixteenth century to the early seventeenth and included Delicado in 1529, Fracastoro less than twenty years later, Gabrielle Falloppio in 1563, and the apothecary of the hospital of San Giacomo in Rome in 1613.[62] As we have seen in Chapter Five, the wood was broken into small pieces like sawdust and added to water. This mixture was boiled up to produce three different substances: the foam created during the process, which was skimmed off; the concentrated solution produced at the end of the process; and finally a weak solution which was obtained by reboiling the wood with more water. The first was used as a drying powder on sores; the second was the main part of the treatment and was drunk at regular intervals during the cure; and the third was taken during meals.[63] The purposes of giving the wood were many: to dry the body and induce sweating, to liberate and cleanse the body from peccant matter, and to promote resistance to putrefaction and to disease through the action of resin. Other elements of the treatment reinforced the virtues of the wood: the patients were placed in well-covered beds, all the windows and the exits were sealed, stoves were lit and left burning to promote sweating, and laxatives were administered to rid the body of its impurities.[64] Given the heat generated by this treatment, it was normally supplied only during the warmer months of the year. A cynical interpretation could claim that this was a cost-cutting exercise but, although the expense of the treatment was a very real consideration, there were also important medical reasons. They were summarised by the 1574 statutes of the Florence hospital of SS. Trinità: 'to supply the [holy] wood from mid-February until the end of October . . . and this is because seeing that the patients have been in a place so hot, they should not be allowed to go outside in the coldness of winter'.[65] In Padua and Venice the treatment also lasted during the spring and autumn, but in other places such as Bologna and Rome the tendency was to restrict it still further to just two to three months from April or May.[66] Further afield, at the Hospital General of Valencia the same reasons were provided for seasonal treatment by those who ran the pox wards, even though mercurial compounds rather than guaiacum were administered to their patients.[67]

Diet was also an important part of the treatment. Food intake was reduced gradually in order to help the action of Legno Santo in purging the body of its peccant matter. Patients were allowed to drink only watered-down wine and to eat only dry biscuits, although towards the end of the treatment a more sustaining diet of meat and chicken soup was introduced.[68]

Treatment was overseen and administered by a professional medical staff. In common with most general hospitals, Incurabili hospitals employed two medical men, a physician and a surgeon, who were required to visit the patients daily.[69] In a contract between the Florentine hospital and a surgeon, Maestro Giovan Pavolo d'Allegro da Vercelli, he was instructed 'with diligence and charity [to] look after well the sick who are in this hospital . . .'.[70]

At San Giacomo in Rome visits were instead made twice a day, probably because of the size of the hospital, and the medical men were required to examine the patients' urine, to recommend the appropriate food and drink and to prescribe the relevant simples to treat their condition. From 1584 it was further required that the medical staff should also meet every Sunday evening at seven o'clock in order 'to consult together about the treatment of the gravely sick'.[71]

Holy Wood treatment quickly became fashionable and was adopted all over Europe during the 1520s.[72] Its reputed miraculous effects were trumpeted by practitioners and patients alike, not least because there were far fewer side effects than there were from the mercurial treatment. Francisco Delicado, for example, was so enthusiastic about the Holy Wood that he published in 1529 a treatise on its excellent effect because, as Pope Clement VII said in his introduction,

> Our beloved son Francisco Delicado . . . suffered for a while in the Arcispedale of San Giacomo Apostolo, of our noble city, the greatest pains and almost incurable sickness as a result of the *Morbo Gallico*, and through the gracious intervention of God and of the Apostles, to the amazement of everybody, has recovered his original health.[73]

People from all social levels took this miraculous cure. High-ranking prelates, for example, were among those who suffered, as one can see from the letter written from Rome to the Duke of Mantua in 1534: 'The Cardinal de' Medici has been taking the wood from the Indies for four days and has been fasting for fifty days. However, he is much burdened with Mal Francese and the poor gentleman is very patient and hopes to be cured completely'.[74]

While the Medici cardinal, Ippolito, in common with the more affluent throughout Europe, could afford to be treated at home,[75] the majority of patients at San Giacomo were poor, and indeed Legno Santo was provided free to many hundreds, later thousands, of people. They arrived after having seen or heard about the posters which were pinned to the doors of churches throughout Rome 'with details of the day and hour that the sick had to appear to be admitted into the hospital, and information that they had to come prepared with testimony that they had confessed and taken communion'.[76]

However, because the treatment had become so popular and so many people collected in front of the hospital, measures had to be taken to control the crowds. The captain of the Swiss Guards sent half his troops, 'who guarded the main entrance during the day while they received the sick', and a palisade was erected outside the door of the hospital in order to avoid a riot.[77]

One of the main problems associated with the treatment was its enormous expense, as was underlined by the governors when they made an appeal for financial help:

> In the Hospital of San Giacomo degli Incurabili it is normal every three or four years or more to give the Acqua del Legno generally to all the people who come there; they always numbered more than a thousand, all wretched, and are those who do not have the wherewithal to pay to take this medicament, and in this way over and above the charity to those poor people who invade the city we ensure the greater health of many. . . .[78]

In 1562, for example, the cost of treating 754 males and 300 females was 3,059 *scudi*. This was a very considerable sum. It was equivalent to 1.3 per cent of total papal expenditure for the Papal State and the Church fourteen years later, or almost one and a half times more than the papacy spent on alms in 1590.[79] The largest single expense was for the purchase of 7,287 lb of Legno Santo (357 *scudi*), followed closely by 'diverse simples for the said wood'. The other main items purchased were the ingredients for the patients' diet, including 12,685 lb of Passerina grapes, 268 barrels of wine, meat for the soup and more than 96 bushels of grain, as well as 100 wool covers for the beds and cloth for sheets, bedwear, and napkins.[80]

The expenses, however, were clearly regarded as worth while because alms continued to pour into the coffers of the hospital and patients continued to queue up in great numbers to receive the treatment. The sections which follow will examine in more detail those admitted to San Giacomo, whose archive is unique among Italian Incurabili hospitals for its patient registers, which have survived virtually intact from the mid-sixteenth century. The rest of this chapter presents a preliminary analysis of these registers from the second half of the sixteenth century. Obviously it has not been possible to analyse more than a sample of the patient registers from the second half of the sixteenth century, given that well over 50,000 patients were admitted.[81] We shall therefore examine the aggregate totals of admissions and exits for each year for the whole period 1554 to 1600, and this general picture will provide the background against which to study four sample years: 1561, 1562, 1569 and 1570.[82]

The Patients at San Giacomo, 1550–1600

Analysis of the registers on which this discussion is based is far from straight-forward, as we shall see when we come to examine in more detail each characteristic of the patients as recorded by the scribe. A representative page of the register is reproduced as Plate 8.13, which records admissions for males in May 1561. They have been entered according to the prescriptions of the hospital's statutes, which are rigorous in the detail required:

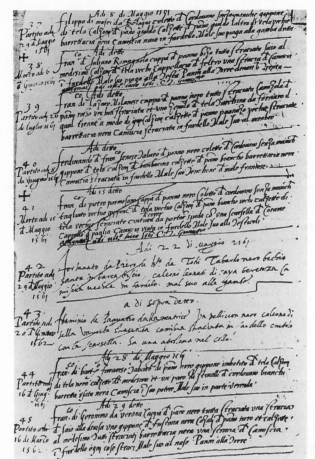

Plate 8.13 Patient register, male admissions, May 1561, Spedale di San Giacomo, Rome

[The prior] must keep a book in which are written in alphabetical order the Christian name, surname, provenance, the name of the father of the patient who entered the hospital, the day he came, month and year, and the clothes that he was wearing, piece by piece, and this should be done in the presence of the same patient and of the wardrobe official, to whom he must consign the bundle. . . . once the bundle is made up, they give to the patient a ticket on which all his clothes in the bundle are noted, so that if the patient gets better everything in its entirety can be restituted to him.[83]

In addition to these details the scribe also recorded two other pieces of information: an indication of the sickness for which the patient was admitted, in the form of a symptom and often the part of the body which was affected, and finally the date and condition on leaving the hospital, whether alive or dead.

The fourth entry on this folio reads in translation as follows:

40. [Entered] On the 8 May 1561

Ferdinando, son of Francesco from Siena: long tabard of black cloth, Morocco leather jerkin without sleeves, linen doublet, cotton hose, white cloth stockings, old black cap, ragged shirt in a bundle. Sick from abscesses in the groin from the French Disease.

Left on 8 June 1561.[84]

Although this may seem quite a detailed account of the patient and his appearance, there are considerable problems of interpretation. This is especially true of the records for women, where the details about their illnesses are particularly scant. Perhaps the least problematic information provided are the dates of admission and exit, together with the exit condition, whether an individual was alive or dead. For our sample years only 10 per cent of the 4,697 patients had to be excluded from analysis because they did not have this information.

Admissions

Two very clear patterns emerge from an analysis of these patient registers over this fifty-year period. The first is that an increasing number of patients were admitted to San Giacomo in the second half of the sixteenth century. This is reflected in the five-year annual averages of admissions during the thirty years from 1555: 617, 852, 1,162, 1,568, 1,535 and 1,755. Even though the first two figures omit females – their records do not survive before 1569 – Figure 8.1 shows that there was a significant increase in the number of males admitted. By the early 1580s annual admissions reached as high as nearly 2,500 (1581: 2,208; 1583: 2,472). Thereafter the patient registers cease to be an accurate guide to the totals admitted because the names of patients admitted for the *cura con il legno* were probably recorded in separate registers and not, as in earlier years, also included in the main admission books.[85] This hypothesis is confirmed by notes made in separate account books for 1590. The main register records only the admission of 630 patients, whereas in fact the total males and females admitted in May and June alone for the *cura* was 1,141.[86]

Bearing this last reservation in mind, these records do reflect a continued rise in patient admissions throughout this period. In general terms, as in late sixteenth-century Valencia, the increased numbers reflect growing levels of poverty within the city.[87] More specifically this can be related to the provision of Holy Wood treatment. The link between demand and the supply of the *cura* is reflected in the peaks in 1562 and from 1567 onwards, and then in particular by the jagged see-saw motion of the years 1575 to 1583 when the Holy Wood was administered every two years. Indeed, as can be seen from Figures 8.2 and 8.3, there was a very clear surge between March and June

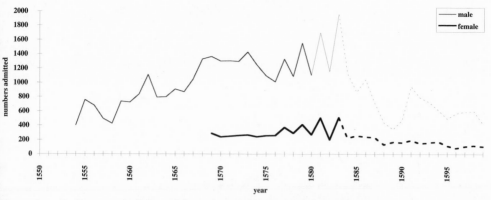

Figure 8.1 S. Giacomo degli Incurabili: male and female admissions, 1554–1599
Source: ASR, S. Giacomo degli Incurabili, 384–418 (. . . years excluding admissions for Holy Wood)

1562 and in May 1569 and May 1570. This led to a 25 per cent jump in admissions over the previous year. At the end of the decade the same pattern can be seen for both spring 1569 and 1570; this also shows that female admissions followed a similar seasonality.

The second pattern which emerges from the graph is the enormous disparity between the number of males and females; the women always represented less than 20 per cent of the total. The reasons for this difference are not made clear by the hospital's records. To a certain degree this reflects contemporary practices in Italian hospitals. Studies of three hospitals in Florence and Prato show that admission policies were generally biased towards men, with women presumably being instead nursed at home.[88] However, given Rome's peculiar status as the capital of Christendom and the Church, the sex ratio of San Giacomo's patients was also influenced by the highly masculinised nature of the population. This is reflected in two censuses of Rome in the final decade of the sixteenth century: in 1592 only 37 per cent of the population was female, increasing slightly by 1599 to 40 to 43 per cent.[89] This imbalance between the sexes was a peculiarly Roman phenomenon, as is shown by a comparison with the sex ratios of other Italian cities around this time: females represented as much as 51 to 55 per cent of cities such as Bologna, Florence, Messina and Palermo.[90]

Even a skewed sex ratio in Rome does not fully explain the emphasis on males and suggests that San Giacomo's admission policy reflected the characteristics of the applicants themselves. Certainly studies of patients in pox hospitals in Spain and Germany imply no such male bias in morbidity rates.[91] This is a point to which we shall return when considering the social status of patients in our sample years. Next, however, we shall look at the other set of aggregate figures, the death rate of patients, to see how far Incurabili hospitals were regarded as places in which to deposit the moribund.

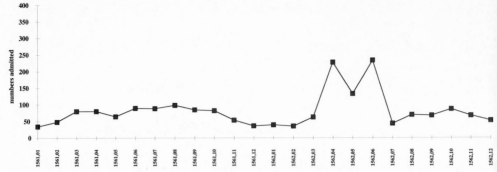

Figure 8.2   S. Giacomo degli Incurabili: male admissions, 1561–1562
Source: ASR, S. Giacomo degli Incurabili, 386

Mortality

Despite the fluctuations in mortality at San Giacomo, the underlying level bore little resemblance to Michel Foucault's characterisation of early modern hospitals as 'portals of death', and are not far out of line with findings for pox hospitals in early modern Germany.[92] Taking the number who died as a percentage of admissions, the combined male and female rates over the whole period were no more than 12 per cent.[93] However, this worsens after 1584 to an average of 16 per cent. This reflects, on the one hand, a deterioration in conditions in the city with a greater prevalence of epidemics and dearth. But more important was the fact that these registers now excluded those people admitted for Holy Wood treatment, and they had a lower mortality than those admitted during the rest of the year. Another general feature of Figure 8.4 is that, while males and females shared the same overall pattern of mortality, the latter were consistently higher; male mortality as a percentage of admissions was 12 per cent and female 16 per cent. This difference was

Figure 8.3   S. Giacomo degli Incurabili: male and female admissions, 1569–1570
Source: ASR, S. Giacomo degli Incurabili, 390–2

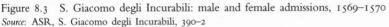

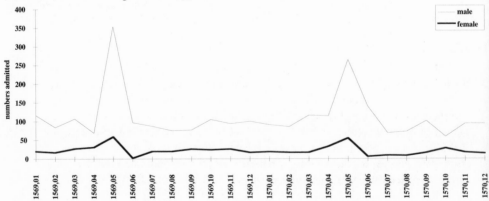

Figure 8.4 S. Giacomo degli Incurabili: percentage mortality of admissions, 1554–1599
Source: ASR, S. Giacomo degli Incurabili, 384–418 (from 1584, admissions for Holy Wood treatment excluded)

exaggerated during the fifteen years after 1584 when the averages were 13 per cent and 18 per cent respectively.

The reasons for higher female mortality are not immediately obvious. They could be related to a different policy in the type of complaint treated, but details about the sicknesses suffered by women are very sparse compared with those for men. It is also possible that women were offered a lower standard of care in a smaller, more crowded ward than men, as has been suggested was the cause of higher female mortality at S. Maria Nuova in Florence.[94] This is, however, difficult to prove, although an answer to this problem may become clearer when we come to the 1590s, the period of the greatest disparity between male and female deaths.

Taking those years when combined male and female mortality exceeded 15 per cent of admissions, San Giacomo was evidently much affected by exogenous factors in Rome. As in most pre-industrial cities, the most serious problems for the poor were epidemics and dearths. It is, however, often difficult to separate out which of a series of factors was the principal cause of a rise in mortality in the city in general and in an institution such as San Giacomo in particular. In the first place the disease categories used by chroniclers were often vague and different contemporaries recorded the presence of different epidemic diseases in the city in the same year. Also, as the Abbot Segni remarked after a decade of crisis in the late sixteenth century, 'the majority of the poor' were always struck down by some form of sickness at times of dearth.[95] The hardship and malnutrition associated with severe shortages may, furthermore, have caused the premature death of the chronically sick who frequented a hospital such as San Giacomo.

Rome in the second half of the sixteenth century experienced many epidemics, some of which were linked closely with extreme weather conditions and others with periods of shortage.[96] The most common was the general category of fevers, either *febbre tertiane* or *febbre maligne* or *morbo di febbre*. These recurred three to four times in each of the decades in the second half of the sixteenth century.[97] Contemporaries also recorded a number of epidemics during these fifty years in colder, wet weather, such as *infermità catarrale*.[98] Fevers tended to be associated with high temperatures in the summer or early autumn or alternatively, as in 1590–3, with poor harvests. Bad weather and periods of shortage also led to an increase of intestinal diseases with the deterioration in the quality of food and water. But perhaps the single biggest killer in these years – plague was absent from Rome at this time – was petechial fever, often occurring during dearths.[99] This was one of the most prevalent epidemic diseases in late sixteenth- and seventeen-century Italy and affected mostly those at the lower levels of society living in unhygienic conditions.[100] Although, as Carlo Cipolla reminds us,[101] the connection between an outbreak of petechial fever and a dearth was not automatic, it was more likely within the context of Italian cities, given that their normally insanitary conditions were worsened by the crowds of poor beggars who flooded into the towns in search of food. Rome was perhaps the worst hit in these circumstances, given that it was seen by contemporaries as 'the international capital of the poor', especially in the late sixteenth century with the repeated failure of harvests in the Roman Campagna.[102]

Figure 8.4 shows a number of peaks of mortality during these fifty years, the majority of which can be linked to epidemics in Rome or the Campagna. Diseases associated with colder weather were present in the city in 1554, 1557, 1569–70, 1580 and 1597; *catarri* and 'fevers' in Rome and the Campagna in 1572 and 1574, and petechial fever in 1569–70 and the period 1587 to 1593. The timing of dearths can be correlated even more closely with peaks in San Giacomo deaths. In 1557, for example, the price of all basic foodstuffs was so high that by the autumn the *Avvisi*, an unofficial journalistic record of events in the city, stated that the only way the poor could obtain food was through violence.[103] Similar problems characterised 1569–70, as we shall see in the next section, but worst of all were the dearths between the late 1580s and the early to mid-1590s. One contemporary, the biographer of Camillo de Lellis, described graphically the scenes in the streets during the *mortalità* at the time of the dearth in 1590:

> just in the city of Rome and its region, 60,000 people died, partly through hunger, partly through cold. It is horrible even to read of such a disaster. Imagine then how heartbreaking it must have been for those who saw men in the *contrade* of the city dying under the benches of the butchers and other shops, reduced to feeding on grass like sheep in the fields and to eating even cats and dead dogs and any filthy food they could find; so that our [religious] recorded more than once a dead body with his mouth full of grass. . . .[104]

While one should be careful to avoid using a hagiographical biography too literally, especially in relation to the numbers who died and the common *topos* of eating domestic animals, all contemporaries did agree on the gravity of the situation. Part of the papal programme to deal with the crisis was to use hospitals, as another contemporary records for 1591: 'all the hospitals of the city of Rome were so full of the sick that there was not enough space and so the poor workers from elsewhere and the poor found themselves in the streets, many abandoned and often were found dead there'.[105] The recently founded Spedale dei Mendicanti was severely overcrowded; 2,000 poor people were admitted in January 1591 alone.[106] San Giacomo, too, admitted large numbers, even if they were not reflected in Figure 8.1, since, as noted above, the registers on which it is based omitted all those taking the Holy Wood. Mortality increased as well and would have reflected the deaths of some of the many starving malnourished beggars with the additional burden of an incurable disease.

It is in the last decade of the century that the disparity between male and female mortality is most obvious, apparently associated with the continued shortage and high prices. During these years the price of wheat was between 50 and 100 per cent higher than the normal level in the second half of the century.[107] Indeed high prices over the previous decades were one of the main factors which distinguished the years of excess female mortality, suggesting that female 'incurables' admitted to San Giacomo may have been more frail and malnourished than men.

To look at this phenomenon in more detail we shall turn to the sample years of 1561–2 and 1569–70. Even though at the beginning of the decade we possess data only for males, there does appear to have been some relationship between mortality and price levels within the city: 11 per cent in 1561, 6.8 per cent in 1562 followed by 13 per cent in 1563, although we must not forget that lower mortality in 1562 reflected the lower death rates for those who were admitted for guaiacum-wood treatment.

In fact, the decade had opened at the tail-end of a period of high prices and severe shortage. The price of wheat was still high, but fell during the harvest of 1561, so that by October the author of a letter from Rome to Vincenzo Gonzaga in Mantua could write that the city in summer 1562 had 'a superabundance of grain, wine and other necessities, and the feeling of general contentment is universal'. However, there was a sting in the author's pen when he continued: 'Persons of good conduct and talent are highly esteemed, and worthless characters have either to change their ways or submit to punishment, if they do not prefer to go of their own accord into banishment.'[108] Once again we are presented with a picture through the eyes of the upper echelons of society. They maintained an intolerant attitude towards the floating masses of beggars who thronged the streets of Rome, though once patients were safely tucked up in the beds of the city's hospitals they became objects of Christian charity. The following year conditions in the city in fact deteriorated; the price of grain doubled and in the summer the city was afflicted by *catarri* and 'epidemic coughs'; according to one probably exaggerated account over 12,000 people died in the city during these months.[109]

At the end of the decade, 1569–70, male mortality at San Giacomo remained at the overall average of 11 per cent, but female deaths rose to 15

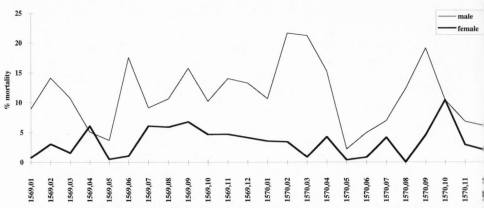

Figure 8.5   S. Giacomo degli Incurabili: percentage mortality of total admissions, 1569–1570
Source: ASR, S. Giacomo degli Incurabili, 390–2

to 16 per cent of admissions. As we have seen, between 1567 and 1570 the city was afflicted by a series of bad harvests caused by the poor weather.[110] The *Avvisi* recorded in June 1569 that there was 'an extreme shortage of everything in the city. . . . for some days it has been impossible to obtain bread except through violence'.[111] Even the normally prosperous cardinals and wealthy prelates were forced to sack some of their personnel. Pope Pius V was concerned enough about the situation in the following spring to have food distributed to the indigent and through a physician, barber–surgeon and apothecary to provide free medical treatment for the poor, who were suffering from sicknesses related to dearth.[112] Obviously, though, his main aim was to maintain order within the city, so that, as he said in his proclamation of 12 March, 'they [the poor] do not travel around begging and disturbing' their social betters.[113] Then when the harvest arrived it was insufficient; prices did not fall until the following June.[114] The same period also saw an outbreak of fevers in July 1569, which gave way to another epidemic disease from August, and petechial fever broke out during the subsequent months of winter and spring, followed by 'fevers' the following summer in the Campagna.[115]

Very broadly, mortality at San Giacomo seems to have reflected some of these influences. Figure 8.5 plots mortality for male and female patients as a percentage of the total admissions. If this has the effect of deflating female mortality, it has the advantage of ironing out the extreme cases, as in June 1569, when even if a 50 per cent mortality was recorded this simply represented the death of one of two people admitted.

In the case of males the seasonality of their mortality does appear to have mirrored the influence of the sicknesses associated with high prices in February 1569, fevers in the summer and the 'influenza' epidemic from August followed by petechial fever during the harsh winter and spring of 1570, and fevers in the Campagna in the summer and probably another epidemic in the autumn.[116] The striking dip in May can be explained by the hospital admin-

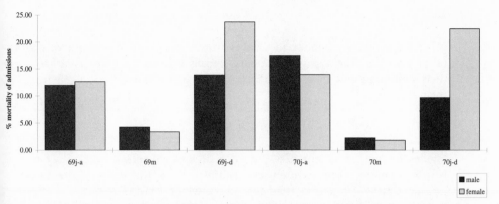

Figure 8.6 S. Giacomo degli Incurabili: mortality of Holy Wood admissions cf. normal admissions, 1569–1570. Admission period: j–a (Jan–Apr); m (May); j–d (Jun–Dec) (Holy Wood admissions mainly occur in May)
Source: ASR, S. Giacomo degli Incurabili, 390–2

istrators' policy of either dismissing the so-called *impiagati normali* (normal sores) from San Giacomo, or, at the very least, of transferring some to a separate ward, the *hospitaletto*, to make room for those admitted for the forty-day period reserved for guaiacum.[117]

While variations in female mortality broadly follow those for males, in many cases there appears to have been a lag of about a month before women were apparently affected by the same exogenous influences. While not too much weight should be placed on these differences, given the fact that the number of women who died was so low, this may point again to the fact that they were admitted later and so were more sick than men.

This examination of mortality at San Giacomo has revealed a number of significant characteristics of the patient population. First, the overall rate was relatively low: 12 per cent over these fifty years. Second, the rises can be linked to exogenous factors, in particular epidemic diseases and dearths. Third, female mortality was higher than male, particularly at times of dearth; and fourth, even though there were increases in mortality of up to 10 per cent, exogenous factors were not as disastrous for the majority of the patient population as they would have been if an outbreak of plague had broken out in the hospital. Finally, those who were admitted for Holy Wood treatment had a much lower rate of mortality than those who entered during the rest of the year, as is reflected clearly in Figure 8.6. Furthermore, this also shows that while there were no significant differences in mortality between the sexes for those admitted for guaiacum treatment, females suffered a higher death rate in the second half of the year, especially during the colder months.

All this suggests that the hospital had a very specific admission policy concerning the types of diseases admitted and how long patients were allowed to remain; above all, it would not admit many of the truly moribund. The following sections will examine this policy and then see how far the more

general statements of policy in statutes were reflected in the length of stay
of inmates and the types of patients actually admitted, in terms of both
their symptoms and their social backgrounds as far as can be judged from
their clothing.

Length of stay

Figures for the actual length of stay of male patients entering San Giacomo
largely confirm their written regulations. Thus the hospital's statutes
instructed the Guardians to 'send away those who are not in need so that they
do not eat the bread of the other needy poor'.[118]

Figure 8.7 plots the frequency of length of stay of all the patients in our
four sample years, ignoring, however, the stays for longer than four months.
Evidently even if the hospital was designed for 'incurables', it was not a place
where the terminally sick remained very long. The vast majority of patients
in these four years left within forty days (66 per cent), and indeed a significant
proportion (37 per cent) left within twenty days. This more rapid turnover
was, moreover, a process which accelerated over this decade. In 1561, 56 per
cent of patients left within forty days; this rose to 61 per cent in the following
year and then increased to 71 per cent in 1569 and 75 per cent in 1570. The
contrast between 1561 and 1562 reflects the fact that it was only in the second
year that guaiacum was provided, depressing the overall length of stay because
of the fixed forty-day period for the treatment. This was also behind the more
rapid turnover at the end of the decade; Legno Santo was provided in both
years. But this does not provide the entire explanation for the increase of 15
per cent between 1561 and 1570. Instead these figures indicate that at this
time of rising admissions the hospital administrators were anxious to treat
more people in the same space, given that it was not until later in the century
that another ward was constructed.

All this suggests that the 1560s saw growing pressure on the hospital from
patients requesting admission, especially with the attraction of the more
regular administration of guaiacum. The governors appear to have responded
to this demand with a policy which had much in common with contemporary Tuscan hospitals for acute conditions. They made sure that the majority
of their patients did not remain for longer than forty days and also aimed to
avoid accepting the truly moribund.[119] These general principles were not
always put into practice: Figure 8.7 shows that some people remained in the
hospital for considerably longer than the forty-day average. In addition to
those who stayed at San Giacomo for up to four months, there was also, as
in other Italian Incurabili hospitals,[120] a small number who remained for
longer. In the case of males this represented only about 2 per cent of all those
admitted during the four sample years combined. One way that this could be
made more acceptable to the governors was when, in common with San

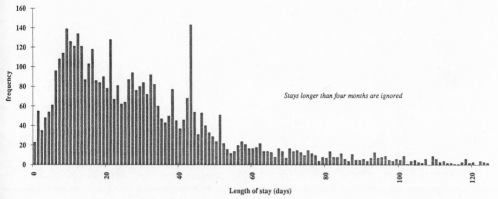

Figure 8.7 S. Giacomo degli Incurabili: frequencies of lengths of stay, male and female, 1561–1562 and 1569–1570

Source: ASR, S. Giacomo degli Incurabili, 386, 390–2

Camillo, the patient took on the role of serving his fellows and in this way was able to help repay the institution for its service.[121]

If some patients stayed well beyond the normally acceptable period, a comparison of the length of stay of male and female patients admitted in 1569–70 with their mortality demonstrates that here too there were those who fell outside the desired prescription for an average patient (see Figure 8.8). Evidently the physicians must have accepted some people who were fairly near to death for, although some inmates continued to die over a long period, the majority did so within the first two weeks of entry. This was especially true of the men; after the first week female mortality remained consistently higher, confirming our suggestion above that they may have arrived at the hospital in a more decrepit state than their male counterparts. To examine this point in more detail we now need to turn to the hospital's admission policy and the symptoms of San Giacomo's patients.

San Giacomo Admissions and Patient Symptoms

Contemporaries suggest that by the middle decades of the sixteenth century the vast majority of patients of Italian Incurabili hospitals arrived voluntarily, a pattern reflected in Valencia.[122] The enforced treatment for vagrants evident in the early days appears to have become a feature of the past. The reasons for this change, to which we shall return in conclusion, have much to do with the perceived benefits of the guaiacum-wood treatment.

The majority of patients admitted to San Giacomo were self-referrals, who simply presented themselves at the door of the hospital either individually during the year or as a member of the crowds attracted to San Giacomo in the spring, having seen or heard about the posters which were plastered on

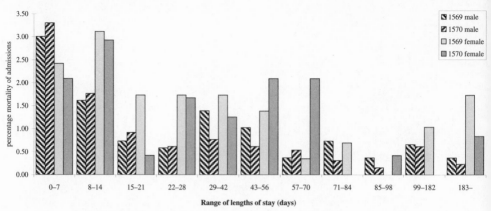

Figure 8.8   S. Giacomo degli Incurabili: mortality compared with length of stay (days), 1569–1570
Source: ASR, S. Giacomo degli Incurabili, 390–2

church doors throughout Rome. But it was also possible to by-pass the normal admission procedure; about ten beds were specially reserved 'to give satisfaction to some superior or patron who recommends somebody'.[123] This was presumably why Francisco Delicado was treated at San Giacomo. Each one in this special category arrived with a letter of presentation; Antonio Maria Manzuoli, for example, wrote, 'Dominico Genovese, my old servant, through his bad luck has fallen into a Male Francese and desires to be treated.' Another patron wrote: 'You will find here this sick man, Cesare di Tatacola, who through his great poverty and through the uselessness of the physicians has not been able to be treated for this sickness he has.'[124] In addition, some of the smaller Incurabili hospitals, such as at Padua and Bologna, also provided an out-patient service, although there is no evidence of this practice at San Giacomo since presumably such a substantial hospital already had high enough expenses incurred by admitting in-patients.[125]

On arrival at San Giacomo, as at most other Incurabili hospitals, patients were vetted by a physician or surgeon, and since this was a specialised hospital applicants had to fulfil certain criteria before admission.[126] Indeed the Guardians had to make sure that: 'when a poor person enters he must be seen by the doctors and if they say that he is only very needy and not incurable then the doctors must not receive him'.[127]

An important condition for admission, which helped to sort out the moral sheep from the immoral goats – and also those without parishes – was that potential patients had to 'come prepared with testimonies of having been confessed and having communicated'.[128] Then just to make doubly sure, when the sick were admitted and before they were put to bed, they had to be confessed and then the following morning they had to take communion.[129] The statutes of the Florentine Spedale della SS. Trinità were even more specific in their regulations, presumably because their facilities were on a smaller scale than those in Rome: 'they shall bring testimony from the physician of the place of having need to take the wood and also testimony from their parish priest that they are of a poor sort who cannot themselves afford to pay for medication . . . '.[130]

Patients admitted to these hospitals, therefore, had to fulfil four basic conditions: they had to have an 'incurable' disease; they had to be poor; they had to provide written proof that they were spiritually in grace; and, as the Bolognese Incurabili hospital put it in 1570, they had to show that 'they have been rejected and abandoned by all other types of hospitals'.[131]

These general remarks help us to determine the patients' material and spiritual state, but take us no closer to understanding their physical condition, except through the general statement of their incurability. Occasionally, as we saw in the previous chapter, commentators in the early sixteenth century did provide a more specific idea of the types of diseases treated, as in Naples in 1520, where the patients of the Spedale degli Incurabili were seen as 'sick from Mal Francese, cancers, and other incurable diseases'.[132] Incurabili hospitals also, as the 1515 bull *Salvatoris Nostri* demonstrates, made it a policy not to receive those suffering from plague and leprosy.[133] Later in the century San Giacomo's statutes were even more explicit: they should not receive '*impiagati* from wounds or *rognosi* [with scabies], lepers, wounded, nor those suffering from a fever'.[134] Indeed it can be seen from Table 8.3 below that this policy was carried out in practice; only twenty-two people were admitted with 'fevers' in 1569–70 and none in 1561–2, which represented only 1.3 per cent of all those listed with symptoms.

It is clear, therefore, that although an Incurabili hospital such as San Giacomo was open to treat a wide range of incurable diseases there were certain restrictions on the conditions of those they were prepared to admit. But this may also have varied according to the institution. The largest hospitals, in Naples and Rome, were forced by demand to restrict their intake; hence their clearer categorisation. Evidently the smaller hospitals were more flexible, as long as the patient admitted was perceived as suffering from an incurable condition. Thus in 1538 the Spedale di S. Francesco in Padua is recorded as having 'observed true hospitality and received there continuously with charity the poor sick and other wretched people who flocked there'.[135] But this may have been a special case because they apparently did not have the funds to supply guaiacum before 1582 and therefore might have attracted a wider clientele.[136] Even so, the Bolognese Spedale di S. Giobbe, which did provide guaiacum from an early date, described its clientele at the end of the century in generic terms. The hospital was 'full of the poor sick with sores', described in another document as 'all the poor sick with ulcers of each sex'.[137] This suggests a different point: that although the famous guaiacum wood was best known for the treatment of the pox, even Girolamo Fracastoro said that it had a much wider application, 'for any old and cold complaint of the head, nerves, stomach and joints'.[138]

In order to take these general points further and to see which diseases were catered for by the largest Incurabili hospital in Italy, that of San Giacomo in Rome, we must turn to an analysis of the symptoms of patients admitted during our sample years.

It will be seen that even the detailed patient registers of San Giacomo appear to confirm the observations made about other Italian Incurabili hospitals. In other words, the Incurabli hospitals, which had made their initial reputation as specialists in Mal Francese, in fact received a much wider clientele. But it will be seen that it is not a simple task to identify the illnesses of the sixteenth century. There is not just the problem of terminology, but also the lack of really exact descriptions of symptoms. The second problem is related to the first, the difficulty of identifying complaints of the patients, even within sixteenth-century terms.

Symptoms

With this general framework in mind, we will turn to the actual symptoms and sicknesses of the patients in these years. Plate 8.12, which is an extract from the patient register for May 1561, provides some idea of the variety and often the vagueness of these descriptions. Five of these nine men were described simply as 'sick' (*male*) in a particular part of their body, as in the case of Fortunato di Piero, who had something wrong with his legs. Four others, however, had particular symptoms, including sores, swellings or apostemes, and abscesses. Only the last mentioned were linked specifically to Mal Francese: 'Ferdinando di Francesco Senese . . . male suo tenchone di Male Franchese', abscesses in the groin associated with the pox. But the appearance of three others with complaints in the genital area (member, testicles and venereal region) might suggest that they had some kind of venereal disease, the symptoms of which were not linked immediately to Mal Francese.

Evidence about the symptoms of male patients admitted to San Giacomo in 1561–2 and 1569–70 is summarised in Tables 8.1 and 8.2. There was considerable variation in the amount of detail provided about the complaints of individuals, especially between the beginning and end of the decade. In 1561–2 it is possible to discuss the symptoms associated with all male patients admitted. In 1569–70, however, virtually no additional information was provided once a male had been identified as having Mal Francese and in the case of females only 13 to 15 per cent were recorded with symptoms; most were simply described as *malata* or sick.

The first most striking feature of the 4,612 patients identified with symptoms was that only 20 per cent had any which the admitting doctors and surgeons associated specifically with Mal Francese. This confirms our earlier observation that, although the driving force behind setting up the Incurabili hospitals may have been the need to cope with the *mal franciosati*, these institutions treated a large number of incurable diseases.

Secondly, a comparison between Tables 8.1 and 8.2 shows that there was a very clear distinction in the minds of the admitting physicians between those male patients who had and those who did not have Mal Francese. Table 8.1 shows that 85 per cent of male patients with the pox in 1561 had one of three main symptoms: pustules, pains and *tincone*, or abscesses in the groin. Table 8.2 shows, on the other hand, that only 10 per cent of non-pox patients were identified with these ailments in 1561.

It is more difficult to know how to interpret the data for the women, since only 43 of 288 admitted in 1569 were listed with a symptom or disease. Given this inexactness it may not be surprising that only one was described as having Mal Francese and three in the following year. Some of these women may, of course, have subsequently been identified as having the disease, given that 8.4 per cent had the pustules or pains familiar from contemporary symptomatologies. But the lack of information about their symptoms may be explained partly by problems of diagnosis. Thus physicians when they admitted patients may have found Mal Francese more difficult to detect in women than in men. This may have been particularly true in the case of prostitutes admitted with Mal Francese for they would no doubt have wanted to hide the disease for as long as possible in order to continue to ply their trade. Unfortunately we know virtually nothing about the professions of women patients and so cannot estimate how many were prostitutes, although it may not be irrelevant that a significant percentage of the women appearing in a more detailed early seventeenth-century admission register (1616–17) were unmarried; they were listed with their Christian names and the names of their fathers.[139]

To understand better the symptoms associated here with Mal Francese we need to compare them with a contemporary symptomatology. One of the most detailed is contained in Girolamo Fracastoro's famous treatise *De Contagione*:

in the majority of cases, small ulcers began to appear on the sexual organs [and they were] intractable and would not depart. . . . Next the skin broke out with encrusted pustules. . . . they soon grew little by little till they were the size of the cup of an acorn, which they in fact resembled . . . . Next these ulcerated pustules ate away the skin. . . . and they sometimes infected not only the fleshy parts but even the very bones as well. In cases where the malady was firmly established in the upper parts of the body, the patients suffered from pernicious catarrh which eroded the palate or the uvula or the pharynx or tonsils. In some cases the lips or nose or eyes were eaten away, or in others the whole of the sexual organs. Moreover, many patients suffered from the great deformity or gummata which developed on the members; these were often as large as an egg or a roll of bread. . . . Besides all the above symptoms, as if they were not bad enough, violent pains attacked the muscles. . . . these pains were persistent,

Table 8.1   S. Giacomo degli Incurabili: symptoms of male patients identified with Mal Francese, 1561–1562, 1569–1570

Symptom	1561		1562		1569		1570	
	no.	%	no.	%	no.	%	no.	%
bolle/pustules	46	21.1	22	3.2	0	0.0	0	0.0
doglie/pains	69	31.7	355	52.1	0	0.0	0	0.0
gomme/gummata	9	4.1	6	0.9	0	0.0	0	0.0
piaghe/sores	4	1.8	2	0.3	0	0.0	0	0.0
rogne/scabs	6	2.8	6	0.9	0	0.0	0	0.0
tincone/★	71	32.6	41	6.0	0	0.0	0	0.0
altri/other	13	6.0	249	36.6	7	100.0	32	100.0
totals	218	100.0	681	100.0	7	100.0	32	100.0

★ abscesses in groin
Source: S. Giacomo degli Incurabili, 386, 390–2

Table 8.2   S. Giacomo degli Incurabili: symptoms of male patients not identified with Mal Francese, 1561–1562, 1569–1570

Symptom	1561		1562		1569		1570	
	no.	%	no.	%	no.	%	no.	%
bolle/pustules	6	1.0	5	1.2	58	4.3	37	2.9
doglie/pains	29	4.7	6	1.4	59	4.3	156	12.3
gomme/gummata	12	1.9	2	0.5	15	1.1	5	0.4
piaghe/sores	310	50.2	229	53.4	20	1.5	21	1.7
rogne/scabs	15	2.4	3	0.7	10	0.7	56	4.4
tincone/★	27	4.4	12	2.8	63	4.6	84	6.6
altri/other	41	6.6	31	7.2	84	6.2	55	4.3
malato/sick	177	28.7	141	32.9	1,050	77.3	855	67.4
totals	617	100.0	429	100.0	1,359	100.0	1,269	100.0

★ abscesses in groin
Source: S. Giacomo degli Incurabili, 386, 390–2

Table 8.3 S. Giacomo degli Incurabili: symptoms
and illnesses of female patients, 1569–1570

Symptom	1569		1570	
	no.	%	no.	%
bolle/pustules	12	4.2	5	2.1
doglie/pains	12	4.2	4	1.7
gomme/gummata	0	0.0	0	0.0
piaghe/sores	0	0.0	0	0.0
rogne/scabs	2	0.7	3	1.3
tincone/★	2	0.7	1	0.4
altri/other	14	4.9	16	6.7
mal francese	1	0.3	3	1.3
malato/sick	245	85.1	208	86.7
totals	288	100.0	240	100.0

★ abscesses in groin
Source: S. Giacomo degli Incurabili, 391

tormented the sufferer chiefly at night, and were the most cruel of all the symptoms.[140]

Pustules were among the first and most readily observable symptoms to those admitting men with Mal Francese to San Giacomo, especially, as Fracastoro related, they grew 'to the size of the cup of an acorn'.[141] While abscesses in the groin were not discussed by Fracastoro, they were by Falloppio in his contemporary treatise *De Morbo Gallico* of 1563, where he says it is one of the names for a *bubone gallico*.[142] The third symptom, pains, was mentioned by all observers, Fracastoro calling it 'the most cruel of all'. The appearance of these three conditions suggests that San Giacomo concentrated on the patients with the more, if not the most, advanced stages of Mal Francese, when they had developed the more ugly and deforming symptoms of pustules and abscesses rather than simply the small ulcers. There was, however, one major difference between 1561 and 1562, those years with most details about symptoms; there was a considerable increase in the number of male patients who had pains. This suggests that guaiacum, which was administered only in the second year, was seen as especially efficacious in treating pain, which Fracastoro says occurred when the disease became more 'deeply rooted'.[143]

It was principally, of course, the debilitating nature of the pox and its effect on the outward appearance of the sick which drove the sufferers in desperation to San Giacomo. As we have seen from contemporary reactions, from chroniclers to papal bulls, this also awoke feelings of disgust among those who saw these wretched people in the streets, especially when recalling Fracastoro's vivid description of the erosion of eyes, noses and genitals. But one of the most disfiguring of the symptoms of Mal Francese mentioned by Fracastoro, the appearance of gummata 'as large as an egg or a roll of bread', did not figure prominently among this sample, especially considering that Fracastoro had noted that this symptom had become particularly characteristic of *mal franciosati* by the mid-sixteenth century.[144] Why this should have been the case is not clear from the records. It may simply have been a function of recording practices, but it is also possible that the hospital administrators had decided not to admit those who were more hideously deformed and therefore completely beyond help. This hypothesis is given extra weight if one remembers the low mortality rate at San Giacomo; the most disfigured would also have been those most likely to have died shortly after admission.

If male patients were not identified as having Mal Francese, they were very rarely labelled with any disease category at all. Instead the admitting physicians recorded only their symptoms, which of course makes it very difficult to pin down what were the other incurable diseases treated at San Giacomo. However, there is one symptom which clearly acted as a distinguishing mark of non-pox patients, *piaghe* or sores. A comparison between Tables 8.1 and 8.2 shows that while a mere 2 per cent of *mal franciosati* had sores, over 50 per cent of those with some other type of incurable disease were identified with this symptom. Indeed by the early seventeenth century a contemporary commentator, Camillo Fanucci, recorded that the main reason for admission to San Giacomo was that patients were 'sick with sores from an incurable disease'.[145] At the same time the regulations for the acceptance of those admitted for Holy Wood make a clear distinction between these patients and their more regular clientele, the *impiagati normali* who were transferred to the *hospitaletto* in order to make room for the crowds.[146] The best-known example of a patient admitted with this symptom in this period was Camillo de Lellis with his 'incurable sore', which none of his biographers ever have had the temerity to attribute to the pox!

The predominance of *piaghe* as a symptom can also be seen graphically in Figure 8.9, which plots the admissions of non-pox sufferers from January 1561 to December 1562. In 1561 admissions from this symptom remained high after the second month and indeed peaked in March and June to August, only falling at the end of the year. The reasons for this seasonal pattern must remain conjectural. They probably just reflect admission policies rather than any exogenous influences, especially, as we have seen, because not only was this a period of relative health and prosperity, but also San Giacomo was likely to have concentrated more on incurable conditions than on acute diseases generated by epidemics. The second year, on the other hand, demonstrates a different pattern with admissions of those with sores falling in the

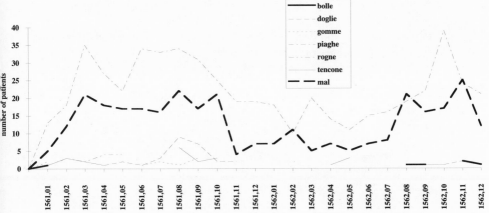

Figure 8.9 S. Giacomo degli Incurabili: symptoms of male patients (excluding those with Mal
Francese) admitted 1561–1562
Source: ASR, S. Giacomo degli Incurabili, 386

late winter and early spring. Then, although there was a slight increase in
March, the numbers fell as the hospital began to prepare for the large number
of people to be admitted for Holy Wood treatment. Only after these seasonal
admissions had all left in July did the non-Mal Francese patients enter once
again, with a surge of the *piaghati* towards the end of the year.[147]

Diseased body parts

If the symptoms provided by the patient registers remain vague, another way
to add flesh to the profile of the hospital's clientele is to examine the
information concerning the parts of the body affected by their complaints.
Indeed outward physical disfigurement was the feature which was remarked
on most by contemporaries and was potentially a general problem associated
with any incurable disease. It will be remembered from accounts of reactions
during the first few decades after the outbreak of the epidemic that all
commentators registered their horror of the physical decay associated with
Mal Francese. One of the most trenchant was in Leo X's *Salvatoris Nostri*,
which talked about the sick crippled by their disease and 'giving offence to
the sight and smell' of passers-by in the streets.[148] Later commentators who
remarked on the sicknesses of San Giacomo patients always stressed the
incurable sores, which must have been the symptom most visible to visitors.[149]
This can, in fact, be confirmed by linking the symptoms of male patients
recorded in the hospital's registers with the parts of the body affected for our
sample years, 1561–2 and 1569–70.

This analysis is far from straightforward. First, details were not recorded for
the body parts of over a third (37 per cent) of the 4,615 male patients
admitted, including both those who were and those who were not identified
as suffering from Mal Francese. Furthermore, no information was provided

Table 8.4 S. Giacomo degli Incurabili: symptoms and known body parts of male patients admitted 1561–1562 and 1569–1570

Body part	Symptom	1561	1562	1569	1570	total no.	total %
1. body							
	– no symptom	24	39	19	25	107	3.7
	ascesso/abscess	2	4	2	1	9	0.3
	storpiato/crippled		1			1	0.0
	fistola/fistula	5		9	2	16	0.6
	doglie/pains	11	115	1	2	129	4.4
	pelarella/peeling skin	1	2			3	0.1
	taroli/pustules	11	8	2		21	0.7
	rogne/scabs	13	3			16	0.6
	piaghe/sores	10	9		1	20	0.7
	tincone★	2	1			3	0.1
	gomme/gommata	20	4	6	2	32	1.1
	misc.	1				1	0.0
Sub-total						358	12.3
2. head							
	– no symptom	13	11	76	50	150	5.2
	ascesso/abscess	3	3		1	7	0.2
	cecità/blindness			1		1	0.0
	catarro/catarrh			1	1	2	0.1
	muto/dumb			1		1	0.0
	fistola/fistula				1	1	0.0
	doglie/pains	2				2	0.1
	taroli/pustules	1			1	2	0.1
	tigna/ringworm	1			1	2	0.1
	piaghe/sores	18	8	1	1	28	1.0
	gomme/gommata		4	3	1	8	0.3
	ferita/wound	1	1		1	3	0.1
	misc.			1		1	0.0
Sub-total						208	7.2
3. genital area							
	– no symptom	101	77	84	84	346	11.9
	ascesso/abscess			1		1	0.0
	non può orinare/ cannot urinate			1		1	0.0
	storta/deformed		1			1	0.0
	fistola/fistula	3		3		6	0.2
	doglie/pains	17	13			30	1.0
	taroli/pustules	1				1	0.0
	tincone★	95	52	69	83	299	10.3
Sub-total						685	23.6

Table 8.4   *Continued*

Body part	Symptom	1561	1562	1569	1570	total no.	total %
4. limbs							
	– no symptom	32	24	523	476	1,055	36.3
	ascesso/abscess	10	8	8	3	29	1.0
	storpiato/crippled			2	1	3	0.1
	frattura/fractures		3			3	0.1
	morigini/marks				1	1	0.0
	doglie/pains	16	8		2	26	0.9
	paralitico/paralysis			3	1	4	0.1
	taroli/pustules	1	1	1		3	0.1
	rogne/scabs		1			1	0.0
	piaghe/sores	289	216	7	7	519	17.9
	tincone*	1			1	2	0.1
	gomme/gommata	1			2	3	0.1
	ferita/wound		1			1	0.0
	misc.	1		1		2	0.1
Sub-total						1,652	56.9
TOTAL						2,903	

* abscesses in groin
Source: ASR, S. Giacomo degli Incurabili, 386, 390–2

about the symptoms of 2,566 or 56 per cent of the total. Whether this was due to sloppy record-keeping or because no very obvious symptom was evident is difficult to determine. However, it cannot be irrelevant that 28 per cent of those men admitted whose records contain no information about their body parts were described as having 'pains', a condition which is so generic as to make a specific diagnosis difficult. This would also help to explain why no part of the body was specified when the whole of an individual's body was wracked with pain.

In Table 8.4 we have taken only those entries in our sample years where a body part is specified and summarised the symptom categories for the main areas: from the most generic of 'body' to head, genital area and limbs. In this way we have reduced our sample by about a third by excluding any entry where no body part is specified (1,712 of 4,615).

The majority (57 per cent) had diseased limbs: arms, hands, legs and feet. These were the most visible parts of the anatomy and most likely to have attracted attention if they were covered with sores, as was the case in the majority of instances where a symptom was listed. This was also true of the head, where abscesses, gommata and sores were identified. These may very well have included the ulcerated pustules mentioned by Fracastoro. In contrast, in those parts of the body which were normally covered with clothes (genitals, chest and back), the main symptoms experienced were pains, derived no doubt from the patients' own descriptions rather than the direct observations of the admitting physician or surgeon. But there were others, albeit in the minority, who were distinguished immediately because their sickness had left them crippled. The early seventeenth-century regulations governing the admission of patients for the Holy Wood talked about first admitting the most wretched because of their condition. Those described as 'the crippled, with sores and the more wretched and beggarly' were placed in the lower ward rather than in the larger one upstairs where people were usually treated with guaiacum. In this way those seriously ill would be provided with their own latrines rather than having to share the 'common places'.[150]

Finally, it is significant for the theme of this book that 24 per cent of cases for which we know the affected body part should have been identified as being 'sick' in the genital area. They may very well have been suffering from Mal Francese, suggested by the fact that the largest number (299 of 685) were labelled as having *tencone*, the abcesses in the groin which medical writers at the time identified as a specific symptom of the French Disease.

Until now we have not gone any further than most contemporary observers who made the automatic assumption that all those patients admitted to San Giacomo with the symptoms discussed above were poor. The next section will examine how far San Giacomo's records can be used to determine more exactly the social status of patients and to what extent they were drawn from that vast floating population of beggars who were such a feature of medieval and early modern Rome. This leads to the further question, of how far San Giacomo performed a mopping-up operation for vagrants with incurable diseases. Or did its admission policy tend to follow that of the general hospitals for acute conditions and concentrate rather on the respectable poor who had fallen on hard times?

Social Status of Applicants

These questions are easier to pose than to answer from the patient records of San Giacomo, given that a negligible amount of information was provided about the occupations of applicants. However, there appears to have been little doubt that San Giacomo, in common with other Incurabili hospitals in Italy as well as Spain, France and Germany,[151] did cater predominantly for the poorer levels of society. From the very beginning, as has been seen from Leo X's bull *Salvatoris Nostri*, San Giacomo was envisaged as a place for *pauperes* and *miserabiles personas*. By the late seventeenth century little seemed to have changed. One contemporary, Carlo Bartolomeo Piazza, characterised the patients of San Giacomo in his book on the charities of Rome as 'poveri incurabili' and 'miserabili impiagati'.[152] These statements, however, beg the wider and more intractable question about how this mass of *pauperes* was constituted and whether there might not have been different types of poor people among this undifferentiated mass of *poveri incurabili*.

We have seen from San Giacomo's admission policy that there were two distinct types of patient: the vast majority who were just categorised as 'poveri' and a smaller more select group who had been especially 'recommended' for treatment. They had ten beds reserved for them.[153] Francisco Delicado obviously was in this second category, but so also were a handful of men and women whose letters of recommendation have chanced to survive for the years between 1575 and 1587.[154]

Most of this sample were male; indeed the percentage of females present (19 per cent of 17) was only slightly higher than the proportion in the hospital as a whole in the second half of the sixteenth century. Many of the letters stressed the poverty of these people caused by their illness, as in the case of Cesare di Tatacola cited above, or the 'pover homo' who was in the unenviable position of 'having consumed what he had and not being able to work and the sickness having increased such that he is forced to travel through the streets begging for his livelihood and one day he will die if he is not helped'.[155] Indeed we can see clearly in these letters the downward spiral of poverty for those who contracted an incurable disease, for it meant that they were unable to work for their living. Although there is little information about their occupations, there was a scattering of servants, particularly those employed in the housholds of wealthly patricians or cardinals who had recommended them for treatment. Hence the example cited above of Dominico Genovese, 'my old servant', or the two boys, described as 'putti', Niccolò and Agostino, 'who served in the house of the Illustrious Signor Mario Sforza'.[156] Others came from a slightly higher professional scale, such as Giovanni Paulo, who worked as 'spenditore' or cashier in the household of Cardinal Maffeo.[157] Employees of cardinals also used their influence with their masters to obtain favours from their relatives, for example the brother of the barber of a cardinal. Connections between individual religious who ran hospitals meant that two chaplains who were employed at S. Spirito were recommended by the prior of the hospital for treatment with Acqua del Legno.[158]

These few letters suggest, then, that if those who carried letters of recommendation came from a mixed social background, many of them were linked through ties of employment to wealthy and influential patrons. The frequent appearance of cardinals in particular underlines their connections not just with each other, but also with the world of charitable institutions, for, as has been seen, all Roman hospitals were headed by cardinal protectors.

Those women who arrived at San Giacomo through recommendation shared the same patronage networks, although, as with the main patient registers, there is less information available about their background. Only one was definitely married, while two of them were children. The first child was Margarita. She was described as the daughter of Gentile – though it is unclear whether he was still alive – and had lost her mother, but was now living with a Monna Domenica da Castello. The older woman had evidently been driven to desperation by Margarita's sickness; she declared that she did not have the 'wherewithal to help her'. The other example is an anonymous letter from a man who had sent his relative to San Giacomo with a 'putta inferma incurabile', revealing at the end that she was 'his own daughter'.[159]

While these examples may have been a better-connected sample than the majority of San Giacomo's clientele, they also underline the fact that even among this category the hospital admitted a wide range of conditions. Thus at one end there were those who were just described as 'sick', like Giovan Domenico da Padova, who had 'been advised by the physicians' to take the Acqua del Legno, while at the other extreme there was the man who had pains in his 'arms, shoulders and legs' so that 'he was not able to work in any way'.[160] This points, then, to the connection between sickness and poverty, which might reduce even a man or woman with a respectable profession to the level of financial destitution so that they came to be characterised by contemporary observers as 'poor' or 'wretched'. Unfortunately the patient registers of San Giacomo provide little information about the occupational and social background of its clientele, so it is difficult to guage the accuracy of these general labels. One additional piece of information, the clothes which patients wore on admission, does, however, provide some extra indication of social status and it is to the results of a very preliminary analysis that we shall now turn.

Patients and their clothes

As has been indicated, the description of patients' clothes is more detailed than any other piece of information in the records; it had to be exact enough for the hospital servants to identify the bundle on the patient's exit. This can be seen in the case of the Corsican Matteo, who was wearing the following when he entered San Giacomo on 20 November 1562: 'a cape of grey cloth, worn according to the fashion of a *contadino*, a leather jerkin, a doublet of old linen and an undergarment of old red cloth, an old black cap, a sword belt of white leather, canions of old black cloth, hose of old torn linen, an old shirt in a bundle . . . and a leather purse'.[161] This entry summons up an exact and vivid picture of this man, who had come to San Giacomo in search of treatment for a sore on his left leg. Clearly, though, Matteo was much more sick than the bare statement of his symptom – 'sore' – would lead one to believe; he died in hospital only seven days later. Whether or not he had come specifically to Rome from Corsica for treatment at San Giacomo is impossible to say. More likely, given his sword belt, he had at some time in the past been employed as a mercenary and had fallen on hard times as a result of his illness, which may have been related to his profession. His financial position is suggested by the repeated use of the word 'old' to describe his clothes, some of which may, like the jerkin of Morocco leather, have originally been of good quality.

The same type of picture of clothes in a ragged condition emerges when one looks at how the women were dressed in 1569–70: 'Joanna from Milan, who is sick around her waist, a black cloak of old black cloth, a man's old jacket, an old grey strip across her dress, white cloth stockings and a shirt in a bundle'.[162] Two main differences emerge between male and female dress. The first is that women were on the whole dressed in duller colours, tending to wear black, grey and white rather than the brighter colours of the men. The second is that women appear to have arrived at San Giacomo with even fewer clothes, which by their very scarcity underline their poverty. This is exemplified by the case of Isabetta from Ancona, who entered on 12 April 1570, only to die two days later, and whose clothes had all been reduced to rags. Or Maria from Anguillara, who had something wrong with her feet and was wearing only 'a torn dress of red cloth, girdle of torn black cloth, a shift in a bundle'.[163]

These examples emphasise the strong connection between disease and poverty. Those dressed in ragged clothes probably came from that vast floating population of beggars for which Rome was so well known in the early modern period.[164] It would, however, be a mistake to generalise from these examples and characterise all the patients admitted to San Giacomo as destitute. There were obviously as many categories of poor people as appeared in the famous contemporary descriptions of beggars, from the worthy, deserving poor to the rascal who pretended to be sick or maimed in order to excite the compassion of passers-by to provide him with alms.[165]

Even so, when a patient is described in the records as wearing rags or ragged clothes it is probably safe to assume that he or she came from the poorest levels of society. It is therefore interesting to note that the proportion of people who fell into this category did not remain constant but changed from year to year. Thus there was a considerable difference between the percentage of male patients in the first two sample years whose clothes, either individually or in total, were described as 'tutti stracciati': from 42 per cent in 1561 to 27 per cent in 1562. The reason for this reduction must have been related to, if not directly caused by, the differences between those who were admitted for Holy Wood treatment (1562) and those who were not (1561). Evidently admissions in 1561 came from a poorer pool of people who suffered from an 'incurable' disease which did not necessarily need to be treated with guaiacum as in 1562. An example of one of these poorer types admitted in 1561 is a man called Biego di Leonardo from Parma, who entered on 24 March and was wearing 'a ragged black cape, a gown of white cloth, all torn, a bodice of the same linen, canions of linen, all torn, livery hose, that is one of white cloth, and the other of linen, all torn, an old black beret, a ragged shirt in a bundle'.[166] However, it is interesting that, although he is described as being ragged in appearance, his clothes indicate that at one stage he had been in respectable employment. Originally he probably worked in the household of a nobleman, hence his livery hose, but now through illness and misfortune he had fallen on very hard times.

This relationship between social class, as reflected in the basic distinction between those wearing ragged or non-ragged clothes, the patients' known symptoms and the treatment provided is explored further in Figures 8.10 and 8.11. In 1561 almost half (42 per cent) of male patients were dressed in ragged clothes. This suggests that there was a relatively high incidence of the very poor among the hospital's clientele in this year when Holy Wood was not provided. The major symptom was the generic category of *piaghe*; the 'incurable sores', as we have seen, had become the identifying mark of the majority of the clientele. In the case of the other symptoms which might be identified more closely with Mal Francese, there was a predominance of those who were slightly better dressed.

This association between the less ragged and Mal Francese in particular and those conditions treated with Holy Wood in general is confirmed in 1562. In this year when patients were admitted for guaiacum-wood treatment the proportion of ragged patients dropped to 27 per cent. Moreover, there was a massive increase in those with pains, the main symptom associated with Mal Francese. Indeed nearly half of those identified with the pox in 1562 were better dressed.

The two years from 1569 to 1570 saw a similar pattern, though even more exaggerated: a reduction of those in rags from 36 to 13 per cent. This cannot be explained simply by reference to guaiacum, because this treatment was provided in both years. Instead we have to look for wider explanations, in particular to the extreme shortage of food in 1569, which may have reduced a higher proportion of the clientele to penury, leaving them with even less available cash to spend on clothes.[167] In both years those people with symptoms associated predominantly with Mal Francese (*tincone* and *doglie*) were again in less ragged attire.

The same overall pattern seems to have been true of women, although with the sparsity of information about their symptoms it is difficult to be as precise about the relationship between particular conditions and their dress. There was a clear drop in those wearing ragged clothes during the spring months of each year at the time patients were admitted for guaiacum. Despite this similarity with male admissions, a much lower proportion of females were recorded as dressed in ragged clothes (19 to 21 per cent). It is unclear why this should have been so; it may simply reflect the lower standards of recording information about women rather than the possibility that they were more affluent than their male counterparts. Indeed, judging by their entries, women

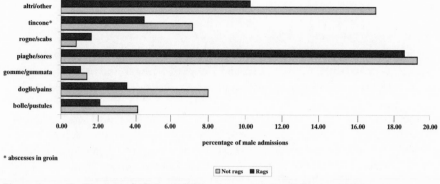

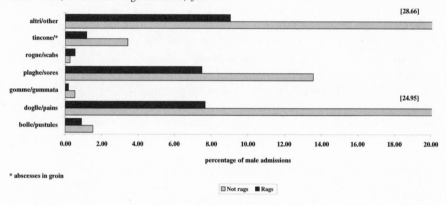

appear to have been poorer than the men, given that they arrived with even fewer clothes.

The greater poverty of female patients has also been noted by a study of a more general hospital in fifteenth-century Florence. Here, although there were fewer women wearing torn clothes, almost double were recorded with no clothes at all. Even if it is extremely doubtful that they arrived wearing nothing, their level of clothing must have been very low indeed if they were recorded as not even being dressed in rags, since hospitals tended to record virtually every stitch of clothing which might have been worth selling on the death of a patient.[168]

To take this analysis further we need to examine in more detail the types of clothing worn by San Giacomo's patients; we shall concentrate on the male records for our sample years because they provide a greater range of information. As we have seen from the entries in the registers for the Sienese Ferdinando and the Corsican Matteo, there was some variation in terms of type and colour of clothing worn by men entering the hospital. However, once we move away from examining individual entries to a broad analysis of all the males admitted in our sample years we discover that the majority of patients wore some or all of the following types of clothes depending on their financial status: shirt, doublet, breeches, stockings, shoes and an overgarment.

Obviously within these wide categories there was a range not just in the type of material and garment, but also in the condition. Thus poorer patients wore fewer and more ragged clothes and the less impoverished wore garments which were heavier and of better quality. Table 8.5 presents a preliminary analysis of what seems to be the most distinctive types of clothing worn by male patients – in addition, that is, to those basic garments worn by everybody. The clothing has been divided up into five major types, two of which (2 and 3) might indicate that the individual exercised a particular occupation, a third (4) might show that the individual was a traveller or pilgrim, and the other two (1 and 5) reflected some social or financial standing.

The two main occupational groupings, as far as one can judge from the clothing, were ecclesiastical and military. As we have seen in the case of Francisco Delicado, San Giacomo admitted priests for Holy Wood treatment, and here they have been identified wearing either a scapular (*pazienza*) or a cassock (*sottana*). Although there were relatively few clerical patients, more were admitted in 1561, the year when guaiacum was not administered, suggesting that perhaps by this time clerics were less likely to receive Holy Wood treatment in hospital than their secular brothers. However, the borderline between clerical and lay was clearly rather indistinct; those men recorded as wearing a *pazienza* or *sottana* were not actually described as priests in the records, perhaps because they were only in minor clerical orders.

More numerous were the men whom we have categorised as from a military background, because they were wearing either a soldier's hat or a sword-belt, although, of course, one has to be careful when interpreting these data given that somebody could easily have bought these items second-hand. Even bearing in mind this reservation, it cannot be insignificant that 19 per cent of all male patients who entered in 1561 and 20 per cent in 1562 wore a sword-belt. Although no more information is available about these men admitted in 1561–2 to help associate them more closely with a military background, once we move to the end of the decade a clearer identification is possible. The majority of the men wearing sword-belts in 1569–70 were described as members of the pope's Swiss Guards. As we have seen, the connection between the papal guards and San Giacomo was already strong, since they helped to maintain order during periods when patients were admitted for guaiacum treatment. However, these men were not just staying overnight during their guard duty, but were genuinely sick. The majority of the twenty-five who entered in 1570 had something wrong with their legs, which presumably rendered them immobile or at the very least unable to perform their duties properly. What exactly they were suffering from is unclear, but it cannot be irrelevant that a fifth of the 1,110 male patients

Table 8.5 S. Giacomo degli Incurabili: selected items of clothing worn by patients admitted 1561–1562 and 1569–1570

	1561 male		1562 male		1569 male		1570 male		1569 female	1570 female
	no.	%	no.	%	no.	%	no.	%	no.	no.
Overgarments										
cappotto	16	3.4	7	1.6	61	19.3	37	13.5		
gabbano	24	5.0	23	5.2	8	2.5	11	4.0		
saio	120	25.2	88	19.7	65	20.6	36	13.1		
saltimbarca	45	9.4	52	11.7	58	18.4	15	5.5		
Military										
cappello d'arme	4	0.8	3	0.7	1	0.3	0	0.0		
cintura da portare spada	159	33.3	223	50.0	10	3.2	25	9.1		
Ecclesiastical										
pazienza/sottana	27	5.7	0	0.0	5	1.6	5	1.8		
Knapsack – zaino	19	4.0	9	2.0	0	0.0	0	0.0		
Shoeless – senza scarpa	117	24.5	83	18.6	117	37.0	149	54.4	8	14
minus Duplicates	54		42		9		4			
Total known	477		446		316		274		8	14
Unknown	359		664		1,049		1,027		281	225

Source: ASR, S. Giacomo degli Incurabili 386, 390–2

admitted to San Giacomo in 1562 wore sword-belts and of these 68 per cent had Mal Francese.

Turning instead to the first category we see a variety of overgarments, from the more generic *cappotto* or cloak of heavy material to the *gabbano* or heavy travelling cloak or mantle, to the *saltimbarca* or loose cape worn over the shoulders. While it is sometimes difficult now to capture the exact differences between these terms,[169] clearly they all carried a precise significance to the recording clerks. They also tell us something of the provenance of those who wore them. For example, in one context a *saltimbarca* was a term used by Florentines to denote a cloak or mantle without sleeves worn by Tuscan *contadini*, though in time it came to be used as a term for a sailor's cloak which apparently, because it was sleeveless and worn over the head, allowed them considerable liberty of movement.[170]

All these various types of overgarment were, then, well adapted for travellers and, as with those who arrived at San Giacomo with knapsacks, suggest that many of the patients came from outside Rome. This suggestion is confirmed, as we shall see, by our analysis of the geographical origins of the patients, most of whom derived from outside Rome. Indeed it would not have made sense for those who were resident in the city to wear such heavy garments, especially in the spring and early summer when the Holy Wood patients were admitted. Instead it is probable that those who fell into the 'shoeless' category were more likely to have been living in Rome and possibly came from the crowds of beggars who thronged the city. They, however, never made up more than 14 per cent of the total intake and, like those in rags, tended to be most numerous in 1561 when Holy Wood was not on offer.

This discussion of patients' clothes can be taken one stage further, although here we move from a quantitative to a qualitative analysis. This will represent a snapshot of individuals by combining patient records from San Giacomo with the Perugian collection of mid-sixteenth-century watercolours depicting people sick with Mal Francese. These pictures represent men and women from a wide range of social backgrounds from the poor and destitute to the more affluent in the initial stages of the disease.

At the lower level are two men who must be in the advanced stages of the disease since both are crippled and unable to walk except with the aid of crutches (Plate 8.14). The first man is slightly better dressed than the second. He is shown wearing a collar, a shirt, hose, stockings and shoes, as well as a *saio* or loose tunic which falls from the shoulders to above his knees. The second is clearly the poorer of the two because he is wearing very simple garments: a shirt which is caught at the waist with a belt and over his shoulder a cloak or wrap. His sores, which are evident on his right leg, are covered with bandages on his left leg. Whether because of poverty or because it is too painful for him to wear anything on his feet, he is represented as shoeless. He might very well have been taken to represent Antonio da Bologna, who

Plate 8.14   Crippled male Mal Francese patients

entered San Giacomo on 15 October 1561. He was simply dressed in 'an old woollen gown, old torn linen stockings, an old black beret, a torn shirt'. He is recorded with sores on his legs and in fact died in hospital the following April.[171]

Slightly higher up the social scale are the next two men (Plate 8.15). The second is evidently in discomfort, with his left arm in a sling, and he is already beginning to lose his hair, either as a result of mercury treatment or because he is in the more advanced stages of Mal Francese. The second is supporting himself on a crutch. Both hold out their right hands to the viewer to show their spots. In each case they are dressed in a shirt and doublet with a trunk-hose, shoes and stockings, suggesting some level of respectability equivalent to the status of Ferdinando di Francesco the Sienese, whose entry appears in Plate 8.13 and who was sick from the abscesses in the groin attributed specifically to Mal Francese.

Next we encounter two reasonably affluent young men who, judging by the spots on their faces, are probably suffering from the early stages of Mal Francese (Plate 8.16). The dress of the second is in particular quite elegant, with a ruff around his neck, a doublet and a slashed jerkin or *colleto*, a cloak, hose, canions and garters, stockings and shoes, and a sword to denote his social if not his professional status.

Finally, we come to examples of two women, both of whom are clearly begging in the streets and are discomfited by their spots and ulcers, caused by Mal Francese (Plate 8.17). The one lying recumbent is dressed very simply in an undergarment with a skirt and some type of gown, but she has rolled up her sleeves to show off the spots on her arms in order to excite pity and

Plate 8.15   Male Mal Francese patients

hopefully alms. Such was Barbara from Modena, who entered San Giacomo on 14 September 1569 suffering from 'male suo per la vita' and dressed simply in 'a beige gown, black hose, shirt', and who died only three days later.[172]

This discussion of clothing has suggested that the vast majority of patients at San Giacomo in this period were poor. However, this was not uniform poverty. Not only were some more privileged groups admitted on the recommendation of patrons, but there were those who had followed professions in the army and Church and others who had been involved in agricultural trades.

These conclusions are inevitably tentative given the inexactness of the sources and the fact that the clothing worn by patients may not always have reflected their actual occupations, not least because of the importance of the second-hand clothes market among the poor. Indeed hospitals were one source for dealers in second-hand clothes; these institutions generated extra income through selling off the garments of patients who had died.[173] Even with this qualification, the records do provide a useful guide to the social status of those admitted for treatment. However, when comparing the way that San Giacomo was run and the way its patients were admitted with the results of the few studies which have been undertaken of more general hospitals in Italy in this period, the question remains how different was the clientele of San Giacomo given the nature of the diseases treated and the contemporary perception of Rome as a centre for the poor.

Plate 8.16 Affluent male Mal Francese patients

If a comparison between San Giacomo's clientele in Rome with those of general hospitals in Florence has disclosed roughly similar levels of mortality, the social status of the *incurabili* in Rome was clearly much lower, as revealed by their ragged appearance. This may very well have been a function of the diseases which had been contracted by their patients, though this can be answered only by comparison with other Incurabili hospitals in Italy. But undoubtedly an important related factor which determined the social level of applicants was Rome's peculiar status as the capital of Christianity. The poor were therefore attracted to Rome as a profitable place to beg and to San Giacomo as the largest Incurabili hospital in the peninsula. The strength of these two factors can be examined further through the records of the geographical origins of their patients.

Geographical Origins of Patients at San Giacomo

Contemporary comments about the provenance of patients treated at San Giacomo reveal a different policy from that adopted by other Incurabili hospitals in Italy. Camillo Fanucci and Carlo Bartolomeo Piazza remarked in their surveys of Roman charitable institutions that the inmates of San Giacomo were from 'ogni natione'.[174] That this was not just a perception of outsiders is confirmed by the records of the hospital itself, which described its

Plate 8.17   Female Mal Francese patients

patients in 1568 as 'the weak poor [*poveri languenti*] both men and women and from many countries'.[175]

This open-door policy was strikingly different from that of Incurabili hospitals elsewhere. The principle adopted in Florence, Genoa, Naples and Pavia was the same.[176] The Florentine statutes of 1574 reveal, for example, that their main priority was the 'inhabitants of Florence and in the country-side. But as far as other foreigners are concerned normally the Prior decides on whether to admit them according to the cause of their poverty'.[177]

These general comments about the provenance of the clientele of San Giacomo when compared with Incurabili hospitals elsewhere would seem to be supported by the fact that in our sample years the percentage of male patients from Rome itself was only 5.6 per cent, though somewhat higher for women at 11.7 per cent (see Table 8.6).[178] However, establishing their provenance is not straightforward, and indeed there is a growing literature which underlines the complexity of the problem. It is difficult to know whether or not an individual described, for example, as a Florentine was a recent arrival or had been living in Rome for a while. Some medieval historians of Rome distinguish between, for example, Florentines described in contemporary records as 'da' or 'di Firenze' and those described simply as a 'Fiorentino'.[179] The former are taken to have been genuine recent arrivals from Florence, whereas the others are seen as longer-term residents who had come to Rome some time before, or whose fathers had done so. This is undoubtedly a complex question and the answer probably varies according to both the type of records consulted and the period concerned.

In the case of San Giacomo's mid-sixteenth-century patients,[180] we have decided to treat these two categories of provenance as the same. The justifi-cation for this is three-fold. The first and most general justification is expressed in the statement of the mid-sixteenth-century chronicler Marcello Alberini that 'It is clear that the Romans only form a minority in the city, since it is the refuge for all nations and a common home to the entire world.'[181] Secondly, the records of San Giacomo tend to use these terms interchangeably. Thus in one register a patient might be described as a 'Fiorentino' and in another as 'di' or 'da Firenze'. This suggests that not only was there no hard-and-fast rule concerning recording practices, but there may have been little distinction in the minds of either the administrators or the patients themselves. This conclusion is further borne out by correlating the survival rates of both categories. Thus it might be expected that the survival rate of residents of Rome would have been higher, especially compared with those coming from abroad. However, an analysis of all these categories shows that there was an almost perfect match – the correlation was virtually 100 per cent – between the proportion of those who lived and died regardless of how their origins were described. This was true for both males and females.

Leaving aside for a moment the problem of how recently patients had arrived in Rome, we can see from Table 8.6 that people were attracted to San Giacomo from all over Italy. Very broadly if one divides the peninsula into three main blocks (north, centre and south), the percentage of patients who came from each region was 44, 38 and 19 (including Rome). Perhaps most surprising is the fact that relatively few people came from the southern province, especially given that there were many more large Incurabili hospitals north than south of Rome. This pattern probably reflects the lower levels of population in these areas and also the complementary role of another substantial Incurabili hospital not far south of Rome in Naples.[182] As one might expect, nearly half of patients from the south came from Lazio (if one excludes those from Rome), followed by Campania and Abruzzo.

Patients from areas in the top third of the peninsula, the most distant from Rome on mainland Italy, accounted for almost half of the total (44 per cent). At first sight this seems rather curious given that it was these areas where, as we have seen, the majority of Incurabili hospitals had been founded. But the reason may be linked to the fact that these were the most urbanised regions of Italy and, as we have seen, there were close connections between the Incurabili hospitals in each city. Furthermore, the very presence of these institutions in these areas may have served to raise awareness of availability of treatment for incurable diseases, perhaps leading to disappointment for those who were turned away because of these hospitals' lack of resources and geographically restrictive admission policy. The incurably sick poor who came from outside the large urban centres would therefore have been forced to travel to Rome to the largest and most affluent treatment centre, which, moreover, welcomed rather than rejected non-residents. The same would also have been true of the central Italian provinces. Here there was a particularly strong attraction from Tuscany. This area was in fact more highly represented than any other part of Italy, with 26 per cent of the total. The reasons for this

Table 8.6 S. Giacomo degli Incurabili: known geographical origins of discharged patients from Italy (including Sicily) 1561–1562 and 1569–1570

Province	Live						Dead						Overall totals			
	male		female		total		male		female		total		male		female	
	no.	%	no.	%	no.	%	no.	%	no.	%	no.	%	no.	%	no.	%
North																
Emilia Romagna	407	13.9	54	16.2	461	14.2	60	16.4	14	20.3	74	17.1	467	14.2	68	16.9
Friuli	3	0.1	1	0.3	4	0.1							3	0.1	1	0.2
Liguria	53	1.8	3	0.9	56	1.7	7	1.9	6	8.7	7	1.6	60	1.8	3	0.7
Lombardia	465	15.9	14	4.2	479	14.7	60	16.4	2	2.9	66	15.2	525	16.0	20	5.0
Piemonte	180	6.2	9	2.7	189	5.8	24	6.6	2	2.9	26	6.0	204	6.2	11	2.7
Savoia	39	1.3	1	0.3	40	1.2	4	1.1	1	1.4	5	1.2	43	1.3	2	0.5
Adige	28	1.0	1	0.3	29	0.9	2	0.5	1	1.4	2	0.5	30	0.9	1	0.2
Val d'Aosta	1	0.0			1	0.0							1	0.0		
Veneto	103	3.5	18	5.4	121	3.7	16	4.4	1	1.4	17	3.9	119	3.6	19	4.7
Sub-total	1,279	43.8	101	30.2	1,380	42.4	173	47.4	24	34.8	197	45.4	1,452	44.2	125	31.0

	N	%	N	%	N	%	N	%	N	%	N	%	N	%	N	%
Centre																
Marche	215	7.4	19	5.7	234	7.2	34	9.3	8	11.6	42	9.7	249	7.6	27	6.7
Toscana	657	22.5	102	30.5	759	23.3	77	21.1	18	26.1	95	21.9	734	22.3	120	29.8
Umbria	231	7.9	39	11.7	270	8.3	25	6.8	5	7.2	30	6.9	256	7.8	44	10.9
Sub-total	1,103	37.8	160	47.9	1,263	38.8	136	37.3	31	44.9	167	38.5	1,239	37.7	191	47.4
Roma	171	5.9	42	12.6	213	6.5	13	3.6	5	7.2	18	4.1	184	5.6	47	11.7
South																
Abruzzo	52	1.8	5	1.5	57	1.8	4	1.1	2	2.9	6	1.4	56	1.7	7	1.7
Basilicata	15	0.5			15	0.5	2	0.5			2	0.5	17	0.5		
Calabria	43	1.5	3	0.9	46	1.4	4	1.1			4	0.9	47	1.4	3	0.7
Campania	91	3.1	6	1.8	97	3.0	8	2.2	2	2.9	10	2.3	99	3.0	8	2.0
Catania	1	0.0			1	0.0							1	0.0		
Lazio	113	3.9	16	4.8	129	4.0	20	5.5	2	2.9	22	5.1	133	4.0	18	4.5
Puglia	13	0.4			13	0.4	1	0.3	3	4.3	4	0.9	14	0.4	3	0.7
Sicilia	40	1.4	1	0.3	41	1.3	4	1.1			4	0.9	44	1.3	1	0.2
Sub-total	368	12.6	31	9.3	399	124.3	43	11.8	9	13.0	52	12.0	411	12.5	40	9.9
Totals	2,921	100.0	334	100.0	3,255	100.0	365	100.0	69	100.0	434	100.0	3,286	100.0	403	100.0

Source: ASR, S. Giacomo degli Incurabili, 386, 390–2

bias are not made obvious from internal evidence in the hospital's records and the argument from geographical proximity is not a complete explanation, given that Umbria, which is equally close, contributed only 9 per cent of the patient population. As we have noted, this was not quite so true of female patients, many more of whom came from Rome and central Italy (59 per cent) than was true of men (43 per cent).

The reasons for these biases must also be sought in the economic and cultural links between particular parts of the peninsula and the city of Rome itself.[183] Many of these links can be attributed to the influence of individual popes, who attracted large numbers of people from their own provinces in general and their own cities in particular. These included the architects, artists and sculptors associated with the grand building and decorative projects promoted by many popes, as well as important commercial and financial interests which helped to finance these enterprises. Others from a more humble background were also attracted to Rome in the wake of these movements of the more famous and better heeled. These would have included suppliers and artisans, as well as many servants and staff for the households of popes and cardinals, who frequently lived in lavish style.

The effect of the influence of a series of fifteenth- and sixteenth-century popes on the provenance of the residents of the city can be seen very clearly in the 1527 Census of Rome; although forty years earlier than our registers it represents the nearest Census to the date of our records. In Table 8.7 we have compared the declared geographical origins of San Giacomo patients in the mid-sixteenth century with the 3,496 household heads whose provenance was recorded in 1527 before the famous sack of the city.

The broad geographical distribution between Italians and non-Italians in the city was of roughly the same order of magnitude, with slightly fewer (5 per cent) patients from abroad. Within Italy there were two marked differences between the two samples. First, there were fewer patients recorded as originating from Rome and Lazio, suggesting that San Giacomo's patients were more itinerant than the population at large. But more significant was the even greater bias of San Giacomo patients towards central Italy: 33 per cent compared with 19 per cent. The process through which Tuscans were attracted to Rome had been accelerated in the late fifteenth and early sixteenth centuries with the election of the two Medici popes, Leo X (1513–21) and Clement VII (1523–34). They brought with them large numbers of Tuscans and in particular Florentines.[184] The bias in San Giacomo's patients towards Tuscany obviously reflects these general factors, exaggerated in the case of the hospital by the strong association between the Medici popes and the Incurabili hospitals, especially those in Rome and Florence, which they helped to promote.

The considerable attraction of the north among both sample populations can also be explained by the long-standing economic and political links

Table 8.7 Known geographical origins of patients of S. Giacomo degli Incurabili, 1561–1562 and 1569–1570, and household heads from Census of City of Rome, 1527

	S. Giacomo		City of Rome	
	no.	%	no.	%
Mainland Italy				
North	1,577	36.4	1,221	34.9
Centre	1,430	33.0	666	19.1
Rome and Lazio	382	8.8	573	16.4
South	255	5.9	142	4.1
Sub-total	3,644	84.2	2,602	74.4
Offshore islands				
Corsica	1	0.0	38	1.1
Sardinia	8	0.2	5	0.1
Sicily	45	1.0	168	4.8
Sub-total	54	1.2	211	6.0
Outside Italy				
Spain and Portugal	171	4.0	234	6.7
France	268	6.2	176	5.0
Flanders	37	0.9	13	0.4
Germany	49	1.1	152	4.3
Switzerland	80	1.8	0	0.0
Poland	2	0.0	5	0.1
Greece	5	0.1	17	0.5
'Schiavoni' and Albania	6	0.1	44	1.3
Turkey	4	0.1	10	0.3
Others	8	0.2	32	0.9
Sub-total	630	14.6	683	19.5
Total	4,328	100.0	3,496	100.0

Source: ASR, S. Giacomo degli Incurabili, 386, 390–2; for census: J. Delumeau, *Vie économique et sociale de Rome dans la seconde moitié du XVIe siécle*, 2 vols, Paris, 1957, i, pp. 190–213.

between the papacy and these regions. This was especially obvious in the case of Emilia-Romagna, which contained an important part of the Papal States from where people would have travelled freely to Rome. Furthermore a very specific event had swollen the Lombard population of Rome in precisely the years of our sample of patients: in 1559 a Milanese, Pius IV, was elected pope and subsequently a large number of Milanese travelled to Rome in search of employment during the four years he held office, especially when he initiated his considerable construction programmes.[185]

It was also largely the influence of individual popes which led to the establishment of communities of non-Italians in Rome. The two most significant in both sample populations were Spain (with Portugal) and France, reflecting their close economic and political connections with Rome. These links were reinforced by the presence of important national communities within the city, which themselves had grown considerably under the influence of French and Spanish popes and cardinals over the previous hundred years. The majority of the latter had arrived in Rome in the late fifteenth century with the Borgia popes.[186] It was precisely during Alexander VI's pontificate that Mal Francese first assumed its epidemic form, and partly no doubt in consequence of this the pope's physicians Gaspar Torrella and Pere Pintor became experts in it. Thirty years later, as we have seen, the Spanish priest Francisco Delicado was treated in San Giacomo and later in the century the Spanish cardinal Bartolomé de la Cueva (1499–1562) became the hospital's cardinal protector.[187] Finally the presence of the Swiss contingent at San Giacomo can be explained by the presence of the Papal Guards. Evidently free treatment for their incurable diseases was a form of repayment for their help in controlling the crowds wishing to take guaiacum.

All these general reasons, then, for non-Romans to come and live in the city must also have applied to the patients of San Giacomo, a supposition reinforced by the relatively close correlation between their main areas of origin. While it may be impossible to decide finally what percentage of patients were residents or non-residents of Rome, a substantial proportion probably came from that floating population of the poor and sick attracted to Rome as a thriving centre of institutional charity. The significant numbers of San Giacomo patients, moreover, who wore heavy garments such as overcoats and travelling cloaks also suggest that they were from outside Rome rather than local residents. This was all the more probable given that so many dressed in this fashion were admitted for Holy Wood treatment during the warmer late spring and early summer months, when local residents were unlikely to have worn their heavy clothes to hospital. Indeed it was the provision of free guaiacum to large numbers of the sick without any residence restrictions which served to make San Giacomo so popular among non-Romans.

Conclusion

This discussion of patients admitted to San Giacomo has underlined the difficulty in establishing the exact identity of diseases treated in sixteenth-century hospitals, even in their own terms. It is clear, though, that the majority of patients had to fulfil two basic criteria in order to be admitted:

first, they had to be poor and, second, they had to be in need of treatment for a range of ailments which the physicians defined as 'incurable'. Those who suffered from the stock-in-trade conditions of the general hospitals, acute diseases such as fevers, were definitely not permitted entry, nor were those suffering from two diseases which, though incurable, had to be treated elsewhere, leprosy and plague.

If incurability was the defining qualification for acceptance into hospitals such as San Giacomo in Rome – excepting lepers and plague victims – this shows that when these institutions were established the new disease of Mal Francese was regarded as incurable. Indeed we have argued that it was the emergence of the pox in epidemic form from the 1490s that was one of the main incentives behind the movement which led to the establishment of this new type of hospital in Italy. Thus although San Giacomo treated a wide range of incurable conditions, the single largest category of symptoms were those associated with Mal Francese.

It was, then, the very perception of Mal Francese as 'incurable' which led contemporaries to give such a rapturous reception to guaiacum, which was believed to have miraculous curative properties. This in turn led to the expansion of Incurabili hospitals, the main centres for treatment with the wonder drug. As we have seen, Francisco Delicado is supposed to have been cured of Mal Francese at San Giacomo in the 1520s through this treatment.[188] Later in the century Camillo de Lellis travelled to Rome owing to the reputation of the medical treatment offered at San Giacomo. On his second visit he was allegedly 'almost cured from his sickness', an 'incurable' sore on his leg.[189]

There is conflicting evidence from as early as the 1520s about the extent of the incurability of the pox, especially after the introduction of Holy Wood. It may be, of course, that the length of time a patient survived, or how long the disease remained in remission, depended in some cases on his or her social standing; a Delicado was more likely to have been better cared for both within and outside the hospital than the average patient admitted to San Giacomo. But this question becomes more complex with the second and third generations of pox sufferers. By the time Fracastoro was writing *De Contagione* in the 1540s he could observe that 'though the contagion is still flourishing today, it seems to have changed its character since those earliest periods of its appearance'.[190] The laity also recorded changes in the nature of the disease, most famously Francesco Guicciardini in his *Storia d'Italia*: 'But after many years the sickness became less serious, whether it was because of astrological influence, or through the long experience of the doctors, or the appropriate remedies to treat the sickness, or it had found itself able to transform itself into other types of diseases different from the original.'[191]

If Fracastoro had emphasised that the symptoms of the pox had changed over the first half of the sixteenth century, Guicciardini suggested that the disease had become less serious. It must have been this perception that led the protectors of the hospital of the Ridotto in Genoa to affirm in 1552 that 'the Mal Francese was reputed to have been an incurable disease, and now they say it is curable'.[192] Whether this really was the case or whether the periods between each stage of the illness had simply grown longer is impossible to determine.[193] But the same phenomenon was also true in southern Germany; by 1548 in the *Blatternhaus* in Ulm, for example, only the 'curable' were admitted.[194] Whatever was the actual change in the nature of the illness, the important thing was contemporary perception that it was now possible to recover from Mal Francese. This perception was necessary if the Incurabili hospitals were to continue to receive the financial support necessary to underwrite the cost of the expensive treatment they offered. For guaiacum was evidently seen by some as having played an important role; the 1574 statutes of the Florentine Incurabili hospital, for example, stated categorically that the Legno was 'the cause of very good results'.[195]

Even if not everybody thought guaiacum was as miraculous as was suggested by its protagonists,[196] it continued as the main treatment provided by Incurabili hospitals for incurable diseases, in which category most commentators still included the pox. Moreover, popular perception of its curative properties must have been widespread, judging by the extraordinary crowds which jostled for admission to San Giacomo in Rome during the period when Holy Wood was provided. But we also have to look to the broader social context for the reasons why the Incurabili hospitals such as San Giacomo continued to expand in the second half of the sixteenth century. The increase in numbers admitted must also have reflected the growth in poverty and begging, associated with the series of natural crises, dearth and epidemic disease which afflicted the city.[197]

Certainly the authorities saw the role of the major hospitals of Rome as complementary and San Giacomo as playing an important part within the city's overall poor-relief policy. For example, Clement VIII at the end of the century saw San Giacomo as the home for those suffering from a *male incurabile*, while others listed included S. Antonio for the aged, the Hospitale di Porta Angelica for the *rognosi e tignosi*, and S. Sisto for the *poveri miserabili*.[198] Furthermore, at times of emergency San Giacomo, along with the others, played an important role in state policy for controlling the crisis. During the epidemic of petechial fever in the summer of 1566 the magistrates of the city council had a special kitchen opened at San Giacomo to prepare meat for distribution to the sick poor. Then in 1629 San Giacomo was viewed, with the Spedale dei Mendicanti of S. Sisto, as an appropriate place within which to shut up beggars when Rome was threatened with plague.[199]

In time, therefore, the Incurabili hospitals, despite their names, had come to be seen as places in which it was possible at worst to receive beneficial treatment and at best to be cured. Thus as the disease was seen to have changed and become less severe the more coercive nature of these institutions dwindled. Although some of their inmates were, as the Incurabili hospital of

Venice had it, 'persone da chativo governo et da mal far',[200] the role of custodians and *inquisitores* of the early part of the century was no longer emphasised. This had much to do with contemporary perception of the changed nature of the disease, the subject to which we shall turn briefly in the conclusion to this study.

Chapter Nine

Catching the Pox: contagion

Introduction

As we have seen in earlier chapters, many people were involved in a practical way with the pox, whether attempting to deal with it in hospitals or taking some form of civil action to contain it. It was plain enough to such people, whatever the origins of the disease, that it was passed from person to person. It was, in short, infectious or contagious: while contagion implied contact, the essential meaning of both terms was that a poison or taint of some sort was passed from a sick to a healthy person, perhaps indirectly, through the air or contaminated objects. In this respect the pox resembled the plague, which prompted the most vigorous strategies of avoidance by communities and individuals.

Yet the theory of medicine was ill equipped to deal with these two great medieval catastrophes. It rested on a scheme of bodily function adumbrated by Galen in the second century AD and refined by the scholastic masters of the thirteenth century and the first half of the fourteenth – until indeed the plague itself began to change European medicine in more ways than one.[1] Much of the Greek practice of medicine had relied on controlling the diet, exercise, sleep and so on of the patient, that is, his regimen. This largely Hippocratic practice had been rationalised by Galen on the basis of Aristotelian natural philosophy, and the scholastics found that they could refine theoretical medicine in the same kind of way, aided by medieval developments in logic. When they had established their medicine in the universities and had claimed, with some success, that it was superior to other kinds, the university-trained physicians formed a medical elite.[2] They were able to command higher fees and in some cases become attached to a court on an annuity, like those we have met who became members of the pope's 'family'. This all suited the style of medicine they favoured. It was based on regimen and a close study of the patient and his or her circumstances: the peculiarities of the body's constitution, the age and sex of the patient, the seasons of the year, the nature of the environment and so on. These things, technically the 'naturals' and 'non-naturals', determined how the doctor ordered the patient's treatment and regimen, from seasonal prophylactic bleeding and purging to the choice of digestible meats. The doctor juggled the naturals and non-naturals to restore the balance of qualities that was lost when the patient became ill.

Medical care of this kind took time and was exercised ideally by a permanent medical adviser, whether employed by the civic authorities of a town or in the retinue of a prince. It suited the medical elite. But it did not suit the plague. On its first calamitous arrival in 1348 it killed perhaps a third of the population of Europe. It killed quickly, generally within three days of the appearance of the first symptom. Regimen, diet, prognosis and prophylactic treatment were irrelevant. It also killed the well-to-do as well as the poor, who were anyway less important in the kind of medicine practised by the university-trained physicians. The plague frequently returned, up to and beyond the arrival of the French Disease, and experience of the two diseases jointly altered European medicine. This is the subject of these two final chapters.

Complexional Medicine

Medicine before the plague centred on complexion.[3] This English word, together with 'temper' and 'temperament', are linguistic vestiges of a scheme of bodily function that seemed natural and obvious in the middle ages. The world, after all, was made of four elements, earth, air, fire and water, each with a pair of qualities, so that fire was hot and dry and water cold and wet. Philosophers and medical men agreed that Aristotle and Galen had been right in asserting that these qualities were active and that their interaction accounted for the existence and behaviour of natural bodies compounded from the elements. These bodies included the human body and its four humours (black bile, yellow bile, phlegm and blood), each of which had a pair of qualities like the elements. For the medical man food, medicines, places and the seasons also had elementary qualities, and the interaction of these with the qualities of the body and its humours determined when medical action should be taken and what kind of regimen the patient should adopt. The essence of illness was disturbed complexion, either of the parts of the body or of the humours. The disturbance had come about, the doctor traditionally argued, by some congenital defect in the patient, from his unhealthy surroundings or from defects in his mode of life, his regimen. A disturbed complexion – one with a quality in excess – was treated simply by application of the opposite quality. In the case of a disturbed humour, the doctor attempted to evacuate it by purging his patient or removing blood, sweat, urine or vomit from his body. The long-term aim was to correct the deficiencies in the patient's regimen and non-naturals.

Thus traditional medical theory and treatment was based on Aristotelian elementary qualities and the complexions of the body and its parts, and of foods and medicines. This did not explain how plague and the French Disease were caused. Experience showed that a very small cause like touching or even looking at an infected person had huge and catastrophic effects, from painful and disfiguring symptoms to death. Most educated men had been through a university arts course, which taught them how the hot and the wet caused generation and corruption and why things grew in the spring and died down in the autumn. Whether educated or not, men could feel what was cold and dry, and there was little reason to doubt that the manifest qualities had the manifest effect that the philosophers said they had. Except, that is, in infectious diseases.

Galen, like the medieval doctors who followed him, had good professional reasons for maintaining an Aristotelian rationality.[4] Medical theory was not only an intellectual tool that guided practice, it was a guarantee to society that the doctor was learned and based his medicine on fundamental principles. The learned doctor in the middle ages was also in competition with other kinds of practitioner, especially at times of an epidemic like the French Disease, and had to insist on his own learning as a sign of superiority. Fundamental to the rationality of the learned doctor was the belief that the elementary qualities described by Aristotle – the Hot, the Dry, the Wet and the Cold – produced the basic actions of the body. These were the 'manifest qualities' and with their actions – understood by all educated men – were irremovable from orthodox medicine. Yet what about infectious disease, especially indeed the French Disease, with its disproportion between cause and effect and lack of manifest quality? Galen had recognised an exception to action by manifest quality in the case of certain drugs, which, like infectious disease, produced an effect out of all proportion to their quantity and quality. He said that these drugs act by virtue of their 'whole substance'.[5] It was not possible to break down such drugs to their elementary components and explain their power in terms of manifest qualities: it was only the whole drug, in its complete form, that had a special, non-manifest quality. This doctrine provided a way of explaining how the French Disease could spread from one person to another, producing enormous effects from a slight cause, without the action of manifest qualities. There were many ways in which this was done. We shall look at these explanations in some detail in this chapter, since they were central to how people came to understand the disease, that is, how they pushed it into contemporary categories. But so great was the impact of the French Disease that some categories had to be changed. Understanding the French Disease was inextricably bound to forms of dissent from the orthodox natural philosophy of manifest causes.

Sympathies and Subtleties

The contagious nature of the French Disease compelled the medical men to find an explanation. The doctor not only had to maintain his reputation as rational and learned but also of course had to try to stop the spreading of the disease. He accordingly expressed the problem as one of cause and effect, a formulation widely accepted: the cause was in the sick patient, and was small and sometimes distant from its effects in the recipient. The learned doctor knew of several kinds of actions of this kind. One was involved in the old doctrine of 'sympathy', which explained how a part of the body suffered with another, but without a direct local cause. Another was the new notion of 'subtlety', a name invented to cover natural actions that could not be explained by manifest qualities. These two related topics were employed by a variety of medical men in explaining the contagion of the French Disease. The use to which they were put depended on the orientation of the author concerned to standard school natural philosophy and its manifest qualities, and even on his religious orientation. Let us look at such things in those who wrote about the contagion of the pox.

The search for 'subtleties' was not confined to Italy. The recognised leader of the neoterics in medicine – the men who deliberately sought alternatives to traditional theory – was Jean Fernel (1506/7–58). Educated in Paris and later (1534) a teacher of medicine there, he was in an influential position. What he thought and wrote on the French Disease, its identity and causes, had a large audience across Europe, including Italy. He is important enough for us to divert our gaze to Paris for a while.

Any learned physician who departed from orthodox medical doctrines necessarily had to have something else to put in their place, if only to maintain the image of learning. It was in identifying the natural-philosophical causes of the pox that the school physician distanced himself from the unlearned practitioner. As Fernel said, the one thing that makes the physician superior to the apothecary and herbalist is his knowledge of causes.[6] Like the Italian philosopher Cardano, who was important in developing the notion of 'subtlety'[7] Fernel wrote a treatise on hidden causes.[8] He addressed it to his king and explained to him why it was time to stop slavishly following the ancients in things philosophical. Fernel felt himself to be in a culture that was flowering in philosophical, economic, practical and military ways that out-stripped the arts of antiquity. How superior are printed books to the wax tablets and papyri of antiquity! he exclaimed. As for his remarks on the discovery of things completely unknown to the ancients, like the compass and the New World, Fernel seems like Cardano to feel that new horizons made the philosophical world of the ancients somewhat parochial. As with Cardano, the old system of the elements and qualities seemed incomplete, for the old *ethnici* (pagan) philosophers had not taken into account the subtle and invisible powers of the natural world.

Fernel is also claiming superior, theoretical, knowledge of the pox when he says that it exists in different people at different states of intensity, depending on their constitution. The first level, or kind, of the disease is that which affects only the head and the beard. The second kind, says Fernel, is worse, and disfigures the skin with a multitude of flat pock-marks of a reddish or yellow colour. Here the malign quality lies in the thinner blood, and no further symptoms appear. In the third kind the pocks become pustules covered with a dry crust, degenerating into ulcers 'if neglected', says Fernel. They spread from the head to the rest of the body; and, when the disease reaches the liver, the fleshy parts begin to decay: this, says Fernel, is a true *lues*. The fourth stage is when the disease affects the solid parts and a malign excrement collects in the membranes, nerves and especially the bones and joints. This stage ends in death.

In making such distinctions between the manifestations of the disease Fernel is saying that only the learned practitioner can understand such things; and understand them, moreover, on the basis of a new kind of natural philosophy. Fernel deals with it separately, in the dialogue on the hidden causes of things. The conversation is an allegory of the times, when philosophical dissent was being expressed outside the schools. A major theme is woven round Brutus (the physician-figure), who has a problem with a *sententia* from Hippocrates, that all diseases have something of the divine in them.[9] Brutus tells Philiatros of his problem, explaining that the divine causes within disease are part of the subtle powers of the natural world that are not to be explained by mixtures of the elements and their manifest qualities. Together, they go off in search of Eudoxus to seek clarification.[10] The allegory continues as Eudoxus (the philosopher-figure) welcomes them to his sodality, that is, to his circle of like-minded philosophers who have come together to discuss the new dissenting philosophy. Like the real sodalities of the Germans we met above, Fernel's imaginary group is expressly[11] an elite group, looking down at the crowd of vulgar philosophers (of the schools). Their own philosophy is mathematically demonstrative[12] and Platonic.[13]

New subtle and hidden causes dominate Fernel's treatment of the pox. He deals with it in two major locations in his writings. First he gives it space in his systematic treatise on diseases and symptoms.[14] Carefully avoiding giving it the common name it had in other countries, the 'French Disease', he calls it instead the *lues venerea*. What we call the clinical description is very brief, for Fernel says that it is a contagious, non-localised, painful disease with ulcers. Clearly it is not his intention to solve any perceived problem of recognition. By calling it a contagious disease he meant that it was not self-generated, arising within the individual from for example a weakness of the naturals or a poor regimen of non-naturals. It was in other words something that was passed from one person to another, a poisoned, malign quality that spread throughout the body, even to the spirits, from a small point of contact. Or, more precisely, what was passed on was the efficient cause of the disease. Fernel thought that while the most important mode of transmission was sexual contact, it could also be transmitted by skin contact, by the breath and from mother to unborn child.

His principal explanation of the mechanism of contagion of the *lues* is a modification of the Galenic doctrine of 'whole substance'. While Galen had discussed the whole substance of certain drugs, Fernel turns the doctrine around and argues that some diseases, like the pox, act on the whole substance of the parts of the *body*. This is a major category of disease in Fernel's new scheme, and it adds to the traditional categories of 'faults of matter' (constitutional disorder) and faults in the complexion of manifest qualities.[15]

Such actions are 'occult' for Fernel,[16] partly in that they are hidden from the senses of the doctor and partly in that they are hidden from his reason. While manifest qualities were handled in medical discussion in standard logical ways, hidden, occult or subtle qualities were not necessarily open to analysis by reason. It was enough that everyone agreed that their effects occurred, and the literature of the time had many instances of subtle and powerful forces in nature. A favourite example was the electric eel, *torpedo*, which passed a quality through the trident of the fisherman and numbed his arm. The story comes from Galen, and in the same place[17] Galen talked of the attraction exerted by the lodestone for iron. Stones that attracted, drugs that attracted or repelled (like rhubarb), poisons and the shock of the *torpedo* were all actions that resulted from whole substance.[18]

Fernel deals with these matters again in the bigger treatise on the cure of the pox.[19] Because of the disagreements among the doctors, he felt obliged to spell out carefully what the apparently new disease was. This is another way in which he pressed the pox into a formal and here largely classical apparatus of theory, in order to be able to understand it and treat it. His argument begins with the Galenic distinction between diseases of the similar parts (those compounded from the elements) and of the organic parts (made up of similar parts). It was an organising principle that gave shape to doctors' thinking up to the eighteenth century and which was clearly a useful guide in the difficult area of distinguishing diseases, causes, symptoms and signs. Every disease, began Fernel, is primarily and *per se* in a particular part of the body either similar or organic. But the pox cannot be limited to an organ, for it does not have shape, size or restricted location. If it did primarily and *per se* attack the organic parts (continues Fernel) then it would not be a single disease, but multiple (from Galen's definition). It followed for Fernel that the pox was therefore a disease of the similar parts, and he here reasserts his claim about the three kinds of 'similar' diseases. As we have seen, of these pox was an occult disease of the whole substance.

So, in order to get an intellectual, academic and learned hold on the pox, Fernel has developed Galen's doctrine of the whole substance of poisons and pressed the new disease into two different parts of the apparatus of theoretical medicine. At the very least he was now in a respectable position to address his learned and rational colleagues. Almost certainly he now believed he had correctly categorised and analysed the disease and so could proceed to the business of cure. This relationship between theory and practice is made clear when he begins to address the business of cure, for he claims that previously those attempting a cure had ignored the essence of the disease and had sought only to get rid of the symptoms.[20] This of course is a powerful rationalist argument against experiential medicine, and Fernel is once more defending learned and rational medicine, albeit in a rather new way. Here he argues that empirical practice, guided by the symptoms rather than the essence, suggested attacking the pustules and ulcers with stiptic substances to burn away pathological excrescence. Then, because the empirics found that another appeared as soon as they had destroyed one, they took to an ointment of the same kind spread on all at once, as was the practice with other conditions. (Fernel has a strong historical sense with which he helps to define the nature of the pox and medical thought.) All this failing (he says), they turned to mercury, which 'our predecessors took from the school of the Arabs'[21] and which had been used for malign ulcers and scabies. This they beat up with oils and powders to make an ointment, sometimes applying it to the joints as much as four times a day. The patient was shut up in an *estuarium*, where he could be conveniently and extensively heated, to sweat for twenty or thirty days. 'This empirical mode of cure has been followed up to now by almost all physicians and surgeons, not without great damage to the Republic',[22] exclaimed Fernel indignantly, apparently referring to the damage inflicted on the public; but he was probably also concerned with the 'republic of [medical] letters', his own learned profession. He accordingly tries to limit the damage with a rationalist account of the powers of mercury, its various forms and its effects on those (like painters,[23] goldsmiths[24] and tanners[25]) who accidentally absorbed it and on those (like pox patients) who on a course of mercury were put through tortures by their doctors.

Fernel's preferred remedy is a decoction of the guaiacum wood. His account of its discovery in the Indies does not dwell on the fact that it was used empirically and successfully by the natives. But, for all his neoteric theory of occult causality, his explanation of the mode of cure is almost entirely traditional. He proceeds[26] to allot to guaiacum the traditional elementary qualities by which (he says) all medicines have their actions. His explanation of its action includes its ability to promote sweat and to humidify, but does not go beyond the traditional actions of the qualities. It is an explanation that would fit well enough into the first principles of theory that we have seen him anxious to set up; indeed, in his sense his whole account of how to prepare and apply a decoction of guaiacum is derived from first principles. That is to say, what looks to us like a fortuitous and empirical discovery of a (supposed) remedy, which Fernel forces into a standard account of how medicines act, was for him a real act of understanding: understanding was by means of first principles.[27]

Plate 9.1 illustrates the guaiacum treatment. It is a moral story of a rake's progress, beginning with the picture on the wall of the sickroom which portrays the victim leading a young woman from the festive table to the bed.

9.1 A line engraving of 'A Man in Bed Suffering from the French Disease' showing stages of acum-wood treatment, 1580s, by P. Galle after Jan van der Straet known as 'Stradanus'

After he has been exposed to contagion, the symptoms appear in the patient and the guaiacum is purchased. Pieces are cut from the log by the seated man, while two women weigh the requisite quantities and boil them in water over the fire. The circle is completed by the figure of the patient in his bed, drinking the decoction, attended by the physician and an assistant.

We cannot leave Fernel's view of the disease-without-a-name, the *lues*, without a consideration of the part played by his religion in his new theories of disease. Just as the early perception of the French Disease incorporated the notion that it was a punishment from God, so now, in a post-Reformation period, notions of the divine were not separable from other areas of thought. Thus in his *Therapeutices*[28] Fernel confidently describes how the laws of nature, laid down directly by God, produce the 'universal consent and sympathy' among natural things. For him natural law was eternal, immutable, good and centred on God; to attack it was to to lack *faith*.[29] The natural law that was fundamental to medicine was that there was something divine in diseases. The 'subtlety' of the pox was indeed partly this, and for Fernel 'occult' causes are partly hidden from reason because they are God's action. Fernel, through Eudoxus, maintains[30] that magnetism, the action of rhubarb in purging bile and the ability of the ostrich to digest iron are occult, essentially unknowable and inexpressible in words. This is a stronger formulation of the term 'occult', which as we have seen was often used to indicate merely something that was not explicable in terms of manifest Aristotelian qualities.

Fernel maintained too that there something divine in the 'whole substance' action by which diseases like the pox affected the organs. 'Substance' as Fernel uses it is close to the scholastic notion that it is matter shaped by its form. But 'form' for Fernel also meant 'soul' in the Christian as well as the philosophical tradition.[31] All animal actions including reaction to contagion, Fernel insists,[32] are ultimately divine. 'Whole substance' actions thus had something divine in them for Fernel; this is what 'whole substance' diseases like the pox acted on.[33] The more orthodox position, held by commentators of Fernel's time like Da Monte and Sylvius,[34] was that the Galenic faculties, and hence animal actions, arose primarily from complexion, the mixture of elementary qualities.

Fernel's deliberate rejection of parts of orthodox medical theory was not admired by everyone. Opinion for and against the ancient writers had been polarised by the attack made during Fernel's lifetime by Vesalius on Galen. Galen's defenders said that Vesalius had 'broken faith' with the great ancient teacher, and their language owed much to the bitter arguments of the Reformation.[35] Galen was defended particularly in France, and we are concerned here with the elder Jean Riolan (c.1538–1605). Riolan's critique of Fernel's[36] doctrines on the nature of contagion is an attempt to reconcile it with Galenic theory. He does so, expressly, by presenting the new scheme as a refinement of the old. He complains that Fernel's account of contagion (in his description of the three ways in which similar parts can become diseased) is too 'metaphysical', reflecting, no doubt, Fernel's bringing the divine into 'whole substance' action. Riolan nevertheless tacitly adopts Fernel's account of disease 'of the whole substance', like pox. Riolan says such diseases seek out and destroy the 'formal principles', *formalia principia*, of human life. Such a disease in his terminology then becomes a *morbus formalis*. However, he does not go so far as Fernel and asserts only that the formal principles are the innate heat and the spirits, and he lacks the detail and coherence employed by Fernel in relation to contagion, the occult nature of disease and the involvement of forms.

He extends this purpose by arguing that the ancients had a perfectly adequate description of the *effects* of contagion by occult and *formales* diseases. It was a characteristically humanist device to argue, as Riolan now does, that the ancients 'were not ignorant' of something (in this case of the transmission of occult and poisonous qualities and the categories of their effects). But their knowledge, he says, was 'of the thing', not 'on account of which'. He means that the ancients knew the thing simply, or in the terms of the Latin tradition they had knowledge *quia*. Knowledge *propter quid* in contrast was rational knowledge of the causes of the thing (that is, which Riolan believed he knew). Riolan uses the Greek equivalents, which were coming into use at this time.[37] In other words, for him later medicine may refine, but does not replace, the knowledge of the ancients.

The urgency of the questions of the nature of contagion in relation to the pox compelled Riolan to face these questions in commenting on Fernel's work. In following Riolan here we are brought to face yet another alternative to orthodox medicine and its school natural philosophy. This is medical Platonism, the novelty of which appears perhaps more clearly from Riolan's commentary than from Fernel's carefully argued dialogues.

To make the contrast between medical Platonism and traditional orthodoxy sharper, let us first remind ourselves of the power and persistence of the traditional picture of contagion. For example the series of lectures given in Bologna in 1563 by Antonio Fracanzano (d.1567) were entirely traditional.[38] Fracanzano denied that the pox was a disease of whole substance because, he said, 'substance' was either substantial form or elementary. 'Whole substance' action for him was simply what resulted from the balance of elementary – manifest – qualities within a substance.[39] He accordingly defined pox in humoral terms – it was hot and dry – and held that the action of guaiacum was a simple purging. Although Fracanzano used the terms *fomites* and *lues* to explain contagion, he meant little more than a direct and material transfer of manifest qualities. At the same time Galen's definition of disease remained a powerful one for many authors. While we can argue that experience of plague and pox forced men who gave their attention to contagious diseases to think in other ways, the attractions of traditional Galenic medicine were strong for those who wrote textbooks and systematic expositions of medicine. Laurent Joubert opened his textbook of practical medicine with the Galenic definition of disease, and it acted as a structure for what followed.[40] Leonhart Fuchs likewise followed Galen closely in his *Institutiones* of medicine,[41] and claimed that the Galenic definition of disease was very widely held.

In contrast the medical Platonists had radically different ideas about the mechanism of contagion of the French Disease. They claimed there were two kinds of contagion, one of which was formal and qualitative. This was 'physical' in the sense of belonging to traditional Aristotelian natural philosophy, where form and matter gave reality and corporeality to the world. But the other was corporeal and quantitative contagion, which can be called (if you want, says Riolan) mathematical. Mathematics was held by the Aristotelians to give no guide to the essences of things, and the development of the topic within medicine was a business of the Platonists. Clearly for them mathematics had some relationship with matter, but the principal advantage of mathematics in questions of contagion seems to be that it could explain contagion at a distance. It did so by the doctrine of 'mathematical form', a concept apparently developed in opposition to the standard 'form' of Aristotelian theory of substance (which was informed matter). It is, Riolan says, the numerous medical men established in the schools of the Platonists who extol mathematical forms: 'Mathematical forms, because they are freer of matter, time and place, are more divine than Physical forms, and are similar to metaphysical.'[42] The doctrine was taken up by Fernel's countryman André du

Laurens, who lectured on the pox and its contagion in 1587–8. He too held
that contagion was of two kinds, physical (the contiguity of two quantities)
and mathematical (a 'communion of potency'). In mathematical 'contagion'
the communicating bodies need not be in touch, according to Du Laurens,
and clearly no matter was thought to be transmitted.

Riolan was less enthusiastic. He was not sure that he approved of all
neoteric 'subtlety'.[43] He was prepared to accept traditional stories of sympathy
and antipathy from Pliny, but did not succumb to the attractions of imagining
a world full of unknown powers; after all, he says, man is the measure of all
things and the world was made for him; his powers are equal to the task of
understanding them. As with the authors he is criticising, the pox was a
prominent example of contagious diseases. Riolan will not accept that contagion can happen at a distance, because 'action' is involved and every *agens*
within an action acts by contact. But he allows that there is an essential
difference between, on the one hand, corporeal and quantitative contagion
and, on the other, formal and qualitative, of which mathematics could give no
causal or essential account.

Medical Platonism seems to have been associated with a new piety. While
the Christian philosopher found the paganness of the peripatetics troubling,
there was something appealing about the Platonists. Fernel believed that the
late Platonists like Proclus, Iamblichus and Plotinus had borrowed material
from the Christians John, Paul and Dionysius and so approached the truth
more clearly. Indeed, part of the superiority of the sixteenth-century world
for Fernel was that it was also illuminated by a truth more certain than that
of any philosophical system, particularly the pagan ones of the past. It is
through Christ, he says,[44] that we know things unknown to the past. 'Who
does not know the domicile, power and immortality of our souls?' It was this
religious–philosophical understanding that Fernel brought to the natural
world and its medicine. Many of the subtle and invisible powers of the world
he derived from divine sources, some mediated through the soul. Platonism,
the soul, Fernel's kind of Christianity and departure from some aspects of
school natural philosophy were all important in his understanding of the pox.

Contagion and Seeds

Having followed the French Disease and its subtleties in France, we must
return to Italy and follow a parallel story. The notion of 'seeds of disease' was
a third contender in an arena where doctrines of whole substance were
opposed to the more traditional accounts relying on manifest elementary
qualities. One of the advantages of the doctrine of seeds was that it gave a
good account too of contagion. Pietro Trapolino (1451–1509: the *ordinarius*
teacher of theory at Padua)[45] also uses 'seedbed', *seminarium*, as equivalent to
fomes. The *fomes* themselves do not constitute the disease and may remain

dormant for the entire life of the person who carries them. It is like an architect, says Trapolino, who has no cement, stones or wood and so cannot build a house. The implication is that the *seminaria* of the pox need the appropriate material to build the 'house' of the disease. Leonardo Botallo (b.1530),[46] the anatomist student of Falloppio and Vesalius, readily accepted that contagion was an 'impression' made upon the body by seeds, and that the disease consequently spread 'like an occult flame' through the *fomites* of the body. In the earlier part of the century those who discussed seeds of disease had generally found the term in Galen. It was not until well into the second half of the century that the work of Fracastoro became widely read. Da Monte's opposition to the idea was also well known and influential. Struthius,[47] writing on the pulse in the French Disease, used Fracastoro's term, *seminaria*, for the atom-like seeds by which the pox was spread. He took note of Da Monte's objection that the notion looked like a fragment of Epicurus but defended it by returning to those passages in Galen in which earlier doctors had found mentions of seeds.

So let us look briefly at the poem *Syphilis*, largely completed by 1525 and published in its final form in 1531.[48] It was this poem that gave the name which historians used for the disease we are here calling the pox; this is some measure of the reception given to Fracastoro's poem.

As we saw above, to compose a poem in classical Latin style, even one on a disease, was to announce oneself as a learned humanist. Italian humanists like Fracastoro were not creatures of the schools, and his poem distances itself both from renaissance theology and from school natural philosophy. Although a medical man and so trained in the schools[49] he was ready to abandon peripatetic natural philosophy, the theoretical underpinning of medicine. To explain the transmission of the pox, Fracastoro invoked the idea of 'seeds', *semina*. Only by such means, he believed, could the rapid spread of the disease be explained: simple contagion would have been too slow.[50] What was behind Fracastoro's perception of the pox was, as with others, the fundamentals of his world-picture. As a humanist it was the classical pantheon and not a vengeful Old Testament God who inflicted the disease upon man.

Fracastoro addresses Urania, the Muse of Astronomy,[51] when discussing the astrological circumstances of the disease's appearance. As a humanist, he found the arguments of the Greeks powerful, and he adopts the philosophers' argument of the eternity of the world: in the *aeternum aevum* of the world, he says, everything possible must have happened, including the pox. But cultural decay – so clear to the humanists and hellenists of his time – had blotted the memory of it and its name from men's minds.[52] It followed, for Fracastoro, that the pox did not originate in the New World, but was simply temporally and geographically more frequent there.

In giving a prominent place to the seeds of the disease, Fracastoro was departing somewhat from the Galenic model, where a disease was disordered function. In addition, renaissance medical men in Fracastoro's time found that the ancients had used some words as technical terms, such as *angina* or *phthisis*: to the renaissance doctor these looked like disease entities. Fracastoro seems to have looked on pox as a disease entity that, like a plant, could propagate itself.

Some historians have seen Fracastoro's 'seeds of disease' as part of a development that led to theories of germs.[53] It is better related to the other non-standard parts of his view of the world. To some of his contemporaries, the seeds of disease looked like the atoms of the philosophers so disliked by Aristotle and Galen. To Fracastoro they were part of his dissent from the doctrines of these same authors. As agents of contagion, the action of the seeds of the pox was directly related to what he thought about sympathy and antipathy and his unAristotelian physical principles of the natural world. Indeed, the text on sympathy was published as one of a pair, the other being on contagion.[54]

Contagion and Sympathy

The doctrine of seeds that Fracastoro put into *Syphilis* belonged to the early 1520s. By 1546 he wanted to express this doctrine as part of an extended natural philosophy which was derived from fundamental principles of action in the world and which was applied to the question of contagion. The natural philosophy was not Aristotelian, but served the purpose that peripatetic natural philosophy served, to link a world-view to medical practice in a convincing way. Contagion was explained by sympathy and the French Disease by contagion; Fracastoro said that he was writing to supply many things he had missed out of *Syphilis*, and certainly the three works reinforced each other. Let us look at the two later works in the order that Fracastoro wanted.

'Sympathy' in its broadest sense was a fellow feeling between two natural parts of the world, a communication of an often unknown mechanism. One of its sources was Galen's discussion of pathology, in which localised, limited damage was identified as 'idiopathy'. But idiopathic disorders could also produce pain or damage elsewhere, by sympathy. The doctrine became formalised in medicine, and sympathies were thought to arise by a number of mechanisms and to exist in a number of categories.[55] One of them was by transmission of a quality, whether Aristotelian or occult. Because sympathies and subtleties involved some form of action at a distance they interested medical men who wanted to explain contagion generally, which was so important a feature of the French Disease.

Sympathies and antipathies of the world at large were very numerous. Listen to Fracastoro: drums made of wolfskin when beaten rupture those made of lambskin; angry bulls become calm when tied to fig trees; lightning melts the gold, but leaves the cash-box intact;[56] adamant is softened only by goat's blood; the lion is terrified only of the cock, especially when crowing;

cabbage and rue will never grow when sown together. It sounds a little like Pliny and a little like folklore; but what is clear is that these are mechanisms of action that have nothing to do with Aristotelian natural philosophy and its manifest elementary qualities. However, they do have a great deal to do with the subtlety that lay behind new explanations – particularly Fracastoro's – of how the French Disease has its effects in the body and how it is transmitted from one body to another.

It is possible that some of these instances of sympathy had Pliny's authority. There is abundant evidence for the huge popularity of his *Natural History* in the universities, partly the large number of early editions.[57] That it was expected reading in the universities is shown by the editions of Tübingen and Paris, printed for sale by the Paris university stationer. In Wittenberg the theological objections to Aristotle meant that the younger students were taught their 'physics' of the natural world from Pliny's second book of the *Natural History*.[58] The sheer volume of editions and the accessibility and interest of Pliny's subject matter to those outside the universities too suggest that many in fact gathered their notions about the real world from him. It is important also to remember the attractions of Neoplatonism, the cosmic sympathies within which resemble those we are discussing here. Pliny's stories would sit well within a Neoplatonic intellectual framework. So would Fracastoro's doctrines.

For Fracastoro sympathy was evidence that there is some attraction at a distance between (in a medical instance) the individuals who are infected. This is true of all cases of sympathy. That 'miracle unknown to the ancients', the ship's compass, demonstrates the sympathy of the needle for the pole.[59] The lodestone has a sympathy for iron, and polished amber attracts chaff. What is common to all these sympathies and antipathies? What explanation is there? Fracastoro's answer is that the *whole universe* acts 'sympathetically' or in consent (*consensus*). The most immediate example of this, he says, is that sympathetic union of parts of the world is so great that nothing can separate contiguous parts and so form a vacuum. This is the stuff of Aristotelian commentary, but Fracastoro's language is distant from that of the schools; in comparing the sympathising parts of the world to those of a living body, he seems to be drawing on the Platonic tradition. He does indeed have standard arguments about a vacuum, that is, that nature does nothing in vain, that a vacuum is a negation of existence and that the purpose – the final cause – of universal sympathy is that there should not be a vacuum. 'But if anyone should not be satisfied with that, but should actively enquire what it is that resists the pulling apart, and how, it will not be easy to give him an answer.'[60] The problem was that the parts of the universe, although involved in a purposeful 'sympathising', had no recognition of the purpose, no natural appetite which could act in achieving such a thing. Nor, said Fracastoro (in opposition to others), are these parts directed by something that does know the final cause.

In view of these difficulties about the final cause, Fracastoro limits his enquiry to 'proper and particular causes'. He believed that matter was entirely passive, without action or resistance. Nor in his scheme of things was there action at a distance. While the elements moved to their natural places by sympathy, this did not, he repeats, involve recognition. And while the purpose of the elements moving to their natural places was self-conservation by the mutuality of similars and the avoidance of a vacuum, it is not purpose that moves the parts: all action is by contact, and matter is passive and not sentient.

In the treatise on contagion Fracastoro develops these doctrines and explores their medical applications. He opens the work by asserting the links between sympathy and contagion and he deals again with the French Disease in the second book of the treatise: contagion is central. How did Fracastoro see it? He begins with a distinction that has been lost to us. Because our attention is centred on the infective organism we distinguish 'infection' from 'contagion' only by the mode by which it reaches us, normally through the air or by contact, respectively. But in the sixteenth century both words meant the passing of a taint or poison, and were often interchangeable. For Fracastoro contagion is a 'certain infection', but of a special kind, person to person. Simple infection was for example when someone died from drinking poison.[61] This was not contagion, nor was it when pieces of meat, or milk, began to putrefy on being left standing in the air.[62] The essential thing about contagion was that it took place between different things (not different parts of the same thing) and that something unpleasant but always similar was passed between them, *simile quoddam vitium*.[63]

Thus contagion was not limited to living things and Fracastoro is asserting that, like sympathy, it is a universal principle. It is a principle that operated among 'mixed' bodies, that is, those made up from simpler bodies. Traditionally the simplest parts were the four elements, but now for Fracastoro the simplest parts were the smallest particles – invisibly small – into which a body could be resolved. It was these particles that were transmitted in contagion: in their new location, or person, they began a corruption that ultimately spreads to the whole of the mixed body. Fracastoro wondered in passing whether this corruption was caused by the introduction of 'contraries' which the 'form' of the body could not tolerate, or if it was a dissolution of the mixed body, as in putrefaction. It will be noticed that for all the novelty of the 'smallest particles', which look as if they had been inspired by Lucretian atomism,[64] Fracastoro keeps to the Aristotelian category of form and to what is perhaps a medical category of 'opposites' (as in 'opposites cure opposites': a cool medicine for a hot disease). He also retains 'substance' and 'accidents', through which alone all natural action proceeds.[65] His final elaborate definition of contagion is 'a certain similar corruption of a mixed body according to substance, passing from one to another by an infection in insensible particles'.[66]

This has to be understood in the context of a natural philosophy which, although retaining some Aristotelian terms, has radically different elements. Because it is at the basis of Fracastoro's understanding of the French Disease, we must look briefly at it. He says that, of the ten categories of natural things, only substance and quality (which is manifest in accidents) are active. Substance has form and so looks rather Aristotelian, but Fracastoro says that it produces only local motions – up, down, round, and rarefaction and its opposite. The qualities are no longer elementary but are 'material'. The first four of them are the traditional hot, cold, wet and dry, but the list continues with light, smell, taste and sound.[67] These look at first like sensory actions, and Fracastoro has to explain that what he means is the thing that causes the sensation, for which there is no name. Certainly we have *lux* and *lumen* for 'light', he says, but there is no name for the material quality we smell by means of *odor* unless we invent one, *odorimen*. We should also have to invent *saporimen* and *sonimen*.

Fracastoro argues that the traditional material qualities are involved in many actions in the natural world, for example in the usual sense in 'generation'. Their action is by the opposition they have for each other. The 'second' qualities, *lux*, *odor* and so on, do not interact in this way but are responsible for many actions deriving from the senses and, in man, from the intellect. Here he makes a cross-reference to *De Sympathia* and clearly wants to build a unified picture of the world. The same is true where he introduces a whole new group, the 'spiritual species', which he had discussed at some length in *De Sympathia*. In that work he was explicit that species were atomic simulacra emerging from the surface of things and either perceptible to the senses or effecting physical action: they combined tenuity with the ability materially to move sympathising and antipathising parts.

With this in mind, Fracastoro sets out to explain the three different kinds of contagion.[68] The first sort of contagion is by touch alone, and his image here is of apples crowded together in storage, where one rotten one infects the rest. As with the French Disease, the *first* appearance of rottenness is not by contagion but has some other cause. Fracastoro says the cause is a 'foreign heat', *aliena caliditas*, which causes the innate heat and humidity of the apple to evaporate, so bringing about the dissolution of the composed body. The process becomes contagious when the invisibly small particles of the first apple move to the second, causing a further evaporation. He calls them *seminaria*.[69]

This basic model of contagion is developed in Fracastoro's second category, contagion through *fomites*. Here the small particles (which still have the power to infect by direct touch) are able to survive in things like clothes and wood. Those of plague and phthisis are small, *subtiles*, and can survive for two or three years in the *fomites* and still be infective. Surely here is a voice informed with the collective experience of trade and commerce: practical people knew empirically that diseases could be caught from inanimate objects that had been exposed to disease elsewhere and earlier.

Fracastoro's third category of contagion is that which happens at a distance. His examples are plague and phthisis again, and *lippitudo* (in classical usage a bleariness of the eyes). This is transferred, according to Fracastoro, simply by a glance from the affected person, or when a healthy person looks at him or her. The cause of this is a different order of things, says Fracastoro; it comes from a different *principium* like the glance of the catablepha, the animal whose look can kill. No quality is exchanged, not even an occult quality, explains Fracastoro, for whom 'occult' was a word used by people to hide their ignorance.[70] Certainly the manifest and gross elementary qualities of hot or cold were not transmitted. What is transmitted is 'what is called species', *vocatas species*, and the simulacra of things.[71] These are what in *De Sympathia* he had described as swarms of atoms: although he did not want to revive the medieval theory of 'species', subtle images emerging from the surfaces of things used to explain vision, his thinking is guided by the atomism of Lucretius.

Indeed, Lucretius is another source of the 'subtlety' which was so often used in opposition to the coarse manifest qualities of Aristotelian natural philosophy. His text was rediscovered only towards the end of the previous century and provided a wholly new account of what the world was made of.[72] In some quarters Lucretius was welcomed as an ornament of Latin culture, which sometimes seemed in need of defence against the hellenists. That he wrote in verse encouraged the humanists to do likewise, and new verse on a technical philosophical or medical topic was in some sense Lucretian. We met earlier the poems of Pirckheimer and Brant on gout and pox, and Fracastoro in writing his own poem had them as examples.

'Syphilis or the so-called French Disease'[73] is a conspicuous example of contagion of the second kind for Fracastoro in his work on contagion. Its seeds, he says, are dense and slow-acting, lying latent in the body for up to four months.[74] The theory of disease seeds allows him to explain other features of the pox as he perceived it. He believed that the current outbreak of the pox was caused by astrological circumstances in the first instance, and obviously, then, not by contagion. The disease that arose 'spontaneously' in this way was more vigorous, he thought, and had since become milder, as it passed from person to person by means of the seeds, which were gradually becoming drier, earthier and less virulent. He gives more clinical details of the disease than do many medical writers, and argues that during the previous twenty years the pustules had become less frequent (and even rare in the previous six years), the pain had diminished, there was more white 'phlegm' in the sores and now (he says) the disease newly causes the loss of hair and the loosening of teeth. (Compare the situation in the Incurabili in Rome in Chapter Eight above.) In short, he thought that the disease was in its old age and in the absence of astrological causes would shortly disappear.

It had also been about twenty years since Fracastoro had written his poem on pox and he now had more to say about it.[75] Part of this is concerned with the seeds of the disease. The disease's most obvious characteristic, he says,[76] is the white phlegm that emerges from the ulcers, a phlegm that was shown by post-mortem dissection to be associated with the nerves and muscles, where the pain of the disease had been located in life. Fracastoro, arguing from analogy, asserts that the seeds must be of the same nature. He now says that their first appearance was in the air, following bad aspects of Saturn, Jupiter and Mars. Entering the body, the seeds generate more of themselves, producing the disease and the possibility of contagion.

Fracastoro's discussion of the treatment of the pox also centres on his unorthodox principles. Since the disease was due to seeds, the most effective treatment was to destroy them.[77] Fracastoro makes the telling point that the pox can be caught by a perfectly healthy person: that is, the disease is not a result of poor regimen or innate constitution, as in traditional medicine, but was an invasive entity. It followed that its treatment required *special* remedies, specific to the nature of the disease. Here Fracastoro invokes his basic physical principles of sympathy and antipathy, and his ideal remedy is that which has special and also spiritual antipathy to the seeds.[78] The mechanisms involved here are like the ways in which (he says) the species of poisons and antidotes act on the body. (In fact Fracastoro does not have a long list of things specifically antipathetic to the pox seeds and centres on cold as nullifying the acrimony of the seeds and on drying medicines which reduce its moisture.)

Conclusion

A principal feature of the French Disease was that, however it was originally caused, it was obviously passed on from person to person. The same had been true of the plague, and European medical thinking undoubtedly changed as a result of the experience of these two epidemics. At the time of the French Disease, however, many new theoretical positions were available in which to discuss the mechanisms of contagion. The urgency of the problem compelled the doctors, who had the greatest stake in finding an explanation of contagion, to 'medicalise' these theoretical positions: that is, to draw them into a broad framework of medical learning and rationality. Above all, the doctors had to decide what was being transmitted in contagion: was it a cause in some traditional sense, or was it a thing? We shall look at the ontology of disease in the next chapter.

Chapter Ten

The French Disease Grows Old

Introduction

We saw in the last chapter that experience of the French Disease compelled medical men to offer new explanations of contagion. A related change in the perception of the disease was its new ontological status. The disease was not a condition of the individual, it was a thing. Something awful had swept out of the East or the New World, or had been imposed upon them by God's wrath. This thing, this disease, was something that could be recognised, fled from, perhaps stopped by quarantine or confined to hospitals; if all failed, it was a thing that reached you directly from another patient, or indirectly through his possessions, and perhaps killed or maimed you.

Diseases were now things with histories (and futures). We need to remember this if we are to understand the reaction of people to the French Disease in the sixteenth and early seventeenth century, for it is one of the ways in which traditional Western medicine of the late middle ages was changed by experience. But orthodox, 'establishment' medicine changed slowly, and we shall see below some reasons why the doctors resisted change.

Epidemics and Empirics

Different kinds of practitioner reacted differently to the French Disease. Its victims, unlike those of the plague, remained alive but very obviously in need of medical attention. While during attacks of the plague the empirics and others had but a little time to sell medicines claiming to be preventive, in the case of the pox a new medical market, for cures, arose around the long-suffering patients. The empirics had some advantages here. Their remedies were cheaper than the physicians' fees. They did not claim to bring a vast knowledge to bear on the individual nature of the patient, but sold something that, like the disease itself, applied without discrimination to everyone. They claimed that their medicines were specific to the *disease* rather than to the patient. (Indeed empirical medicines came to be known as 'specifics'.) They could also claim quick cures, while the physicians' traditional treatment was a drawn-out affair. They seem to have had less hesitation than the physicians in dealing with cases of pox.

The learned doctors both resented and were anxious about the situation. But they also misrepresented it, and have often been followed by historians. The university-trained physicians reinvented the term 'empiric' (found in Galen's discussion of the medical sects of Rome) and applied it pejoratively to practitioners who had not been through a university medical faculty. But many such practitioners were legitimately licensed[1] by civic authorities. Many such licences were for limited areas of practice, and sometimes made no demands about literacy. The physicians could do nothing except become indignant. The German writer Johannes Benedictus (1483–1564) found the empirics who dealt with the pox 'truculent'.[2] He also called them 'impious', meaning most likely that they had no faith in the revered fathers of medicine in antiquity. This was the language of controversy, and the main charge made against Vesalius, for example, for his attack on Galen was that of 'breaking faith' with this ancient teacher.[3] Part of the problem was that the empirics practised their medicine while carrying on other trades, as one might expect of a specialist. To the learned physicians they were secretly practising internal medicine. The same was true in France, where Prospero Borgarucci (*fl.* 1560–70), physician to Charles IX, was resentful of the arrogance of such people that led them to 'usurp' the business of real doctors: the pharmacists, the barbers, the wrestling-school men, the oil-massagers, the midwives, the little old ladies who gather round the sickbed and so on. Anyone who falsely claimed to be a *medicus*, said Borgarucci, should be seized, placed on a decrepit ass, preferably one with scabies, and carried round the city for people to jeer and spit at him. Rain blows and rubbish on him, urged Borgarucci; lead him to the city gate and tell him never to return.[4] Borgarucci was in France only for the year (1567) in which he published on the French Disease. Earlier he had taught anatomy in Padua, and it was probably there too that the enemies of the monopoly of practice claimed by the university physicians annoyed him so intensely.

The trouble was that the practitioners without full licences, and especially those without licences at all, could claim quickly and loudly that their remedies worked, while the university doctors were still wondering how to fit the French Disease into their theoretical apparatus and so construct a case of their own. Desperate victims naturally went to those who claimed to be able to cure it. The city physician of Strasbourg, Lorenz Friese (1490–c.1531), whose book was published in 1532, recalled that the ferocity of the disease when it first arrived was such that the very lepers recoiled from it and refused to live with those infected. Those victims too poor to secure protection were turned out to live in the fields and woods, he said, adding that the doctors turned their backs on the disease, refusing to inspect, treat or visit the victims.

According to Friese, just as the disease had come from France so now in this situation and with divine sanction some *empirici vel medici* came from France (and Naples) to treat the disease. His words echo the opportunity that we may suppose some empirics found in a situation where the university doctors could not fit the pox into their medicine and would not run the risks involved in treating it. For a German writer like Friese, the disease was French not only because it originated in that country but because these 'empirics or doctors' came from there too.[5] The empirical remedy he was principally concerned with was the guaiacum, about which he had written in 1525, in the vernacular: he was concerned about the plight of the poor, who were unable to afford the escalating cost of treatment with the wood. His advice is direct and empirical.[6]

Friese was a friend of Paracelsus (or, at least, Paracelsus stayed with him during his travels, just before they both wrote on the pox),[7] whose empiricism was of a different kind: the rejection of his own education. By whatever route, Paracelsus shared some of the empirics' features. The French Disease, like others, had its own ontology: it was an entity. It was an entity with specific features and had to be fought with specific remedies. Paracelsus and the empirics used no medical theory or syllogising or talk of anatomy and wasted little affection on the learned physicians. Friese did not share these attitudes: while Paracelsus committed Avicenna's *Canon* to the flames, Friese defended it against the humanists.[8]

Another German medical man whose path crossed that of Paracelsus was Wendelin Hock von Brackenau (*fl.* 1502–14). Paracelsus is said to have avoided a debate with him on anatomy,[9] and certainly Hock had no pretensions to Paracelsian empiricism. He had in any case written his tract on the pox some time before, in 1514.[10] Like Friese, he reports on the behaviour of the doctors when the French Disease arrived. He had read that in Rome the panic caused by the appearance of the disease had paralysed the city's medical profession, and that literate people had fled from the disease, exclaiming about the doctors' ignorance of it. In their place, says Hock, came the illiterates, the sellers of spices, the collectors of herbs, the mechanics, vagabonds and *trusatores*[11] who claimed to be able to cure the disease perfectly. Because they knew nothing, says Hock, they doubted nothing and claimed all; to hear them you would think they could raise the dead. The learned doctor was in a difficult position: the empirics were using ointments and so could not be accused of prescribing internal medicine and so infringing the physicians' monopoly; they were 'ignorant of the secrets of medicine', a state of ignorance which the physicians had striven to maintain; they claimed success should anyone with the help of God or nature (says Hock) begin to get better, and so were beginning to rival the physicians seriously. The contemporary medical ethics of the physicians reserved its strongest censure for those who commerced with empirics.[12]

Whether or not doctors elsewhere were hesitant about treating pox cases, they soon found it advantageous to denigrate the empirics' practice. In Italy, Benivieni claimed that, rather than their refusal to treat the disease, it was the physicians' failure in curing it that drove patients to the empirics. Borgarucci too recorded the early failure of the physicians to cure the pox and held that as a result they were thought despicable throughout Europe.[13] Benivieni and Friese thought that the rough treatment of the patients by the empirics made all the symptoms worse, turning small nodes into stinking ulcers. Leonhart Schmaus, professor of medicine in Vienna, writing in 1518, thought that many had died simply from empirical treatment.[14]

But the physicians were also uncomfortably aware that some of the empirics appeared to be successful. After all, both major treatments for the pox, mercury and guaiacum, were empirical remedies. Borgarucci, who was a surgeon himself, praised the bravery of the surgeons who had first faced the dangers of treating pox and who had used mercury.[15] Friese too recalled the rash courage of the first empirics in treating the pox, and attributed their successes to their courage rather than their skill.[16] Convinced that the world was full of undiscovered remedies of which there was no *a priori* knowledge, Pietro Trapolino found it natural that sometimes the empiric cured better than the most learned man, and that often the pox was cured only by empirics and barbers.[17]

Schmaus had a particular reason to be familiar with empirical remedies, for he was a member of a commission sent by the Emperor Maximilian to Spain to observe experiments being made with guaiacum. Maximilian, whom we met in an earlier chapter and who at first thought the pox was God's punishment for blasphemy, had now caught it himself and began to think about its cure. Nicolaus Pol (1470–c.1532), Maximilian's personal physician, reported back in December 1517[18] and a year later the substance of the report leaked out in a Latin and a vernacular tract by Schmaus. It described in simple terms the preparation and use of the guaiac-water and makes no use of the learned apparatus.

In the face of the empirical challenge, the strategy of the learned doctors was therefore double. They first had to take the apparently successful remedies of the empirics and incorporate them into learned medicine, arguing that only by the theory of medicine could the remedies be understood and used most effectively. We have seen some evidence of this strategy already. Second, they stressed the learnedness and rationality of their own medicine. This happened in two ways, which seem to represent two different kinds of practitioner. Each centres round an adjective used to illustrate what was so good about university medicine. For some, good medicine was 'canonical'. Sometimes this was used as an equivalent of 'regular', that is, following a set of rules. In discussing how the rational doctor treats pox so much better than the empiric, the Spanish author Joan Almenar (*fl.* 1500), for example, uses the phrase *regulariter operari*.[19] The term 'canonical' also implied 'orthodox', following intelligible and rational rules in a medical world where many were driven to 'occult' explanations by the obscurity of the causes of the pox.[20] The term also has resonances of conventual life, where canons and others were 'regular' in ordering their lives according to rules of conduct. Canons of behaviour were wider than this, however, and in the medical profession the term surely was consciously used to reflect the orderliness, utility and authority of the *Canon* of Avicenna.[21]

When many renaissance medical title-pages refer to Galen as the 'Prince of Physicians, second only to Hippocrates', it is humanist or hellenist advertising. The 'Prince' to many of the authors who wrote on pox was in fact Avicenna. Giorgio Vella of Brescia,[22] Marino Brocardo of Venice,[23] Benedetto Rinio (1485–c.1565) of Venice[24] and Pietro Trapolino in Padua[25] all call Avicenna the 'Prince', often side by side with Galen and generally without seeking conflict between them. Lorenz Friese made a point of promoting Avicenna as the Prince among the German physicians. In contrast were those, beginning with Leoniceno, who found Avicenna an unsatisfactory author; we have seen that Leoniceno attacked Avicenna. For the hellenists the Prince was Galen, and when they also mention Avicenna it is often enough to explain Galen's superiority. Among our authors Antonio Scanaroli, disciple of Leoniceno, is an example; he regarded his tract as an extension of the debate in Ferrara.[26]

The other adjective used by the learned physicians in promoting their own kind of medicine when dealing with the French Disease was 'methodical'. This has clear connections with 'canonical' in implying a set of rules for proper rational and learned procedure. It too seems to relate to the title of an important medical text, the *De Methodo Medendi* of Galen. Giovanni Battista da Monte (1498–1551) uses the term for a systematised technique of teaching different arts;[27] Bernadino Tomitano (1506/17–76) of Padua, writing on the French Disease, treats method as a set of rules, enlightened with reason, to be followed by the medical man.[28] Borgarucci called his entire book on the pox a method, *Methodus de Morbo Gallico.*[29] For him, method was partly a means of enquiry into natural things that were obscure (like the pox) and partly what structures good practice in medicine.

In general the employment of 'method' continued throughout the sixteenth century to be the strategy whereby the learned and rational physician medicalised the empirical treatments of the surgeons and others. For example Domenico Leone (d.1592), a medical teacher in Bologna, used the term (in 1562) in medicalising cures for fevers and tumours;[30] in the same university Giovanni Zecchi (1533–1601), the teacher of theoretical medicine, explained (in 1586) that treatments like fumigation for the pox were first discovered by empirics and were not safe; but 'corrected and handled by a particular method' they were now successful.[31] Likewise, Nicolò Macchelli (c.1494–1554) called his work on the pox a *Tractatus Methodicus*, and it is partly an attempt to provide rationalisations of a heat- or spirit-based contagion.[32]

Many of the points made above are illustrated by the French writer Jacques de Béthencourt in 1527.[33] A humanist and hellenist, he railed against the surgeons and little old women whose ignorance of the first principles of medicine was so dangerous. The surgeons' use of guaiacum (he said) was punishment and their application of mercury purgatory. He saw it as his job to bring Hippocratic and especially Galenic methodical and canonical reasoning to these empirical practices. He writes with the high style of the self-conscious humanist and clearly would have preferred to have been writing in Greek. Galen was the *humanissimus* of authors, he says, Greek in language and Greek by nation, like Hippocrates; we draw our medicine from such wellsprings, but in translation, like barbarians. The canon and method will be Galen's reasonings, his understanding of the whole body and what is natural: the very things of which the surgeon and the empirics are ignorant. It was not simply the case for Béthencourt that Galen was Greek, but that he had written with divine inspiration. Not only was he the *summus* doctor (after Hippocrates) but the *veracissimus*, his truth partly divine: Galen was to be revered in medicine as St Paul was in religion; his medical works are a bible, *probatissima biblia*. Like Sylvius (also in Paris), who accused Vesalius of 'breaking faith' with Galen,[34] Béthencourt uses the language and imagery of religion to support his medical opinions.

Béthencourt was indeed one of the few authors to extend an argument into the religious area. Even though the pox was widely seen as a divine punishment, most physicians expressly denied that it fell into their territory to discuss its divine origins. There would have been little advantage in doing so. While the physicians could usefully 'medicalise' empirical remedies and claim them for their own, they did not poach on the theologians' ground. Sometimes a doctor like Johannes Benedictus would make the obvious moral that divine anger and disease could be avoided by leading a morally good and physically clean life – *mens sana in sano corpore* – but as in Benedictus' case the advice comes from Avicenna, not from Christian sources. It partly depended on who was being addressed. We have seen in the case of Torrella that a doctor addressing a political magnate could suggest controlling the disease by rounding up all the prostitutes. But if the doctor was writing a *consilium* for an archbishop who had contracted the pox it would not do to dwell on the manner of its contagion. The doctor in question, Benedetto Rinio (c.1485–1565),[35] appropriately dwells on the changes in the air that caused the disease, as similar changes caused tertian fevers. Such universal causes involved no vice of personal behaviour, whether whoring or mishandling one's regimen. That such changes were, additionally, 'specific' and *occultae* rather than manifest made them somehow even less avoidable. Guillaume Rondelet (1507–66) gives some plain advice on modifying diagnosis according to the patient. If the patient has pustules on the *pudenda* or face and a liking for loose women then you may be quite sure, says Rondelet, that he has the French Disease. But these symptoms present difficulties when present in a virgin or a man of religion; then the doctor, says Rondelet, speaking, as regius professor and chancellor, for all doctors, expresses doubt 'and we blush to say what the disease is'. Instead, it is called perhaps a certain 'heat of the liver' or 'pimples' or some other *exanthemata*; or if some other condition appears at the same time then all attention is given to that instead, so that in the confusion the French Disease will lie hidden.[36]

What Is Disease?

The Galenic model

Thus the doctors attempted to prevent their professional rivals from taking over the new disease as their own. The doctors had to 'medicalise' the remedies of the empirics and assert again the superiority of their own rational and learned method. This meant withdrawing somewhat from the perception of lay people, civil authorities and the empirics that the pox was a thing, an entity, a disease of which there could be an ontology. The empirics stoutly asserted that the pox was an entity and that they had its antidote. This simple one-to-one relationship did not suit the physicians at all, and, as they struggled to complicate the situation, they again used the resources of their learned tradition.

The most common medical notion of disease was Galen's. A disease was what impeded a natural operation of the body. Its causes lay almost all within the body of the individual. They could be in his most basic parts, where they were a simple imbalance of elementary qualites, a *dyscrasia* or *intemperies*, 'distemper'. Or they could be in the organic parts, and might be congenital. There was also actual physical separation of parts, the 'solution of continuity'. There was a general relationship between these causes and the way the individual behaved – his diet, exercise, sleeping and so on. The effects of the causes and the actions of remedies all varied with the age, sex and qualitative disposition of the individual and the seasons, places and (by the time of the pox) the astrological circumstances. The learned doctor at the time of the pox laid much emphasis on the assessment of the individual patient and his needs. It was part of his claim that it was he, and not the empiric with his specifics and blanket remedies, who *understood* the patient and how remedies affected him.

In addition, Greek medicine included a range of named diseases, like *phthisis* and *pleuresis*, which were generally those where certain causes had similar effects in similar individuals. They were simply multiple cases of 'particular' diseases, that is, of individuals. The ancients also knew of 'epidemics', where large numbers of people were affected at the same time. The Hippocratic writings did not offer theoretical explanations of this to our pox authors, who in choosing between an astrological, natural and theurgical cause generally settled for a change in the air so powerful as to force itself on many differing individuals. To a limited extent then there was an ancient awareness of a disease as an entity, but what made the ontology of disease such a feature of sixteenth-century medicine was the obvious spread of the French Disease, from one human body to another. Contagion, which we looked at in the last chapter, is the key word in understanding how an ontological doctrine of disease developed. Contagion too is the central topic as we round off, in this final chapter, two stories that have emerged as we have followed the history of the French Disease: the questions of 'occult' causes and of dissent from orthodoxy.

Names, essences and quiddities

An ontological view of disease naturally centres on its essence. We have seen that, because the French Disease did not have a proper name, it was difficult for the learned physicians to fit it into their theory of medicine. It was not simply that they could not look it up in their books, but that a vernacular name carried *no meaning*. There were many, even among the learned physicians, for whom this was not a matter of great concern. They took as their text the well-known opinion of Galen, that physicians should not dispute about names, but about things. This is what we might call the 'realist' position, centred on the 'thing', the *res*, adopted for example by Trapolino. He calls the physician an *artifex realis*, a craftsman who works with things and consciously avoids disputes about mere names. This corresponds to the view of Antonio Scanaroli, that medicine, the business of the *artifex*, was a *scientia realis* in which the important distinctions were *reales* rather than dialectical.[37]

Thus a 'realist' physician could afford to ignore the vernacular names of the French Disease because, he argued, he was concerned with things rather than names. For Giovanni Pascale (*fl.* 1534) the vernacular names were not worth serious thought. 'Besides the joke'[38] of the vernacular names, he says, we should be aware that names follow opinion only, not the reality of things. Only in some cases are they well grounded and certain, such as squinancy, pleurisy, cholic, sciatica and peripneumonia. Other names follow from the resemblance between the disease they signify and some animal, as leprosy can be 'leonine', or a disease might be called *elephantia*, *testudo* or *glandula*. Or a disease might be named from similarities to the actions of animals, like *cancer*, *lupo*, *anthrax* and *bubo*; or from simple non-animal things, like *pruna*, *ignis persicus*, *sephiros*, *schirrus*, *nodus* and *scrophula*.

Pascale does not go further into the matter but it is clear that his argument throughout is that names are simple labels, historical accidents that have become customarily attached to things. Quite opposite is the view of Wendelinus Hock, and we may call it the nominalist position. 'You should know first that names are imposed on diseases and on other things to denote their substance or quality,'[39] he says, relying on Avicenna. This is not the earlier medieval view that somehow the etymology of its name revealed the essence of a thing, but it is a belief that gave a great deal of importance to names in the medical rationality of the day. A name may be taken from cause or effect, says Hock. If from the cause, then sometimes from the material cause, as 'pleurisy' from the membrane of the ribs (*pleura*) or 'melancholy' from the melancholic humour. Sometimes the name may be taken from the formal or efficient cause, or from a related form, like *elephantiasis*; or *serpigo* from *serpendo*.

A more extreme 'nominalist' position was taken by Marino Brocardo, who began with the Galenic advice to seek the essence of the disease first.[40] But for Brocardo the name preceded the essence: *praecognitio* of the name comes before that of the thing, he says. It followed that the 'French Disease' and all the other vulgar names could not lead to a knowledge of the essence and that in the absence of a real name the cause and *principia* must remain unknown. Brocardo argues that in practice the doctor seeks the essence of the disease from the senses, constructing it *a posteriori*, but again denies that causes and origins are knowable, hinting from Avicenna that they might be forms sent from heaven.

Whatever the status of names, most physicians agreed that the first item on the agenda of understanding and treating the French Disease was to understand its essence. The argument was Galen's – that first we must recognise what we are dealing with. The variation in terms used by renaissance doctors in interpreting this throws some light on what they thought a 'disease' was. They looked for essences, principles, quiddities and causes. The difficulty was that the essence of any disease was hidden within the diseased body. All that was visible were symptoms of one or more kinds, some of which may have served as signs to the doctor and others of which were simply 'accidents'. As the authors struggled to define the disease and so put themselves on a proper Galenic footing, many ended up with brief descriptions of observable events which could be used dialectically but which gave little support to an ontology of disease. A good example is Benedetto Vittori (d.1561), who first announces in his preface the necessity of finding the quiddity of the disease, and does so in a rather grand manner from Plato and Aristotle. But his first chapter, on quiddity, is little more than an assertion that the French Disease is epidemic, in affecting many people at the same time, but not pestilential, since chronic rather than acute.[41]

Vittori wrote this at mid-century. By then many writers had taken the matter a great deal further than the simple Galenic model of disease. There were a number of reasons for this. One was that the pox was often asserted to be a new disease. This meant that gaining knowledge about it was gaining *new* knowledge or making a discovery. The philosophers and physicians who wrote about the French Disease often enjoyed writing about the acquisition and evaluation of knowledge, and sometimes their discussions touched on the question we are interested in here: the ontology of disease. Jacopo Cattaneo (*fl.* 1510) faced the questions squarely. He wanted like others to find out first the 'what is?' that lies at the heart of every *scientia*. In the case of the pox, he says, this will lead him to answer the question of whether the disease can be an entity in nature, *ipsumque morbum Gallicum ens esse possibile in natura.*[42] It is again a question of recognising the essence. But the essence was hidden, and the only way of gaining knowledge about it was that adopted by Aristotle when discussing the soul: essences are recognised by their operations and the accidents proper to them. Wendelin Hock was in just the same position and took the argument further. It is because the disease is new that generating knowledge about it is *discovery*, passing from the known to the unknown.[43]

For Wendelin Hock this intellectual process was philosophical. But we can see that, much more than in the rather static body of school philosophy, it was in medicine that real urgency was felt about discovery. There was nothing in our sense 'philosophical' about the plague and the French Disease. When Hock says that the beginning of all philosophical (in his sense) discovery is *admiratio*,[44] he meant not only the wondering ignorance of the medical man but also his urgent anxiety to make discoveries about essences and cures. In moving from the known to the unknown therefore Hock begins with the 'accidents' of the disease – the results of its operations. He takes this from Avicenna, and in the relevant passage Avicenna distinguishes between manifest diseases (those which depend on changed elementary qualities) and 'occult'. In the case of the latter, concludes Hock, no true demonstration of the disease was possible. By 'demonstration' he means full philosophical knowledge of the thing and its causes, especially the final cause, the *purpose* of what was being generated. Hock uses the contemporary term *demonstratio propter quid* for this and asserts that it is not possible in the case of the French Disease. This is occult and we can only know about it by a *demonstratio quia*, that is, from its effects.

In arguing like this Hock was leaving open the question of whether the essence of the disease was some kind of imperceptible entity. It was a question that some doctors preferred not to deal with. It was possible to take a professional medical line and argue, often against the philosophers, that medicine was a *scientia* of things rather than names or dialectic. Marino Brocardo of Venice argued that the medical man was an *artifex sensitivus* in whom prominence had to be given to the senses. He looked therefore for the essence of the pox from its effects, *a posteriori*. Brocardo maintained that in the case of pox the process failed and its essence remained unknowable.[45] Others saw the difficulty, but felt the need to be able to know the essence. Giovanni Pascale, like so many, understood the force of Galen's admonition first to discover the essence, but he saw that the essence *per se* was not available to the senses and had to be constructed by the mind. The *canonicus* and *rationalis* doctor, thought Pascale, therefore begins with the intelligible and often visible causes and mentally constructs the essence, taking into account too the symptoms and signs, which are also available to the senses.[46]

Is the Pox a Disease at All?

In their search for the nature of the French Disease perhaps the majority of physicians refused to be driven to hidden natures or occult qualities. Those like Tomitano, who stuck to the Galenic method, argued the case for intelligible and manifest changes of elementary qualities. Important teachers like Rondelet, Manardi and, especially, Da Monte denied occult qualities.[47]

But often the French Disease could not be forced into a Galenic framework, and the attempts to do so clearly had a significant effect in changing sixteenth-century medicine. Let us take the case of another important teacher, Gabriele Falloppio (1523–62).[48] Like many others, he begins his discussion with a list of the alternative names of the French Disease. The absence of a real classical name and the plethora of vernacular alternatives leads his rhetoric towards a crisis of identity. It is a crisis that is heightened by his further argument that the French Disease does not fit into the Galenic model of disease – it is not a disturbance of qualities, a fault in conformation or an interruption of operation. Falloppio's conclusion is stark: the French Disease is not a disease.

But Falloppio was a man of the schools, and has engineered a paradox to make his resolution of it the more dramatic. He first asserts a simple faith that the pox is after all a disease – *Tamen credo esse morbum* – but if so, what *is* a disease? – *sed quisnam erit morbus?* How, in other words, was the pox to be squeezed into the apparatus of theoretical medicine and so be made a fit and proper topic for the rational and learned doctor? It was unthinkable to deny the definition 'of Galen and of nature' that a disease is what damages function. Falloppio's resolution of the paradox is a 'determination' of a disputed question by 'distinction' – he draws out of the term 'function' a meaning consistent with a new theoretical apparatus. He says the body's function is damaged in its 'whole form'. This allows him, like the French authors we have already met, to employ the category of changes taking place by means of 'whole substance' action, by which some agents, like poisons, affect the body in a way that was not manifest and did not rely on changes in elementary qualities. This could be found in Galen, as Falloppio knew; he also knew that to say that *diseases* or the body's reaction were 'whole substance' things was a neoteric idea. Falloppio argues that such things were not noted by Galen because Galen in his extant writings was working methodically, that is, according to the canons of natural philosophical rationality and intelligibility.

Classification of Disease

The net result of arguing for a 'whole substance' disease was to push the mind a little towards the notion of disease as an entity. It was unknown, to be sure, and its mode of action perhaps unknowable; but in the sixteenth century that did not diminish its reality. A disease that behaved according to its 'whole substance' was at least more than a collection of manifest causes producing intelligible symptoms within the body, which is what the methodical doctor saw. 'Whole substance' diseases acted 'irrationally' in not being amenable to cures chosen by means of reason. Falloppio says that this is why the French Disease was often cured best by empirics; and he stresses the long practical experience necessary for the recognition of 'whole substance' diseases. Significantly, he included the plague in this discussion: it is clear that for him at least the collective impact of the plague and the French Disease extended the Western perception of 'disease' from the Galenic, or methodical, to the 'occult' or hidden.

To the extent that diseases could be thought of as things and so discussed dialectically, they could be classified. For someone like Cattaneo, classification of diseases was a logical exercise and his discussion of the identity of pox, *lepra*, *elephantiasis*, *lichen* and so on is mostly syllogistic. He draws some authority from Porphyry and in practice his argument means that what one can predicate about is a thing, here a disease entity.[49] Classification was a useful device for the learned and rational doctor. It was a set of relationships of which use could be made in a rational medicine. To say that one disease was a species of another extended the definition of each and strengthened the doctor's intellectual grip on each. To say that the pox was a species of some known genus was a useful way of squeezing it into the apparatus. Since it had some symptoms that looked similar to symptoms of another disease, these symptoms could be called generic; symptoms unique to the pox were its specific symptoms. A disease that was a species of a genus known to the ancients looked a little less new and a little more acceptable to orthodox physicians.

Diseases connected by a species-genus relationship also invited similar treatment, so that to insert a new disease into a classification helped the doctor to further knowledge about it in this way too. In particular, Avicenna's *Canon*, as a highly systematised account of the body and diseases, gave more significance to the classification of disease. To put the pox in its proper slot in the *Canon* was to learn more about it. Some of our authors, like Johannes Benedictus, call this process 'capitulation', that is, giving the French Disease its proper 'chapter'. Benedictus thought that the pox was a species of scabies: *apud nostros ad capitulum scabiei reduci potest*, 'With us it is possible to reduce it to the chapter of scabies.'[50] The same language is used by Brocardo[51] in arguing that it was *not* possible to 'reduce it' to a chapter. We can guess from these authors and from Trapolino[52] that 'capitulation' was attempted for the pox only in relation to Avicenna, who, as Trapolino says, makes *propria capitula* for his named diseases. Just as species and genera were logical relationships made on the basis of the 'operations and accidents' of diseases with an eye on Aristotle and the commentators, so 'chapters' of diseases were subdivisions of Avicenna's discussion of diseases, recognised by the schoolmen of the sixteenth century just as they recognised other cardinal divisions of the text.

In short, neither species–genera relationships nor 'capitulation' were intended to reveal similarities between disease entities, but simply between their symptoms, signs and 'accidents' in general. The same point can be made from the fact that it was not uncommon for the renaissance doctor to assert that one disease could change into another. Naturally enough many diseases shared similar causes in regimen, diet, condition of the air and so on, and shared many symptoms. It followed that if the causes intensified, let us say, then a long-standing disease might alter its symptoms to the extent that the doctor recognised it as another disease. For the Galenist this was not some switch from one essential nature of a disease to another, for the essence of a disease was how far it could be logically shown to follow part of Galen's three-fold definition of disease as *dyscrasia*, bad conformation and damage to function.

We should have a similar caution in mind when reading about authors of our period who describe the pox as a multiple or compound disease. For the Galenist a disease was double if it was manifest in two of Galen's categories, let us say, *dyscrasia* and solution of continuity (a loss of physical cohesion). It did not consist of some combination of disease entities. An ontological conception of disease was more available to those who maintained a belief in some hidden disease process, such as that of 'whole substance'. We should recall that the Galenic model for this was poison and medicines which act by whole substance: attention was focused on the material basis of the 'substance' precisely by reason of the paradox that its manifest qualities were insufficient to explain the nature and extent of its action in the body. Naturally when reading about 'whole substance' things outside the body, and transferring the principle to diseases and the body itself, our doctors would have thought of a material basis of disease, in which the whole substance resided, and which came much closer to an ontology of disease.

A New Disease?

We have seen that there was no general agreement among the authors about whether the pox was a new disease. The topic relates directly to that of the ontology of disease, for clearly something which is new is freer of relatedness to other things and more autonomous in its being. To the extent that the doctors could not find its name, its place in the theoretical apparatus or its essence, they could not supply its relationships to other parts of medical knowledge. It stood apart.

Although these factors may have played a part in the way that the French Disease came to be seen as an entity, especially outside the medical profession, there were drawbacks for the physicians in accepting that it was new in any direct sense. It was their business to demonstrate that learned and rational medicine *could* understand and deal with the disease and, as we have seen, that meant forging links between the disease and other areas of medical knowledge. In particular the hellenists did not want to believe that the Greeks had not known the disease. They suffered in an acute form the difficulty of explaining why the disease was not named and described in the ancient literature, if it were not new. The way out of the difficulty was to say that the disease was only apparently new or was new in some heavily qualified sense. This gave the doctors the opportunity to remedicalise a disease of which the name had been lost.

Various strategies were available for this purpose. It could be argued that the astrological circumstances that gave rise to the disease returned so rarely that knowledge and the name of the disease were lost in the intervals. Perhaps the same thing applied to the human vices which called down God's wrath. Hellenists like Leoniceno liked to think that Hippocrates had described the disease, without naming it, in the third section of the *Aphorisms*. Those not of a hellenist persuasion, like Pistoris in Leipzig and Trapolino in Padua (in 1505) denied that the disease was to be found in this text. Another strategy was to claim that the disease was ancient, but only in the New World. Another possibility was to explain that the degeneration of modern man had made what were trifling inconveniences for the ancients serious diseases now.[53] Some thought that the pox was a new combination of old diseases, a strategy which like the others gave the doctor authority in medicalising it.

Other apparently new diseases prompted a similar reaction. One of them was the 'English Sweats', an acute and savage fever. The first appearance of the Sweats is said[54] to have been in Milford Haven in 1486, from where it reached London. After further outbreaks, it reached the Continent in 1529 (but was always confined to northern Europe). It created alarm in Antwerp and elsewhere, causing the city fathers to call a meeting of the physicians for their advice.

The physicians' reaction was characteristic. Like the French Disease, the English Sweats had only a vernacular name, and the doctors had to squeeze the disease into their learned apparatus. They were detailed in their explanation of the causes and nature of the Sweats. Many of these details would have fitted the plague equally well, and the pox almost perfectly. Thus we learn from Simon Riquin (*fl.* 1529) that the Sweats are God's scourge on those without the right religion or piety. The doctors made efforts to understand its causes, a major one of which was a corrupt state of the air, as with pox. Like the pox too, it was preceded by floods and storms and a particular astrological situation. As they were to do for the pox, humanists wrote verses about it; and doctors attempted to cure it in the way they came to treat the pox, by sweating.[55]

We have argued above (Chapters Two and Three) that the apparent newness of the French Disease was perceived differently by the doctor and layman. The layman saw clearly the doctor's inability to name the disease and he did not have the doctor's professional need to show that the disease was only apparently new and that medicine therefore had the resources to cope with it. What was important for the layman was that old things like plague happened from time to time and new ones like the English Sweats and the French Disease had happened recently. The men whose job it was to prevent these diseases causing devastation in their cities had to treat them as 'things'. Such an ontological view of disease was perhaps also encouraged by the use of specifics by unlicensed practitioners: a specific, after all, was aimed at the disease, not the patient. In learned medicine, as we have seen, the patient was the centre of the doctor's activity and around the patient were organised the elaborate theoretical structure and practical regimen of traditional medicine. This was controlled by the doctor and was part of the image he generated for professional purposes. Specifics cut through all this and the doctors had either to stigmatise them (along with their users) or to bring them into learned medicine by explaining them. Possibly such considerations about new diseases, with a new ontology and new specific cures that did not have known mechanisms of action, can help to explain the rise of medical dissent.

When this dissent appeared it indeed took the form of claiming that some diseases were really new. Later in the century some of our French Disease authors were using examples of new diseases deliberately to show that Galenic medicine was incomplete. Three examples seem to have caught the imagination. The first is two old observations by Gentile da Foligno (who had died during the plague of 1348) of stones generated in the gut and voided through the mouth. The story is given by Trapolino and Rinio[56] and the point is that what Gentile saw twice, Galen never saw at all. Trapolino adds to the list of new diseases two new fevers, a 'seventh' and a 'ninth', no doubt so called from the period of their critical days, like the traditional tertians and quartans. The second new disease discussed by these two authors was the worm generated between the skin and the flesh, unknown to all authors. Trapolino discusses intestinal worms in the same place, but does not claim that they, like the flesh-worm, were unknown to Galen. Perhaps this is another story from Gentile, for certainly he is the source of the third new disease given by these two authors. This was a cough caused by small animals in the lungs. They were *mustilliones* (perhaps resembling vinegar-flies) and as they moved so they brought on the cough, giving relief as they stopped. Here was a disease entity of another sort.

The French Disease Changes

There is a sense, in the sixteenth-century discussions about the coming of the French Disease, in which it was seen not only as a new disease, but also as a *young* disease. Like most young things, it was at first vigorous and then slowly became weaker (see also Chapter Seven). In this way too it was seen as an entity, having some of the characteristics of other natural kinds. When Luigini made his collection of old and new accounts of the pox in 1566 the disease was about seventy years old and seemed to be showing its age. Alessandro Trajano Petronio (d.1585) recalled how savage it had been at its first appearance, and how it had spread by indirect contagion, sparing no classes of victim.[57] Its only cure at that stage, he said, was mercury, with all its attendant evils. But Petronius held that the more successful medicine, guaiacum, had somehow wrought a change on the disease, making it weaker, more bearable to the patient, and curable. His sense is that the relationship is between the wood and the pox, not that individual *patients* are now routinely made better. The disease, he says, has become 'more accustomed', *mansuetius,* with the result that fewer precautions against contagion are necessary, for it is no longer transmitted by indirect contagion through clothes and similar things, nor even by simple skin contact. His words imply that he thought of the disease as some enduring entity which passed from body to body and which had been weakened by the medicines used there. This entity can hardly be other than the *fomes* and *seminaria* that he envisaged as the agents of indirect contagion which we met above. He thought that the major changes that had made the disease shorter in duration and had removed its pustules had occurred in the previous thirty-five years. Perhaps indeed (he added) what was experienced now was a mere simulacrum of the pox; perhaps the pox, like some particular diseases, can change into other diseases and was now doing so.[58]

Antonio Musa Brasavola (1500–55) was another author who thought that the pox had changed during its European career.[59] This helped him explain how he disagreed with Leoniceno, his teacher. He was able to declare that Leoniceno's description of the pox at the end of the previous century had been correct, but that since then it had begun to change in a number of ways. Sometimes it appeared without pustules, with only pain; at other times it manifested itself in hard tumours instead of pustules. Not only that, but Brasavola thought that about twenty years before he wrote new symptoms had appeared. Brasavola was the man who drove himself almost to distraction by constructing a huge index to the works of Galen, and his categorising instincts appear here in his scheme of classification of the forms of the French Disease. For him it was above all a multiple or compound disease: not a collection of disease essences or entities, but something that manifests itself at different levels in the Galenic account of 'disease'. With permutations of the symptoms Brasavola makes new species (in this sense) within the genus of the French Disease. Pain on its own is 'French pains' while pustules without other symptoms are 'French scabies'. 'French tumours' are the hard tumours on their own; and these three simple species can exist in combination. For Brasavola the new symptoms are five other species and follow either the changes in the disease or its decline. Brasavola says that these species generally follow in sequence, so that they behave as a stages in a sequence. They are characterised by loss of hair, of teeth, of nails, blindness and gonorrhoea. Permutation of the symptoms of these five species with those of the three simple species gives Brasavola a *refertissimus* list of varieties of the pox (it attracted some criticism from less tidy-minded doctors).[60]

Later still in the century more authors agreed that the pox had changed. They were not old enough to remember its first appearance and necessarily relied on older accounts, on textbooks and perhaps on other sources. One of these newer doctors, interviewing an old man who had lived through the appearance of the pox, was told by him that it had begun as a result of cannibalism during the notable periods of famine that we saw accompanied the arrival of the 'Neapolitan Disease'. (The old man was in a hospital in Naples, and the story was reported by André du Laurens (1558–1609), who did not like to call it the 'French Disease'.)[61] We have seen that other accounts of the early days of the pox described it as very savage and often fatal. The doctors of the later sixteenth century were acting as historians in looking at this early literature, and in looking at it – and indeed in collecting it together, like Luigini – for *medical* purposes, had perhaps misinterpreted their sources.

At all events, doctors like Laurent Joubert (1529–83), who had been taught at Montpellier by Rondelet and who was in 1577 chancellor of the university, had firm ideas about the decline of the disease.[62] He gave an oration in or about that year (it was published in 1581) in which he declared that the pox was simply a species of *variola* that had grown vigorous under the skies of the Indies but which was now declining and would vanish in European conditions. 'By passing through various bodies this exotic affection is now much milder, so that, declining and growing old, it will gain the apppearance of simple *scabies*, which is contagious in a similar way.'[63] The view that the disease was in decline was shared by Zecchi, the theoretician of Bologna (1586),[64] and Girolamo Mercuriale (1530–1606), the *practicus* in Padua (writing about 1587) who argued that other diseases had also disappeared. By Mercuriale's time the strict classicism of the successful hellenists of mid-century had given way somewhat to a resurfacing and perhaps Counter-Reformation Christian piety.[65] When a hellenist wanted to refer to divine agencies, it was often the thunderbolt of Zeus and the pantheon, but for Mercuriale the possibility that the pox was the wrath of the *Deus Optimus Maximus* of the Christian tradition was as real as it had been for the first authors who had attempted to explain the new disease. For Mercuriale the divine source of the pox was an explanation also of why it was weakening and might disappear.[66] He also held that the ancients had discussed the principle that new diseases could arise (as a result of changes in regimen and the non-naturals), which was an added justification for thinking that the disease was mutable.

Another reason given by Mercuriale for the diminished power of the disease in his day is that experience of it has taught man to be more careful in his habits, diet and sexual activities. Cities, he says, used to be dirtier and so less healthy; we are better at avoiding contagion and at curing disease. The same reasons, he asserts, explain why the plague is now rare. This is good evidence for the argument of this chapter, that experience of medical disasters in the form of communicable diseases occurring in a comparatively short space of time did change the way people thought about disease: diseases are *things* and experience of them goes towards building up a civil and personal climate in which cleanliness of the person and of the streets is identified with health. Disease very easily carried a social, moral stigma, and now it was plain that, if you were not clean and continent, it would come and get you.[67]

Clearly whatever grows old and feeble, passing through many bodies and weakened by medicines, must have been seen as an entity. André du Laurens in Montpellier made the natural connection that a changed and weaker pox was less contagious.[68] Believing early accounts that it could be transmitted with the breath of an infected person he held that in his day (he wrote in 1587) contagion was possible only by means of a liquid medium in direct contact with the infected person. By now too Fracastoro's poem was becoming better known among the medical men[69] and perhaps his belief that even by mid-century the disease was weakening was becoming known.

The Material Basis of Disease

In the previous chapter we considered the mechanisms of contagion envisaged by physicians, and here we should look at a related matter, the 'matter of the disease', the substance inside the body that caused the symptoms. A number of people thought that the intractability and contagiousness of the French Disease demanded a material explanation. In a sense the traditional humours could be seen as a material basis for the disease, but what mattered was the disturbance of their *qualities*, not their substance. Johannes Benedictus[70] shows how it was possible to attribute a greater importance to the substance of the humours. Declaring the divine and astrological causes of pox, as a doctor he concentrates on the lower and material causes. He uses the phrase 'matter of disease', which shows that he is thinking of more than just a humoral imbalance. It was part of his thinking, and of medical theory in general, that the humour which had been made malign should be driven out of the body by nature. Driven to the surface, such matter formed the pustules in pox. This too was standard theory, as was Benedictus' assertion that some of the matter became lodged in the nerves, membranes and bones, causing the notorious pains of the French Disease. These bodily parts were customarily nourished by the more melancholic part of the blood, and it seemed then to Benedictus that the 'matter of the disease' was melancholic; its dry and earthy qualities made it very difficult to evacuate.

In pursuing this topic it will be useful to look at Scanaroli in a little more detail. He had been a pupil of Leoniceno and his work on the pox was partly a defence of his teacher's views against the criticism of Natale Montesauro and that aired during the dispute in Ferrara. Scanaroli called his treatise on the pox a 'useful disputation' and we are reminded again of the importance of the disputation, whether in a university or a court, as an opinion-former. As Scanaroli says, the French Disease was the concern of all Europe and was still *sub judice*, the subject of much argument.[71]

Scanaroli dismisses astrology contemptuously as a refuge for those ignorant of manifest causes; he is obliged therefore to say what those manifest causes are. His answer is that there are both external and internal pustules, formed as nature tries to expel the peccant humour, and that the internal ones can be found by dissection. A number of our authors report post-mortem findings, and it is evidence of a feeling that some 'matter of disease' with manifest qualities would be found. Scanaroli says that the internal pustules can be found close to the joints and nerves. Schmaus (1518) also said that, as a single disease, it is the same matter that causes the pustules and the pains; those without external pustules, he says, have internal ones, as can be seen in post-mortem anatomies.[72]

It was more usually reported from anatomies made upon those who had died while suffering from the French Disease that a white viscous 'matter of disease' was found associated with the nerves and membranes of the joints, where the pains had been felt. A doctor writing on the pox had to be able to explain these pains and indeed to decide whether they on their own consti-tuted a separate disease. Wendelin Hock thought that the French Disease was indeed compound and that part of it was Pliny's *mentagra*. Hock was very firm that the cause of the pain was a peccant phlegmatic material, found in quantity in the joints as the bones were separated in a post-mortem in Rome. Because this substance was phlegmatic, its source for Hock had to be in the brain, and he defined the French Disease accordingly.[73] In contrast Trapolino, who held that the disease was multiple and partly depended on 'whole substance' changes, had on neither account a need to find the same 'matter of disease' causing pains and pustules. In his account of post-mortem examina-tion he denies the existence of internal pustules and, while remarking on the extenuated appearance of the parts, has nothing to say on a phlegmatic substance at the joints.[74] Another author who claimed that the matter of disease was a viscid phlegm collected on the nerves, membranes and muscles was Josephus Struthius (1510–68), in 1555.[75] He claims that this is seen in post-mortem examinations, but he is probably relying on other people's accounts of dissection; the same is probably true of Giorgio Vella, who thought that the *gumma* on the bones was rather dry.[76] In the case of the anatomist Nicolò Massa, however, it is clear that first-hand knowledge was involved. Like Struthius he held that the matter of disease was a viscid phlegm that could be seen emerging from the pustules and ulcers. Massa had done some dissections and found that the white phlegm was collected where the pains were in life. Sometimes it was soft, he said, and at other times hard; he cites in particular a dissection he carried out in 1524, when he found the white matter adhering to the membranes of the bones of the lower leg and in the joints.[77]

Some authors abandon the humours entirely in giving explanations about the 'matter of disease'. Those who preferred 'whole substance' explanations necessarily required some substance in which the manifest qualities (so important in the humours) were not important. Trapolino made a big issue of the question of whether efficient causality (with manifest qualities) or the matter of disease was the more important consideration. He introduces terms that seem designed to distance his discussion from those about manifest qualities. He thought that what made a particular individual liable to contract the French Disease was a sort of ignitable quality, tinder, *fomes (verbi causa) morbi Gallici* generated within that person from corruption. This could be 'set on fire' by some contagious spark from another sufferer. Giorgio Vella also thought that infection could happen in the manner of a spark that ignited something in the new victim. For him, this was almost an immaterial contagion and he talks of a 'symbolic' transfer of putrefaction.[78]

While the 'matter of disease' was readily seen as that which nature was attempting to evacuate through the pustules, it was less often argued that the matter of disease was the agent of contagion. For Massa there *was* a close correlation, for he claimed that any material disease generated an evil vapour,[79] and that the French Disease was spread in this way even through inanimate intermediaries such as clothing and food. (He claimed to have treated the disease caught in this way in children of three, six and eleven years of age.) As an anatomist Massa made a great deal of what he called *anatomia sensata*, where it was the job of the anatomist to report only things actually seen in dissection. This seems obvious enough to us but in the first half of the sixteenth century it was a radical sensory epistemology that denied the use of authority in anatomy and so in the eyes of many contemporaries it was incomplete or even empirical. In the case of the post-mortem of the pox patient Massa presents himself as obliged willy-nilly – *velimus nolimus* – to accept the evidence of his eyes that the phlegm was the material basis of the disease. Yet even on this basis, with a material basis of both the disease and contagion, Massa invokes subtlety to explain how the contagious vapour generates the disease again in a new body and how the matter of disease has its effects.

There is a similar hesitation about identifying the matter of disease and the agent of contagion in the discussion about the pox by Pietro Andrea Mattioli (1500–77). He frames it in the form of a dialogue between Andreas (who represents Mattioli) and Franciscus. Andreas reports on a period he spent with Bernadinus Hispanus at the Incurabili of San Giacomo in Rome, where many died infected with the French Disease.[80] Andreas says that he performed dissections in search of a *pituita* or phlegm, but did not always find it. His account of the cause of the disease accordingly gives a limited role to a matter of disease, which he says is not in itself damaging. But it has its effect in an occult way, and so opens the pores of the body, allowing entry to the agent of contagion, a *virus* that reaches the liver.

Other authors also used terms that show that they were anxious to get away from explanations based solely on manifest qualities. Leonardo Botallo (b.1530), the anatomist, called the French Disease a *lues*, a general word for 'pestilence' or 'corruption'.[81] The French writers did the same, and Luigi Luigini (b.1526), the man who collected together all the previous work on the disease in 1566, said (in addressing the anatomist Massa) that it was a *lues* that spread its *virus* by contagion. *Virus* is 'slime' or 'poison' and Luigini is seeking to express the idea of a substance that is the agent of transmission from one person to another. The same term is used by Cattaneo in explaining that the origin of the pox is a poisonous substance developed from menstrual blood. This poison infects the entire mass of blood of the woman and also infects the man. Cattaneo needed some material thing to explain how infection happens by a material agent, *ab re*, which indeed explains how this infective disease is different from others (like *lepra* and scabies).[82] The *virus* was this material agent and Cattaneo has other analogies to explain how it effects contagion. It is like a ferment, he says, or like the bites of wild animals and poison. Like a ferment, it *changes the nature* of what it infects so that it becomes like itself: the ferment reproduces itself. The same doctrine and the term *virus* were also used by Mattioli.[83]

Sennert

Our last major author is Daniel Sennert. He was born (in Breslau) in 1572, by which time many authors had decided that the disease, an entity in itself and contagious in a material way, was growing old. Traditional natural philosophy was still in place in the schools, although under increasing attack from outside. Sennert died in 1637, the year in which Descartes published his *Discourse on Method*. Some natural philosophers had already decided, like Descartes, that the world, once full of sympathies and subtleties, was a *machine*. The argument applied to the human body as well: faculties and attractions were replaced by passive particles moved by contact. In the *Discourse* Descartes chose the motion of the heart as the principal example of the machinery of the body.

Many of the new philosophers were protestants. So was Sennert, who was educated at Wittenberg and became a professor there in 1602. He saw his business as reconciling the new particulate philosophy, including chemistry, with parts of the old. He worked hard at this in Wittenberg, where he remained until he died (he was rector six times), and produced a huge synthesis in his *Opera Omnia*.[84]

On the eve of a wholly mechanical medicine, Sennert's work serves to sum up the intellectual and cultural changes we have observed, each of which had some effect on the way people thought about the French Disease. The new Platonism, hermeticism and atomism of the late fifteenth century were a fecund source of new doctrines throughout the sixteenth. The Reformation and Counter-Reformation changed people's ideas about the relationship of man to God and about the nature of the human body. Italian civic humanism provided a base outside the universities for an alternative culture. Even within the universities there were ways of side-stepping the statutory peripatetic texts of the arts-course natural philosophy. Many began to see not only that traditional natural philosophy played an important role in imparting common belief and hence stability in society, but also that it did not represent the physical truth of things. Those who searched for a new truth had nothing so complete as what they wanted to replace and agreed on little except that matter was probably made up of particles that moved by contact.[85] Medicine, recognised as an extension of natural philosophy, also changed and here we look at how different notions of contagion and the nature of disease in general were used to explain and deal with the French Disease.

An important group of people who differed from orthodox medicine and natural philosophy were the chemists, who became numerous by the end of the sixteenth century. Many of them owed some allegiance to Paracelsus and were ready to dispense with the traditional elements and humours. Sennert adopted some of the chemists' teaching, and approved of Paracelsus' internal use of mercury in the treatment of the French Disease, but he thought it erroneous to depart from the traditional four humours.[86] The chemists believed that chemical remedies were more effective than simples, and that the essence of plants could be separated and concentrated by distillation. The inability of traditional physicians to deal effectively with the French Disease was proof to the chemists that stronger medicines were needed; it was useless to use Galenic methods to treat a disease that Galen had not known.[87] In protestant countries part of the appeal of the new chemistry was that it avoided the classical authors, who were increasingly seen as too heathen. By the early seventeenth century in England the chemical physicians had organised themselves and posed a real threat to the orthodox College of Physicians.

In discussing the French Disease, Sennert presents himself as a traditionalist. Indeed, he attacks his enemies with the charge that it is they, not he, who are neoterics, *novatores* and *paradoxologi* who abandon admirable antiquity.[88] But he made many enemies by the novelty of some of his doctrines, a number of which were derived from the chemists.[89] In his explanation of the transmission and nature of the pox he used the term 'miasma', a word appropriated by many historians for all theories about transmission that were employed before the germ theory. But Sennert was perhaps the only author among all those we have met who used the term. Nor did he mean by it some sort of poisonous vapour that collected in certain places. He held that the miasma was a medium of transmission, not the agent of infection. What was transmitted through this medium was particulate. He called the particles *semina* and *seminaria*, the 'seeds' of the French Disease that earlier writers had described. They are analogous to the seeds of plants and contain within themselves the whole nature of the disease, and once in the body they impose a *diathesis* upon it, attacking its whole substance and so disposing its parts that they are slowly assimilated to it, as plants draw from the soil.[90] The doctrine that the pox is like a plant, with seeds that germinate in and nourish themselves from the body as they grow, is one that Sennert developed from his review of the literature on the French Disease, much of which we have now examined. It is a strong statement about the ontology of disease, greatly influenced by accumulated experience of contagious diseases since the plague, and informed by current natural philosophy. That is, Sennert's 'seeds' are more than the *seminaria* of earlier writers: they were, he said, more like atoms, and could become lodged in clothes and other items that helped to spread the French Disease.

But Sennert's atomism is not of the Lucretian kind. He draws more upon the doctrines of 'subtlety' that had been used by those who disliked school natural philosophy. The particles that he thought were responsible for spreading the French Disease were very like *species*, the superficial images projected from the surface of things, used to explain perception in the thirteenth century. Sennert expands the comparison: *lumen*, light, is the image of *lux*, its source; the image in the mirror is the species of the observer. Sennert calls these species 'spiritual' (probably from his reading of Fracastoro on sympathy). He wanted to make it clear that they had little in common with the old material qualities. The latter are in their subject and move with it, are received successively by it and are bound to it. Spiritual species in contrast continually radiate off from their subject, forming a sphere and diffusing away into the universe. Some of them can cross solid bodies, like sound and the species of the magnet. Although they have some features of corporeality, like limitation of size and having some material effects, they are quite distinct from the atoms with which a number of people are wont to explain effects in a non-Aristotelian way and which Fracastoro discusses in his account of sympathy (says Sennert).[91] For Sennert such spiritual species are essentially occult, in having visible effects without visible means of acting, and he is not over-concerned to explain how they do act. But there are, he is sure, many of them, invisible to the senses and responsible for many of the appearances of what was (elsewhere) called the magnetical philosophy and many of the surprising effects of sympathy.

Although very like spiritual species, the seeds of the French Disease were different, in not radiating out into a sphere and in needing a material medium for transmission. It is plain that he is modifying a basic physical principle to explain the special case of this contagious disease. His explanation is detailed and entirely consistent with other parts of his natural philosophy. His systematic coverage owes much to the fact that he was a university teacher for a long time. Having been teaching his doctrines of occult and poisonous disease since 1607, and largely by disputation, Sennert provides much material that had doubtless found use as the disputed questions of theses. Certainly an authoritative teacher had to be able to settle questions of this kind, and undoubtedly Sennert did so. Often enough a teacher would establish a whole doctrine by having his pupils defend (and thus prove the correctness of) a series of related theses that could be later assembled as a textbook. It was as a teacher too that Sennert showed himself to be a master of the literature on the pox. Sometimes his accounts of other people's teaching form a little history of his topic, leading up to his own doctrines. He does not hesitate to name and attack his enemies.

So then, within Sennert's systematic coverage, in what way did the cause of the French Disease differ from a species? To provide an answer Sennert brings in a whole range of things that share the characteristics of the cause of the French Disease. To list a few of them here will serve to remind us of what we have met in discussing other authors in this book, and to remind us that every act of understanding the pox meant employing part of natural philosophy, which could vary greatly from one group of doctors to another. Sennert says the cause of the French Disease has occult, poisonous, contagious and particulate properties, each shared by some other things and events. It is occult, in being hidden to the senses and in involving only very small amounts of matter, like the spiritual species that passes up the fisherman's spear from the electric eel, *torpedo*, and is not a material quality nor atoms. Poisons in general, he adds, may work in the same way (although some are clearly material). The important part of the mechanism of poisons was 'whole substance' action, and this was a major kind of occult action for Sennert as for the authors discussed above. Sennert systematises his position on occult qualities as follows.[92] First are occult qualities occurring in all examples of the kind. This derives from their specific form – their form as a living species – and an example is the *echeneis* or *remora*, a fish said by Pliny to be able to stop ships under sail. Another is the electric eel, harmful in life but eatable after death. In itself, says Sennert, the example of the eel is slight, yet irrefutable; it is a signpost to a whole field of 'alternative' explanation of nature, sympathies and antipathies. So systematic and so influential was Sennert that these alternatives have almost become the new orthodoxy.

The most important part of Sennert's account of the cause of the pox is the ontological status of the seeds of the disease. The point will bear repeating. The seeds were particles, but not passive ones like Lucretian atoms. In a generally particulate natural philosophy in which there were active qualities and sympathies, Sennert endowed the *semina* with characteristics of a living organism.[93] They implanted themselves in the substance of the body and grew like plants, changing the nature of the body to that of themselves, as plants draw material from the soil. Not only was the pox an entity, it was one that feeds on the flesh and grows at its expense. Like other plants the *semina* produced more seeds that could infect other bodies by way of the miasma. There was in other words continuity of substance from generation to generation and the pox passed through many bodies. Like others before him Sennert thought that this process weakened the pox, which was growing old like an individual. He argued that it had been a new disease when it first appeared (at least in the Old World). Inevitably, writing in the early seventeenth century about a literature that had begun in the late fifteenth, Sennert was partly thinking in historical terms, and he counted over eighty works on the topic. Like Luigini in the middle of the sixteenth century, and like the other collectors mentioned in chapter one of this volume, Sennert had to decide which written works were about the French Disease; correspondingly to a certain extent what was in the books determined what the French Disease was. Collections, bibliographies and reference works mutually reinforce the authority of what they contain. But what was in the books did not agree with Sennert's experience. When writing on the pox he had thirty-four years' experience of treating it in Wittenberg. He knew that in the individual the disease could last as long as thirty years, with a late recrudescence of symptoms, while in contrast some of the early works stress the high and rapid mortality in the disease. Comparing his own experience with the early literature, Sennert thought that the disease had changed: it now caused fewer pustules and the pain was less, but it produced more gummy eruptions and greater loss of hair.

Thus the perception of the French Disease by Sennert was very different from that of the participants in the disputations at Ferrara and Leipzig at the end of the fifteenth century. The pox had become a thing, constructed in the image of a new philosophy, a living thing that had once had a vigorous youth and was now in old age. A central question in Leipzig was: could elementary air become corrupt in its qualities? While qualities remained active in Sennert's philosophy, they were very different kinds of things. Sennert the teacher is well aware of the difference and he compiles a short history of this central topic, beginning with Galen's distinction between manifest elementary qualities and 'whole substance' action and running down through Cardano, Scaliger and Fernel, whose doctrine he adopts and extends.[94] Sennert's enemy is Thomas Erastus (1524–83), who savagely attacked Paracelsus[95] and insisted that all effects came from manifest qualities. Nothing in philosophy is more damnable, says Sennert. He has at his disposal a long list of things that cannot be supposed to act by change in elementary qualities: the magnet, purges, opium, poisonous animals and contagious diseases among them. He emphasises more than had previous writers that these act in an entirely different *kind* of way. To attract iron, to purge bile, to induce sleep, to kill very quickly with very small amounts of matter, has nothing in common with the slow changes brought about by elementary qualities.

Sennert elevates the qualitative difference between manifest and occult action into a law of nature. 'Nothing acts beyond the powers of its kind', *nihil agat ultra vires suae speciei*.[96] Thus by mixing four colours, a whole range of other colours is produced, but they remain colours. This infallible law of nature meant that even those who accepted the existence of occult qualities but derived them from prime qualities were wrong. Nor could Sennert allow that occult qualities always derived from 'specific' form, for opium and rhubarb are but parts of plants and so do not have specific form.[97] He lived in a new philosophical world. For him qualities were active, but some of them – he calls them intentional – are simply sensations that we contrive, like letting light shine through a bottle of wine and appearing red, or dressing ourselves or our walls in green. He is using Scaliger's exercises on Cardano's *De Subtilitate* where intentional qualities are distinguished from real, which are material. It helps us to understand Sennert's departure from school natural philosophy to see from which intellectual tradition he drew parts of his own philosophy.

Conclusion

This book has examined the early history of what the vast majority of contemporaries regarded as a new disease, the Mal Francese or the French Disease. Even though perceived as new, reactions of both the medical and non-medical worlds were based to a large degree on existing practices and ideas about coping with disease. Nevertheless, the French Disease did lead to the emergence of new civic and intellectual strategies.

Our approach differs from that of the majority of earlier writers on the subject in that we concentrate on contemporary understanding and perception of the disease, rather than making the assumption that the pox was the equivalent of the syphilis of the laboratory and germ theory. We have seen in these chapters that the French Disease was a more complex thing than the simple presence of a pathogen, projected backwards in time by people who know about pathogens.

We have also tried to portray more than the perceptions and reactions of the people at the time to the French Disease, and to give some account of how and why medicine changed. Rather than looking for medical progress, we have been concerned with finding causes of change in medicine.

The difference between these two approaches is clear, especially in periods when medicine did not seem to be conspicuously successful. For all the publications, the civil and religious reactions, the professional emergencies and contortions, the building and funding of hospitals, the ransacking of libraries and dissections of bodies, the poxed patient taking the best medical advice could only secure himself or herself in a desperately hot place and choose between drinking the juice of boiled sawdust or taking some danger-ous compound of mercury, perhaps slaked by the spittle of a hungry person. The reader might feel that a detailed analysis of such nonsense tells him or her nothing about the true nature of the disease or about the progress of medicine. The historian, of course, wants to know why guaiacum and mercury seemed like a good idea at the time; but he should also want to know the *kinds* of motive and external influences that drove doctors to this or any other answer. We have seen that these driving forces were of many different sorts, including religious, intellectual, professional, social, cultural and economic.

Many of these factors operate also in our society, not least those that give authority to the doctor and encourage the belief that medicine is powerful because it relies ultimately on the correct interpretation of the natural world – in our case, 'science'. We too as a society have diseases, some of them like the pox transmitted sexually, which medicine cannot cure. The intractability of a disease naturally draws attention to the logistics of the attack upon it, the resources and strategies of the people who find themselves teaching about it, treating it, suffering from it, organising help or attempting to prevent it.

The people who reacted to the French Disease normally did so as members of groups – often they belonged to more than one – and their actions varied with the nature of the group and its common interest. The biggest of such groups was the nation. The characteristic act of a nation is to distinguish itself from the eccentricities of foreigners. It is a truism of such societies that bad and new diseases come from somewhere else. They are generally brought by people with bad habits, especially your neighbours. Thus the Italians so effectively blamed the invading French that the 'French Disease' became a general name. The French blamed the Neapolitans, but with less success. Nothing was newer, more distant or more foreign than the New World and to many it came to seem natural that the new disease, and its empirical remedy, should have originated there.

Another important kind of grouping of people was that round a ruler, his court. The papal court was in many senses supra-national and at the time of the arrival of the pox claimed the religious allegiance of Europe. The court was also necessarily a political, economic and intellectual centre, and what its doctors thought and did about the French Disease was important. The courts of the Italian princes also gave more status in the region to their medical men and so offered models that could be followed by other doctors.

In Italy and Germany the important political group was the city and the area it controlled. Within a city, the group with fewest economic or political resources was the urban poor. Many of them depended in part on institutional charity, which became progressively more exclusive by the late fifteenth century, making distinctions, not only between the disabled and able-bodied poor but also between locals and outsiders. The city as a political unit might be defined in the person of the lord of the place or in the oligarchy of its important citizens, and it was not in the commercial or military interests of authority to succour citizens of competing cities. Only Rome, as the mother of Christianity, provided help to the sick poor from distant places. The strategy of the poor was to be conspicuous, perhaps pushing their smelly and objectionable bodies about on little trollies as they got in the way of decent folk. These were among the reasons why the pope encouraged the foundation of the network of Incurabili hospitals throughout Italy; if the sick poor were not cured therein, at least they were fed and housed (and the Church had a captive audience).

The city also controlled directly some forms of medical practice, for example by giving partial licences, on the basis of proven ability, to various kinds of uneducated specialists. The surgical guilds also maintained the right of surgeons to practise. Within the city the group with the greatest pretension to medical authority was the faculty of the *studium*: we have seen that the university-trained physician, whether in Rome, Ferrara or Leipzig, agreed with his colleagues and with his clients that the best medical answer to the pox was the learned and rational medicine that had been refined by university teachers since the thirteenth century. The superiority of this kind of medicine was part of the argument by which the doctor had inserted his subject into the new universities and developed it there, and in normal times it served him well. But new epidemics are out of the ordinary and university medicine was not a perfect resource for the university doctor competing in a medical marketplace. It lent itself best to long-term strategies of regimen based on the individuality of the patient and was unsuited to a situation where many different individuals quickly acquired the same disease.

In this situation some doctors simply refused to treat the disease, as their colleagues noted later with regret. The doctors also regretted that uneducated practitioners seized the opportunity for their own practice. They too were a group, and one not merely characterised by privation of the medical degree, for as we have seen they were often partially licensed in many European towns. Their resources were less cumbersome than the weight of learning of the universities and often included a specific or nostrum that was aimed strategically not at the individuality of the patient but at the disease the patients had in common.

Even the doctors admitted that this empirical strategy sometimes worked better than learned medicine. But it was professionally unthinkable that such a remedy should simply be adopted by the learned doctors. They had to make it a complex matter. They feared the competition of, and despised the practice of, the nimbler unlicensed practitioners. The characteristic action of the university doctors had to be to identify the French Disease and draw it into their apparatus of theory, that is, to understand it and to claim authority in handling it: in a word to 'medicalise' it. All of them agreed that this resource of learning was the only road to the correct treatment of the disease, and all agreed that all other kinds of practitioner were wrong: this was another reason for the reaction of the group as a whole being characteristic, the *quaestio disputata* of our Preface.

But not all was unity in the group of university-trained physicians. They could not agree on a mode of treatment, and while they in common deplored the fact that the two most widely used remedies, mercury and guaiacum wood, were of empirical origin, they could not agree on how they should be medicalised. Among the group of physicians as a whole, there were those who gave allegiance primarily to Greek, Arabic or Latin authors because they also belonged to groups of another kind, for example the hellenists or the defenders of the *res Latina*. Their resources were different and their strategies had to be different.

Because the university-trained physicians depended on their learning and rationality for their professional image, it was natural that they should seek to deal with the French Disease in a way characteristic of their group: by disputation, where learning and dialectical argumentation were recognised as the proper way of reaching the truth. We have seen that in Leipzig they agreed to dispute and that different allegiances of the disputants led to different conclusions. All men educated in a university had disputed at some stage and agreed on the utility of the disputation. Even in the less academically structured environment of a ducal court, like that at Ferrara, the disputation gave form to the argument about the nature and treatment of the French Disease.

While the university-trained doctors were a professional group, we may think of the hospital as an institutional group. It was also an institution that left many records, both written and architectural. And, as in the case of the learned doctors, those engaged in the founding and funding of hospitals had group characteristics. Pious men and women believed that the disease was God's vengeance and should be met by both the appropriate religious actions and practical social action that God allowed. The religious aspect of the disease and its moral side – it was often seen as a shameful thing to have – were as much parts of its identity as the pustules and the pain. Religious confraternities, such as the Italian Companies of Divine Love that raised money for Incurabili hospitals, were expressly groups of people with similar perceptions of the disease and shared ideals of action. They might be prompted into action by inspired preaching, and drew upon the wealth of patricians to implement their ideals. The religious confraternities existed in a society where the charitable distribution of aid was good for the person who received it, good for the immortal soul of the giver, and good for his standing in society. It was also good for his group that the streets were cleared, at least temporarily, of pitiable, disgusting and dangerously contagious sick poor. All these purposes could be met, and could be seen to be met, by the construction of a purpose-built hospital. That these were 'incurable hospitals' emphasised their charitable nature but did not prevent medicine from being practised within them. The doctors and surgeons who worked there extended their own practice in a new way.

Groups with common interests and a defining body of doctrine or practices tend to change slowly. Highly structured groups, like the university or the medical faculty within it, used public rituals of disputation, graduation and human dissection to display externally what distinguished them as a group – for the physicians it was largely learning and a rationality, in our period, based on anatomy. These things lent stability – or, if preferred, conservatism – to the structure of the institution, for it continued to meet the expectations of people with interests in it. A medicine that met expectations was also stable and in many senses successful.

But over the period covered in this book sources of authority alternative to those of the universities became available. Italian civic humanism and non-Aristotelian natural philosophy were outside the walls of the university. These two things were important to medicine and its understanding of the French Disease and both were treated differently by the new Reformed religion of the sixteenth century. Dissent took many related forms, and within medicine made the possibility of change greater.

Over this period too the perception of the French Disease changed. Cumulative experience of it gave it an ontology it did not have earlier. Part of its character was that it had had a vigorous youth and was now decaying in old age. It began to have a history. Medical men began to collect the literature of the disease, generally with a view to improving the understanding and therefore the treatment of it, or to give authority to a favoured mode of treatment. Handling the increasingly large body of literature had a number of results. One was the development of biographical and bibliographical techniques, which fed directly into the history of medicine as a discipline. Another was that the doctor gained authority from this extension to his learning and used it to his advantage: we have seen in this book a number of ways in which doctors could be perceived as successful despite being ignorant of germs. In other words medicine changed – it would be out of context here to say that it progressed – not essentially by an improved technical content, but by how far it did what people expected of it. This was partly engineered by the doctors themselves acting as a group, and their continued success in a changing world was a question of how they managed their relationship with other social and professional groups, each characterised by its own under-standing of the French Disease.

There is also a sense in which the French Disease contributed to a shift in the perception of the poor in the early modern period. Indeed, we have argued that the pox helped to create an increasingly intolerant attitude towards the poor. Unlike plague, which killed its victims rapidly, those sick with the French Disease remained to litter the streets and importune passers-by with their pathetic cries for alms. The hospitals established for their treatment were only one of a series of strategies adopted, especially in southern Europe, to cope with those sick from an incurable disease. But attitudes changed as the French Disease came to be seen as less incurable. Strategies adopted to deal with its victims took on a less specific character as these people merged with the growing mass of the poor, whose ability to survive became less certain with the increasing pressure on resources prompted by expanding populations in many parts of Europe.

Notes

Abbreviations

ADF   Archivio Diocesano di Ferrara
ASB   Archivio di Stato di Bologna
ASE   Archivio Segreto Estense
ASF   Archivio di Stato di Firenze
ASG   Archivio dell'Ospedale di San Giacomo in Augusta degli Incurabili
ASM   Archivio di Stato di Modena
ASR   Archivio di Stato di Roma
BCAP Biblioteca Comunale Augusta, Perugia
DFA   *Diario Ferrarese dall'anno 1409 sino al 1502 di autori incerti*
DFZ   *Diario Ferrarese dall'anno 1476 sino al 1504 di Bernardino Zambotti*
GDLI Battaglia, *Grande dizionario della lingua italiana*

Chapter One: Syphilis and the French Disease

1. (*Treponema pallidum*).
2. A. Cunningham, 'Transforming Plague: the laboratory and the identity of infectious disease', in A. Cunningham and P. Williams, eds, *The Laboratory Revolution in Medicine*, Cambridge, 1992, pp. 209–44; L. S. King, *Medical Thinking: a historical preface*, Princeton, 1982, esp. pp. 187–223; K. Codell Carter, 'Causes of Disease and Causes of Death', paper at the Conference on the History of Registration of Causes of Death, Indiana Univ., Bloomington, Nov. 1993; M. Nicolson, 'The Methastasic Theory of Pathogenesis and the Professional Interests of the Eighteenth-Century Physician', *Medical History*, 32 (1988), pp. 277–300; J. Arrizabalaga, 'Facing the Black Death: perceptions and reactions of university medical practitioners', in L. García-Ballester et al., eds, *Practical Medicine from Salerno to the Black Death*, Cambridge, 1994, pp. 237–88.

3. See C. E. Rosenberg, 'Disease in History: frame and frames', in C. E. Rosenberg and J. Golden, eds, *Framing Disease: the creation and negotiation of explanatory schemes*, Millbank Quarterly, 67, Suppl. 1 (1989), pp. 1–16.

4. For laboratory medicine see Cunningham and Williams, eds, *The Laboratory Revolution*.

5. On this new causal system and its philosophical origins, see C. Delkeskamp-Hayes and M. A. Gardell Cutter, eds, *Science, Technology, and the Art of Medicine: European–American dialogues*, Dordrecht, 1993, esp. pp. 57–162. For an interesting nineteenth-century case illustrating contemporary reluctance to abandon the old causal system see C. Hamlin, 'Predisposing Causes and Public Health in Early Nineteenth-Century Medical Thought', *Social History of Medicine*, 5/1, (1992), pp. 43–70.

6. Cunningham, 'Transforming Plague', pp. 210, 242.
7. Cunningham, 'Transforming Plague', p. 240.
8. On this topic, see L. G. Stevenson, 'Science Down the Drain: on the hostility of certain sanitarians to animal experimentation, bacteriology and immunology', *Bulletin of the History of Medicine*, 29 (1955), pp. 1–26.
9. Cunningham, 'Transforming Plague', pp. 238–42.
10. For the history of medical historiography, see among others, L. García-Ballester, 'Historia de la Historiografía médica', *Memoria de oposición a la Agregación de Historia de la medicina de la Universidad de Valencia*, Valencia, 1971 [typescript], 30 pp.; P. Laín-Entralgo, 'Vida, muerte y resurrección de la Historia de la Medicina', in A. Albarracín-Teulón, J. M. López-Piñero and L. S. Granjel, eds, *Medicina e Historia*, Madrid, 1980, pp. 9–24; J. M. López-Piñero, 'Los estudios históricosociales sobre la medicina', in E. Lesky, ed., *Medicina social. Estudios y testimonios históricos*, Madrid, 1984, pp. 9–30, and bibliography cited in these works.
11. *Aureum opus et sublime ad medellam non parum utile Plinii philosophi et medici integerrimi. Nonnullasque opuscula videlicet Joannis Almenar . . .*, Pavia, 1516; *Contenta in hoc volumine sunt infra notata. Marci Gattinarie . . .*, Venice, 1516; *Contenta. Nicolai Massae . . .*, [n.p.], 1532; *Liber de Morbo Gallico, in quo diversi celeberrimi in tali materia scribientes, medicine continentur auctores videlicet Nicolaus Leonicenus . . .*, Venice, 1535; *Morbi Gallici curandi ratio exquisitissima, a variis, iisdemque peritissimis medicis conscripta, nempe Petro Andrea Mattheolo Senensi . . .*, Basel, 1536; Lyon, 1536.
12. Aloysius Luisinus [Luigi Luigini], *De Morbo Gallico omnia quae extant apud omnes medicos cuiuscunque nationis, qui vel integris libris, vel quoquo alio modo huius affectus curationem methodice aut*

empirice tradiderunt, diligenter hincinde conquisita, sparsim inventa, erroribus expurgata, et in unum tandem hoc corpus redacta. In quo de ligno Indico, salsa perillia, radice Chynae, argento vivo, caeterisque rebus omnibus ad huius luis profligationem inventis, diffusissima tractatio habetur . . . Opus hac nostra aetate, qua Morbi Gallici vis passim vagatur, apprime necessarium, 2 vols and an appendix to the first, Venice, 1566–7.
13. Luigini, *De Morbo Gallico*, i, f. 2r.
14. Luigini, *De Morbo Gallico*, i, f. 3r.
15. Luigini, *De Morbo Gallico*, i, f. 2v.
16. Luigi Luigini, *Aphrodisiacus, sive de Lue Venerea in duos tomos bipartitus, continens omnia quaecumque hactenus de hac re sunt ab omnibus medicis conscripta. Ubi de ligno Indico, salsa perillia, radice Chynae, argento vivo, caeterisque rebus omnibus ad huius luis profligationem inventis, diffusissima tractatio habetur. Opus haec nostra aetate, qua morbi gallici vis passim vagatur, apprime necessarium, ab excellentissimo A. L. Utinensi, medico celeberrimo novissime collectum. Indice rerum omnium scitu dignarum adornarum. Editio longe emendatior, et ab innumeris mendis repurgata*, 2 vols in one, Leyden, 1728. According to several early modern sources, this collection had had two previous editions (1559 and 1599), although both appear to be lost.
17. Luigini, *Aphrodisiacus*, ff. [1r–11v].
18. Luigini, *Aphrodisiacus*, ff. 1r–v, 4v.
19. Christian Gottfried Gruner, ed., *Aphrodisiacus, sive de Lue Venerea in duas partes divisus quarum altera continet eius vestigia in veterum auctorum monimentis obvia, altera quos Aloysius Luisinus temere omisit scriptores et medicos et historicos ordine chronologico digestos. Collegit notulis instruxit glossarium indicemque rerum memorabilium subiecit D.C.G.G. . . .*, Jena, 1789.
20. Gruner, ed., *Aphrodisiacus*, p. ii.
21. Christian Gottfried Gruner, ed., *De Morbo Gallico scriptores medici et historici partim inediti partim rari et*

notationibus aucti. Accedunt morbi gallici origines maranicae. Collegit, edidit glossario et indice auxit D.C.G.G., Jena, 1793.

22. Gruner, ed., *De Morbo Gallico,* pp. v–xvii. We have not used a third volume containing sources on the venereal disease which Gruner published under the title *Spicilegium scriptorum de morbo gallico,* Jena, 1799–1802.

23. Conrad Heinrich Fuchs, *Die ältesten deutschen Schrifsteller über die Lustseuche in Deutschland von 1495 bis 1510, nebst mehrerer Anecdotis späterer Zeit, gesammelt und mit literarhistorischen Notizen und einer kurzen Darstellung der epidemischen Syphilis in Deutschland,* Göttingen, 1843. For the medical works, see pp. 1–302; for the additional sources collected, pp. 303–78; for the two appendices, pp. 381–414 and 415–54.

24. A. Corradi, 'Nuovi documenti per la storia delle malattie veneree in Italia dalla fine del quattrocento alla metà del cinquecento', *Annali Universali di Medicina e Chirurgia,* 269/808 (1884), pp. 289–386. Little has been written on this important medical historian, but see for now: *Dizionario biografico degli Italiani* (ongoing), Rome, 1983, xxix, pp. 313–15, and J. Henderson, '"A Certain Sickness with Suspicion of Contagion": physicians, plague and public health in early modern Florence', in W. Bynum and B. Fantini, eds, *The History of the Concepts of Infection, Contagion and Miasma,* forthcoming.

25. As to Sudhoff's historical method, sixty years ago Oswei Temkin, very expressively, said: 'All available facts had to be assembled, no detail had to be overlooked or despised, and however strongly an opinion might be maintained, it had to be based on these facts, and only then was a broader outlook allowed and required. This method is the requirement of real historical scholarship, which distinguishes it from dilettantism. Thus Sudhoff became the founder of modern critical history of medicine.' See O. Temkin, 'Karl Sudhoff, the Rediscoverer of Paracelsus', *Bulletin of the Institute of the History of Medicine,* 2/1 (1934), pp. 16–21: p. 20.

26. See also K. Sudhoff, *Graphische und typographische Erstlinge der Syphilisliteratur aus den Jahren 1495 und 1496,* Munich, 1912; *Aus der Frühgeschichte der Syphilis. Handschriften- und Inkunabelstudien epidemiologische Untersuchung und kritische Gänge,* Leipzig, 1912; *Zehn Syphilis Drucke aus den Jahren 1495–1498,* Milan, 1924.

27. K. Sudhoff, *The Earliest Printed Literature on Syphilis, being ten tractates from the years 1495–1498* [in complete facsimile with an introduction and other accessory material by K.S.; adapted by Charles Singer], Florence, 1925, p. xvii. See n. 26.

28. J. Astruc, *De Morbis Venereis libri sex in quibus disseritur tum de origine, propagatione et contagione horumce affectuum in genere, tum singulorum natura, aetiologia et therapeia, cum brevi analysi et epicrisi operum plerorumque quae de eodem argumento scripta sunt,* Paris, 1736; 2nd edn: *De morbis venereis . . . scripta sunt . . . Editio altera, auctior et emendatior, in qua additae sunt duae dissertationes novae,* 2 vols, Paris, 1740. Astruc's work was repeatedly published in Latin and translated into several European languages (French, English and Spanish, among others). Its vernacular editions were partly full translations, partly adapted and abridged versions.

29. See Astruc, *De Morbis Venereis,* 1736, pp. i–x; 1740, i, pp. i–xii.

30. The chronological distribution of the authors in the different books is as follows, 1st edn, bk 5 (1495–1599) and bk 6 (1600–1735); 2nd edn, bk 5 (1495–1549), bk 6 (1550–99), bk 7 (1600–49), bk 8 (1650–99) and bk 9 (1700–49).

31. J. K. Proksch, *Die Geschichte der venerischen Krankheiten,* 2 vols, Bonn, 1895.

32. J. L. Choulant, *Bibliotheca Medico-Historica sive catalogus librorum historicorum de re medica et scientia naturali systematicus*, Leipzig, 1842; H. Haeser, *Bibliotheca epidemiographica sive catalogus librorum de historia morborum epidemicorum cum generali tum speciali conscriptorum*, 2nd edn, Gripeswolda, 1862.

33. J. K. Proksch, *Die Litteratur über die venerischen Krankheiten von den ersten Schriften über Syphilis aus dem Ende des Fünfzehnten Jahrhunderts bis zum Jahre 1889*, 5 vols, Bonn, 1889–1900.

34. *Index Catalog of the Library of the Surgeon General's Office*, 5 ser., Washington, DC, 1880–1961: ser. I, xiv/1, pp. 89–93; ser. II, xvii, pp. 413–15; ser. III, x, pp. 40–2; ser. V, iii, p. 1488. Ser. IV stopped before 's'.

35. A. Gerbi, *La disputa del Nuevo Mundo. Historia de una polémica, 1750–1900*, 2nd edn, México, 1982, esp. pp. 102, 196–7.

36. See Gerbi, *La disputa*, pp. 77, 123, 150, passim. For the discussions on the origin of venereal disease–syphilis, see F. Guerra, 'The Dispute over Syphilis: Europe versus America', *Clio Medica*, 13/1 (1978), pp. 39–61.

37. C. de Pauw, *Recherches philosophiques sur les Américains, ou mémoires interessants pour servir à l'histoire de l'Espèce humaine*, Berlin, 1768–9.

38. On De Pauw's views, see Gerbi, *La disputa*, pp. 66–101; Guerra, 'The Dispute', pp. 47–8.

39. See also the discussion by A. Foa, 'The New and the Old: the spread of syphilis (1494–1530)', in E. Muir and G. Ruggiero, eds, *Sex and Gender in Historical Perspective*, Baltimore and London, 1990, pp. 26–45.

40. Compare Shakespeare: 'This precious stone set in the silver sea . . .', a 'fortress built by Nature for herself Against infection and the hand of war'. What is natural is what is at home and infection comes from elsewhere. Quoted in the useful study by J. Fabricius, *Syphilis in Shakespeare's England*, London, 1994, p. xi

41. A. Nunes Ribeiro Sanches, *A Dissertation on the Origin of the Venereal Disease; proving that it was not brought from America, but began in Europe by an epidemical distemper (translated from the original manuscript of an eminent physician)*, London, 1751; *Dissertation sur l'origine de la maladie vénérienne, pour prouver que ce mal n'est pas venu d'Amérique, mais qu'il a commencé en Europe, par une épidémie*, Paris, 1752. In addition to this work, which was repeatedly reissued, he also published *Examen historique sur l'apparition de la maladie vénérienne en Europe, et sur la nature de cette épidémie*, Lisbon, 1774, to support his former thesis with new arguments.

42. D. Willemse, *António Nunes Ribeiro Sanches – élève de Boerhaave – et son importance pour la Russie*, Leyden, 1966, pp. 20–2, 180–1; E. Jeanselme, *Histoire de la syphilis, son origin, son expansion. Progrès réalisés dans l'étude de cette maladie depuis la fin du XVe siècle jusqu'à l'époque contemporaine*, Paris, 1931, p. 4.

43. A Spanish translation of Clavijero's dissertation was published separately in Madrid in 1785 and was followed soon by the Benedictine Martín Sarmiento's leaflet on the same topic. See Martín Sarmiento, *Antigüedad de las bubas*, Madrid, 1787. On De Pauw's followers and opponents, see Gerbi, *La disputa*, esp. pp. 102–558; Guerra, 'The Dispute', pp. 49–50.

44. C. Girtanner, *Abhandlung über die venerische Krankheit*, 3 vols, Göttingen, 1788–9.

45. P.-G. Hensler, *Geschichte der Lustseuche, die zu Ende des fünfzehnten Jahrhunderts in Europa ausbrach*, Altona, 1783. Conceived as a two-volume work, only the second part of the second volume eventually appeared under the title *Über den West-indischen Ursprung der Lustseuche*, Hamburg, 1789.

46. See R. K. French, *Ancient Natural History: histories of nature*, London, 1994, chs 3 and 5.

47. Gruner related the arrival of this disease in Spain either with the first arrival there of some African Moors, 'perhaps mixed with Jews', who had escaped from their original cities having become suspected of practising a hidden religion, or with a 'more serious trade of things and bodies'.

48. *Morbi Gallici Origines Maranicae*; Gruner, ed., *De Morbo Gallico*, pp. iii–xxxvi.

49. See Foa, 'The New and the Old', pp. 37–42.

50. See V. Nutton, 'The Reception of Fracastoro's Theory of Contagion: the seed that fell among thorns?', *Osiris*, 6, 2nd ser. (1990), pp. 196–234. We shall meet numerous examples of these terms in the authors discussed in the following chapters.

51. J. Rosenbaum, *Geschichte der Lustseuche im Alterthume . . .*, Berlin, 1839. It was repeatedly published in Halle: 1845, 1882, 1883, 1888, 1892, 1893; Berlin: 1904, 1921, as well as translated into French: Brussels, 1847, and English: Paris, 1901.

52. Gruner, ed., *De Morbo Gallico*, pp. xiii–xiv.

53. Gruner, ed., *De Morbo Gallico*, pp. xvii–xviii.

54. J. Rosenbaum, *The Plague of Lust, being a History of Venereal Disease in Classical Antiquity . . .*, trans. from the 6th German edn, Paris, 1901, p. xvii: 'The question at issue is nothing less than that of gaining a clear insight into the nature and origin of the operation of a Disease that destroys the very marrow of Nations. Without such insight the Physician cannot hope, whether in the particular or speaking generally, to obtain a radical cure; and of all forms of Disease the Venereal is pre-eminently that where obscurity in the history of the malady conditions obscurity in its curative method.' This quotation comes from the preface of the first German edition of this work.

55. Gruner, ed., *De Morbo Gallico*, pp. xvi, xviii.

56. For a list including many physicians who contributed to this historical controversy, see Guerra, 'The Dispute', esp. pp. 50–3.

57. This might, for instance, explain to some extent some of the late nineteenth- and early twentieth-century contributions to this topic by Spanish and Latin American physicians, most of whom were in favour of exempting America from the charge of being the origin of venereal disease or syphilis. On the other hand, Claude Quétel's *History of Syphilis*, Cambridge, 1990 (originally published as *Le Mal de Naples* in Paris in 1986) provides a recent example illustrating the impact of nationalism on the studies of this topic. Quétel's ironical comments apropos the knowledge of the disease possessed by some of the earliest Spanish–Italian practitioners (pp. 19–22) are entirely inappropriate from an historical point of view. In addition the title of the book refers to a name for the French Disease the ephemeral fortune of which was restricted to late fifteenth- and early sixteenth-century France.

58. See most recently O. Dutour, G. Pálfi, J. Berato and J. P. Brun, eds, *L'Origine de la syphilis en Europe: avant ou après 1493?*, Actes du Colloque International de Toulon, 25–28 Nov. 1993, Toulon and Paris, 1994.

59. J. Arrizabalaga, 'Syphilis', in K. F. Kiple, ed., *The Cambridge World History of Human Disease*, Cambridge, 1993, p. 1029. For an overview of this dispute, see Guerra, 'The Dispute'.

60. See among others E. H. Hudson, *Non-Venereal Syphilis*, Edinburgh and London, 1958; Hudson, 'Treponematosis and Man's Social Evolution', *American Anthropologist*, 67 (1965), pp. 885–901; T. A. Cockburn, 'The Origin of the Treponematoses', *Bulletin of the World Health Organization*, 24 (1961), pp. 221–8; Cockburn, *The Evolution*

and Eradication of Infectious Diseases, Baltimore, 1963, pp. 152–74; C. J. Hackett, 'On the Origin of the Human Treponematoses (Pinta, Yaws, Endemic Syphilis and Venereal Syphilis)', *Bulletin of the World Health Organization,* 29 (1963), pp. 7–41; M. D. Grmek, *Les Maladies à l'aube de la civilisation occidentale,* Paris, 1983, pp. 199–225.

61. See R. K. French, 'Surgery and Scrophula', in C. Lawrence, ed., *Medical Theory, Surgical Practice: studies in the history of surgery,* London, 1992, pp. 85–100.

Chapter Two: The Arrival of the French Disease in Renaissance Italy

1. On this see A. Corradi, *Annali delle epidemie occorse in Italia dalle prime memorie fino al 1850,* 5 vols, Bologna, 1865–92 (facs. repr.: Bologna, 1972), i, pp. 338–60; iv, pp. 212–54; v, pp. 265–74.
2. On Charles VIII's invasion of Italy and its consequences, see L. von Pastor, *The History of the Popes from the Close of the Middle Ages,* 40 vols, London, 1891–1953, v (1898), pp. 434–81; C. M. Ady, 'The Invasions of Italy', in D. Hay, ed., *The New Cambridge Modern History,* i: *The Renaissance, 1493–1520,* Cambridge, 1961, pp. 343–67; and I. Cloulas, *Charles VIII et le mirage Italien,* Paris, 1986.
3. On all these events, particularly the floods, see Nicolò Leoniceno, *Libellus de Epidemia quam vulgo Morbum Gallicum vocant,* Venice, 1497, sigs d1r–v. For the Roman floods, see Pastor, *History of the Popes,* v, pp. 475–81. On the outbreak of pestilential diseases, cf. Corradi, *Annali,* i, pp. 349–53; iv, pp. 228–40; v, pp. 269–71. On Florence see J. Henderson, *Piety and Charity in Late Medieval Florence,* Oxford, 1994, ch. 9.
4. Antonio Benivieni, *De abditis nonnullis ac mirandis morborum et*

sanationum causis, Paris, 1528, *observatio* 57 (Fames valida), f. 12v.

5. Henderson, *Piety and Charity,* ch. 9.
6. The best collection of lay sources on Mal Francese from late fifteenth- and early sixteenth-century Italy is still that of A. Corradi, 'Nuovi documenti per la storia delle malattie veneree in Italia dalla fine del quattrocento alla metà del cinquecento', *Annali Universali di Medicina e Chirurgia,* 269/808 (1884), pp. 289–386. It has to be stressed that only one – a chronicle of Cremona – of the fifty sources reported by Corradi gave the date of the outbreak of the disease in Italy as 1495 (p. 361) – in contrast to the historians who have often placed it as early as 1493. As for the phrase Mal Francese, we have adopted the present-day Italian spelling in view of the many variations appearing in contemporary sources: *male franzoxo, mal francioso, male franzoxe, male franzoso, male franzese, mal francexo, mal françoxo, mal franzoxo* and *mal franzoso,* among others.
7. See, for example, A. G. Carmichael, *Plague and the Poor in Renaissance Florence,* Cambridge, 1986, ch. 5.
8. See some of the entries relating to Mal Francese in *Diario di Ser Tommaso di Silvestro* in *Ephemerides Urbevetanae dal Codice Vaticano Urbinate 1745 (AA. 1482–1514),* ed. L. Fumi, ii, in *Rerum Italicarum Scriptores,* Bologna, 1925, xv/5.
9. F. Guicciardini, *Storia d'Italia,* ed. S. S. Menchi, 3 vols, Turin, 1971, Bari, 1929, i, p. 233. Guicciardini appears in the contributions of the two most recent historians of Mal Francese in Italy: A. Malamani, 'Notizie sul mal francese e gli ospedali degli incurabili in età moderna', *Critica storica,* 15 (1978), pp. 193–4; A. Foa, 'The New and the Old: the spread of syphilis (1494–1530)', in E. Muir and G. Ruggiero, eds, *Sex and Gender in Historical Perspective,* Baltimore and London, 1990, p. 33.
10. Cf. R. Ridolfi, *The Life of Francesco*

Guicciardini, London, 1967, pp. 3, 259.

11. A. Corradi, 'Nuovi documenti', pp. 289–386.

12. See below for the additional sources consulted.

13. *Diario Ferrarese dall'anno 1476 sino al 1504 di Bernardino Zambotti*, ed. G. Pardi, in *Rerum Italicarum Scriptores*, Città di Castello and Bologna, 1934–7, xxiv/7 (henceforth *DFZ*) , pp. 267, 276–7; *Diario Ferrarese dall'anno 1409 sino al 1502 di autori incerti*, ed. G. Pardi, in *Rerum Italicarum Scriptores*, Città di Castello and Bologna, 1928–33, xxiv/7 (henceforth *DFA*), pp. 199–200, 204–5.

14. Archivio Arcivescovile di Ferrara: Fondo della Compagnia di S. Job de Ferrara 5, f. 2r (21.v.1499); S. Giobbe 4A (20.iii.1502); 13 (17.vii.1525).

15. See Chapter Three below.

16. *Diario di Gaspare Nadi*, ed. C. Ricci and A. Bacchi della Lega, Bologna, 1886, repr. 1969, p. 213; Fileno dalle Tuatte, 'Historia di Bologna principiando dalla sua origine, sino all'anno 1511', Biblioteca della Università di Bologna MS 1439, f. 422v, cf. Corradi, 'Nuovi documenti', p. 346; Friano degli Ubaldini, 'Cronaca dalla creazione del mondo fino all'anno di N.S. 1513, nella quale non lasciare di scrivere tutta l'istoria della sua Patria', Biblioteca della Università di Bologna MS 430, f. 77v: cf. Corradi, 'Nuovi documenti', pp. 245–6; Anon, 'Cronica Bianchina', unpublished: see Corradi, 'Nuovi documenti', p. 344; C. Ghirardacci, *Della Historia di Bologna*, ed. A. Sorbelli, *Rerum Italicarum Scriptores*, Città di Castello, 1915, xxx/iii/1/1, pp. xi–xii, 291–2.

17. Friano degli Ubaldini, 'Cronaca', f. 77v; Anon, 'Cronica Bianchina', p. 344; see below.

18. E. Cavriolo, *Dell'istorie della città di Brescia*, Venice, 1744, pp. 222, 364; Marin Sanudo, *I Diarii*, ed. R. Fulin et al., 58 vols, Venice, 1879–1902, i,

pp. 233–4; Jacopino de' Bianchi, *Cronaca Modenese*, in *Monumenta di Storia Patria delle Provincie Modenesi*, Parma, 1861, i, p. 153; L. Landucci, *Diario Fiorentino dal 1450 al 1516*, ed. I. Del Badia, Florence, 1883, repr. 1985, pp. 132, 134, 141, 143, 211; Piero di Marco Parenti, 'Istorie Fiorentine', in Corradi, 'Nuovi documenti', p. 342 (unpublished); Raffaello da Volterra, *Commentariorum Urbanorum*, Leipzig, 1603 edn, pp. 909–10; Sigismondo dei Conti da Foligno, *Le storie de' suoi tempi dal 1475 al 1510*, 2 vols, Rome, 1883, ii, pp. 271–2.

19. Como: F. Muraltus, *Annali a Petro Aloisio Donino*, Milan, 1861, pp. 46–7; Cremona: *Cronaca di Cremona dal MCDXCIV al MDXXV*, ed. A. Ceruti, Milan, 1876, i, p. 191; Orvieto: *Diario di Ser Tommaso di Silvestro*; Perugia: 'Cronaca della città di Perugia dal 1492 al 1503 di Francesco Matarazzo detto Maturanzio', ed. A. Fabretti, *Archivio Storico Italiano*, ser. I, 16/2 (1851), pp. 32–6; Pisa: 'Memoriale di Giovanni Portoveneri dall'anno 1494 sino al 1502', ed. F. Bonaini, *Archivio Storico Italiano*, ser. I, vi/2 (1845), pp. 337–8.

20. *Storia di Milano*, ed. G. Treccani degli Alfieri, 16 vols, Milan, 1958, xi, pp. 622–5; viii, p. 409. The letter by Nicolò Squillaci has been republished recently by G. Del Guerra and P. L. Mondani, 'I primi documenti quattrocenteschi sulla sifilide e le lezioni pisane di Luca Ghini (secolo XVI)', *Scientia Veterum*, 20 (1970), pp. 5–11.

21. Bernardino Zambotti of Ferrara was a notary, though he had a cousin who was a physician (*DFZ*, pp. v, x–xi); the editor of the anonymous diarist of Ferrara suggests that the author was a notary: *DFA*, p. xvii; both Luca Landucci of Florence and Jacopino de' Bianchi of Modena were apothecaries: Landucci, *Diario*, p. viii, Jacopino de' Bianchi in Corradi, 'Nuovi documenti', p. 360;

Sigismondo dei Conti da Foligno was papal secretary to a series of popes, but was best known for his service to Julius II (*Le storie*, pp. xiii–xxv); the two patricians were represented by Piero di Marco Parenti of Florence (M. Phillips, *The Memoir of Marco Parenti: a life in Medici Florence*, Princeton, 1987, pp. 37–8, 45, 48–9), and the well-known Venetian, Marin Sanudo.

22. Friano degli Ubaldini, 'Cronaca', pp. 245–6; Anon, 'Cronica Bianchina', p. 344.

23. Landucci, *Diario*, p. 143: 11.i.1497.

24. *Diario di Ser Tommaso di Silvestro*, p. 69; Francesco Matarazzo of Perugia also left an exceptionally detailed account of Mal Francese, although there is no internal evidence to suggest that he contracted the disease: Matarazzo, 'Cronaca', pp. 32–6.

25. Friano degli Ubaldini, 'Cronaca', f. 717v; *DFA*, pp. 199–200.

26. Landucci, *Diario*, p. 132; Parenti in Corradi, 'Nuovi documenti', p. 342.

27. Sigismondo de' Conti, *Le storie*, pp. 271–2. This is discussed by Foa, 'The New and the Old', pp. 34–8.

28. B. Senarega, *De Rebus Genuensibus Commentaria ab anno MCDLXXXVIII usque ad annum MDXIV*, ed. E. Pandiani, *Rerum Italicarum Scriptores*, Bologna, 1929, xxiv/8, p. 54.

29. B. Cirillo, *Annali della città dell'Aquila con l'historie del suo tempo*, Rome, 1570, cc. 96r–v; Guicciardini, *Storia d'Italia*, i, pp. 204–5. See T. Pennacchia, *Storia della sifilide*, Pisa, 1961, pp. 7–19; A. W. Crosby, *The Columbian Exchange: biological and cultural consequences of 1492*, Westport, Conn., 1972, ch. 4; Foa, 'The New and the Old', pp. 29–33; and A. G. Carmichael, 'Syphilis and the Columbian Exchange: was the new disease really new?', in M. G. Marques and J. Cule, eds, *The Great Maritime Discoveries and World Health*, Lisbon, 1991, pp. 187–90.

30. On the origins of the pox see F. Guerra, 'The Dispute over Syphilis:

Europe versus America', *Clio Medica*, 13 (1978), pp. 39–6.

31. Fileno dalle Tuatte, 'Historia di Bologna', f. 422v; Sigismondo dei Conti, *Le storie*, p. 272. Cf. also Foa, 'The New and the Old', pp. 36–42.

32. Raffaello da Volterra, *Commentariorum Urbanorum*, pp. 909–10; B. Senarega, *De Rebus Genuensibus*, p. 55.

33. Jacopino de' Bianchi, in Corradi, 'Nuovi documenti', p. 360; Landucci, *Diario*, p. 132.

34. *Diario di Ser Tommaso di Silvestro*, p. 100.

35. Sigismondo dei Conti, *Le storie*, p. 272.

36. Matarazzo, 'Cronaca', p. 33.

37. Anon, 'Cronica Bianchina', in Corradi, 'Nuovi documenti', p. 344; Sigismondo dei Conti, *Le storie*, p. 272.

38. Matarazzo, 'Cronaca', p. 35.

39. Parenti, 'Istorie', in Corradi, 'Nuovi documenti', p. 342.

40. See J. Henderson, '"A Certain Sickness with Suspicion of Contagion": physicians, plague and public health in early modern Florence', in W. Bynum and B. Fantini, eds, *The History of the Concepts of Infection, Contagion and Miasma*, forthcoming, at n. 47. See also on V. Nutton, 'The Seeds of Disease: an explanation of contagion and infection from the Greeks to the renaissance', *Medical History*, 27. (1983), pp. 25–7, and Nutton, 'The Reception of Fracastoro's Theory of Contagion: the seed that fell among thorns?', *Osiris*, 6, 2nd ser. (1990), pp. 201–5. J. Arrizabalaga, 'Facing the Black Death: perceptions and reactions of university medical practitioners', in L. Garcia-Ballester et al., eds, *Practical Medicine from Salerno to the Black Death*, Cambridge, 1994, pp. 237–88.

41. *Diario di Ser Tommaso di Silvestro*, p. 69.

42. *Diario di Ser Tommaso di Silvestro*, p. 101.

43. Nadi, *Diario*, p. 213; Fileno dalle

Tuatte, 'Cronaca', in Corradi, 'Nuovi documenti', p. 346.

44. Friano degli Ubaldini, 'Cronaca', f. 717v; Anon, 'Cronica Bianchina', in Corradi, 'Nuovi documenti', p. 344.

45. Anon, 'Cronica Bianchina', in Corradi, 'Nuovi documenti', p. 344; *DFZ*, p. 267.

46. Nadi, *Diario*, p. xvii; Friano degli Ubaldini, 'Cronaca', f. 717v.

47. Nadi, *Diario*, p. 213; Friano degli Ubaldini, 'Cronaca', f. 717v.

48. *Diario di Ser Tommaso di Silvestro*, p. 100: 1498.

49. *Diario di Ser Tommaso di Silvestro*, p. 169.

50. Fileno dalle Tuatte, 'Cronaca', f. 422v; Landucci, *Diario*, p. 141.

51. Sigismondo dei Conti, *Le storie*, p. 272.

52. G. Torrella, *Tractatus cum Consiliis contra Pudendagram seu Morbum Gallicum*, Rome, 1497, ff. c4v–d2v and the discussion below in Chapter Six; J. Cattaneo, *Opus de Morbo Gallico*, Genoa, 1522, c. 12r.

53. *Diario di Ser Tommaso di Silvestro*, p. 101.

54. Matarazzo, 'Cronaca', p. 35.

55. Biblioteca Comunale Augusta di Perugia MS 472 (G 61). Unfortunately there is no surviving evidence to suggest the provenance of the manuscript, although some of the scenes suggest that patients may have been in a hospital. We are grateful to the Vice-Director of the library, Dr Mario Roncetti, for information about the MS. See also his 'The Public Library of Perugia (Biblioteca Augusta del Comune di Perugia): a list of medical manuscripts and incunabula', in *Rivista Storico-Medica*, 2 (1973), p. 239; and M. Zini, 'Le cure mediche all'Ospedale di S. Giobbe', in G. Maiolo and G. Raversi, eds, *Il Credito Romagnolo fra Storia, Arte e Tradizione*, Bologna, 1985, pp. 456–70, who reproduces many of these illustrations.

56. Cited in A. Tosti, *Storie all'ombra del malfrancese*, Palermo, 1992, pp. 56–60, esp. p. 57.

57. A. Luzio and R. Renier, 'Contributo alla storia del Malfrancese ne'costumi e nella letteratura italiana del sec. XVI', *Giornale storico della letteratura italiana*, 5 (1885), pp. 412–13.

58. Cf. R. Palmer, 'L'assistenza medica nella Venezia cinquecentesca', in B. Aikema and D. Meijers, eds, *Nel regno dei poveri. Arte e storia dei grandi ospedali veneziani in età moderna, 1474–1797*, Venice, 1989, p. 40, on Nicolò Massa's *Liber de Morbo Gallico*, and 'Nicolò Massa, his Family and his Fortune', *Medical History*, 25 (1981), pp. 391–4.

59. Luzio and Renier, 'Contributo', p. 412.

60. Ser Silvestro's *Diario* ends in 1514, though we do not know when he died: *Diario di Ser Tommaso di Silvestro*, pp. 1–2 n. 1; on the Gonzaga see: Luzio and Renier, 'Contributo', p. 416, and for Soderini: K. J. P. Lowe, *Church and Politics in Renaissance Italy: the life and career of Cardinal Francesco Soderini (1453–1524)*, Cambridge, 1993, pp. 65, 141, 166.

61. P. Cassiano da Langasco, *Gli ospedali degli Incurabili*, Genoa, 1938, pp. 43–4: says that the morbidity rate was much higher than the case fatality rate, even though contemporary chroniclers mention that 'the majority die from it' or that it killed an 'infinite' number of people (cf. *DFZ*, p. 267; Muraltus, *Annali*, p. 47; *Cronaca di Cremona*, i, p. 191; Guicciardini, *Storia*, i, p. 233. Survival rates also probably depended on treatment; the rich did not die as readily as the poor because they had better care. See Sigismondi dei Conti, *Le Storie*, pp. 271–2; Anon, 'Cronica Bianchina', in Corradi, 'Nuovi documenti', p. 344; and Senarega, *De Rebus Genuensibus*, pp. 54ff.

62. *Diario di Ser Tommaso di Silvestro*, p. 100.

63. *Diario di Ser Tommaso di Silvestro*, p. 84.

64. Carmichael, 'Syphilis', p. 193.
65. *Diario di Ser Tommaso di Silvestro*, pp. 127–8.
66. Carmichael, 'Syphilis', p. 193.
67. Friano degli Ubaldini, 'Cronaca', f. 717v; Matarazzo, 'Cronaca', p. 36; Portoveneri, 'Memoriale', p. 337; Nadi, *Diario*, p. 213; *Diario di Ser Tommaso di Silvestro*, p. 100.
68. See the ongoing research of Ann Carmichael, of which her article 'Syphilis' is a foretaste.
69. Friano degli Ubaldini, 'Cronaca', f. 717v.
70. G. Torrella, *Dialogus de Dolore cum tractatu de Ulceribus in Pudendagra evenire solitis*, Rome, 1500, sig. d4v.
71. A. Pazzini, *Storia dell'arte sanitaria dalle origini a oggi*, Rome, 1973 edn, i, pp. 836–7; A. Castiglioni, *A History of Medicine*, New York, 1947 edn, pp. 464–5; Cassiano da Langasco, *Gli ospedali*, pp. 37–41, 56–7; Malamani, 'Notizie', pp. 13–14; Corradi, 'Nuovi documenti', pp. 346, 384. See, though, for more enlightened views Foa, 'The New and the Old', pp. 27–8, 39–40, and B. Pullan, 'Per la difesa del corpo sociale: gli ospedali', in N.-E. Vanzan Marchini, ed., *De Natura*, Milan, forthcoming.
72. Portoveneri, 'Memoriale', p. 138.
73. Sanudo, *I Diarii*, xxxiii, pp. 233–4.
74. Matarazzo, 'Cronaca', p. 36.
75. *Diario di Ser Tommaso di Silvestro*, pp. 69, 100.
76. Anon, 'Cronica Bianchina', in Corradi, 'Nuovi documenti', p. 344; Friano degli Ubaldini, 'Cronaca', f. 717v.
77. G. Fracastoro, *De Contagione et Contagiosis Morbis*, ed. and trans. W. C. Wright, New York and London, 1930, pp. 3–21 on the different types of 'contagion'. On these theories see M. D. Grmek, 'Les Vicissitudes des notions d'infection, de contagion et de germe dans la médecine antique', *Mémoires de Centre Jean Palerme*, v: *Textes Médicaux Latins Antiques*, Sainte-Etienne, 1984, pp. 53–70; Nutton, 'The Seeds of Disease', pp. 1–34; Nutton, 'The Reception of

Fracastoro's theory', pp. 196–234; Henderson, '"A Certain Sickness"'; Arrizabalaga, 'Facing the Black Death'.
78. For example: E. Capriolo, *Dell'istorie della città di Brescia*, Venice, 1744 edn, p. 214; Matarazzo, 'Cronaca', p. 36; and Friano degli Ubaldini, 'Cronaca', f. 717v.
79. Cited in F. Puccinotti, *Storia della medicina*, Livorno, 1859, ii/2, p. 505.
80. Fileno dalle Tuatte, 'Historia', f. 422v.
81. Cf. Foa, 'The New and the Old', p. 29.
82. With a few exceptions, historians of the French Disease in France in this period have tended to repeat accounts of measures taken in Paris. See, for example, E. Jeanselme, *Histoire de la syphilis. Son origine, son expansion*, Paris, 1931, pp. 83–90; C. Quétel, *History of Syphilis*, Cambridge, 1990, pp. 24–5; A. Saunier, *'Le Pauvre Malade' dans le cadre hospitalier médiéval. France du Nord, vers 1300–1500*, Paris, 1993, pp. 231–3. Saunier, 'Le Pauvre Malade', p. 231, does, however, mention measures taken by Abbeville and Montdidier in northern France, as does L. Le Pileur, *La Prostitution du xiiie au xviie siècle*, Paris, 1908, pp. 80–1, for the south, especially Orange.
83. J. Fabricius, *Syphilis in Shakespeare's England*, London, 1994, p. 58.
84. Saunier, 'Le Pauvre Malade', p. 231; K. Sudhoff, *Aus der Frühgeschichte der Syphilis*. See Ch. 1, n. 26 for full title. Leipzig, 1912, pp. 12–22; A. Kinzelbach, '"Böse Blattern" oder "Franzosenkrankheit": Syphiliskonzept, Kranke und die Genese des Krankenhauses in oberdeutschen Reichsstädten der frühen Neuzeit', in M. Dinges and T. Schlich, eds, *Neue Wege in der Seuchengeschichte*, Stuttgart, 1995, pp. 54ff.
85. R. Jütte, 'Syphilis and Confinement: early modern German hospitals for syphilitics', in N. Finizsch and R. Jütte, eds, *The Prerogative of Confinement*, Cambridge, 1995, table 1; and

Kinzelbach, '"Böse Blattern"', pp. 43–69. On Strasbourg see E. Wickersheimer, 'Les débuts à Strasbourg, de l'hospitalisation des syphilitiques', *Comptes Rendus du XVIe Congrès International d'Histoire de la Médecine*, ed. F.-A. Sondervorst in *Bulletin et Mémoires de la Société Internationale d'Histoire de la Médecine*, n.s. 1 (1959), pp. 187–97; and P. Adam, *Charité et assistance en Alsace au Moyen Age*, Strasbourg, 1982, pp. 207–13.

86. See B. Pullan, 'Support and Redeem: charity and poor relief in Italian cities from the 14th to the 17th century', *Continuity and Change*, 3 (1988), pp. 177–208.

Chapter Three: God's Punishment

1. See *Diario Ferrarese dall'anno 1476 sino al 1504 di Bernardino Zambotti*, ed. G. Pardi, in L. A. Muratori, ed., *Rerum Italicarum Scriptores*, Città di Castello and Bologna, 1934–7, xxiv/7 (in appendix) (henceforth DFZ); *Diario Ferrarese dall'anno 1409 sino al 1502 di autori incerti*, ed. G. Pardi, in Muratori, ed., Città di Castello and Bologna, 1928–33, xxiv/7 (henceforth DFA). The notary Bernardino Zambotti was a member of a Ferrara bourgeois family which included many notaries, apothecaries and physicians. Doubtless, his cousin and close friend Zaccaria Zambotti, one of the family doctors of Duke Ercole d'Este, was the main source for the abundant information about the court in his diary. For more information on the authors of both diaries, see Giuseppe Pardi's introductions in DFA, pp. iii–xix, and DFZ, pp. iii–xxxvi.

2. This internal correspondence is in the Archivio Segreto Estense (henceforth ASE), housed in the Archivio di Stato di Modena (henceforth ASM). See ASM, ASE, Archivio per Materie, Medici e Medicina 19. Most letters were summarised by C. Foucard, who also

mentioned others now lost: *Documenti storici spettanti alla Medicina, Chirurgia, Farmaceutica conservati nell'Archivio di Stato in Modena*, Modena, 1885.

3. For these letters, see A. Cappelli, 'Fra Girolamo Savonarola e notizie intorno il suo tempo', *Atti e Memorie delle RR. Deputazioni di Storia Patria per le provincie modenesi e parmesi*, 4, (1868), pp. 301–406 (passim); R. Ridolfi, *Le lettere di Girolamo Savonarola*, Firenze, 1933, pp. 75, 104–5, 110–13, 117–19, 156–7, 180–1, 219–20, 228–31, 235–9; L. Chiappini, 'Ercole d'Este e Girolamo Savonarola', *Atti e Memorie della Deputazione Ferrarese di Storia Patria*, ser. II, 7/3 (1952), pp. 45–53.

4. On the long Estense dominion over Ferrara, see A. Frizzi, *Memorie per la storia di Ferrara . . .*, 5 vols, Ferrara, 1791–1809; L. Chiappini, *Gli Estensi*, Milano, 1967; W. L. Gundersheimer, *Ferrara: the style of a renaissance despotism*, Princeton, 1973; G. Papagno and A. Quondam, eds, *La corte e lo spazio: Ferrara estense*, 3 vols, Rome, 1982.

5. On fifteenth-century Ferrara, particularly at the time of Duke Ercole I d'Este, in addition to the references quoted above see Gundersheimer, 'The Patronage of Ercole I d'Este', *Journal of Medieval and Renaissance Studies*, 6 (1976), pp. 1–18; A. Piromalli, *La cultura a Ferrara al tempo di Lodovico Ariosto*, 2nd edn, Rome, 1975; G. Pardi, *Lo Studio di Ferrara nei secoli xv e xvi*, Ferrara, 1903; D. B. Ruderman, *The World of a Renaissance Jew: the life and thought of Abraham ben Mordecai Farissol*, Cincinnati, 1981.

6. On this particular point, cf. Chiappini, *Gli Estensi*, pp. 183–9; Gundersheimer, *Ferrara*, pp. 225–7. On the strong influence of French fashions in late fifteenth-century Ferrara, see DFA, pp. 144, 171.

7. The anonymous diarist records very severe weather conditions from the beginning of December: the Tiber overflowed; there was an earthquake

in Ferrara and floods from the Po when it broke its banks; the rain then turned to snow and hail; the subsequent rise in the price of grain caused a severe dearth. See *DFA*, pp. 165–208 (passim).

8. For the relationship between moral and natural disorder in the 'longue durée' see J. Delumeau, *Le Peché et la peur: la culpabilisation en Occident (XIIIe–XVIIIe siècles)*, Paris, 1983, pp. 152–8.

9. *DFA*, p. 166.

10. *DFA*, p. 168.

11. *DFA*, p. 168.

12. L. Pastor, *The History of the Popes from the Close of the Middle Ages*, 40 vols, London, 1891–1953, v (1898), pp. 480–1. In contrast to the Ferrarese diaries which did not record the Roman portent, a proof of Ercole's concern about it is the fact that it was the theme of a Latin poem that the humanist Francesco Rococioli dedicated to Duke Ercole. See Francesco Rococioli, *Libellus de monstro Romae in Tyberi reperto anno Domini MCCCCLXXXXVI*, Modena, 1501. This portent, however, was not recorded by any Ferrarese diary.

13. Gundersheimer, *Ferrara*, pp. 184–99.

14. On the relationship between the Duke of Ferrara and the Dominican friar, see Chiappini, *Gli Estensi*; Gundersheimer, *Ferrara*, pp. 197–9. Also see J. Burckhardt, *The Civilization of the Renaissance in Italy: an essay*, London, 1965, pp. 301–3.

15. On Savonarola see: F. Villari, *La storia di Girolamo Savonarola e de' suoi tempi*, 2 vols, 2nd edn, Florence, 1887–8; R. Ridolfi, *Vita di Girolamo Savonarola*, 2 vols, 4th edn, Florence, 1974. On Savonarola's activities in Florence, see Pastor, *History of the Popes*, vi (1898), pp. 3–54; D. Weinstein, 'Millenarianism in a Civic Setting: the Savonarola movement in Florence', in S. L. Thrupp, ed., *Millennial Dreams in Action: essays in comparative study*, The Hague,

1962, pp. 187–203; Weinstein, *Savonarola and Florence*, Princeton, 1970; B. McGinn, *Visions of the End: apocalyptic traditions in the middle ages*, New York, 1979, pp. 277–83.

16. See the works referred to in the notes above.

17. This enclosed a further letter that Savonarola sent to Ercole through the Estense orator. Cappelli, 'Fra Girolamo', p. 391.

18. Chiappini, *Gli Estensi*, p. 45. For the contents of this letter, see Cappelli, 'Fra Girolamo', pp. 330–2. From November 1494 onwards, Manfredi kept Ercole d'Este well informed about Savonarola's activities in Florence.

19. Chiappini, *Gli Estensi*, pp. 45–6; Cappelli, 'Fra Girolamo', pp. 347–8.

20. Cappelli, 'Fra Girolamo', p. 345.

21. Ridolfi, *Vita*, pp. 228–9.

22. Ridolfi, *Vita*, pp. 220, 230–1, 235; Cappelli, 'Fra Girolamo', pp. 362–3. Written during spring and summer 1495, the *Compendio di revelazioni* was published soon after in two versions: the Tuscan, which was printed in Florence at least three times before the end of the year, and once more in 1496, and the Latin, which was also printed in Florence in 1495, and re-edited in Florence, Paris and Ulm the following year. See Hain-Copinger, #H.14332 to #H.14337, and #C.5274; *Indice generale degli incunaboli delle biblioteche d'Italia*, 6 vols., Rome, 1943–81, v, pp. 36–7 (#8681).

23. Chiappini, *Gli Estensi*, p. 46.

24. Ridolfi, *Vita*, p. 104.

25. ASM, ASE, Cancelleria Ducale, Gride Manoscritte I (1350–1560). This edict also recalled the prevailing rules concerning fiscal immunity of ecclesiastics, identification of Jews and sanctification of the relevant feasts. The *DFA* (p. 174) printed a substantial section of this *grida*, recording that it was read out in public the following day (Monday 4 April 1496). Cf. Burckhardt, *The Civilization*, p. 302.

26. Ridolfi, *Vita*, p. 111.
27. Ridolfi, *Vita*, p. 112.
28. Ridolfi, *Vita*, p. 156.
29. Ridolfi, *Vita*, p. 157.
30. Ridolfi, *Vita*, p. 239.
31. Chiappini, *Gli Estensi*, pp. 49–51. See also Cappelli, 'Fra Girolamo', pp. 385–6, 390–1, 393–5, 397–9, 401–2.
32. ASM, ASE, Camera Ducale Estense, Mandati, Registro 36, f. 163r: 'Magistro Joanni Iusti chirurgico libras quatuor marchesinas, pro eiusdem mercede curandi et liberandi infirmitate Francigene.' Though erroneously dated 16 October 1496, this document was quoted by Foucard, *I documenti*, p. 84.
33. See F. Valenti et al., 'Archivio di Stato di Modena', in *Guida Generale degli Archivi di Stato Italiani*, Rome, 1981, I/ii, pp. 1016–17.
34. A. Corradi, 'Nuovi documenti per la storia delle malattie veneree in Italia dalla fine del quattrocento alla metà del cinquecento', *Annali Universali di Medicina e Chirurgia*, 269/808 (1884), pp. 289–386: p. 347.
35. *DFZ*, p. 267. According to S. Battaglia, *Grande dizionario della lingua italiana*, Torino, 1961- (henceforth *GDLI*), ii, p. 396, *brozole* are pustules, itching blisters.
36. *DFA*, p. 198.
37. L. Stephen and S. Lee, eds, *Dictionary of National Biography*, 22 vols, Oxford, 1917, xix, pp. 72–3.
38. F. Guicciardini, *Storia d'Italia*, ed. S. S. Menchi, 3 vols, Turin, 1971, i, pp. 252, 268, 283.
39. Luca Landucci, *Diario fiorentino dal 1450 al 1516*, ed. I. del Badia, Florence, 1883, p. 143; Marin Sanudo, *I Diarii*, ed. R. Fulin et al., 58 vols, Venice, 1879–1902, i, cols 485, 567; Jacopino de' Bianchi, *Cronaca modenese*, ed. C. Borghi, Parma, i, 1861, pp. 165–6.
40. This first reference to the French Disease in the anonymous diary appeared two months after the earliest one in Zambotti's diary. This combined evidence suggests that Mal Francese was unknown in Ferrara until the beginning of February 1497. This reinforces the idea that Da Linago's and Zambotti's previous references to the French Disease in Ferrara may have reflected the medical 'discovery' of the disease within the courtly circles close to the Estense family.
41. *DFA*, p. 199.
42. *DFA*, pp. 199–200.
43. At least, the *DFZ* reported that another autopsy of someone who was executed was performed on 17 December 1478 after the ducal permission: *DFZ*, p. 57.
44. N. Leoniceno, *Libellus de Epidemia quam vulgo Morbum Gallicum vocant*, Venice, 1497, sigs d3r–v.
45. *DFA*, pp. 204–5.
46. *DFZ*, pp. 276–7.
47. *DFA*, pp. 204–5.
48. Sanudo, *I Diarii*, ii, col. 399. See also *DFA*, pp. 214, 219.
49. *DFA*, p. 219.
50. *DFA*, p. 224.
51. *DFA*, p. 240.
52. Quoted by Corradi, 'I nuovi documenti', p. 332. Except for his Spanish origins, we know nothing about his identity or qualifications.
53. G. Bertoni, *La Biblioteca Estense a la cultura ferrarese ai tempi del duca Ercole I (1471–1505)*, Torino, 1903, p. 192. According to Bertoni, this document is in ASM, ASE, Camera Ducale Estense, Mandati, 1505, f. 38v, though we have been unable to confirm this.
54. Archivio Archivescovile di Ferrara, Compagnia di S. Giobbe di Ferrara, A4: 20.iii.1502; A5: 20.iii.1505.
55. There are eight letters: ASM, ASE, Archivio per Materie, Medici e Medicina 19. Most of them were edited or excerpted by Foucard, *Documenti*, pp. 47, 56–7, 86, 93–4.
56. *DFA*, p. 188.
57. *DFA*, p. 188.
58. On Zaccaria Zambotti, see G. Pardi, *Lo Studio di Ferrara nei secoli XV e XVI*, Ferrara, 1903, p. 142.

59. ASM, ASE, Archivio per Materie, Medici e Medicina 19, in Foucard, *Documenti*, pp. 93–4.

60. Cf. also A. Corradi, 'I documenti storici spettanti alla Medicina, Chirurgia, Farmaceutica, conservati nell'Archivio di Stato in Modena, ed in particolare della malattia di Lucrezia Borgia e della Farmacia nel secolo XV', *Annali Universali di Medicina e Chirurgia*, 273 (1885), pp. 438–71; 275 (1886), pp. 21–56: 275, pp. 24–5.

61. See note 32 above.

62. Foucard, *Documenti*, p. 56. We have not been able to trace the original in the ASM.

63. ASM, ASE, Archivio per Materie, Medici e Medicina 19: 29.iii.1498, in Foucard, *Documenti*, p. 56: 'Essendo hoci sira stato ad visitarmi magistro Ludovico Carro, fra li altri discorsi chel fece cum mi ara el regimento et cura ho ad tenire per recuperatione de la salute mia, il me dixo chel gli parcun molto conveniente per molte regione deducte per lui, et chel mi conferiria assai, il farme levare li capilli; cussi, per essere disposto fare quanto mi sera recordato per li medici per la liberatione mia, ho facto tosarmi, et so bene lo ho prima facto che advisarni et chiudere licentia a Vostra Excellentia.'

64. ASM, ASE, Archivio per Materie, Medici e Medicina 19: 22.viii.1499, in Foucard, *Documenti*, pp. 56–7.

65. ASM, ASE, Archivio per Materie, Medici e Medicina 19: 30.iv.1498, in Foucard, *Documenti*, p. 86.

66. ASM, ASE, Archivio per Materie, Medici e Medicina 19: letter of Cardinal Ippolito d'Este and of his secretary Antonio Costabili to Duke Ercole, 14.iv.1498; letter of Agostino Benzi, Ippolito d'Este's physician, to Duke Ercole, 25.iv.1498, in Foucard, *Documenti*, p. 47.

67. *DFA*, p. 207; *DFZ*, pp. 278–9.

68. *DFA*, p. 224.

69. *DFA*, p. 240.

70. See B. Pistofilo, *Vita di Alfonso I*, ch.

58, quoted by A. Cappelli, *Lettere di Lodovico Ariosto, con prefazione storico-critica, documenti e note*, 3rd edn, Milan, 1887, p. LXVIII.

71. ASM, ASE, Archivio per Materie, Medici e Medicina 19: 3.x.1499, in Foucard, *I documenti*, p. 86.

72. We deal at length below with Coradino Gilino.

73. Coradino Gilino, *De Morbo quem Gallicum nuncupant*, Ferrara, c. 1497/8, f. 1v.

74. Gilino established a close link between the new firearms and the very destructive nature of the wars. The contrast between the old hand-weapon, 'ironarm', and the new firearm was a well-known topic. In this controversy, the critics of firearms attacked them because they symbolised the coward in contrast to the brave fighter who used only a lance, bow and sword; Gilino seems to have taken the side of the latter, as did another Ferrarese courtier, the poet Lodovico Ariosto (1474–1533) in the episode of his *Orlando furioso* (started about 1505, published in 1516) when the King of Friesland Cimosco tried to kill Count Orlando. See Lodovico Ariosto, *Orlando furioso*, ix, 28–9, 68–78. See the English edition in 2 vols, Harmondsworth, 1977, i, pp. 295, 305–7 (we are grateful to Mr José Luis Gil-Aristu for this reference).

75. *DFZ*, p. 267.

76. *GDLI*, x, p. 755. See also M. Doria, *Grande Dizionario del dialetto triestino storico etimologico fraseologico*, Trieste, 1987, pp. 384–5.

77. J. A. Brundage, *Law, Sex, and Christian Society in Medieval Europe*, Chicago and London, 1987, pp. 6, 167, 212.

78. We are grateful to Jole Agrimi for this suggestion.

79. J. Delaney, M. J. Lupton and E. Toth, *The Curse: a cultural history of menstruation*, 2nd edn, Urbana and Chicago, 1988.

80. *GDLI*, x, p. 755.

81. Corradi, 'I nuovi documenti', pp.

346–7, wrongly transcribed *donne immonde* ('dirty women') instead of *donne in mona* when he published this paragraph 100 years ago.

82. J. Rossiaud, *La prostituzione nel Medioevo*, Rome and Bari, 1984, pp. 167–204, 209–12; L. L. Otis, *Prostitution in Medieval Society: the history of an urban institution in Languedoc*, Chicago and London, 1985, pp. 25–45, 111–13; M. S. Mazzi, 'Il mondo della prostituzione nella Firenze tardo medievale', *Ricerche storiche*, 14/2–3 (1984), pp. 346–7, and *Prostitute e lenoni nella Firenze del Quattrocento*, Milan, 1991.

83. See note 25.

84. See note 47.

85. On the figure of Job in Jewish and Christian religions, cf. S. Terrien, 'Job', in M. Eliade, ed., *The Encyclopedia of Religion*, 16 vols, New York, 1987, viii, pp. 97–100; J. R. Baskin, *Pharaoh's Counsellors: Job, Jetho, and Balaam in rabbinic and patristic tradition*, Chico, Calif., pp. 7–43, 129–43.

86. For additional information on the significance of Job in the Christian spirituality, see C. Kannengiesser, 'Job (Le Livre de)', in M. Viller et al., eds, *Dictionnaire de spiritualité ascétique et mystique: doctrine et histoire*, Paris, vols i–(1937–), viii (1974), cols 1201–25: col. 1201.

87. See L. L. Besserman, *The Legend of Job in the Middle Ages*, Cambridge, Mass., 1979, pp. 64–5; L. Menzies, *The Saints in Italy: a book of reference to the saints in Italian art and dedication*, London, 1924, pp. 137–8.

88. See A. Sorbelli, ed., *Corpus Chronicorum Bononiensium: Cronaca di Bologna detta Varignana*, 4 books, in Muratori, ed., *Rerum Italicarum Scriptores*, Città di Castello, 1905–24, xviii/1: book 4, pp. 551–2 (*malo de San Job*); C. G. Gruner, ed., *Aphrodisiacus sive De Lue Venerea*, 3 vols, Jena, 1789, iii, p. 54, 'Sent Iobs Krenkde' in the 'Cronica van der Hilligen Stat Coellen'.

89. A. Franceschini, *Il sapore del sale.*

Ricerche sulla assistenza ospedaliera nel sec. XV in una città di punta: Ferrara, Ferrara, 1981, p. 112; Archivio Archivescovile di Ferrara, Compagnia di S. Giobbe A.5: 28.iii.1505. In 1503 this brotherhood asked Ercole d'Este to declare a feast on the day of St Job. See Archivio di Stato di Ferrara, Archivio Storico Communale, Serie Patrimoniale, busta 12, inserto 12 ('Registro delle Commissioni Ducali dall'anno 1501 sino al 1506'), ff. 78v–79r (this document was kindly passed to us by Maestro Adriano Franceschini).

90. See Chapter Seven below.

91. In this respect, compare Job 1 and 42 with the remaining verses, 2–41. See Baskin, *Pharaoh's Counsellors*, pp. 8–9.

92. On this question see Besserman, *The Legend*.

93. *DFZ*, p. 267: 'il quale male [male franzoxe] pare incurabile, per essere il male de Santo Job'; *DFA*, p. 199: 'uno male chiamato mal franzoso o male de Sancto Job, a lo qualle male li medici non sano remediare'.

94. The adjective 'incurable' as applied to the disease of Job can be found only in the current editions of the Bible, Book of Job, 34: 6. Indeed, where the Vulgate said: 'Violenta sagitta mea absque ullo peccato', both Authorised and Revised English translations use the phrase 'my wound is incurable'.

95. Job, 2: 7–8. For other passages of the same book where Job himself referred to his illness, see ibid., 7: 5 ('My flesh is clothed with worms and clods of dust; my skin is broken, and become loathsome'; Revised Version: 'closeth up and breaketh out afresh'), 30: 30 ('My skin is black upon me, and my bones are burned with heat'; Revised: 'My skin is black and falleth from me . . .'), 30: 16–17 ('My bones are pierced in me in the night season: and my sinews take no rest'), 19: 17–20 ('My breath is strange to my wife. . . . My bone cleaveth to my

skin and to my flesh, and I am escaped with the skin of my teeth').

96. We have explored the patristic commentaries, by St Jerome (c. 347–420), S. Augustine (354–430), Giuliano de Eclano (c. 380–c. 445), S. Gregory the Great (c. 540–604), S. Pietro Damiano (1007–72), S. Bruno de Segni (1049–1123), and Rupertus Tuitiensis (d. 1135), the Glossa ordinaria (XII2), and the exegetical, by Thomas Aquinas (1224–74). For the patristic commentaries, cf. Migne, *Patrologia Latina*, xxiii, cols 1469–1552, xxvi, cols 655–850, xxix, cols 63–118 (S. Jerome); xxxiv, cols 825–86 (S. Augustine); Suppl. I, 1579 (Giuliano de Eclano); lxxv, cols 499–1162, lxxvi, cols 1–782 (S. Gregory the Great); cxlv, cols 1129–30 (S. Pietro Damiano); clxviii, cols 963–1196 (Rupertus Tuitiensis); clxiv, cols 551–696 (S. Bruno de Segni). For the commentary to the Book of Job in the Glossa ordinaria, cf. ibid., cxiii cols 747–840. For that of Thomas of Aquinas, cf. Thomas of Aquinas, *In Iob librum . . . historia dilucidaque Explicatio. Opuscula Omnia*, Lyon, 1562, pp. 571–650.

97. Aquinas, *In Iob librum*, p. 577.

98. Job, 5: 18.

99. Terrien, 'Job', viii, pp. 99–100.

100. See Besserman, *The Legend*, pp. 44–5.

101. Job, 1: 20. The fact that Job took this measure before – not after - having received the proof of his terrible illness need not be contradictory to our hypothesis.

102. Migne, *Patrologia Latina*, lxxv, cols 569–70, 583–4.

103. Thus on 20 August 1495 Savonarola sent to Lodovico Carri and Ercole d'Este a copy of his *Sommario delle sue prediche e visione*. Then in a letter sent to Ercole five months later along with a draft of his *De simplicitate Christianae vitae* Savonarola asked Ercole to let him know through master Lodovico Carri about any objection which

anyone could make to his work. Ridolfi, *Vita*, p. 220. For the full text of this letter, see Cappelli, 'Fra Girolamo', pp. 362–3. In an acknowledgement of receipt written the day after (23 August 1495) Ercole informed Manfredi that he had already passed the copy of Savonarola's book to Carri (Cappelli, 'Fra Girolamo', p. 363). See also Ridolfi, *Vita*, pp. 104–5: p. 104. Additionally, a further pilgrimage that Alfonso d'Este made to the Mary's sanctuary at Loreto in May 1500 would be in the same way a resort to divine remedies to face divine diseases. See *DFA*, p. 253; *DFZ*, p. 263. On the sanctuary of Loreto, a centre of devotion to Mary and where numerous sick people and well-known pilgrims came in the late middle ages, see F. Cabrol and H. Leclercq, *Dictionnaire d'archéologie chrétienne et de liturgie*, 15 vols, Paris, 1924–53, ix/2, cols 2473–511.

104. L. Martines, *Power and Imagination: city-states in renaissance Italy*, Harmondsworth, 1979, pp. 387–415.

105. Indeed Zambotti's diary reported that in April 1494 Duke Ercole came out 'con tuta la corte' to receive D'Aubigny when the latter arrived at Ferrara, 'per essere il duca nostro bon franzoxe et bon vasallo del re Carlo christianissimo e benignissimo' (*DFZ*, p. 232). On the other hand, in February 1496, the *DFA* said: 'Ferrarexi quasi tuti universaliter tengono et sono partesani del Re di Franza' (p. 171).

106. *DFA*, pp. 155, 157, 161.

Chapter Four: The Medical Dispute at the Court of Ferrara

1. See M. McVaugh, 'Medicine, History of', in J. R. Strayer, ed., *Dictionary of the Middle Ages*, New York, 1982–, viii, p. 253.

2. On hellenism see D. J. Geanokoplos, *Greek Scholars in Venice*,

Cambridge, Mass., 1962; and *Interaction of the 'Sibling' Byzantine and Western Cultures in the Middle Ages and Italian Renaissance, 330–1600*, New Haven and London, 1976.

3. K. Sudhoff, *The Earliest Printed Literature on Syphilis, being ten tractates from the years 1495–1498*, Florence, 1925 (henceforth *Tractates*), pp. ix–xlv, esp. pp. xxix–xxxi, xliv–xlv.

4. For a recent instance of this historiographical tendency, see the suggestive article by D. Mugnai-Carrara, 'Fra causalità astrologica e causalità naturale. Gli interventi di Nicolò Leoniceno e della sua scuola sul morbo gallico', *Physis*, 21 (1979), pp. 37–54.

5. For the works of these physicians, see Nicolò Leoniceno, *Libellus de Epidemia quam vulgo Morbum Gallicum vocant*, Venice, June 1497 (henceforth *Libellus*); Natale Montesauro, *De Dispositionibus quas vulgares Mal Franzoso appellant*, Bologna, 1497/8 (henceforth *De Dispositionibus*); Antonio Scanaroli, *Disputatio utilis de Morbo Gallico et opinionis Nicolai Leoniceni confirmatio contra adversarium eandem opinionem oppugnantem*, Bologna, 26 March 1498 (henceforth *Disputatio*). There are facsimile reprints of all these works in Sudhoff, *Tractates*, pp. 119–82 (Leoniceno), 281–311 (Montesauro), 315–45 (Scanaroli).

6. Our historical reconstruction relies on the information provided by medical printed works and, additionally, by letters, chronicles and diaries, all of them contemporary. The disputation was well known in Bologna.

7. For the works of the first three physicians, see Sudhoff, *Tractates*. For Dall'Aquila's, which was written about 1497/8, although not published until more than a decade after, see Sebastiano dall'Aquila, *Interpretatio Morbi Gallici et Cura*, in Marco Gattinara et al., *De Curis Egritudinum particularium noni Almansoris practica uberrima . . .*,

Pavia, 1509 (henceforth *Interpretatio*), ff. 184r–202v. All four authors echoed this disputation right at the beginning of their relevant works. See Leoniceno, *Libellus*, sig. a2r; Montesauro, *De Dispositionibus*,[f. 1r]; Scanaroli, *Disputatio*, sig. a2r; Dall'Aquila, *Interpretatio*, f. 184r.

8. Coradino Gilino, *De Morbo quem Gallicum nuncupant*, [Ferrara, 1497/8], (henceforth *De Morbo*), [f. 1r]. For the facsimile reprint of this work, see Sudhoff, *Tractates*, pp. 253–60.

9. Dall'Aquila, *Interpretatio*, f. 184r.

10. Dall'Aquila, *Interpretatio*, f. 186r.

11. *Diario Ferrarese dall'anno 1409 sino al 1502 di autori incerti*, ed. G. Pardi, in L. A. Muratori, ed., *Rerum Italicarum Scriptores*, Città di Castello and Bologna, 1928–33, xxiv/7 (henceforth *DFA*), pp. 199–200: 'lo qualle fu donato a' medici per fare nothomia, perche havea il mal franzoso, per vedere onde procedeva tale infermita'. Since Dall'Aquila placed this post-mortem 'soon after' (*paulo post*) the disputation, we have evidence that it took place in late March or early April 1497, when we know that the French Disease had become a health problem in that northern Italian city. From Leoniceno's *Libellus* we also know that the date of the dispute was set some time before, no doubt (like university disputations) to give the antagonists time to prepare their arguments. The early notice given of the dispute and the importance of the topic must have combined to raise much interest in the discussion (see Leoniceno, *Libellus*, sig. a2r).

12. The 'Latin establishment' physician is discussed in Chapter Six below on the papal court.

13. See D. B. Ruderman, *The World of a Renaissance Jew: the life and thought of Abraham ben Mordecai Farissol*, Cincinnati, 1981, pp. 57–60.

14. On Sigismondo d'Este, see L. Chiappini, *Gli Estensi*, Milan, 1967,

pp. 563–4; W. Gundersheimer, ed., *Art and Life at the Court of Ercole I d'Este: the 'De Triumphis Religionis' of Giovanni Sabadino degli Arienti*, Geneva [Travaux d'Humanisme et Renaissance, no. 127], 1972, pp. 40, 42, 48; W. Gundersheimer, *Ferrara: the style and life of a renaissance despotism*, Princeton, 1973, pp. 122, 290.

15. Montesauro, who lectured at the faculty of medicine of Bologna, and Scanaroli, who practised medicine at Modena, seem to have known about the disputation only through Leoniceno's *Libellus*. Each of these contemporaries referred to the disputation in different ways: Montesauro mentioned it in a peevish way, not even condescending to mention Avicenna's detractor by name (Leoniceno); while in his preface addressed to the lecturer at the medical faculty of Bologna, Nestore Morandi, Scanaroli treated this disputation as well known in Bolognese university circles.

16. Leoniceno, *Libellus*, sig. a2r.

17. Leoniceno, *Libellus*, sig. a6r.

18. R. K. French and F. Greenaway, *Science in the Early Roman Empire: Pliny the Elder, his sources and influence*, London, 1986, pp. 252–81.

19. Although the statement that Leoniceno taught at that university for sixty years has become a commonplace, there is only evidence of his lecturing at the university of Ferrara for the academic years as follows, 1466–7, 1468–74, 1474–5(?), 1485–6, 1487–8, 1501–2, 1504–5, 1511–16. He also lectured at the University of Bologna on philosophy (1482–3) and later on medicine (in the afternoons) and on philosophy (on feast days) in 1508–9. See C. Foucard, *Documenti storici spettanti alla Medicina, Chirurgia, Farmaceutica conservati nell'Archivio di Stato in Modena*, Modena, 1885, p. 29; D. Vitaliani, *Della vita e delle opere di Niccolò Leoniceno vicentino*, Verona, 1892, p. 6; G. Secco-Suardo, 'Lo Studio di Ferrara a tutto il secolo xv', *Atti e Memorie della Deputazione Ferrarese di Storia Patria*, 6 (1894), pp. 25–294: p. 288; G. Pardi, ed., *Diario di Ugo Caleffini (1471–1494)*, 2 vols, Ferrara, 1938–40, i, pp. 78–9, 84–5, 108–9, 112–17; G. Pardi, *Titoli dottorali conferiti dallo studio di Ferrara nei secoli xv e xvi*, Lucca, 1901 (facs. repr., Bologna, 1970), pp. 78–9, 84–5, 108–9, 112–17; A. Franceschini, *Nuovi documenti relativi ai docenti dello Studio di Ferrara nel sec. XVI*, Ferrara, 1970, pp. 6, 13. For his lectures in Bologna, C. Malagola, *Della vita e delle opere di Antonio Urceo*, Bologna, 1878, pp. 106, 451–2; Vitaliani, *Della vita*, pp. 78–80; D. Mugnai-Carrara, 'Profilo di Nicolò Leoniceno', *Interpres*, 2 (1979), pp. 169–212: pp. 180–1.

20. He did so at least in the years 1472 and 1476. See Pardi, ed., *Diario di Ugo Caleffini*, i, pp. 15–16, 132; Mugnai-Carrara, 'Profilo', p. 177. The almost complete absence of Leoniceno from the payroll of physicians at the Estense court was explained by Vitaliani as a consequence of his being an independent spirit who 'had as a maxim never to entry the courts of the great', and of the fact that he considered as very difficult the art of healing ill persons so that he preferred to teach those who later would devote themselves to this task'. See Vitaliani, *Della vita*, pp. 86–7.

21. From Greek into Italian: Diodorus Siculus, Appian, Arrian, and fragments of Polybius, Dio Cassius and Procopius; from Latin to Italian the *Roma instaurata* of Flavio Biondo, in addition to translating into Italian several works of the Greek Lucian, among them his *Dialogues*. Daniela Mugnai-Carrara has provided us with exhaustive information and bibliography in this respect. See Mugnai-Carrara, 'Profilo', pp. 177–9. Little wonder that the earliest printed editions of these translations did not appear until the period 1525–40, and in some cases even

later on, since the dukes of Ferrara, as well as their contemporary Medici, showed very little interest in the press during the late fifteenth and early sixteenth centuries. On this attitude towards the press and its possible reasons, see D. Fava, *La biblioteca Estense nel suo sui luppo storico*, Modena, 1925, pp. 86–7; L. Balsamo, 'L'industria tipografico-editoriale nel ducato estense all'epoca dell'Ariosto', in P. Rossi, ed., *Il Rinascimento nelle corti padane. Società e cultura*, Bari, 1977, p. 280; Balsamo, 'La circulazione del libro a corte', in G. Papagno and A. Quondam, eds, *La corte e lo spazio: Ferrara estense*, 3 vols, Rome, 1982, ii, pp. 659–81, esp. pp. 679–80.

22. Leoniceno translated the works of Galen as follows, *De Elementis secundum Hippocratem, De Naturalibus Facultatibus, De Motu Musculorum, De Inaequali Intemperie, De Morborum Causis, De Morborum Differentiis, De Febrium Differentiis, De Crisibus, Ars Medica, De Arte Curativa ad Glauconem, In Hippocratis Aphorismos Commentaria.*

23. It is hoped that a chapter developing this theme will appear shortly in a volume on medicine from the Black Death to the French Disease.

24. For instance versions by Pietro d'Abano, Nicolò da Reggio and Burgundio da Pisa, and others from the late fifteenth century (by Lorenzo Lorenzano and Giorgio Valla).

25. Mugnai-Carrara, 'Profilo', p. 201.

26. Franceschini, *Nuovi documenti*, pp. 17–19. It was also some time before his translations were printed (between the years 1508 and 1542). See R. J. Durling, 'A Chronological Census of Renaissance Editions and Translations of Galen', *Journal of the Warburg and Courtauld Institutes*, 24 (1961), pp. 230–305: pp. 281–2, 284, 285, 286, 287, 294, 297 (passim); Mugnai-Carrara, 'Profilo', p. 200.

27. See G. Bertoni, *La Biblioteca Estense*

e la cultura ferrarese ai tempi del Duca Ercole I (1471–1505), Turin, 1903, p. 189.

28. The enemy he said was ignorant, shameless yet unpunished and 'stuttered' in their writing and speech. Bonacciuoli uses the verb *balbutire*, which Greekifying hellenists sometimes used to mean the use of Latin, a 'stuttering' language; he says that a parrot speaks like this. Compare Martin Pollich's attack on Simon Pistoris described in Chapter Five.

29. *vetus medicina que olim in clarissima luce versabatur, nunc autem in libris barbarorum multis iacet obruta tenebris, tandem exerat caput et in pristinam claritatem atque splendorem revocetur.* See *Articella*, Venice, 1523, f. 4rb.

30. *Huic tam laudabile tam vite necessario operi, ne desis humanissime princeps.* See *Articella*, f. 4rb.

31. *Verum hic mihi occurret aliquis philophaster e numero illorum, qui bonas odere litteras, qui in ea heresi sunt, non posse quemquam et recte loqui, et recte philosophari, atque ita inquiet: hoc genus argumentandi sumptum ex loquendi norma, non est philosophorum aut medicorum, sed grammatistarum proprium. Nos non istas curamus rhetoricis, vel potius pedagogicis, qui non eloquentiam, sed sapientiam querimus.* See *Articella*, f. 81v.

32. In Leipzig Pistoris disputed with Pollich in these terms. See Chapter Five below.

33. On Leoniceno's participation in other disputes, see for instance Daniela Mugnai-Carrara, 'Una polemica umanistico–scolastica circa l'interpretazione delle tre dottrine ordinate di Galeno', *Annali dell' Istituto e Museo di Storia della Scienza di Firenze*, 8/1 (1980), pp. 31–57.

34. On Leoniceno's role at the dispute on Pliny, see R. K. French, 'Pliny and Renaissance Medicine', in French and Greenaway, eds, *Science in the Early Roman Empire*, pp. 252–81, and the bibliography cited there.

35. On Venetian pharmacy in the six-

teenth century see Richard Palmer, 'Pharmacy in the Republic of Venice in the Sixteenth Century', in A. Wear, R. K. French and I. Lonie, *The Medical Renaissance of the Sixteenth Century*, Cambridge, 1985, pp. 100–17.

36. In addition to the Venetian *editio princeps*, also printed by Aldo Manucio in June 1497, there was a Milanese edition printed by Guillaume le Segnerre of Rouen on the order of master Giovanni da Legnano, on the colophon of which the date of 4 July 1497 appears.

37. See M. Lowry, *The World of Aldus Manutius: business and scholarship in renaissance Venice*, Oxford, 1979, p. 223. For more details concerning Manucio's publication of these two works, see ibid., pp. 112, 116, 135–6, 168.

38. A. Dragonetti, *Le vite degli illustri aquilani*, Aquila, 1847, pp. 132–8. For this and other issues referring to Dall'Aquila see: L. Gedda, 'Un trattato di terapia agli inizii dell'evo moderno (Dissertazione di Laurea)', *Rivista di Storia delle Scienze Mediche e Naturali*, 10 (1928), pp. 151–62, 208–41: pp. 225–36. Unfortunately, to the best of our knowledge these are the only relevant works dealing with Sebastiano dall'Aquila.

39. Dragonetti, *Le vite*, pp. 133, 137–8.

40. Gedda, 'Un trattato', p. 226.

41. G. Pardi, *Titoli dottorali conferiti dallo Studio di Ferrara nei secoli XV e XVI*, Lucca, 1901 (facs. repr., Bologna, 1970), pp. 84–5.

42. Pardi, *Titoli*, pp. 96–107. That Dall'Aquila changed his academic position during this period is obvious from the contents of the letter of Lodovico Ariosto to Aldo Manucio referred to below.

43. A. Corradi, *Memorie e Documenti per la Storia dell'Università di Pavia e degli uomini più illustri che v'insegnarono*, 3 vols, Pavia, 1877–8, i, p. 122.

44. Corradi, *Memorie*, i, pp. 110–11.

45. Cf. also Dall'Aquila, *Interpretatio*. His

Questio de febre sanguinis ad mentem Galieni occupies ff. 203r–214r.

46. The places and years of the successive editions are as follows: Pavia, 1509 and 1514; Venice, 1516, 1521, 1559, 1560 and 1575 (the last three not including Dall'Aquila's works); Lyon, 1516, 1525, 1532, 1539 and 1542; Bologna, 1517; Basle, 1537; and Frankfurt, 1604. See Gedda, 'Un trattato', pp. 236–41; R. J. Durling (comp.), *A Catalogue of the Sixteenth Century Printed Books in the National Library of Medicine*, Bethesda, US Dept of Health, Education and Welfare, 1967, pp. 243–4; P. Krivatsy (comp.), *A Catalogue of Seventeenth Century Printed Books in the National Library of Medicine*, Bethesda, 1987, p. 456.

47. Turin, Biblioteca Nazionale, Codice 6 II 3. See P. Giacosa, *Magistri Salernitani nondum editi. Catalogo ragionata della Exposizione di Storia della Medicina aperta in Torino nel 1898*, Turin, 1901, pp. 515–16. In the order in which they appear in the manuscript, the title of these four works are *Utrum secundum Galieni sententiam detur unum membrum principalissimum*; *Collecta super questione de subjectis medicine*; *De causa periodicationis humorum secundum Galieni sententiam*; and *Questio de putrescente sanguine*.

48. See A. Cappelli, *Lettere di Ludovico Ariosto, con prefazione storico-critica, documenti e note*, 3rd edn, Milan, 1887, pp. 1–2. In this letter Ariosto asked Aldo Manucio for a volume of Neoplatonist works translated into Latin by Marsilio Ficino – doubtless that of Iamblichos et al., *De mysteriis Aegyptorum, Chaldaeorum et Assyriorum*, Venice, Sept. 1497. On this and other publishing activities of Manucio, see Lowry, *The World*, esp. p. 115. For the printing date of this work (wrongly dated by Lowry to December 1498), see A. C. Klebs, *Incunabula scientifica et medica*, Hildesheim, 1963, # 529.1.

49. Cappelli, *Lettere*, pp. 1–2.

50. ASM, ASE, Archivio per Materie, Medici e Medicina 19, doct. 57. Cf. Gedda, 'Un trattato', p. 229.

51. ASM, ASE, Archivio per Materie, Medici e Medicina 19, doct. 58; cf. Gedda, 'Un trattato', p. 230.

52. J. Cartwright, *Isabella d'Este, Marchioness of Mantua, 1474–1539: a study of the renaissance*, 2 vols, London, 1903, ii, pp. 1–2. On this sculptor, see T. G. Bergin and J. Speake, eds, *Encyclopedia of the Renaissance*, New York and Oxford, 1987, p. 348.

53. Gundersheimer, ed., *Art and Life*, p. 85: 'huomo certo non iniuriando, persona in sua facolta a veruno secondo'.

54. On Lodovico Gonzaga, see G. Pezza-Rosa, *Storia cronologica dei vescovi Mantovani*, Mantova, 1847, pp. 45–6; R. Renier, 'Nuove notizie di Giovanni Sabadino degli Arienti', *Giornale Storico della Letteratura Italiana*, 12 (1888), pp. 301–5; M. Bellonci, *Segreti dei Gonzaga. Ritratto di Famiglia. Isabella fra I Gonzaga. Il Duca nel labirinto*, Verona, 1947, pp. 25–6; M. E. Cosenza, *Biographical and Bibliographical Dictionary of the Italian Humanists and of the World of Classical Scholarship in Italy, 1300–1800*, 5 vols, Boston, 1962, ii, p. 1649. For the extensive praise Sabadino dedicated to Lodovico Gonzaga, see Gundersheimer, ed., *Art and Life*, p. 48.

55. On Nicolò Lelio Cosmico, see G. Vedova, *Biografia degli scrittori padovani*, 2 vols, Padua, 1832–6 (facs. repr., Bologna, 1967), i, pp. 298–9; V. Rossi, 'Nicolò Lelio Cosmico, poeta padovano del secolo XV', *Giornale Storico della Letteratura Italiana*, 13 (1889), pp. 101–58; Cosenza, *Biographical*, ii, pp. 1127–8, v, p. 150. For his praise by Sabadino, see Gundersheimer, ed., *Art and Life*, p. 85.

56. Indeed, he promoted doctoral candidates in arts and medicine during all these periods. For these and other details, see Pardi, *Titoli*, pp. 32–3, 48–9, 66–7, 84–5, 88–91, 94–5, 104–5, 110–11, 114–15; G. Pardi, *Lo Studio di Ferrara nei secoli xv e xvi*, Ferrara, 1903 (facs. repr., Bologna, 1972), p. 142; Pardi, ed., *Diario Ferrarese dell'anno 1476 fino al 1504 di Bernadino Zambotti*, ed. Pardi, in Muratori, ed., *Rerum Italicarum Scriptores*, Città di Castello and Bologna, 1934–7, xxiv/7 (in appendix) (henceforth *DFZ*), pp. 207, 261.

57. Indeed, in his work on the French Disease Gilino referred to the year 1496 as 'last year' (*anno elapso*). On him and his book, see Sudhoff, *Tractates*, pp. xl–xli; C. C. Barnard, 'The "De morbo quem gallicum nuncupant" [1497] of Coradinus Gilinus', *Janus*, 34 (1930), pp. 97–116. Haller referred to another work by Gilino, the *Tractatus Descriptionum Morborum in Corpore Humano existentium cum tractatulo de Viribus*, Benedictae [sic], 1496; unfortunately it is now lost. See Albrecht von Haller, *Bibliotheca Medicinae Practicae*, 4 vols, Bern and Basel, 1776–88, i, p. 479.

58. It seems very unlikely that Gilino's work was in fact addressed to Ercole's son Sigismondo, since apart from the extreme youth of the latter – he was only seventeen years old – and the difference in ages between him and Gilino, there is no evidence of any connection between them nor of special intellectual concerns which could prompt him to ask one of the court physicians to write such a book. Furthermore, the young Sigismondo seems to have fallen ill with the French Disease only in 1498 or 1499, being medically attended during this last year by Lodovico Carri and Magistro Palomarino.

59. An almost unnoticed work in the middle ages, the *De Medicina* of the Roman encyclopaedist Cornelius Celsus, was recovered between 1426 and 1443, first printed at Florence in

1478 and three times more before the end of the fifteenth century (Milan, 1481; Venice, 1492 and 1497). No less than seventeen more editions of *De Medicina* were printed during the sixteenth century.

60. See, for instance, P. O. Kristeller, *Renaissance Thought and its Sources*, New York, 1979, pp. 29–30.

61. On the Florentine Neoplatonist circle of Marsilio Ficino, see A. Della Torre, *Storia dell'Accademia di Firenze*, Florence, 1902; J. Hankins, *Plato in the Italian Renaissance*, 2 vols, Leiden, 1990, and 'The Myth of the Platonic Academy of Florence', *Renaissance Quarterly*, 44/3 (1991), pp. 429–75.

62. D. Mugnai-Carrara, *La biblioteca di Nicolò Leoniceno. Tra Aristotele e Galeno: cultura e libri di un medico umanista*, Florence, 1991, p. 19.

63. *Articella*, f. 81r.

64. Hankins, *Plato*, i, esp. pp. 271–8.

65. On the peculiarities of court medicine and the role of court physicians in spreading new ideas see V. Nutton, ed., *Medicine at the Courts of Europe, 1500–1837*, London, 1990.

66. Kristeller, *Renaissance Thought*, pp. 29–30.

67. Leoniceno, *Libellus*, sig. a3v.

68. Leoniceno, *Libellus*, sig. a3v.

69. Dall'Aquila, *Interpretatio*, f. 184v.

70. Gilino, *De Morbo*, f. 3r.

71. There are a number of works of the general background of the intellectual positions held by university physicians in late fifteenth- and early sixteenth-century Europe. On humanism and on learned culture, see R. R. Bolgar, *The Classical Heritage and its Beneficiaries*, Cambridge, 1954; L. D. Reynolds and N. G. Wilson, *Scribes and Scholars: a guide to the transmission of Greek and Latin literature*, 3rd edn, Oxford, 1991; Kristeller, *Renaissance Thought*; A. Cunningham, 'The Renaissance' [typescript]; J. Stephens, *The Italian Renaissance: the origins of intellectual and artistic change before the Reformation*, London and New York, 1990;

A. Goodman and A. MacKay, eds, *The Impact of Humanism on Western Europe*, London and New York, 1990; Hankins, *Plato*; W. Rüegg, 'Epilogue: the rise of humanism', in H. de Ridder-Symoens, ed., *A History of the University in Europe*. i: *Universities in the Middle Ages*, Cambridge, 1992, pp. 442–68; F. Rico, *El sueño del humanismo (De Petrarca a Erasmo)*, Madrid, 1993. On university medical and natural-philosophical culture in this period, see: Durling, 'A Chronological Census': F. Maddison, M. Pelling and C. Webster, eds, *Linacre Studies: essays on the life and work of Thomas Linacre, c. 1460–1524*, Oxford, 1977; J. J. Bylebyl, 'The School of Padua: humanistic medicine in the sixteenth century', in C. Webster, ed., *Health, Medicine and Mortality in the Sixteenth Century*, Cambridge, 1979, pp. 335–70; R. K. French, 'Berengario da Carpi and the Use of Commentary in Anatomical Teaching', in Wear, French and Lonie, eds, *The Medical Renaissance*, pp. 42–74, 296–8; French, 'Pliny'; N. G. Siraisi, *Avicenna in Renaissance Italy: the 'Canon' and medical teaching in Italian universities after 1500*, Princeton, 1987; V. Nutton, *John Caius and the Manuscripts of Galen*, Cambridge, 1987; Mugnai-Carrara, *La biblioteca*; A. Grafton, *Defenders of the Text: the traditions of scholarship in an age of science, 1450–1800*, Cambridge, Mass., 1991.

72. Leoniceno, *Libellus*, sig. a2r. Gianfrancesco Pico's deep concern about Savonarola's fate is obvious from his *Opusculum de Sententia Excommunicationis iniusta pro Hieronimi Savonarolae viri prophetae innocentia*, Florence, c. February 1498. Pico's dedication of this work to Ercole d'Este embarrassed the Duke of Ferrara politically and forced him to write soon afterwards an apologetic letter to Pope Alexander VI. For further information see R. Ridolfi, *Vita di Girolamo*

Savonarola, 4th edn, 2 vols, Florence, 1974, i, pp. 272–300, ii, pp. 603–16.

73. Leoniceno, *Libellus*, sig. a2r.
74. Leoniceno, *Libellus*, sig. a2r–v.
75. Leoniceno, *Libellus*, sig. a2v.
76. Leoniceno, *Libellus*, sig. a2v.
77. Leoniceno thought that Hippocrates referred to the French Disease at three different places, namely in his *Aphorisms*, section 3, at the beginning of *Epidemics*, book 2, and at the 'constitution' included in *Epidemics*, book 3. See Hippocrates, *Aphorismi*, iii, 21 (Littré IV, 496–7); *Epidemiae*, ii (Littré V, 72–3); iii (Littré iii, 66–103); Galen, *Commentaria in Hippocratis Aphorismos*, iii, 21 (Kühn xvii/2, 618–21); *Commentaria in Hippocratis librum III Epidemiarum*, III (Kühn xvii/1, 646–792). There is no Galenic commentary to the Hippocratic *Epidemiae*, book II, section I (see Kühn xvii/1, 303–12).
78. Leoniceno, *Libellus*, sig. d3v.
79. Leoniceno, *Libellus*, sigs d1v–d3r.
80. Leoniceno, *Libellus*, sigs d2v–d3r.
81. Pliny the Elder, *Naturalis historia*, xxvi 1–2.
82. Leoniceno, *Libellus*, sig. a3r.
83. Leoniceno, *Libellus*, sig. a3r.
84. Leoniceno, *Libellus*, sig. d1v.
85. Leoniceno, *Libellus*, sig. a3r. See also ibid., sig. d1v.
86. Leoniceno, *Libellus*, sig. d3r.
87. Leoniceno, *Libellus*, sig. c8v. This group of diseases had been already described by Hippocrates as 'epidemic diseases' [*Prognosticum*, 25 (Littré II, 188–9)], and disease 'which prevails in an epidemical way' [*De Natura Hominis*, 9 (Littré VI, 54–5)]. See P. Laín-Entralgo, *La medicina hipocrática*, Madrid, 1970, p. 226.
88. Giovanni Pico della Mirandola, *Disputationes adversus astrologiam divinatricem*, ed. E. Garin, 2 vols, Florence, 1946–52, i, pp. 60–3.
89. Leoniceno, *Libellus*, sigs c8v–d1r.
90. Leoniceno, *Libellus*, sig. d1r.
91. Leoniceno, *Libellus*, sig. d1r.
92. Leoniceno, *Libellus*, sig. d1v.
93. Leoniceno, *Libellus*, sig. d3r.

94. Leoniceno, *Libellus*, sigs d2r, d3r.
95. Leoniceno, *Libellus*, sigs d2r, d3r.
96. Leoniceno, *Libellus*, sigs d3r–v.
97. Leoniceno, *Libellus*, sig. d3v.
98. Leoniceno, *Libellus*, sigs d3v–d4r.
99. Leoniceno, *Libellus*, sig. d4r.
100. In the first chapter, entitled 'On the name of this disease' (*De nomine huius egritudinis*), Dall'Aquila set out his view identifying *Morbus Gallicus* with the *elephantiasis* described by Galen, and defended it against the attacks of his opponent(s). In the second, under the heading 'On the unity and the plurality of this kind of disease' (*De unitate et pluralitate huiusmodi morbi*), he dealt briefly with a question which was controversial among the earliest medical writers on the French Disease, namely whether it was actually a simple disease or a compound one. He was more inclined to accept the first option. Finally, in the third chapter (*De modo curationis cum aliquali preservatione*) Dall'Aquila dealt with the treatment and prevention of the French pox, but also with its essence, causes and symptoms. See Dall'Aquila, *Interpretatio*, ff. 184v, 194r, 195v.
101. Marsilio Ficino, *De Vita libri tres*, Lyon, 1560, p. 5. The enclosed translation comes from C. Boer, ed., *Marsilio Ficino: The Book of Life*, Irving, Tex., 1980, p. 1.
102. L. García-Ballester, *Galeno en la sociedad y en la ciencia de su tiempo (c. 130–c. 200 d. de C.)*, Madrid, 1972, pp. 194–205; García-Ballester, 'Galen as a Clinician: His Methods in Diagnosis', in W. Haase and H. Temporini, eds, *Aufstieg und Niedergang der römischen Welt (Geschichte und Kultur R. im Spiegel der neuren Forschung)*, Teil II, Bd. 37.2, Berlin and New York, 1994, pp. 1636–71; P. Laín-Entralgo, *El diagnóstico médico. Historia y teoría*, Barcelona, 1982, pp. 25–34.
103. Among other Galenic works, Dall'Aquila resorted to his *Microtegni*, *De Morbo et Accidenti*, *De Crisi*, *De*

Diffinitionibus Medicine and the spurious *Introductorium Medicine*.

104. Dall'Aquila, *Interpretatio*, ff. 184v–185r. On Galen's and Galenist views on this issue, see J.-A. Paniagua, 'La patología general en la obra de Arnaldo de Vilanova', *Archivo Iberoamericano de Historia de la Medicina y de Antropología Médica*, 1 (1949), pp. 49–119, esp. pp. 102–5; García-Ballester, *Galeno*, pp. 179–84.

105. Dall'Aquila, *Interpretatio*, ff. 185r–188v.

106. Dall'Aquila, *Interpretatio*, f. 185r.

107. Dall'Aquila, *Interpretatio*, f. 185r.

108. Dall'Aquila, *Interpretatio*, ff. 185r–v.

109. Dall'Aquila, *Interpretatio*, ff. 185v–187r.

110. Dall'Aquila, *Interpretatio*, ff. 186v–187r.

111. Dall'Aquila, *Interpretatio*, f. 187r.

112. Dall'Aquila emphasised that in the dissected body the volume of this phlegm in the left knee was double that in the right one, precisely contrary to what would be expected in a healthy individual according to Galen's doctrine. See Dall'Aquila, *Interpretatio*, ff. 186r–v.

113. Dall'Aquila recalled Galen's distinction between those signs appearing at the beginning of the disease and those during its progress. He also recalled the Galenic three-fold classification of these kinds of accidents which damaged function by decrease, by corruption and by ablation. See Dall'Aquila, *Interpretatio*, ff. 187r–v.

114. Dall'Aquila, *Interpretatio*, ff. 187r–v.

115. Dall'Aquila, *Interpretatio*, ff. 187v–188r.

116. Dall'Aquila, *Interpretatio*, ff. 188r–v.

117. Dall'Aquila claimed not to censure the view of the French pox as a compound disease, although he preferred the opposite one. His main aim, he added, was not 'to contradict anyone, but to defend our position'. See Dall'Aquila, *Interpretatio*, f. 195r.

118. Dall'Aquila, *Interpretatio*, f. 195v.

119. Dall'Aquila, *Interpretatio*, ff. 197r–v.

120. Dall'Aquila, *Interpretatio*, f. 196r.

121. Dall'Aquila, *Interpretatio*, ff. 196r–v. For Torrella on this question, see Chapter Six below.

122. For Leoniceno, as we have seen, *Morbus Gallicus* was caused by 'an excessive warm and humid intemperance of the air'. See Leoniceno, *Libellus*, sig. d1r.

123. Dall'Aquila, *Interpretatio*, f. 196v. In order to support his claims on the primitive causes of the French pox, Dall'Aquila resorted to the same authorities (Hippocrates and Galen) as Leoniceno, but the former put more emphasis on Galen, while the latter emphasised Hippocrates.

124. Dall'Aquila, *Interpretatio*, ff. 196v–197r; Leoniceno, *Libellus*, sig. d2r.

125. Dall'Aquila, *Interpretatio*, f. 197r.

126. Dall'Aquila, *Interpretatio*, f. 197r.

127. Dall'Aquila, *Interpretatio*, f. 200r.

128. Dall'Aquila, *Interpretatio*, ff. 197v–198r, 200r, 200v.

129. Dall'Aquila, *Interpretatio*, ff. 198r–v. Dall'Aquila mentioned a little book by Galen on this play (*De parvae pilae exercitio*), which seems to have been very popular at the time, reflected in the large number of printed editions between 1490 and the late sixteenth century. See Durling, 'A Chronological Census', p. 288.

130. Dall'Aquila, *Interpretatio*, ff. 199v–200r.

131. Dall'Aquila, *Interpretatio*, ff. 200v–202v.

132. Gilino, *De Morbo*, ff. 1v–2r. See Cornelius Celsus, *De Medicina*, v/28/4; Galen, *De ingenio sanitatis*, lib. xiv, ch. x, in *Opera*, Venice, 27 Aug. 1490, ii, sig. g4v; Avicenna, *Canon medicine*, iv/iii, tract. i, ch. ix, Venice, 1527, f. 340r.

133. Gilino, *De Morbo*, ff. 1v–2r, 3r.

134. Avicenna, *Canon*, iv/iii, tract. I, ch. ix, f. 340r.

135. Gilino, *De Morbo*, ff. 1r–v, 3r.

136. Gilino, *De Morbo*, f. 1v.

137. Gilino, *De Morbo*, f. 1v. For Gilino's expressive paragraph in this respect,

see our quotation in Chapter Three above.

138. Gilino, *De Morbo*, ff. 2v–3r.
139. Gilino, *De Morbo*, f. 3r.
140. Gilino, *De Morbo*, f. 4r.
141. Gilino, *De Morbo*, f. 3r.
142. Gilino, *De Morbo*, ff. 3v–4v.
143. Gilino, *De Morbo*, f. 4v.
144. Sudhoff, *Tractates*, pp. xl–xli. On the anatomy of the comisura (=sutura) coronalis, and its therapeutic uses by Galenist physicians, see Gabriele de Zerbi, *Liber Anathomie Corporis Humani et singulorum membrorum*, Venice, 1502, ff. 110r–v.
145. Gilino, *De Morbo*, ff. 1v, 2v, 3r, 3v, 4v. In contrast, to Dall'Aquila and Leoniceno, the 'prince of physicians' was Galen, whom Dall'Aquila even once called the 'king of physicians'. See Leoniceno, *Libellus*, sig. 94v; Dall'Aquila, *Interpretatio*, ff. 184r, 189r.
146. Leoniceno, *Libellus*, sig. c7v: 'Therefore, let those who by drawing attention to the quality and brightness of the discourse turn Celsus into a god of medicine, decide, where the Greek denomination of diseases is concerned, whether they prefer to rely on Celsus, the Roman man, rather than on Hippocrates and the remaining Greek authorities [Galen, Paul of Egina], who are famous.'
147. Gilino, *De Morbo*, f. 2r. Pliny the Elder, *Naturalis Historia*, xxvi/5. In his reply, Dall'Aquila, in addition to being ironical about this error, argued that a single remedy could cure different diseases, as in the case of theriac. Dall'Aquila, *Interpretatio*, ff. 193v–194r.
148. Leoniceno, *Libellus*, sigs c3v–c4r.
149. Leoniceno, *Libellus*, sigs a4r–v.
150. Dall'Aquila, *Interpretatio*, f. 193r.
151. Dall'Aquila, *Interpretatio*, f. 192r.
152. Dall'Aquila, *Interpretatio*, f. 192v.
153. Dall'Aquila, *Interpretatio*, f. 191v.
154. Leoniceno, *Libellus*, sigs a5r–v.
155. See Dall'Aquila, *Interpretatio*, f. 190v. For Galen's reference see the *Liber de*

Virtute Simplicis Medicine, lib. XI, ch. I, in *Opera*, Venice, 1490, ii, sigs llL1v–llL2v.

Chapter Five: The French Disease in Northern Europe

1. P. A. Russell, 'Syphilis, God's Scourge or Nature's Vengeance? The German printed response to a public problem in the early sixteenth century', *Archive for Reformation History*, 80 (1989), pp. 286–307: p. 291.
2. Konrad Schellig, *In Pustulas malas Morbum quem Malum de Francia vulgus appellat que sunt de genere Formicarum. Salubre Consilium doctoris Conrad Schellig Heidelebergensis*, Heidelberg, 1495–6. See Charles Singer's adaptation of Karl Sudhoff's collection of early materials on 'syphilis': *The Earliest Printed Literature on Syphilis, being ten tractates from the years 1495–1498*, Florence, 1925. The facsimiles reproduced by Singer are referred to separately in this chapter.
3. Pollich was born in 1450 and died in 1513. On the Leipzig faculty see K. Sudhoff, *Die medizinische Fakultät zu Leipzig im ersten Jahrhundert der Universität*, Leipzig, 1909. Some biographical details of Pistoris and Pollich are given in *Allgemeine deutsche Biographie*, 56 vols, Leipzig, 1888, xxvi. For Pollich's thesis see K. Sudhoff, *Aus der Frühgeschichte der Syphilis*, (see ch. 1, n. 26 for full title) Leipzig, 1912, p. 43.
4. Many of these questions had also been discussed in relation to the plague. The question whether elementary air could become corrupt was derived from the Arabic authors. Like plague too the pox was sometimes thought to be capable of transmission by a glance from the eyes of an infected person. See A. Campbell, *The Black Death and Men of Learning*, New York, 1931, p. 3.
5. Indeed, it is at least possible that he

was involved in the appearance of the book.

6. Martin Pollich of Mellerstadt, *Defensio Leoniceniana,* Leipzig, 1498.

7. Simon Pistoris, *Positio de Morbo Franco,* Leipzig, 1498. This and the later tracts were collected and published by Conrad Heinrich Fuchs, *Die ältesten deutschen Schriftsteller über die Lustseuche in Deutschland von 1495 bis 1510, nebst mehrerer Anecdotis späterer Zeit, gesammelt und mit literarhistorischen Notizen und einer kurzen Darstellung der epidemischen Syphilis in Deutschland,* Göttingen, 1843.

8. The sequence of theses and publication was as follows: (i) Pollich, 'Utrum ex corrupcione aeris causetur fancosica, morbus pestilencialis et invadens', 1496; (ii) Pollich supports Leoniceno, perhaps by thesis; (iii) Pistoris, *Positio de Morbo Franco,* 1498; (iv) Pollich, *Defensio Leoniceniana,* 1498; (v) Pistoris, *Declaratio defensiva cuiusdam positionis de Morbo Gallico,* 1500; (vi) Pollich, *Castigationes in Declarationes D S Pistoris,* 1500; (vii) Pistoris, *Confutatio conflatorum circa positionem quandam extraneam et puerilem a Malefranco,* 1501; (viii) Pollich, *Responsio ad superadditos errores Simonis Pistoris de Malo Franco,* 1501.

9. On Pollich and humanism in Leipzig see G. Bauch, *Geschichte des Leipziger Frühhumanismus mit besonderer Rücksicht auf die Streitigkeiten zwischen Konrad Wimpina und Martin Mellerstadt,* Leipzig, 1899. On the distinction between humanists and hellenists, see the chapter by Roger French on Berengario da Carpi in A. Wear, R. K. French and I. Lonie, *The Medical Renaissance of the Sixteenth Century,* Cambridge, 1985, pp. 42–74.

10. On German humanism see for example P. Joachimsen, 'Humanism and the Growth of the German Mind', in G. Strauss, ed., *Pre-Reformation Germany,* New York, 1972, p. 162; L. W. Spitz, *The Religious Renaissance of the German Hu-*

manists, Cambridge, Mass., 1963, esp. pp. 17 and 113; M. Watanabe, 'Gregor Heimburg and Early Humanism in Germany', in E. P. Mahoney, ed., *Philosophy and Humanism: renaissance essays in honor of Paul Oskar Kristeller,* Leiden, 1976, p. 406.

11. Thus the anatomist Eichmann called himself 'Dryander', the Greek equivalent of his own name, 'Oakman'. The pox author Widman, perhaps for related reasons, gave himself a Latin name, 'Salicetus', meaning 'willow grove'. See the *Allgemeine deutsche Biographie.*

12. For example the lawyer Collenuccio and the surgeon–anatomist Berengario da Carpi in the dispute with Leoniceno over Pliny. See R. K. French and G. Greenaway, *Science in the Early Roman Empire: Pliny the Elder, his sources and influence,* London, 1986, esp. the chapters by Eastwood and French.

13. In his discussion of his first conclusion.

14. In his discussion of his first conclusion.

15. See his discussion of the second corollary of his third conclusion.

16. On this point see the chapter by R. K. French in Wear, French and Lonie, eds, *The Medical Renaissance,* and 'Gentile da Foligno and the Via Medicorum' in J. D. North and J. J. Roche, eds, *The Light of Nature: essays in the history and philosophy of science presented to A. C. Crombie,* Dordrecht, 1985, pp. 21–34.

17. Pollich uses the term *balbutis*: see his discussion of the 'impertinent' conclusion and final corollary of Pistor. The term was not infrequently used by hellenists: see Chapter Four above.

18. See the preliminary matter in Pollich's *Castigationes* of 1500 upon Pistor's *Declaratio.* See Fuchs, *Die ältesten deutschen Schriftsteller,* p. 169.

19. See P. Zambelli, 'Giovanni Manardi e la polemica sull'astrologia', *L'opera e il pensiero di Giovanni Pico della*

Mirandola nella storia dell'umanesimo, Florence, 1965, pp. 205–79.

20. Russell, 'Syphilis', p. 295.
21. Spitz, *Religious Renaissance,* p. 20
22. Spitz, *Religious Renaissance,* p. 12.
23. Spitz, *Religious Renaissance,* p. 67.
24. Brant's *Eulogium* appears in J. Grünpeck, *Tractatus de Pestilentia Scorra sive Mala de Franzos,* Augsburg, 1496.
25. See D. Kurze, 'Popular Astrology and Prophecy in the Fifteenth and Sixteenth Centuries', in P. Zambelli, ed., *'Astrologi Hallucinati': stars and the end of the world in Luther's time,* Berlin and New York, 1986, pp. 178–93: p. 180. See also H. R. Hammerstein, 'The Battle of the Booklets: prognostic tradition and proclamation of the word in early sixteenth century Germany', in Zambelli, ed., *'Astrologi Hallucinati',* pp. 129–51: pp. 129, 131.
26. Grünpeck (c.1472–c.1533) seems however to have been a bachelor of medicine. See Russell, 'Syphilis', p. 293
27. Grünpeck, *Pestilentia Scorra,* ch. 3.
28. Grünpeck, *Pestilentia Scorra,* ch. 10.
29. Grünpeck contracted the pox himself, at an entertainment organised by his fellow humanist Celtis. See Russell, 'Syphilis', p. 294.
30. Joannes Widman, *De Pustulis et Morbo, qui vulgo Mal de Franzos appellatur,* Rome, 1497. The edition of Strasbourg, in the same year, has the shorter title *Tractatus de Pustulis que vulgato nomine dicuntur Mal de Franzos.*
31. See the *Allgemeine deutsche Biographie.*
32. See for example *A Treatise of the donation or gyfte and endowment of possessyons given and granted unto Sylvester pope of Rhome by Constantyne emperour of Rome,* [n.p.], 1532, which includes Valla's denunciation and Hutten's preface. The first edition seems to have been in 1517.
33. Spitz, *Religious Renaissance,* p. 19. On German humanism see also C. Trinkaus, *The Scope of Renaissance*

Humanism, Ann Arbor, 1983; G. Hoffmeister, ed., *The Renaissance and Reformation in Germany: an introduction,* New York, 1977.
34. See in particular S. Wheelis, 'Ulrich von Hutten: representative of patriotic humanism', in Hoffmeister, ed., *Renaissance,* pp. 111–27.
35. See R. S. Munger, 'Guaiacum: the holy wood from the New World', *Journal of the History of Medicine,* 4 (1949), pp. 196–229
36. U. von Hutten, *Of the Wood called Guaiacum, that healeth the French Pockes, and the Palsy, Lepree, Dropsy, fallynge evil and other diseases,* trans. T. Paynel, London, 1536.
37. U. von Hutten, *De Guaiaci Medicina et Morbo Gallico liber unus,* Mainz, 1519 (unpaginated), sig. d3r.
38. Hutten, *De Guaiaci,* sigs a4v, b1v.
39. Hutten, *De Guaiaci,* sig. b1r.
40. Hutten, *De Guaiaci,* sig. b2r; *Wood,* p. 4v. He speaks of his treatment at the hands of the doctors when he was a child. He was born in 1488 and so would have been eight when the first thesis at Leipzig was disputed and thirteen or so when the battle between Pollich and Pistoris petered out. His 'two years' may mean the period that followed Pistoris' thesis of 1498, if he is referring to events in Leipzig. (He probably was, for he was helped in the writing of the book by the dean of the medical faculty there.) If so, he had contracted the pox before he was ten. In any case it provides difficulties for a direct interpretation that the pox was syphilis that it could be contracted by a child, born too early to have the congenital variety but too late to have acquired it by sexual transmission. Hutten records that his father also had the disease, so a non-venereal acquisition seems possible.
41. Hutten, *De Guaiaci,* sig. c1r.
42. Hutten, *De Guaiaci,* sig. c3r.
43. Hutten, *Wood,* p. 15r. See also p. 31r.
44. See the ethical code set out by

Gabriele de Zerbi in 1495: R. K. French, 'The Medical Ethics of Gabriele de Zerbi', in A. Wear, J. Geyer-Kordesch and R. K. French, *Doctors and Ethics: the earlier historical setting of professional ethics*, Amsterdam, 1993, pp.72–97.

45. Hutten, *De Guaiaci*, sig. d4v

46. Hutten, *De Guaiaci*, sig. c3r; *Wood*, p. 15r.

47. See Walter Pagel, *Paracelsus: an introduction to philosophical medicine in the era of the renaissance*, Basel, 1958, p. 24

48. Hutten's references to Stromer are generally favourable. See *De Guaiaci*, sigs d2v, d3r, e3v.

49. On the role of hospitals in general in the German reaction to the French Disease, see R. Jütte, 'Syphilis and Confinement: early modern German hospitals for syphilitics', in N. Finizsch and R. Jütte, eds, *The Prerogative of Confinement*, Cambridge, 1995.

50. Hutten, *De Guaiaci*, sig. g4r: he Latinises the name as Fucheri and mentions their magnificent houses.

51. A. G. Debus, *The Chemical Philosophy. Paracelsian science and medicine in the sixteenth and seventeenth centuries*, 2 vols, New York, 1977, i, p. 52.

52. Pagel, *Paracelsus*, p. 24.

53. See A. Arber, *Herbals: their origin and evolution. A chapter in the history of botany 1470–1670*, 2nd edn, Cambridge, 1953, p. 255.

54. Pagel, *Paracelsus*, pp. 139, 142.

55. He wrote an epitome of anatomy and a description of plants.

56. In Wittenberg there was an attempt to teach physics not from Aristotle, whose views on the eternity of the world were seen as too pagan, but from Pliny, in particular book II of the *Naturalis historia*. This is where Pliny gives his summary view of the heavens and earth, that is, where he covers the same ground as Aristotle in the physical works. While it is in book XXXII (rather than II) that Pliny deals with the *remora* and the

torpedo and their sympathies (see Chapter Nine below), yet the whole subject is so Plinian that we can see why Pliny was attractive to protestant dissenters at Wittenberg. See French and Greenaway, *Pliny*, esp. the chapters by Eastwood and French.

57. L. Fuchs, *Paradoxorum Medicinae libri tres*, Basel, 1535, the address to Hildrick. He deals with the pox on p. 88v.

58. Fuchs, *Paradoxorum*, book 2, p. 89r

59. L. Fuchs, *Institutionum Medicinae, ad Hippocratis, Galeni, aliorumque veterum scripta recte intelligenda mire utiles libri quinque*, Lyon, 1555.

60. Fuchs, *Institutionum*, p. 34. His discussion of what an element is emphasises the fact that an element cannot be resolved into smaller and different parts. An element is thus in one sense at the limits of division, an argument that needed little extension to cover atomism (but this is not Fuchs' intention).

61. Fuchs, *Institutionum*, p. 436.

62. There are a number of signs of a religious unorthodoxy in his later life. His mathematical *Ars Magna* was published in 1545 in Nuremberg by the Lutheran convert Andreas Osiander (1498–1552) (who had also published Copernicus' radical book two years earlier); he turned down the job of teaching mathematics to Pope Paul III, but was the natural target when the protestant Christian II of Denmark wanted a physician.

63. On Cardano see J. Eckman, 'Jerome Cardan', *Bulletin of the History of Medicine*, Suppl. 7 (1946). Although Cardano recanted, observers of the next generation saw him as an atheist. See more recently *The Cambridge History of Renaissance Philosophy*, ed. C. B. Schmitt, Q. Skinner and E. Kessler, Cambridge, 1988, especially A. Ingegno, 'The New Philosophy of Nature', pp. 236–63; M. Fierz, *Girolamo Cardano, 1501–1576: physician, natural philosopher, mathemati-*

cian, astrologer and interpreter of dreams,
trans. H. Nieman, Boston, 1983.

64. On astrology and its terminology see
for example J. Tester, *A History of
Western Astrology*, Woodbridge, Suf-
folk, 1987; W. Shumaker, *The Occult
Sciences in the Renaissance*, Berkeley
and London, 1972.

65. Grünpeck, *Pestilentia Scorra*.

66. Thus Grünpeck. Modern tables
(Tuckerman's) confirm that such a
conjunction occurred between 17
and 27 November 1484. While
Mars, at about 25 degrees, was still in
Aries (its day house, and thus powerful), its position was at about 110
degrees from this conjunction, not a
recognised astrological aspect. The
next conjunction of Jupiter and Saturn was on 26 May 1504: the pox
came almost exactly halfway
between – at its furthest from the
influence of – the two encompassing
evil conjunctions. In other words,
the pox could hardly have happened
at an astrologically more inconven-
ient time. Much of the apparatus of
astrology was in fact exactly analogous to the *rationality* of the contemporary Galenic medicine, where
rationality is a series of arguments
that served to convince the listener
and which were based on some
wider premise, such as the ultimate
nature of the heavens and earth.
Kepler's extension of the traditional
range of aspects had much the same
effect in astrology as the assumption
that planets remained in conjunction
for a number of degrees outside their
strict geometrical equivalence in the
zodiac: both extended the range of
astrological explanation. Since to
observation the heavenly bodies
were very small objects moving in a
very large space, it was professionally
good to multiply the number of occasions on which they interacted.

67. Grünpeck (later perhaps) was also
Joachimite, offering warnings that
the ecclesiastical hierarchy will break
down with the coming of the third

age of the Church, that of spirituality. (On Joachimism see D. Kurze,
'Popular Astrology and Prophecy in
the Fifteenth and Sixteenth Centuries', in Zambelli, '*Astrologi
Hallucinati*', pp. 178–93. More information on astrology and Grünpeck
can be found in E. Garin, *Astrology
in the Renaissance*, London, 1983, and
Hammerstein, 'The Battle'.

68. On Pico against astrology, see L.
Thorndike, *A History of Magic and
Experimental Science*, 8 vols, New
York, 1923–58, IV, pp. 529–43; E.
Garin, *Giovanni Pico della Mirandola.
Vita e dottrina*, Florence, 1937, pp.
169–93; W. Shumaker, *Occult Sci-
ences*, Berkeley, 1972, pp. 16–27;
Giovanni Pico della Mirandola,
*Disputationes adversus Astrologiam
Divinatricem*, ed. E. Garin, 2 vols,
Florence, 1946–52, esp. I, pp. 60–3.
As we will see in Chapter Six, Pico's
work strongly influenced the views
on astrology of the papal physician
Gaspar Torrella, who changed his
mind between 1497 and 1500 as a
result of it. This change of mind is
emphasised by a comparison between Torrella's obvious astrological
concern in his *De Morbo Gallico cum
aliis*, (Rome, *c*.1498, sig. a3v) and his
critical attitude in the *Dialogus de
Dolore cum tractatu de Ulceribus in
Pudendagra evenire solitis* (Rome, 31
Oct. 1500, sigs a5v–a6v).

Chapter Six: The French Disease and the Papal Court

1. On Rodrigo de Borja before and
after becoming Pope Alexander VI,
see L. Pastor, *The History of the Popes
from the Close of the Middle Ages*, 40
vols, London, 1891–1953, v (1898),
pp. 375–523, vi (1898), pp. 3–181;
L. Collison-Morley, *The Story of the
Borgias*, London, 1932, pp. 12–245;
M. Mallett, *The Borgias: the rise and
fall of a renaissance dynasty*, London,
1971, esp. pp. 79–227.

2. On *Morbus Gallicus* at the papal
courts of Alexander VI and Julius
II see Hesnaut [pseud. of Louis
Thuasne], *Le Mal Français à l'époque
de l'expédition de Charles VIII en
Italie, d'après les documents originaux*,
Paris, 1886, pp. 49–50; L. Gualino,
'L'infezione celtica', *Storia medica dei
Romani pontefici*, Turin, 1934, pp.
257–331. For contemporary testimony on the cardinals infected with
the French Disease see Marin
Sanudo, *I Diarii*, ed. R. Fulin et al.,
58 vols, Venice, 1879–1902, i, col.
871 (Ascanio Sforza), ii, col. 749
(Giuliano della Rovere); Johann
Burchard, *Diarium sive Rerum
Urbanarum Commentarii (1483–1506)*,
ed. Louis Thuasne, 3 vols, Paris,
1883–5, ii, p. 521 (Bertomeu Martí),
p. 581 (Joan Borja-Llançol). For
Ippolito d'Este, see above.
3. The other two Spanish physicians
were Alejandro Espinosa and Andrés
Vives. The remaining physicians
were Italian: Filippo della Valle,
Bernardo Buongiovanni and
Giovanni Battista Canani. See G.
Marini, *Degli Archiatri Pontifici*, 2
vols, Rome, 1784, i, pp. 236–80.
See also R. Palmer, 'Medicine at the
Papal Court in the Sixteenth Century', in V. Nutton, ed., *Medicine at
the Courts of Europe, 1500–1837*, London, 1990, pp. 49–78. On Vives see
also G. Bronzino, ed., *Notitia
doctorum, sive Catalogus Doctorum qui
in Collegiis Philosophiae et Medicinae
Bononiae laureati fuerunt ab anno 1480
usque ad annum 1800*, Milan, 1962, p.
1.
4. Among the people put on trial by
the Valencian Inquisition between
1484 and 1530 there were at least
seven members of the Pintor family
and four more of the Torrella family. See R. García Cárcel, *Orígenes de
la Inquisición española. El tribunal de
Valencia, 1478–1530*, Barcelona, 1976,
pp. 284, 300.
5. On this question see J. Arrizabalaga,
L. García-Ballester and F. Salmón,
'A propósito de las relaciones

intelectuales entre la Corona de
Aragón e Italia (1470–1520): los
estudiantes de medicina valencianos
en los estudios generales de Siena,
Pisa, Ferrara y Padua', *Dynamis*, 9
(1989), pp. 117–47; Arrizabalaga,
García-Ballester and J. L. Gil-Aristu,
'Del manuscrito al primitivo
impreso: la labor editora de Francesc
Argilagues (fl. ca. 1470–1508) en el
renacimiento italiano', *Asclepio*, 43
(1991), pp. 3–50.
6. P. O. Kristeller, *Renaissance Thought
and its Sources*, New York, 1979, pp.
29–30.
7. Indeed, Pintor had studied when
young (during the late 1530s and
early 1540s) with master Francesc
Queralt, the ordinary (principal)
teacher, who was then, as Pintor
says, ninety years old. This means
that Queralt's own medical education must have begun as long ago as
1360.
8. For the cultural patronage of the
Borgias in Rome, see Mallett,
Borgias, pp. 216–18 (Cesare Borgia),
233–40 (Alexander VI).
9. For the press in Rome in the
fifteenth century see P. Casciano et
al., 'Materiali e ipotesi per la stampa
a Roma', in C. Bianca et al., eds,
*Scrittura, biblioteche e stampa in Roma
nel quattrocento. Aspetti e problemi (Atti
del Seminario 1–2 giugno 1979)*, 2 vols,
Vatican City, 1980, i, pp. 213–44.
The whole of volume ii consists of
an exhaustive *Indice delle edizione
romane a stampa (1467–1500)*.
10. For the biography of Torrella see J.
M. López-Piñero et al., *Diccionario
histórico de la ciencia moderna en
España*, 2 vols, Barcelona, 1983, ii,
pp. 356–8; J. Arrizabalaga, 'La obra
sifilográfica de Gaspar Torrella:
edición, traducción y estudio de
su "Tractatus cum consiliis contra
pudendagram seu morbum
gallicum" (Roma, 1497)', unpub.
PhD diss., University of Zaragoza,
1983, pp. 27–72. Data that have not
been collected in any of these works
come from L. Zdekauer, *Lo Studio di*

Siena nel Rinascimento, Milan, 1894, p. 181; A. F. Verde, *Lo Studio fiorentino, 1473–1503. Ricerche e documenti*, Florence and Pistoia, 1973–, iii/1, p. 329; iv/1, p. 139; J. Bignami-Odier, *La Bibliothèque Vaticane de Sixte IV à Pie XI. Recherches sur l'histoire des collections de manuscrits*, Vatican City, 1973, pp. 27, 38, 320, 348.

11. M. Gallent Marco, 'La asistencia sanitaria en Valencia (1400–1512)', 2 vols, unpub. PhD. diss., University of Valencia, 1980, ii, pp. 45, 47, 49–50. Pintor entered practice about 1444. For this and his teacher see his *Agregator*, [ff. 4r, 5v] (note 19 below).

12. L. García-Ballester, *La medicina a la València medieval. Medicina i societat en un país medieval mediterrani*, Valencia, 1988, esp. pp. 57–73.

13. The last academic year in which he lectured at the school of surgery was 1484–5. His name appears on a list of converted Jews contributing to a royal Tacha in August 1488 as a former medical practitioner (*olim medicus*). See López-Piñero et al., *Diccionario*, ii, p. 178; J. Guiral, 'Convers à Valence à la fin du XVe siècle', *Mélanges de la Casa de Velázquez*, 11 (1975), pp. 81–98: pp. 81–2, 93.

14. Gaspar Torrella, *Judicium universale de Portentis Presagiis et Ostentis Rerumque admirabilium ac Solis et Lune defectibus et Cometis*, Rome, 1506. On Giovanni Gozzadini (1477–1517), see P. Partner, *The Pope's Men: the papal civil service in the renaissance*, Oxford, 1990, pp. 136–9, 235, passim.

15. Torrella, *Consilium de Egritudine Pestifera et Contagiosa Ovina cognominata nuper cognita quam Hispani Modorrillam vocant*, Rome, 1505; Salamanca, 27 Nov. 1505 (henceforth *Consilium de Egritudine*, R [Rome], S [Salamanca]). On this work, see J. Arrizabalaga, 'El "Consilium de modorrilla" (Roma y Salamanca, 1505): una aportación

nosográfica de Gaspar Torrella', *Dynamis*, 5–6 (1985–6), pp. 59–94.

16. Torrella, *Consilium de Preservatione et Curatione a Pestilentia*, Rome, after 1505. This epidemic was documented by A. Corradi, *Annali delle epidemie occorse in Italia . . .* , 5 vols, Bologna, 1865–92 (facs. repr. Bologna, 1972–3), i, pp. 7–8.

17. Torrella, *Pro Regimine seu Preservatione Sanitatis. De Esculentis et Poculentis dialogus*, Rome, 1506.

18. Torrella, *Dialogus de Dolore cum tractatu de Ulceribus in Pudendagra evenire solitis*, Rome, 31 Oct. 1500 (henceforth *Dialogus*).

19. Pere Pintor, *Agregator Sententiarum doctorum omnium de Preservatione Curationeque Pestilentie*, Rome, 20 Feb. 1499 (henceforth *Agregator*); *Tractatus de Morbo foedo et occulto his temporibus affligente*, Rome, 9 Aug. 1500 (henceforth *Tractatus de Morbo*).

20. Most of Pintor's biographers are repetitive, platitudinous and vague. Among the more useful sources are N. F. J. Eloy, *Dictionnaire historique de la médecine ancienne et moderne*, 4 vols, Mons, 1778 (facs. repr., Brussels, 1973), iii, pp. 568–9; Marini, *Archiatri*, i, pp. 251–7, ii, pp. 247–8; *Dictionnaire des sciences médicales: biographie médicale*, 7 vols, Paris, 1820–5, vi, p. 420; López Piñero et al., *Diccionario* ii, pp. 178–9. Pintor must have been born around 1423, for his epitaph records that he died at eighty (4 September 1503). See Marini, *Archiatri*, i, p. 252). Furthermore, he said that he was seventy-four years and six months old when he finished his earliest book, which he eventually published on 20 February 1499. See Pintor, *Agregator* [f. 1r].

21. Pintor was assigned 100 ducats per year as papal physician in December 1502. See Marini, *Archiatri*, i, pp. 252–3, ii, pp. 247–8

22. See the flattering language used by Pintor in his *Agregator*, sig. o8v; *Tractatus de Morbo*, sig. f4r.

23. He defined the disease as a general

condition of the skin, mostly of the extremities, with pain. See *Tractatus*, sig. a4v. He contrived to draw support from Galen and Avicenna that the disease could take its name from the member in which it first appeared. Cf. *Dialogus*, sig. a6v.

24. There was an analogy with the terms *podagra* and *mentagra* as used by Pliny. For a detailed account of the early names of the pox, see J. Astruc, *De Morbis Venereis libri novem*, 2 vols, Venice, 1748, i, pp. 4–6. Some of these are more fully documented in E. Wickersheimer, 'Sur la syphilis aux XVe et XVIe siècles', *Humanisme et Renaissance*, 4 (1937), pp. 157–207: pp. 159–75. Compare the new name used by the Valencian doctor Joan Almenar: *patursa*, that is, a name compressed from *passio turpis saturnina*, apparently a parallelism to Pliny's *gemursa*. See Joan Almenar, *Libellus ad Evitandum et Expellendum Morbum Gallicum ut nunquam revertatur . . .* , Venice, 13 June 1502, sigs a3v–a4r. Cf. Pliny the Elder, *Naturalis Historia*, xxvi/2 (*mentagra*), 5 (*gemursa*); xxvii/63 (*podagra*).

25. See R. K. French, 'Berengario da Carpi and the Use of Commentary in Anatomical Teaching' in A. Wear, R. K. French and I. Lonie, eds, *The Medical Renaissance of the Sixteenth Century*, Cambridge 1985, pp. 42–74: p. 71.

26. The opinion is found in Guy's *Chirurgia Magna*. See also M. S. Ogden, 'The Galenic Works Cited in Guy de Chauliac's "Chirurgia Magna"', *Journal of the History of Medicine*, 28 (1973), pp. 24–33: p. 24; L. García-Ballester, 'Arnau de Vilanova (c. 1240–1311) y su reforma de los estudios médicos en Montpellier (1309): el Hipócrates latino y la introducción del nuevo Galeno', *Dynamis*, 2 (1982), pp. 97–158: pp. 102–3.

27. Natale Montesauro, *De Dispositionibus quas vulgares Mal Franzoso appellant*, Bologna, 1498, f. 3r.

28. Torrella, *De Morbo Gallico cum aliis*, Rome, c. 1498 (henceforth *De Morbo*), sig. a3v. In the first edition of this work, Torrella located the origin of the disease in France, but some caution may lie in his use of the expression of *ut aiunt*, 'they say'. See Torrella, *Tractatus cum Consiliis contra Pudendagram seu Morbum Gallicum*, Rome, 22 Nov. 1497 (henceforth *Tractatus*), sig. a3v.

29. Torrella, *Dialogus*, sig. a4r.

30. Torrella, *De Morbo*, sig. a2r; *Dialogus*, sigs a4r–v. Note that none of these names was recognised in the first edition of his first work on the topic (1497). Equally, while in 1498 Torrella asserted that 'some call [*Morbus Gallicus*] the "Mal de San Sement"' (Morbus Sancti Sementi), it became just 'Mal de Sement' (Morbus Sementi) in 1500. On the problem of the origin and significance of these names, see J. Rodrigo y Pertegás, 'Mal de sement', *Discursos leídos en la Real Academia de Medicina de Valencia*, Valencia, 1923, pp. 5–53. See also M.-L. López Terrada, 'El mal de siment en la Valencia del siglo XVI: imágenes del morbo gallico en una ciudad mediterránea europea', *Dynamis*, 11 (1991), pp. 119–46.

31. Avicenna, *Canon Medicinae*, iv/vii, tract. iii, cap. vi (De scabie et pruritu) and vii (De cura [scabiei et pruritus]), Venice, 1527, ff. 385v–386v.

32. Pintor, *Tractatus de Morbo*, sigs a3r, a3v–4r, a7v, d7v. In fact in the *Canon* (iv/i, tract. iv, cap. vi) Avicenna is not so explicit as Pintor pretends. He is really discussing *two* species, *variolae* and *morbilli*, and mentions the *aluhumata* only in passing as something intermediate in nature between the two and as more curable than either.

33. Pintor, *Tractatus de Morbo*, sigs av, a1v, a7v–bv.

34. Torrella, *De Morbo*, sig. a3v. Pietro d'Abano, *Conciliator Differentiarum*

Medicorum et Philosophorum, Venice, 1564 (facs. repr., Padua, 1985), ff. 44v–45v diff. xxix.

35. Torrella, *Dialogus*, sig. a5v.
36. Torrella, *Dialogus*, sigs a5v–a6r.
37. Torrella, *Dialogus*, sig. a6r.
38. Torrella, *Dialogus*, sigs a6r–v.
39. Giovanni Pico della Mirandola, *Disputationes adversus Astrologiam Divinatricem*, ed. E. Garin, 2 vols, Florence, 1946–52.
40. On Pico against astrology see L. Thorndike, *A History of Magic and Experimental Science*, 8 vols, New York, 1923–58, iv, pp. 529–43; E. Garin, *Giovanni Pico della Mirandola. Vita e dottrina*, Florence, 1937, pp. 169–93; W. Shumaker, *The Occult Sciences in the Renaissance: a study in intellectual patterns*, Berkeley, 1972, pp. 16–27.
41. Pico, *Disputationes*, i, pp. 60–3.
42. On notions of infection and contagion see Chapter Two above, n. 77.
43. Torrella, *Tractatus*, sig. a4v.
44. Torrella, *Tractatus*, sigs a4v–b1r.
45. Torrella claims him as a servant of Cesare Borgia, but Sudhoff believed that he was Cesare himself. K. Sudhoff, *The Earliest Printed Literature on Syphilis, being ten tractates from the years 1495–1498*, Florence, 1925, p. xxxiii.
46. Torrella, *Tractatus*, sigs c4v–d1r (*consilium* I), e1r (c. III), e2r (c. IV).
47. Torrella, *Dialogus*, sig. a6v.
48. Torrella, *Tractatus*, sig. b1r.
49. Torrella, *Tractatus*, sigs c4v–d1r.
50. Pintor, *Tractatus de Morbo*, sigs a6v–a7v.
51. Pintor, *Tractatus de Morbo*, sigs a7v, b1r.
52. See R. K. French, 'The Medical Ethics of Gabriele de Zerbi', in A. Wear, J. Geyer-Kordesch and R. K. French, eds, *Doctors and Ethics: the earlier historical setting of professional ethics*, Amsterdam, 1993, pp. 72–97: p. 88.
53. Pintor held that the pox was caused by Saturnine conjunctions in Scorpio in October and November

1483. The conjunction of Mars and Jupiter in Libra in 1494 determined which regions were affected. The complexity of the system allowed the astrologers to disagree and Pintor denied that the conjunctions of 1496 (cf. Gilino) were causal.
54. Pintor, *Tractatus de Morbo*, sig. b1v.
55. Pintor, *Tractatus de Morbo,* sigs b1v, b2r, c7r–dr.
56. Pintor, *Tractatus de Morbo*, sig. dv.
57. 'Fugere cito, longe, et tarde reverti': Pintor, *Tractatus de Morbo*, sig. dv.
58. Torrella, *Tractatus*, sig. c4v.
59. Torrella, *Dialogus*, sig. a6v.
60. Torrella, *Tractatus*, sigs b1r–v; b3v–b4v.
61. Pintor, *Tractatus de Morbo*, sigs b2v–b3r.
62. Pintor, *Tractatus de Morbo*, sig. b3r. But he added that in some cases the pus was so corrosive that it acted like cancer.
63. Pintor, *Tractatus de Morbo*, sig. b3r
64. See, for example, M. McVaugh, *Medicine Before the Plague: practitioners and their patients in the Crown of Aragon, 1285–1345*, Cambridge, 1993, esp. ch. 4. Doctors like Jacme d'Agramont and Gentile da Foligno wrote works for the city councils of Lérida and Perugia respectively. See J. Arrizabalaga, 'Facing the Black Death: perceptions and reactions of university medical practitioners', in L. García-Ballester, R. K. French, J. Arrizabalaga and A. R. Cunningham, eds, *Practical Medicine from Salerno to the Black Death*, Cambridge, 1994, pp. 240–1.
65. Torrella, *Dialogus*, sig. d4v.
66. Torrella, *Tractatus*, sig. e6v.
67. M. L. López-Terrada, 'El tratamiento de la sífilis en un hospital renacentista: la sala del *Mal de Siment* del Hospital General de Valencia', *Asclepio*, 41 (1989), pp. 19–50.
68. See J. Rossiaud, *Medieval Prostitution*, Oxford, 1988, pp. 48–51.
69. Pintor, *Tractatus de Morbo*, sig. b6r.

For more information Pintor directs the reader to his *Agregator*, sig. b3v.

70. Pintor, *Tractatus de Morbo*, sigs b5v–b6r.

71. Pintor, *Tractatus de Morbo*, sigs b7r, cr, c2r, c3v, c6r, c6v.

72. Pintor, *Tractatus de Morbo*, sigs b6v–b8v.

73. Torrella, *Tractatus*, sigs c4v–d2v (*consilium* I), d2v–e1r (c. 2), e1r–e2r (c. 3), e2r–e3r (c. 4), e3r–f3v (c. 5).

74. See P. Laín-Entralgo, *La historia clínica. Historia y teoría del relato patográfico*, 2nd edn, Barcelona, 1961, pp. 48–109. The medical *consilium* was a written judgement of a clinical case, with indications of regimen and treatment. Appearing in the thirteenth century, they often appeared in didactic collections, and tended to emphasise the kind of ailment rather than the individuality of the patient (although they evolved over time towards greater individuality in each case). For further details see J. Agrimi and C. Crisciani, *Les consilia médicaux (Typologie des sources du moyen age occidental)*, Tournhout, 1994.

75. Torrella, *Tractatus*, sig. a4r.

76. Ecclesiasticus, 38: 1–15.

77. Torrella, *Tractatus*, sigs e3v–e4r.

78. Torrella, *Tractatus*, sigs a2r–a3v.

79. For an interesting hypothesis about the reasons behind this courtly Platonism, see A. Brown, 'Platonism in Fifteenth-Century Florence and its Contribution to Modern Political Thought', *Journal of Modern History*, 58/2 (1986), pp. 383–413.

80. Torrella, *Tractatus*, sigs c3r–v, d2r, d4r–v, e1v–e2r, e2v, f3r.

81. For the 'intentions' and remedies, see Torrella, *Tractatus*, sigs c1v–c4r, d1v–d2v, d4r–e1r, e1v–e2r, f2v–f3r. Generally speaking, in 1500 he followed the same therapeutical guidelines. See e.g. Torrella, *Dialogus*, sig. e1v–e3r.

82. Avicenna, *Canon Medicinae*, iv/vii, tract. iii, cap. vii, Venice, 1527, ff. 386r–v.

83. Torrella, *De Morbo*, sigs b3v–b4r, b5v–b6r.

84. Pintor, *Tractatus de Morbo*, sigs d5r–d6r. He quotes Galen and Avicenna on the ability of pain to kill.

85. Pintor, *Tractatus de Morbo*, sig. er.

86. Pintor, *Tractatus de Morbo*, sigs er, e3r–v.

87. Pintor, *Tractatus de Morbo*, sigs e4r–f1v. For a detailed study of the division by early medieval physicians of Galen's qualitative classification of remedies into degrees see M. R. McVaugh (ed.) *Arnaldi de Villanova Opera Medica Omnia*, II, *Aphorismi de Gradibus*, 2nd edn, Barcelona, 1992, pp. 1–136.

88. Pintor, *Tractatus de Morbo*, sigs fv–f1r.

89. Pintor, *Tractatus de Morbo*, sigs f1v–f3v.

90. The image of the *stufa* appears in later illustrations, such as the satirical *L'Espaignol affligé du Mal de Naples* printed after the 1647 Neapolitan revolt against Spanish domination, as shown in Plate 6.1.

91. Torrella, *Tractatus*, sig. c3v.

92. Torrella, *Dialogus*, sig. e2r.

93. Pintor, *Tractatus de Morbo*, sig. e4v: 'stupham autem nominamus locum undique vallatum cuius aer et parietes per medium calefiunt sive id ab igne calefiat sive ab aqua aut simplici aut minerali aut composita'.

94. Torrella, *Tractatus*, sigs c3v, d2r, d4r–v, e1v–e2r, e2v, f3r; *Dialogus*, sig. e2r.

95. Pintor, *Tractatus de Morbo*, sig. e5v.

96. Torrella, *Dialogus*, sig. e2v.

97. See e.g. Rhazes, *Ad regem Mansorem*, lib. v, cap. xxviii; lib. vi, cap. xv (Basel, 1544, pp. 125, 153); Avicenna, *Canon Medicinae*, lib. ii, tract. ii, cap. xlvii (*argentum vivum*), iv/vii, tract. iii, cap. vii, xxvii Venice, 1527, ff. 77v, 386r–v, 388r.

98. On the history of mercury and of its therapeutic applications, see E. Lesky, 'Die Arbeiter und das Quecksilber', *Ciba Zeitschrift*, 96, (1959), pp. 3191–3200; J. Schroeter, 'Quecksilber – und Quecksilberver-

bindungen im Wandel der Zeit', *Ciba Zeitschrift*, 96, (1959), pp. 3202–6; L. J. Goldwater, *Mercury: a history of quicksilver*, Baltimore, 1972.

99. On the treatment of the French Disease with mercurial remedies, see Astruc, *De Morbis Venereis*, Paris, 1736, pp. 131–232; G. S. Brock, 'An Early Account of Syphilis and of the Use of Mercury in its Treatment', *Janus*, 6 (1901), pp. 592–5, 645–7; O. Temkin, 'Therapeutic Trends and the Treatment of Syphilis before 1900', *Bulletin of the History of Medicine*, 29 (1955), pp. 309–16: p. 311; E. Lesky, 'Von Schmier- und Räucherkuren zur modernen Syphilistherapie', *Ciba Zeitschrift*, 96, (1959), pp. 3174–89; J. A. Paniagua, 'Clínica del Renacimiento', in P. Laín-Entralgo, ed., *Historia Universal de la Medicina*, 7 vols, Barcelona, 1972–5, iv, p. 100.

100. Pintor dedicated a long chapter to these ointments. *Tractatus de Morbo*, sigs er–e3v.

101. Pintor, *Tractatus de Morbo*, sigs d7r–v.

102. Pintor, *Tractatus de Morbo*, sig. er.

103. Pintor, *Tractatus de Morbo*, sigs ev, e1v, e3r.

104. Torrella, *Tractatus*, sigs c3v, c4r. Curiously, all the preparations including mercury appear in the first part of the book, and no trace of such a remedy can be found in the *consilia* constituting the second part. The significance of this is not clear.

105. Torrella, *Dialogus*, sigs e1v–e2r, f8v, g6v.

106. Torrella, *Dialogus*, sigs e5v–e6v. For the unguent that both physicians excluded, see Pintor, *Tractatus de Morbo*, sig. e1v; Torrella, *Dialogus*, sig. e6r. For the other two reported by both physicians, see Pintor, *Tractatus de Morbo*, sig. ev; Torrella, *Dialogus*, sigs e6r, e6v.

107. Pintor, *Tractatus de Morbo*, sig. e2v.

108. According to J. K. Proksch, *Die Quecksilber-sublimatcuren gegen Syphilis*, Vienna, 1876, pp. 11–13, Gaspar

Torrella seems to have been one of the earliest physicians (if not the first) to use corrosive sublimate (*argentum sublimatum*) as a remedy against *Morbus Gallicus*.

109. Pintor, *Tractatus de Morbo*, sigs e1v–e2v. For Avicenna on quicksilver, see his *Canon*, ii, tract. ii, cap. xlvii (Venice, 1527, f. 77v). There is little wonder that this chapter of the *Canon* supplied enough material for the construction of diverse and even contradictory theses about the complexion, properties and risks of quicksilver.

110. On Bertomeu Martí, see P. L. Llorens-Raga, *Episcopologio de la diócesis de Segorbe-Castellón*, 2 vols, Madrid, 1973, i, pp. 237–42; Burchard, *Diarium*, ii, p. 521; C. Eubel, *Hierarchia Catholica Medii et Recentioris Aevi*, 3 vols, 2nd edn, Munich, 1913–23 (facs. repr., Padua, 1960), ii, pp. 23, 55.

111. Pintor, *Tractatus de Morbo*, sig. ev.

112. Pintor, *Tractatus de Morbo*, sig. ev.

113. Torrella, *Dialogus*, sig. e6r.

114. Torrella, *Dialogus*, sig. e6r: 'Other people only anointed the emunctories with this ointment, and promised wonderful results. If only don Alfonso de Borgia and his brother had had the opportunity to defend themselves publicly from such an accelerated death, and this reckless man had suffered his penalty!' For Pintor's recipe, see his *Tractatus de Morbo*, sig. e1v. Our estimate has been made by comparing the proportions of the different simples included in Torrella's and Pintor's recipes.

Chapter Seven: The French Disease and Hospitals for Incurables in Italy until 1530

1. The most detailed studies of these figures in relation of Mal Francese still remain A. Bianconi, *L'opera delle compagnie del 'Divino Amore' nella*

Riforma Cattolica, Città di Castello, 1914, pp. 33–43; P. Cassiano da Langasco, *Gli ospedali degli Incurabili* (Genoa, 1938), ch. 2, and P. Paschini, 'Le Compagnie del Divino Amore e la beneficenza pubblica nei primi decenni del cinquecento', in *Tre ricerche sulla storia della chiesa nel cinquecento*, Rome, 1945, pp. 11–32. All depend on the contemporary biography: C. Marabotto and E. Vernazza, *Vita mirabile e dottrina celeste di Santa Caterina Fiesca Adorna da Genova*, Padua, 1743 edn.

2. They are printed by P. Tacchi Venturi, *Storia della Compagnia di Gesù in Italia*, 4 vols, Rome, 1930, I/ii, pp. 25–35, and p. 25 for this passage.

3. This theme is discussed in more detail in J. Henderson, *Piety and Charity in Late Medieval Florence*, Oxford, 1994, ch. 1.

4. See P. O. Kristeller, 'Lay Religious Traditions and Florentine Platonism', in *Studies in Renaissance Thought and Letters*, Rome, 1956, pp. 99–122, esp. pp. 113–14. See also P. Pourrat, *Christian Spirituality*, trans. S. P. Jacques, 2 vols, London, 1927, iii, pp. 234–5.

5. See chs ix, x, xi of their early sixteenth-century statutes: Tacchi Venturi, *Storia della Compagnia di Gesù*, I/ii, pp. 30–3.

6. In general on the background to the Observants see Tacchi Venturi, *Storia della Compagnia di Gesù*, I/ii, pp. 219–26, 234–8, 264; B. Pullan, 'Support and Redeem: charity and poor relief in Italian cities from the 14th to the 17th century', *Continuity and Change*, 3 (1988), pp. 177–208: pp. 190–3. On confraternities and the cult of St Jerome see J. Henderson, 'Penitence and the Laity in Fifteenth-Century Florence', in T. Verdon and J. Henderson, eds, *Christianity and the Renaissance*, Syracuse, 1990, pp. 220–49. On the Compagnia di San Girolamo at Vicenza see: Bianconi, *L'opera*, pp. 17–24.

7. On the links between Bernardino da Feltre and Caterina Fieschi in August to September 1492: Paschini, 'Le Compagnie', pp. 12–13. Cf. also ibid., p. 17.

8. Marabotto and Vernazza, *Vita mirabile*, p. 31.

9. Tacchi Venturi, *Storia della Compagnia di Gesù*, I/ii, p. 29: ch. vi.

10. Paschini, 'Le Compagnie', pp. 21–2; Tacchi Venturi, *Storia della Compagnia di Gesù*, I/ii, p. 37 and Bianconi, *L'opera*, pp. 40, 70 and 75.

11. Paschini, 'Le Compagnie', p. 199; Tacchi Venturi, *Storia della Compagnia di Gesù*, I/ii, pp. 36–7.

12. E. Grendi, 'Ideologia della carità e società indisciplinata: la costruzione del sistema assistenziale genovese (1470–1670)', in G. Politi, M. Rosa and F. Della Peruta, eds, *Timore e carità. I poveri nell'Italia moderna*, Cremòna, 1982, p. 66.

13. See C. Marchesini and G. Sperati, *Ospedali Genovesi nel Medioevo*, *Atti della Società Ligure di Storia Patria*, n.s. 21 (1971), pp. 72–99, on the Ospedale di San Lazzaro.

14. 1499 statutes in Langasco, *Gli ospedali*, doct. 1: ch. i: p. 199.

15. Langasco, *Gli ospedali*, doct. 1: ch. xi: pp. 203–4.

16. Langasco, *Gli ospedali*, doct. 1: ch. xi: p. 203.

17. Langasco, *Gli ospedali*, doct. 1: ch. xi: p. 203.

18. Langasco, *Gli ospedali*, doct. 1: ch. xii: p. 204.

19. Langasco, *Gli ospedali*, doct. 1: ch. xii: p. 204.

20. Langasco, *Gli ospedali*, doct. 2: pp. 205–6.

21. Langasco, *Gli ospedali*, doct. 1: ch. xiv: p. 205.

22. For the centrality of Genoa in the geographical spread of plague in the major epidemics in medieval and early modern Italy, see L. Del Panta, *Le epidemie nella storia demografica italiana (secoli xiv–xix)*, Turin, 1980.

23. Grendi, 'Ideologia della carità', p. 66.

24. For example: the works cited above by Tacchi Venturi, Langasco and Paschini.

25. Friano degli Ubaldini, 'Cronaca dalla creazione del mondo fino all'anno di N.S. 1513, nella quale non lasciare di scrivere tutta l'istoria della sua Patria', Biblioteca della Università di Bologna MS 430, f. 717v.

26. See M. Fanti et al., eds, *Gli archivi delle istituzioni di carità e assistenza attive in Bologna nel medioevo e nell'età moderna*, Bologna, 1984, p. 29. A list of members in 1525 contains representatives of some of the most prominent families of the city: Archivio di Stato di Bologna (henceforth ASB), Demaniale 1.6472, f. 1r, and their statutes are in ASB, Archivio degli Ospedali: S. Maria dei Guarini e di S. Giobbe, ser. IV, Misc. 1/3.

27. Anon, 'Cronica Bianchina', in A. Corradi, 'Nuovi documenti per la storia delle malattie veneree in Italia dalla fine del quattrocento alla metà del cinquecento', *Annali Universali di Medicina e Chirurgia*, 269/808 (1884), pp. 289–386: p. 344.

28. Corradi, 'Nuovi documenti', pp. 348–9, prints a short extract from the 1524 statutes of the hospital, which cannot now be found in ASB.

29. For the later statutes see: ASB, Archivio degli Ospedali: S. Maria dei Guarini e di S. Giobbe, ser. IV, Misc. 1/3.

30. 'Cronaca della città di Perugia dal 1492 al 1503 di Francesco Matarazzo detto Maturianzio', ed. A. Fabretti, *Archivio Storico Italiano*, ser. I, 16/2 (1851), p. 34.

31. Matarazzo, 'Cronaca', p. 34. For Ferrara see: C. Brisighella, *Descrizione delle pitture e sculture della città di Ferrara*, ed. M. A. Novelli, Ferrara, 1990, p. 55, and under 'S. Giobbe confraternita'.

32. Archivio Arcivescovile di Ferrara, Compagnia di S. Giobbe di Ferrara 5, f. 4r: 'In questo anno 1503 Zohaine dal' Agnolo fae depingere la chiesa de S. Jobbe dentro da intorno intorno ale istorie de S. Job et altre istorie, come se vede a tutte sue spese. Amore Dei.' See also S. Zamboni, *Pittori di Ercole I d'Este. Giovanni Francesco Maineri, Lazzaro Grimaldi, Domenico Panetti, Michele Coltellini*, Ferrara, 1975, pp. 72–3; and Brisighella, *Descrizione*, p. 55.

33. Archivio Arcivescovile di Ferrara, Compagnia di S. Giobbe di Ferrara 5, f. 2r: 21.v.1499: 'deffenda et liberi questa inclita ci[t]à de Ferrara da ogni et singule persecutione, controversie et infirmità'.

34. Archivio Arcivescovile di Ferrara, Compagnia di, S. Giobbe A4: 20.iii.1502: 'in quo tali morbo gravati se recipere valeant'.

35. Archivio Arcivescovile di Ferrara, A13: 17.vii.1525. For more information on the sicknesses of the Este family see Chapter Three above.

36. On Bologna: Paschini, 'Le Compagnie', p. 47; and Ferrara: E. Peverada, 'Note sulle confraternite e luoghi pii a Ferrara dal 1574 al 1611', in *Ravennatensia*, 4 (1974), p. 325.

37. See, for example, Bianconi, *L'opera*, p. 25, for the involvement of patricians in the Ridotto at Genoa. The list of the members of the Compagnia di S. Giobbe at Bologna in 1525 included Conte Battista Bentivoglio: ASB, Demaniale 1.6472, f. 1r.

38. Paschini, 'Le Compagnie', pp. 27–34.

39. Cf. B. Pullan, 'Poveri, mendicanti e vagabondi (secoli xiv–xvii)', in C. Viventi and R. Romano, eds, *Storia d'Italia. Annali 1: Dal feudalismo al capitalismo*, Turin, 1978, pp. 981–1047; Pullan, 'Support and Redeem', pp. 153–208; B. Geremek, *La pietà e la forca. Storia della miseria e della carità in Europa*, Bari, 1986; L. Fiorani, 'Religione e povertà. Il

dibattito sul pauperismo a Roma tra Cinque e Seicento', *Ricerche per la storia religiosa di Roma*, 3 (1979), pp. 43–131.

40. *Storia di Milano*, ed. G. Treccani degli Alfieri, 16 vols, Milan, 1958, xi, pp. 624–5.

41. *Diario di Ser Tommaso di Silvestro*, in *Ephemerides Urbevetanae dal Codice Vaticano Urbinate 1745 (AA. 1482–1514)*, ed. L. Fumi, ii, in *Rerum Italicarum Scriptores*, Bologna, 1925, xv/5, p. 104: 29.x.1498.

42. Surveyed by A. Malamani, 'Notizie sul mal francese e gli ospedali degli incurabili in età moderna', *Critica storica*, 15 (1978), pp. 193–216.

43. For details of these foundations see below.

44. Vicenza and Verona: Paschini, 'Le Compagnie', pp. 61–2, 64–5.

45. L. Ponnelle and L. Bordet, *St. Philip Neri and the Roman Society of his Times (1515–1595)*, London, 1979 edn, p. 75; cf. Paschini, 'Le Compagnie', p. 51; Ludwig von Pastor, *The History of the Popes from the Close of the Middle Ages*, ed. R. F. Kerr, London, 1928, x, pp. 388–92; J. C. Olin, *The Catholic Reformation: Savonarola to Ignatius Loyola*, New York, Evanston and London, 1969, pp. 16–17.

46. Paschini, 'Le Compagnie', p. 77.

47. See P. Paschini, *S. Gaetano Thiene, Gian Pietro Carafa, e le origini dei chierici regolari teatini*, Rome, 1926, pp. 12–13.

48. For the background see most recently A. Cavaterra, 'L'ospedalità a Roma nell'età moderna: il caso del San Giacomo (1585–1605)', *Sanità, scienza e storia*, 2 (1986), pp. 87–97, and Langasco, *Gli spedali*, pp. 95–120. Bianconi, *L'opera*, pp. 8–123, published a whole series of documents relating to the early history of San Giacomo.

49. Paschini, 'Le compagnie', pp. 32–4; Cavaterra, 'L'ospedalità', pp. 89–90, though neither resolves this problem.

50. *Salvatoris Nostri Domini Jesu Christi*, 15 Aug. 1515, in *Bullarium Romanum a B. Leone Magno usque as S.D.N. Clementem X*, ed. A. M. Cherubino, 15 vols Lyon, 1892, i, pp. 567–71, esp. p. 567; cited in P. De Angelis, *L'Arcispedale di San Giacomo in Augusta*, Rome, 1955, pp. 10–11.

51. *Salvatoris Nostri*, in *Bull. Rom.*, i, p. 567.

52. G. Fracastoro, *De Contagione et Contagiosis Morbis et eorum curatione*, trans. and ed. W. C. Wright, New York and London, 1930, pp. 138–41.

53. J. Delumeau, *Vie économique et sociale de Rome dans la seconde moitié du XVIe siècle*, 2 vols Paris, 1957, i, pp. 403–7.

54. See Henderson, *Piety and Charity*, ch. 10.

55. *Salvatoris Nostri*, in *Bull. Rom.*, i, pp. 567–8.

56. *Salvatoris Nostri*, in *Bull. Rom.*, i, p. 568.

57. *Salvatoris Nostri*, in *Bull. Rom.*, i, p. 568. This at least was the case according to their later statutes in Archivio di Stato di Roma (henceforth ASR), Ospedale di San Giacomo in Augusta degli Incurabili (henceforth ASG), 292/219, f. 23r.

58. *Salvatoris Nostri*, in *Bull. Rom.*, i, p. 568. Cf. Cavaterra, 'L'ospedalità', p. 91.

59. See discussion above, and Fracastoro, *De Contagione*, book 1, on the different kinds of 'contagion'.

60. *Salvatoris Nostri*, in *Bull. Rom.*, i, p. 568.

61. *Salvatoris Nostri*, in *Bull. Rom.*, i, p. 568; summarised by Cavaterra, 'L'ospedalità', pp. 91–3; cf. ASR, ASG 293.37, n. 8, and ASG 359/6, n. 11.

62. *Salvatoris Nostri*, in *Bull. Rom.*, i, p. 569: 14.vii.1516.

63. Cf. Paschini, *S. Gaetano Thiene*, and Pastor, *History of the Popes*, x, p. 418.

64. Sigismondo dei Conti da Foligno, *Le storie de' suoi tempi dal 1475 al 1510*, 2 vols, Rome, 1883, ii, p. 272; cf. A. Foa, 'The New and the Old: the spread of syphilis (1494–1530)',

in E. Muir and G. Ruggiero, eds, *Sex and Gender in Historical Perspective*, Baltimore and London, 1990, pp. 26–45: pp. 34–7.

65. S. Ravicini, *Sulla università dell'opera ospedaliera della S. Casa degl'Incurabili in Napoli. Memorie e documenti storici*, Naples, 1890, pp. 5–9, fails to mention Vernazza. More recently A. Russo, 'L'Ospedale degli Incurabili di Napoli, la sua farmacia ed il ricettario', *Atti e memorie della accademia italiana di storia della farmacia*, 4 (1987), pp. 41–7, places emphasis on Longo, while Paschini, 'Le Compagnie', pp. 52–7, stresses the importance of Vernazza. The most balanced view is the brief account by G. Vitale, 'Ricerche sulla vita religiosa e caritativa a Napoli tra medioevo ed età moderna', *Archivio storico per le province napolitane*, 86–7 (1970), pp. 226–9.

66. Literally, 'love of the bell-tower', a phrase denoting local particularism.

67. Russo, 'L'Ospedale', pp. 43–4.

68. Russo, 'L'Ospedale', pp. 42–3; Vitale, 'Ricerche', p. 226 n. 39.

69. Text of the bull in Ravicini, *Sull'università*, p. 139.

70. Ravicini, *Sull'università*, p. 139: 'unum Hospitale pro pauperibus Incurabilibus ad instar Archihospitalis etiam pauperum Incurabilium Sancti Jacobi de Augusta de Urbe erigere'.

71. Ravicini, *Sull'università*, p. 139.

72. Cited in Corradi, 'Nuovi documenti', doc. xiii: p. 349.

73. Vitale, 'Ricerche', pp. 226–7.

74. G. Richa, *Notizie istoriche delle chiese fiorentine*, Florence, 1759, 8 vols, viii, pp. 317–37; and L. Passerini, *Storia degli stabilmenti di beneficenza e d'istruzione elementare gratuita della città di Firenze*, Florence, 1853, pp. 203–16.

75. Richa, *Notizie*, viii, pp. 319–21; Passerini, *Storia*, pp. 206–10.

76. See H. C. Butters, *Governors and Government in Early Sixteenth-Century Florence, 1502–1519*, Oxford, 1985; and J. N. Stephens, *The Fall of*

the Florentine Republic, 1512–1530, Oxford, 1983.

77. Costs for purchasing property are itemised in Archivio di Stato di Firenze (henceforth ASF), Ospedale degli Incurabili 102, ff. 23v–24r for the period 17.xi.1520 to 19.iv.1522, a total of 2,145 florins and Lire 204–4s–4d. In 1534 Duke Alessandro provided a guaranteed income from the Prestanze; in 1541 Pope Paul III assigned SS. Trinità all the property from the Spedale dei SS. Jacopo e Filippo 'il Ceppo'; the Grand Duchess of Tuscany, Eleanora, gave an annual income plus a lump sum in 1560; and the senator Francesco Capponi provided substantial sums to expand the premises in the 1590s: see Richa, *Notizie*, viii, pp. 321–4; and Passerini, *Storia*, pp. 210–11.

78. Cited in Richa, *Notizie*, viii, p. 319, though the full text does not seem to have survived. Passerini, *Storia*, p. 208, laments that the hospital's statutes were no longer extant (in fact they have survived; see below), but recorded that this bull was in the Diplomatico of Messer Bonifazio, where it is no longer to be found.

79. Mentioned in the Company's statutes as dated 12.i.1521 (ASF, Ospedale degli Incurabili 1, capitoli, ff. 1v–2r), and by Richa, *Notizie*, viii, p. 322, as dated 21.xii.1520.

80. ASF, Ospedale degli Incurabili 1, capitoli, f. 5r.

81. Pastor, *History of the Popes*, x, p. 391; cf. Malamani, 'Notizie', p. 208; Paschini, 'Le Compagnie', p. 51; Olin, *The Catholic Reformation*, pp. 16–17.

82. Cf. K. P. Park and J. Henderson, '"The First Hospital among Christians": the Ospedale di Santa Maria Nuova in early sixteenth-century Florence', *Medical History*, 35 (1991), pp. 164–88.

83. Cited by Pastor, *History of the Popes*, xiii, p. 469, who dates the record to between 1553 and 1558.

84. Paschini, *S. Gaetano Thiene*, pp. 12–13.

85. Paschini, *S. Gaetano Thiene*, p. 36.

86. Pastor, *History of the Popes*, x, p. 418. See also P. Sannazzaro, *Storia dell'Ordine Camilliano (1550–1699)*, Turin, 1986, pp. 29–33.

87. P. Janelle, *The Catholic Reformation*, London, 1971 edn, pp. 96–7.

88. Paschini, *S. Gaetano Thiene*, pp. 12–13, 23, 48–52 and 36. See A. Cistellini, *Figure della riforma pretridentina*, Brescia, 1948, pp. 282–3, who prints a membership list of 1524.

89. On the Compagnia see Bianconi, *L'opera*, pp. 17–24.

90. Paschini, 'Le Compagnie', pp. 61–2, 64–5; Paschini, *S. Gaetano Thiene*, p. 17.

91. Paschini, 'Le Compagnie', pp. 64–5, citing a deliberative record of the confraternity.

92. Paschini, 'Le Compagnie', pp. 64–5; R. Palmer, 'L'assistenza medica nella Venezia cinquecentesca', in B. Aikema and D. Meijers, eds, *Nel regno dei poveri. Arte e storia dei grandi ospedali veneziani in età moderna, 1474–1797*, Venice, 1989, pp. 37, 42 n. 29. Cf. B. Pullan, *Rich and Poor in Renaissance Venice. The social institutions of a Catholic state to 1620*, Oxford 1971, pp. 233–4.

93. See Tacchi Venturi, *Storia della compagnia di Gesù*, 1/ii, chs 10–13; C. F. Black, *Italian Confraternities in the Sixteenth Century*, Cambridge, 1989, pp. 29, 95–9.

94. See Paschini, 'Le Compagnie', pp. 56–7, 70; B. Pullan, *Rich and Poor*, pp. 234–5; B. Aikema and D. Meijers, 'Gli Incurabili. Chiesa e Ospedale del Santissimo Salvatore', in Aikema and Meijers, eds, *Nel regno*, p. 131.

95. There is now a considerable literature on the Venetian hospital, much of which is based on E. A. Cicogna, *Delle iscrizioni veneziane*, 6 vols, Venice, 1842, v, pp. 299–406, who prints most of the relevant contem-porary documentation. For the Sanità's records: Lord Orford, *Leggi e memorie venete sulla prostituzione fino alla caduta della republica*, Venice, 1870–2, esp. pp. 97–8; in English translation in D. Chambers and B. Pullan, *Venice: a documentary history, 1450–1630*, Oxford, 1992, pp. 308–10. See also Pullan, *Rich and Poor*, pp. 234–8; Palmer, 'L'assistenza medica', p. 39; and Aikema and Meijers, 'Gli Incurabili', pp. 131–48.

96. Marin Sanudo, *I Diarii*, ed. F. Stefani et al., 58 vols, Venice, 1879–1903, xxxvi, p. 70: anno 1524; xxxiii, pp. 271–2:15.vi.1522; Cicogna, *Delle iscrizioni*, pp. 305–6.

97. Paschini, *S. Gaetano Thiene*, p. 23.

98. Paschini, *S. Gaetano Thiene*, p. 306.

99. Paschini, *S. Gaetano Thiene*, p. 306.

100. Summarised in Cicogna, *Delle iscrizioni*, v, pp. 306–11.

101. Orford, *Leggi e memorie*, p. 97; trans. Chambers and Pullan, *Venice*, pp. 308–9.

102. See A. G. Carmichael, *Plague and the Poor in Renaissance Florence*, Cambridge, 1986, pp. 106, 124–5; and J. Henderson, 'Epidemics in Renaissance Florence: medical theory and government response', in N. Bulst and R. Delort, eds, *Maladies et sociétés (xiie–xviiie siècles)*, Paris, 1989, pp. 175, 177.

103. The role of putrefaction in contagion is discussed by Fracastoro, *De Contagione*, pp. 40–3. Cf. V. Nutton, 'The Reception of Fracastoro's Theory of Contagion: the seed that fell among thorns?', *Osiris*, 6, 2nd ser. (1990), pp. 205–6.

104. Orford, *Leggi e memorie*, p. 98.

105. Sanudo, *I Diarii*, xxxvi, cols 102–3: 24.iii.1524; Cicogna, *Delle iscrizioni*, v, p. 307; Corradi, 'Nuovi documenti', pp. 93–5.

106. Sanudo, *I Diarii*, xxxviii, p. 111: 1.iv.1525; xxxix, p. 77: 24.vi.1525; xl, p. 407: 24.xii.1525; Cicogna, *Delle iscrizioni*, v, pp. 307–8.

107. Cicogna, *Delle iscrizioni*, v, p. 310.

108. Sanudo, *I Diarii*, xlv, p. 238:

15.vi.1427; Paschini, *S. Gaetano
Thiene*, p. 65, and cf. pp. 60, 65, 69–
70, 75.

109. Pullan, *Rich and Poor*, pp. 259–
60.

110. See Pullan, 'Support and Redeem'.

111. One of the best known writers of
this genre was Pietro di Niccolò di
Tofano di Magio, also known as
Niccolò Campani: *Lamento di Quel
Tribulato di Strascino Campana Senese
Sopra il Male Incognito*, Milan, 1979
edn.

112. This theme is discussed by B. Pullan,
'Per la difesa del corpo sociale:
gli ospedali', in N.-E. Vanzan
Marchini, ed., *De Natura*, Milan,
forthcoming.

113. Summarised in Giuliana Albini,
*Guerra, fame, peste. Crisi di mortalità e
sistema sanitario nella Lombardia
tardomedioevale*, Bologna, 1982, ch. 1.

114. In general see Paschini, 'La
Compagnia', p. 20; for Bologna and
Venice see this chapter above;
Rome: Paschini, 'La Compagnia',
pp. 46–7; Cavaterra, 'L'ospedalità', p.
95 n. 36; Naples: Vitale, 'Ricerche',
pp. 226, 228–9, 264; Florence: list of
founding members in ASF, Ospedale
degli Incurabili 1, f. 1r.

115. In 1500 the governors of the
Ridotto of Genoa approached the
Senate for approval of their statutes
(which was granted): Langasco, *Gli
ospedali*, pp. 21, 205–6: doct. 2; in
1503 they received recognition as a
legal entity, thus enabling them to
receive bequests and in 1511 exemption from gabelles: ibid., pp. 70–2,
76. In Bologna the commune
granted tax exemption in 1520 to
the hospital (ASB, Demaniale, 5/
6476.A). In Ferrara from 1502 a
series of licences was granted by the
Duke to the Compagnia di S.
Giobbe to seek alms 'di reigere uno
spedale in cui cuerarsi gli infetti
di morbo gallico': Archivio
Arcivescovile di Ferrara, Compagnia
di S. Giobbe A4, 5, 8, 11. In Rome
the Spedale di San Giacomo, as has

been seen, obtained approval and
encouragement from the pope
through a series of bulls, beginning
with *Salvatoris Nostri* of 1515. Official interest in the Neapolitan Incurabili was demonstrated from an
early date: in 1521 the viceroy
Ramón de Cardona laid the foundation stone and the hospital came to
be granted revenue from taxes
(Ravicini, *Sulla università*, pp. 7, 53–
4). In Florence the financial backing
of the commune was present from
the beginning: ASF, Ospedale della
SS. Trinità degli Incurabili 102, ff.
1v–22r, lists monies received
from among others the commune
and Giulio de' Medici. Cf. also ASF,
Provvisioni Registri 205, ff. 18v–
19r: 22.viii.1520. Official approval
of the Venetian Incurabili was evident in the fact that the Sanità put
it to immediate use and that the
doge visited the hospital in 1522:
Orford, *Leggi e memorie*, pp. 97–8;
Sanudo, *I Diarii*, xxxiii, pp. 271–2:
15.vi.1522.

116. We have seen that there were
numerous connections between
Incurabili hospitals, as in the case of
Genoa and Rome, Rome and
Naples, Florence and Rome, Venice
and Rome, especially through the
influence of the Medici popes and
the agency of the Companies of
Divine Love and later the Theatines.

117. For Orvieto see *Diario di Ser
Tommaso di Silvestro*, p. 104; *Storia di
Milano*, viii, p. 409; Padua: Paschini,
'Le Compagnie', pp. 71–2.

118. Langasco, *Gli ospedali*, 1499 Capitoli:
doct. 1: chs i, xi: pp. 199, 203–4.

119. *Salvatoris Nostri*, in *Bull. Rom.*, i, p.
567.

120. ASF, Ospedale degli Incurabili 1
(Capitoli), f. 5r: 'poveri infermi che
intenderanno essere oppressi da
alcuna infermità o da morbo gallico
o altra malactia incurabile, excepto
che di lebbra o pesto et quegli che
troverranno infermati di infermità
curabile'.

Chapter Eight: The French Disease and the Incurabili Hospitals, 1530–1600

1. Population levels for major Italian cities are summarised in K. J. Beloch, *Bevölkerungsgeschichte Italiens*, 3 vols, Berlin, 1961, iii, pp. 357–8, though see also A. Bellettini, 'La popolazione italiana dall'inizio dell'era volgare ai giorni nostri. Valutazioni e tendenze', in R. Romano and C. Viventi, eds, *Storia d'Italia*, v, Turin, 1973, pp. 507–9.

2. On the economy see in general R. Romano, 'La storia economica. Dal secolo xiv al Settecento', in Romano and Viventi, eds, *Storia d'Italia*, v: *I documenti*, i, pp. 1885–1907, and for a study of one region see P. Malanima, *La decadenza di un'economia cittadina. L'industria di Firenze nei secoli xvi–xviii*, Bologna, 1982. Studies of the problem of growing poverty in this period include: B. Pullan, *Rich and Poor in Renaissance Venice. The Social Institutions of a Catholic State to 1620*, Oxford 1971. pp. 355–71, and 'Wage-Earners and the Venetian Economy, 1550–1630', in Pullan, ed., *Crisis and Change in the Venetian Economy in the Sixteenth and Seventeenth Centuries*, London, 1968, pp. 153–6, 161–4, 170; J. Delumeau, *Vie économique et sociale de Rome dans la seconde moitié du xvie siècle*, Paris, 1957, i, pp. 403–16; P. Simoncelli, 'Note sul sistema assistenziale a Roma nel xvi secolo', in G. Politi, M. Rosa and F. Della Peruta, eds, *Timore e carità. I poveri nell'Italia moderna*, Cremona, 1982, pp. 137–56.

3. A. Malamani, 'L'Ospedale degli Incurabili di Pavia dalle origini al suo assorbimento nel P. L. Pertusati (1556–1796)', *Archivio Storico Lombardo*, 100 (1974), pp. 147–9. On Miani see Pullan, *Rich and Poor*, pp. 259–62

4. Pullan, *Rich and Poor*, pp. 264–5, and

more generally P. Tacchi Venturi, *Storia della Compagnia di Gesù in Italia*, 4 vols, Rome, 1930, I/i, chs 18–19; and J. O'Malley, *The First Jesuits*, Cambridge, Mass., and London, 1993, ch. 5.

5. E. A. Cicogna, *Delle iscrizioni veneziane*, 6 vols, Venice, 1842, v, pp. 299–300.

6. O'Malley, *The First Jesuits*, pp. 171–3.

7. See M. Scaduto, *L'epoca di Giacomo Lainez, 1556–1565. L'azione* (Tacchi Venturi, *Storia della Compagnia di Gesù in Italia*, iv), Rome, 1974, pp. 637–9.

8. *I Frati Cappuccini. Documenti e testimonianze del primo secolo*, 3 vols, ed. C. Cargnoni, Perugia, 1991, iii/2, pp. 3411–46.

9. *I Frati Cappuccini*, iii/2, pp. 3412–13 n. 6.

10. The words of the seventeenth-century Capuchin chronicler, Boveri, cited in Tacchi Venturi, *Storia della Compagnia di Gesù*, I/i, p. 412; cf. *I Frati Cappuccini*, iii/2, pp. 3423–5.

11. Tacchi Venturi, *Storia della Compagnia di Gesù*, I/i, p. 413.

12. On the role of the Capuchins during plague epidemics see *I Frati Cappuccini*, iii/2, section II/5.

13. ASR, ASG 2/3: 14.vi.1612.

14. G. Vitale, 'Ricerche sulla vita religiosa e caritativa a Napoli tra medioevo ed età moderna', *Archivio storico per le province napolitane*, 86–7 (1970), pp. 228–9.

15. One of the best accounts of the life of Camillo de Lellis was written by his contemporary Sanzio Cicatelli, *Vita del P. Camillo de Lellis, fondatore della religione dei chierici regolari*, Rome, 1615; the latest edition is: P. Sannazzaro, Rome, 1980. See also M. Vanti, *S. Giacomo degli Incurabili di Roma nel Cinquecento. Dalle Compagnie del Divino Amore a S. Camillo De Lellis*, Rome 1938; P. Sannazzaro, *Storia dell'Ordine Camilliano (1550–1699)*, Turin, 1986; cf. Cavaterra, 'L'ospedalità', 113–16.

16. See in general on the more prag-

matic policies of the Roman authorities, Simoncelli, 'Note'.

17. See discussion in Chapter Seven above.

18. Vitale, 'Ricerche', p. 227.

19. On this theme see B. Pullan, 'Per la difesa del corpe sociale: gli ospedali', in N.-E. Vanzan Marchini, ed., *De Natura*, Milan, forthcoming.

20. See S. Cohen, *The Evolution of Women's Asylums since 1500: from refuges for ex-prostitutes to shelters for battered women*, Oxford, 1992; A. Camerano, 'Assistenza richiesta ed assistenza imposta: il Conservatorio di S. Caterinia della Rosa di Roma', *Quaderni storici*, 28 (1993), pp. 227–60.

21. M. L. López-Terrada, 'El tratamiento de la sífilis en un hospital renacentista: la sala del *Mal de Siment* del Hospital General de Valencia', *Asclepio*, 41 (1989), pp. 19–50: p. 34. A possible association in Rome between prostitution and female patients admitted to the Spedale di San Giacomo may also be suggested by the location of the hospital. Via Ripetta was close to the area designated by Pius V in 1566–8 for the creation of a prostitutes' ghetto, although there is no evidence that this project was realised. See Delumeau, *Vie économique*, i, pp. 423–6.

22. ASR, ASG, 854/42.

23. Cicatelli, *Vita del P. Camillo de Lellis*, pp. 40–1.

24. ASR, ASG 386: 6.ix.1562.

25. On concepts of charity in this period see L. Fiorani, 'Religione e povertà. Il dibattito sul pauperismo a Roma tra cinque e seicento', *Ricerche per la storia di Roma*, 3 (1979), pp. 43–87, esp. pp. 81–7.

26. Bologna: ASB, Archivio degli Ospedali, S. Maria dei Guarini e di S. Giobbe, ser. IV, Misc. 1/10 and 2/8; Ferrara: Compagnia di S. Giobbe A: 1521 on lists of licences with permission to raise cash; indulgence in 1560 (33). Florence: L. Passerini, *Storia degli stabilmenti di beneficenza e d'istruzione elementare*

gratuita della città di Firenze, Florence, 1853, p. 211: Paul III in 1541 assigned it some regular income.

27. Florence: ASF, Ospedale degli Incurabili 102, ff. 24v–5r: 1520–39: 'spese di murare per il nostro spedale'; ibid., 1: capitoli, ch. 5 mentions the 'cassette delle limosine'. Bologna: ASB, Demaniale, 1/6472.13: 1570: short of cash 'si trova in estreme necessità et miseria': exhortation to Bolognese to give alms; Demaniale 5/6476/7 1586: members of the confraternity give money for building. Ferrara: ADF, Compagnia di S. Giobbe 4A, 5, 8, 11.

28. Gregory Martin, *Roma Sancta, 1581*, ed. G. B. Parker, Rome, 1969, p. 187. On the feastday see A. Cavaterra, 'L'ospedalità a Roma nell'età moderna: il caso del San Giacomo (1585–1605)', *Sanità, scienza e storia*, 2 (1986), pp. 119–23.

29. Bologna: ASB, Compagnia dell'Ospedale di S. Maria de' Guarini . . . di S. Giobbe, Demaniale 1/6472): 1525: the majority were patricians, including members of the Bentivoglio. Ospedale di S. Giobbe I/1, f. 6r: 1607: Senatore di Bologna. For Florence: ASF, Ospedale degli Incurabili 1: 1521: lists of patricians; the governors of the Incurabili hospital in Naples are listed in their 1538 statutes: Vitale, 'Ricerche', p. 261.

30. C. B. Piazza, *Opere pie di Roma*, Rome, 1679, p. 50.

31. ASR, ASG 292/19, ff. 5r–v (c. 1604 statutes), and *Statuti del venerabile Archiospedale di San Giacomo in Augusta nominato dell'Incurabili di Roma*, Rome, 1659, ch. 10: pp. 24–5.

32. Bologna: ASB, Dem. 1/6472.6: 1520: annual grant of grain and salt; Demaniale 5/6476: 1520: exemptions; 1597: Ospedale di S. Giobbe IV/3: 'una esentione . . . di tutte le robbe che distribuisce la detta casa'. In Pavia the Milanese Senate granted privileges to the Incurabili hospital:

Malamani, 'L'Ospedale', p. 153.
Florence: ASF, Provvisioni Registri
205 (1520), ff. 18v–19r: annual grant
of salt; cf. A. D'Addario, *Aspetti della
Contrariforma a Firenze*, Rome, 1977,
p. 80: in 1534 the Senate granted
income to the Incurabili hospital.

33. Naples: S. Ravicini, *Sull'università
dell'opera ospedaliera della S. Casa
degl'Incurabili in Napoli. Memorie e
documenti storici*, Naples, 1890, pp.
53–4, lists the royal privileges; the
nomination of Governatori was subject to civic approval as were their
statutes: Vitale, 'Ricerche', p. 228;
support of Duchess: 1538 statutes:
Vitale, 'Ricerche', p. 264. For Florence: Passerini, *Storia*, p. 211.

34. See Vanti, *S. Giacomo*, pp. 19–30.

35. See Chapter Two above.

36. On Ferrara: E. Peverada, 'Note sulle
confraternite e luoghi pii a Ferrara
dal 1574 al 1611', *Ravennatensia*, 4
(1974), p. 326 for 1586.

37. The laying of the foundation stone
by the Patriarch of Jerusalem is recorded in ASR, ASG 2/2: 20.v.592.
See G. Giovannoni, *Antonio da San
Gallo il Giovane*, 2 vols, Rome,
1959, i, pp. 238–42; H. Hibbard,
*Carlo Maderno and Roman Architec-
ture, 1580–1630*, London, 1971, pp.
118–21.

38. On the building phases of San
Giacomo in the first half of the six-
teenth century see: Vanti, *S.
Giacomo*, pp. 19–30; and, more spe-
cifically, M. Heinz, 'Das Hospital S.
Giacomo in Augusta in Rom:
Peruzzi und Antonio da Sangallo.
i.G. Zum Hospitalbau der Hochre-
naissance', *Storia dell'Arte*, 41 (1981),
pp. 31–49, and 'Das Hospital von
S. Giacomo in Rom und der
Hospitalbau der Renaissance', PhD
diss., Reinischen Friedrich-
Wilhelms-Universität, Bonn, 1977;
for the later developments see
Hibbard, *Carlo Maderno*, pp. 118–21.

39. Hibbard, *Carlo Maderno*, p. 119.

40. ASR, ASG 853/844, ff. 35v–6r.
'Cariola' is translated literally as
'wheelbarrow'.

41. P. Paschini, 'Le Compagnie del Divino Amore e la beneficenza
pubblica nei primi decenni del
cinquecento', in *Tre ricerche sulla
storia della chiesa nel cinquecento*,
Rome, 1945, p. 35.

42. Cicogna, *Delle iscrizioni*, v, p. 311.

43. B. Aikema and D. Meijers, 'Gli
Incurabili. Chiesa e Ospedale del
Santissimo Salvatore', in Aikema and
Meijers, eds, *Nel regno dei poveri. Arte
e storia dei grandi ospedali veneziani in
età moderna, 1474–1797*, Venice,
1989, p. 134.

44. Aikema and Meijers, 'Gli Incurabili',
pp. 132–3.

45. W. and E. Paatz, *Die Kirchen von
Florenz*, 6 vols, Frankfurt-an-Main,
1940–55, v, p. 394.

46. On Florentine hospitals' design see
R. Goldthwaite and W. R. Rearick,
'Michelozzo and the Ospedale di
San Paolo in Florence', *Mitteilungen
des Kunst Historische Institut in
Florenz*, 21 (1977), pp. 221–306; J.
Henderson, 'The Hospitals of Late
Medieval and Renaissance Florence:
a preliminary survey', in L.
Granshaw and R. Porter, eds, *The
Hospital in History*, London, 1989,
pp. 63–92; and K. P. Park and J.
Henderson, '"The First Hospital
among Christians": the Ospedale di
Santa Maria Nuova in early six-
teenth-century Florence', *Medical
History*, 35 (1991), pp. 164–88.

47. ASB, Ospedale di S. Giobbe IV/3.
See also the record of San Giacomo
in Rome which talks about the lack
of funds because of the demands of
'molto poveri': ASR, ASG 1405:
30.vi.1568.

48. Malamani, 'L'Ospedale', p. 153.

49. Naples: Vitale, 'Ricerche', p. 228;
Venice: Pullan, *Rich and Poor*, p.
375., and Cicogna, *Delle iscrizioni*, p.
311.

50. C. M. Cipolla, *Before the Industrial
Revolution: European society and
economy, 1000–1700*, London, 1978
edn, p. 281.

51. Calculated from ASR, ASG, 381;
ASG 380 lists seventy-seven admis-

sions from August to December 1514 and twelve from January to May 1515, though they probably predated San Giacomo's refoundation as an Incurabili hospital.

52. Calculated from ASR, ASG 384 and 385.

53. The male:female ratio is 5.1 to 1.

54. Calculated from ASR, ASG 403–4; see below for further discussion of this matter.

55. See J. Arrizabalaga, 'Medicina universitaria y *Morbus Gallicus* en la Italia de finales del siglo XV: el arquiatra pontificio Gaspar Torrella (c. 1452–c. 1420)', *Asclepio*, 40 (1988), pp. 25–9. Cf. the use of 'stufe' in early sixteeenth-century Brescia: *Storia di Brescia*, ed. G. Treccani degli Alfieri, 5 vols, Brescia, 1961, ii, p. 364 n. 3: *stufe piccole*.

56. F. Guicciardini, *Storia d'Italia*, ed. S. S. Menchi, 3 vols, Turin, 1971, i, p. 233.

57. R. S. Munger, 'Guaiacum, the Holy Wood from the New World', *Journal of the History of Medicine and Allied Sciences*, 4 (1949), pp. 210–11; Arrizabalaga, 'Medicina universitaria', p. 28. See also P. Vottiner-Pletz, *Lignum sánctum: zur therapeutischen Verwendung des Guajak vom 16. bis zum 20. Jahrhundert*, Frankfurt-am-Main, 1990.

58. F. Delicado, *La Lozana Andalusa*, Milan, 1970, p. 294.

59. Munger, 'Guaiacum', pp. 209–10; A. Corradi, 'L'acqua del legno e le cure depurative nel cinquecento', *Annali Universali di Medicina e Chirurgia*, 269 (1884), pp. 49–82; Cavaterra, 'L'ospedalità', pp. 103–7.

60. Florence: Passerini, *Storia*, p. 209, says that Legno Santo was already adopted by 1533. See also ASF, Ospedale degli Incurabili 49, ff. 59r, 291r for 1563 and 1577; and the 1574 statutes which discuss the treatment: ASF, Ospedale degli Incurabili 1, ff. 14r–v, 15v. Giovanni Martigegni, who was a member of the Florentine Collegio de' Medici,

wrote a short treatise in 1520, 'De Morbo Gallico', in which he recommended the administration of guaiac (Wellcome Institute, Western MS 476, ff. 4v–5v). The tract was dedicated to Goro Gheri, who apparently suffered from Mal Francese and was one of the leading members of the Medici regime. On his role in the period leading up to the death of Lorenzo de' Medici see H. C. Butters, *Governors and Government in Early Sixteenth-Century Florence, 1502–1519*, Oxford, 1985, pp. 278–93, 295–6, 299–300 and 304–6. In Rome clearly the treatment was well established at San Giacomo by 1529 when Delicado published his treatise: Delicado, *La Lozana Andalusa*, p. 303 n.

61. ASR, ASG 382, f. 111v: 'Questo anno [1550] fe incominciò l'acqua del legno ad avere adì primo mai e si finì il dì 14 di junio.' Patients admitted in April 1549 are in ASG 382, ff. 36v–41r, and in April to June 1550 in ff. 107v–10v.

62. Delicado, *La Lozana Andalusa*, pp. 295–300; G. Fracastoro, *De Contagione et Contagiosis Morbis et eorum curatione*, trans. and ed. W. C. Wright, New York and London, 1930, pp. 277–85; G. Falloppio *De Morbo Gallico*, Padua, 1564, chs xlv–xlvii; Laurentius Palmerius Aromatarius, 'Ordini del dare l'acqua del legno': ASR, ASG 853/844. Cf. also the discussion in Nicolò Massa, *Liber de Morbo Gallico*, Venice, 1527, ch. V.

63. Munger, 'Guaiacum', pp. 206–9.

64. Cf. Palmerius, 'Ordini'; Vanti, *S. Giacomo*, pp. 39–54; Cavaterra, 'L'ospedalità', pp. 103–7; and Delicado, *La Lozana Andalusa*, pp. 295–6.

65. ASF, Ospedale degli Incurabili 1: 1574 statutes, ch. 6: 'dare il legno: mezzo febbraio sino a tutto ottobre . . . et questo aciò che sendo stati gl'infermi in luogo così caldo, non habbino a uscir fuori nel asprezza del verno . . .'.

66. R. Palmer, 'L'assistenza medica nella Venezia cinquecentesca', in Aikema and Meijers, eds, *Nel regno*, p. 40; Bologna: 1597: ASB, Ospedale di S. Giobbe IV/3: 'sono curati in due infermerie separate, da due medici eccellenti, uno fisico e l'altro chirusico, et una volta l'anno si li da l'acqua del legno nella stagione di maggio per dui mesi continui . . .'.

67. López-Terrada, 'El tratamiento', pp. 30–1.

68. Delicado, *La Lozana Andalusa*, pp. 298–9; Munger, 'Guaiacum', pp. 208–9.

69. Bologna: ASB, Ospedale di S. Giobbe IV/3; Florence: ASF, Ospedale degli Incurabili 1, f. 14v (1574 statutes); Rome: ASR, ASG 292/19, ch. 17 (mid-sixteenth-century statutes). See also the 1659 printed statutes, which are based on the earlier version: *Statuti* (1659): ch. xiv: pp. 33–4.

70. ASF, Ospedale degli Incurabili 49, f. 304v: 1578: 'tener buona cura degli amalati; con medicarli diligentemente . . . nel far le stufe'.

71. ASR, ASG 292/19, ch. 17 of statutes; Ospedale di San Giacomo 2, f. 2v: 1.vi.1584.

72. Cf. Munger, 'Guaiacum', pp. 209–10.

73. Delicado, *La Lozana Andalusa*, p. 303n.

74. Corradi, 'Nuovi documenti', p. 355.

75. See R. Jütte, 'Syphilis and Confinement: early modern German hospitals for syphilitics', in N. Finizsch and R. Jütte, eds, *The Prerogative of Confinement*, Cambridge, 1995, at n. 31; M. Pelling, 'Appearance and Reality: barber–surgeons, the body and disease', in A. L. Beir and R. Finlay, eds, *London, 1500–1700: the making of a metropolis*, London and New York, 1986, pp. 82–112.

76. Palmerius, 'Ordini', f. 11r.

77. Palmerius, 'Ordini', ff. 12r, 13r.

78. ASR, ASG 811/5 (without date); cf. Cavaterra, 'L'ospedalità', pp. 118–23, on alms received by the hospital between 1585 and 1605.

79. Delumeau, *Vie économique*, ii, pp. 757–8.

80. ASR, ASG, 854/42. Cf. ASG 853/844, ff. 2v–3r: over 3,000 *scudi* were spent in the late sixteenth and early seventeenth centuries, without the cost of 'biancherie et altri mobili, et massaritie necessarie'. Ibid., ff. 3v–6v, lists in detail everything necessary for the treatment.

81. The hospital's patient registers list 49,927 patients admitted between 1554 and 1599, though, as we shall see below, from 1584 those admitted for the guaiacum treatment were not included in these records: cf. ASR, ASG 384–418.

82. During these four years 5,143 individuals were admitted, though 446 of them have been excluded from the following calculations because the records were incomplete.

83. ASR, ASG 292/19, ff. 23r–v: undated, early seventeenth-century statutes.

84. ASR, ASG 386, f. 79r.

85. ASR, ASG 853/845, for example, records the names of all those admitted 'a pigliar l'acqua del legno' in 1569.

86. Calculated from ASR, ASG 853/852; Cavaterra, 'L'ospedalità', pp. 100–1.

87. López-Terrada, 'El tratamiento, pp. 25, 35.

88. L. Sandri, 'Ospedali e utenti dell' assistenza nella Firenze del Quattrocento', in G. Pinto, ed., *La società del bisogno. Povertà e assistenza nella Toscana medievale*, Florence, 1989, pp. 70–1; and G. Paolucci and G. Pinto, 'Gli "infermi" della Misericordia di Prato (1401–1491)', in ibid., p. 126; K. Park, 'Healing the Poor: hospitals and medical assistance in renaissance Florence', in J. Barry and C. Jones, eds, *Medicine and Charity before the Welfare State*, London, 1991, p. 36.

89. Cf. Beloch, *Bevölkerungsgeschichte*, i, p. 17; Delumeau, *Vie économique*, i, p. 422; E. Sonnino, 'Between the Home and the Hospice: the plight

and fate of girl orphans in seventeenth- and eighteenth-century Rome', in J. Henderson and R. Wall, eds, *Poor Women and Children in the European Past*, London, 1994, table 1.

90. Beloch, *Bevölkerungsgeschichte*, i, pp. 16–17; Delumeau, *Vie économique*, i, p. 423.

91. López-Terrada, 'El tratamiento', pp. 22–3; Jütte, 'Syphilis and Confinement', at n. 32.

92. M. Foucault, 'La Politique de la santé au xviiie siècle', in M. Foucault et al., *Les Machines a guérir: aux origines de l'hôpital moderne*, Brussels, 1976, pp. 17–18; Jütte, 'Syphilis and Confinement', at nn. 38–9.

93. Although this does not take into account those who died in the year following their entry, this does not affect overmuch the calculation of annual mortality since the vast majority of patients died in the year they were admitted. These figures may under-estimate the real mortality of the resident population. However, a calculation of the total number of male patients at risk in 1561 suggests that the aggregate figures do not distort the overall pattern of mortality. See table below. Cf. Cavaterra, 'L'ospedalità', p. 102, who has calculated 14.5 per cent for the years 1585–1600.

94. Park, 'Healing the Poor', p. 36.

95. Cited by Fiorani, 'Religione e povertà', p. 84.

96. The following list does not pretend to be complete, but is merely a compilation from secondary sources: A. Celli, *Storia della malaria nell'agro romano*, Città di Castello, 1925, p. 325; A. Ilvento, *Storia delle grandi malattie epidemiche con speciale riguardo alla malaria*, Rome, 1938, pp. 557–61; A. Corradi, *Annali delle epidemie occorse in Italia, dalle prime memorie fino al 1850*, 5 vols, Bologna, 1865–94; 1973 edn, i and iv.

97. Four times in the 1550s (1552, 1555, 1557, 1558), twice in the following decade (1568, 1569), three times in the 1570s (1570, 1572, 1575), three times in the 1580s (1581, 1586, 1589) and three to four times in the 1590s (1590–3 and 1598). See Ilvento, *Storia*, pp. 556–61; Corradi, *Annali*, i, pp. 501–2, 565, 579, 640, 684–6.

98. In 1554, 1557, 1568–9, 1580, 1597: Celli, *Storia*, pp. 323–32; Corradi,

S. Giacomo degli Incurabili: male patients at risk in 1561

1561	at risk (person-days)	deaths in month	deaths per person-day (×1,000)	number admitted	deaths per admission (×100)
Jan.	342	5	14.62	34	14.71
Feb.	483	9	18.63	48	18.75
Mar.	893	8	8.96	80	10.00
Apr.	868	9	10.37	80	11.25
May	713	8	11.22	64	12.50
Jun.	1,160	7	6.03	89	7.87
Jul.	1,079	7	6.49	88	7.95
Aug.	1,103	8	7.25	98	8.16
Sept.	1,201	14	11.66	84	16.67
Oct.	977	10	10,24	82	12.20
Nov.	745	5	6.71	53	9.43
Dec.	440	2	4.55	36	5.56

Source: ASR, S. Giacomo degli Incurabili, 386

Annali, i, pp. 507–8, 634–41, 691; Ilvento, *Storia*, p. 557. 'Infermità catarrale': 1562, 1557, 1572: Corradi, *Annali*, i, pp. 535–42, 551–4, 574–5.

99. See C. M. Cipolla, *I pidocchi e il granduca. Crisi economica e problemi sanitari nella Firenze del' 600*, Bologna, 1979, ch. 1, for a sensitive discussion of the context for the outbreak of the epidemic of petechial fever (which he identifies as typhus) in Florence in 1620–1.

100. Cipolla, *I pidocchi*, pp. 26–7; L. Del Panta, *Le epidemie nella storia demographica italiana (secoli xiv–xix)*, Turin, 1980, pp. 54–63. The worst outbreaks in Rome were in 1557, 1566, 1568–70 and 1591–2 at the time of severe dearths, although some of the 'fevers' mentioned above may also have been petechial fever: Ilvento, *Storia*, p. 557; Corradi, *Annali*, i, pp. 567–8; P. Pecchai, *Roma nel Cinquecento*, Rome, 1948, p. 418; Fiorani, 'Religione e povertà', p. 90; Del Panta, *Le epidemie*, p. 150.

101. Cipolla, *I pidocchi*, pp. 26–35.

102. C. Fanucci, *Trattato di tutte l'opere pie dell'alma città di Roma*, Rome, 1602, p. 79; Delumeau, *Vie économique*, Part 2, ch. 111.

103. Delumeau, *Vie économique*, ii, pp. 605–6; on the *Avvisi* see his ample discussion in ibid., i, pp. 25–36.

104. Cicatelli, *Vita del P. Camillo de Lellis*, pp. 106–7; see also Delumeau, *Vie économique*, ii, pp. 560ff.

105. Archivum Romanum Societatis Jesu di Roma, 127, i, fol. 209, as cited by Fiorani, 'Religione e povertà', p. 90 n. 98.

106. Simoncelli, 'Note', p. 148.

107. Delumeau, *Vie économique*, ii, pp. 694–5

108. L. von Pastor, *The History of the Popes from the Close of the Middle Ages*, ed. R. F. Kerr, London, 1928, xv, p. 130.

109. Delumeau, *Vie économique*, ii, pp. 603–5; Corradi, *Annali*, i, pp. 550–5.

110. Simoncelli, 'Note', p. 143; Delumeau, *Vie économique*, ii, pp. 605–6.

111. Delumeau, *Vie économique*, ii, pp. 606.

112. Delumeau, *Vie économique*, i, pp. 411–12.

113. Pastor, *History of the Popes*, xv, p. 88 n. 2.

114. Delumeau, *Vie économique*, ii, p. 606.

115. Corradi, *Annali*, i, pp. 567–71, iv, pp. 481–2; Ilvento, *Storia*, p. 558; see also Celli, *Storia*, pp. 323–32.

116. Ilvento, *Storia*, p. 558; Corradi, *Annali*, i, pp. 567–71.

117. Palmerius, 'Ordini', ff. 11v–12r.

118. ASR, ASG 293/37/17, c. 7/1.

119. Paolucci and Pinto, 'Gli "infermi"', p. 124, table 3; Park, 'Healing the Poor', p. 36. Cf. Cavaterra, 'L'ospedalità', p. 102.

120. On Venice where patients stayed for up to seven months see, Palmer, 'L'assistenza medica', p. 40.

121. See Cicatelli, *Vita del P. Camillo de Lellis*, pp. 40–1, 48, 50–1.

122. López-Terrada, 'El tratamiento', pp. 33–4.

123. Palmerius, 'Ordini', f. 23v.

124. ASR, ASG, 811/5.

125. Such as at Padua (Palmer, 'L'assistenza medica', p. 40) and Bologna (ASB, Ospedale di S. Maria dei Guarini o di S. Giobbe ser. I/1, f. 3r).

126. Padua: Palmer, 'L'assistenza medica', p. 40; Naples: 1539 statutes: Vitale, 'Ricerche', pp. 263–4. Cf. the 1574 statutes of the Florentine hospital: patients had to bring with them 'fede del medico fisico del luogo di haver bisogno di pigliare il legno' before admission, but did not mention an examination by the hospital's physician: ASF, Ospedale degli Incurabili 1, f. 14r. Cf. Cavaterra, 'L'ospedalità', pp. 110–12.

127. ASR, ASG 293/37/17, c. 8.

128. Palmerius, 'Ordini', f. 10r.

129. San Giacomo, *Statuti* of 1659, p. 26.

130. ASF, Ospedale degli Incurabili 1 (1574 statutes), ff. 13v–14r.

131. ASB, Demaniale, 1/6472: 'pieno di

poveri impiagatti et dali altri hospitalli reietti et abandonatti di sortte'.

132. Corradi, 'Nuovi documenti', p. 349.
133. *Salvatoris Nostri*, in P. De Angelis, *L'Arcispedale di San Giacomo in Augusta*, Rome, 1955, pp. 10–11.
134. San Giacomo, *Statuti* of 1659, pp. 23, 30.
135. Paschini, 'Le Compagnie', p. 71.
136. Palmer, 'L'assistenza medica', p. 40.
137. ASB, Demaniale, 1/6472.13: 1570; ASB, Ospedale di S. Maria dei Guarini o di S. Giobbe, ser. IV/3: 9.iv.1597.
138. Vanti, *S. Giacomo*, p. 41.
139. ASR, ASG 863.
140. Fracastoro, *De Contagione*, pp. 137–9.
141. Fracastoro, *De Contagione*, pp. 136–7, 270–1.
142. Falloppio, *De Morbo Gallico*, ch. xc: p. 53.
143. Fracastoro, *De Contagione*, pp. 272–3.
144. Fracastoro, *De Contagione*, pp. 39–41.
145. Fanucci, *Trattato*, p. 48.
146. ASR, ASG 853/844, ff. 7r, 11r–v.
147. ASR, ASG 853/884, ff. 11r–v.
148. *Salvatoris Nostri Domini Jesu Christi*, 15 Aug. 1515, in *Bullarium Romanum a B. Leone Magno usque as S.D.N. Clementem X*, ed. A./M. Cherubino, 6 vols, Lyon, 1892, i, pp. 567–71: pp. 567–8.
149. Fanucci, *Trattato*, p. 48.
150. ASR, ASG 853/844, ff. 13r, 15v–16r.
151. López-Terrada, 'El tratamiento', p. 21; C. Quétel, *History of Syphilis*, Cambridge, 1990, pp. 12, 24–5; and Jütte, 'Syphilis and Confinement', n. 30.
152. *Salvatoris Nostri*, in *Bull. Rom.*, i, p. 567; Piazza, *Opere pie di Roma*, pp. 45–8.
153. Palmerius, 'Ordini', f. 23v.
154. ASR, ASG 811/5.
155. ASR, ASG 811/5: 5.i.1580.
156. ASR, ASG 811/5: 12.iv.1584.
157. ASR, ASG 811/5: 3.iv.1575.

158. ASR, ASG 811/5: 16.iv.1575 and 15.v.1575.
159. ASR, ASG 811/5: 6.v.1585 and 24.iv.1587.
160. ASR, ASG 811/5: 17.iv.1575 and second without name or date
161. ASR, ASG 386: 20.xi.1562.
162. ASR, ASG 391, f. 77r.
163. ASR, ASG 391, ff. 77r: 12.iv.1570, and 100r: 21.iv.1569.
164. Delumeau, *Vie économique*, i, pp. 403–7; P. Simoncelli, 'Origini e primi anni di vita dell'ospedale romano dei poveri mendicanti', *Annuario dell'Istituto Storico Italiano per l'età moderna e contemporanea*, 25–6 (1973–4), pp. 168–9, provides little information about the sex ratio of those admitted to the Spedale dei Mendicanti, although a similar institution in Florence admitted more women: D. Lombardi, *Povertà maschile, povertà femminile. L'Ospedale dei Mendicanti nella Firenze dei Medici*, Bologna, 1988, p. 136.
165. See *Il libro dei vagabondi*, ed. P. Camporesi, Turin, 1973.
166. ASR, ASG 386: 24.iii.1561.
167. Simoncelli, 'Note', p. 143: Delumeau, *Vie économique*, ii, pp. 605–6.
168. Sandri, 'Ospedali e utenti', pp. 79–80.
169. For this and other discussion of contemporary terminology for clothing we have used in general *Vocabolario della Accademia della Crusca*, Florence, 1733–8; S. Battaglia, *Grande Dizionario della Lingua Italiana*, 18 vols, Turin, 1961; and more specifically R. Levi-Pisetzky, *Storia del costume in Italia*, 5 vols, Milan, 1964, iii.
170. Levi-Pisetzky, *Storia del costume in Italia*, iii, p. 226.
171. ASR, ASG 386: 'A', 15.viii.1561.
172. ASR, ASG 391: 'B' under date.
173. See Sandri, 'Ospedali e utenti', pp. 77–83, in her discussion of the clothes worn by patients admitted to the Spedale di S. Matteo in fifteenth-century Florence.
174. Fanucci, *Trattato*, p. 48; Piazza,

Opere pie di Roma, pp. 48–9, p. 35.

175. ASR, ASG 405: under date.
176. Naples: 1521: Viceroy Ramón de Cardona: 'poveri incurabili del popolo napoletano': Ravicini, *Sull'università*, p. 7; Pavia: 1556 statutes of foundation: patients with 'infermità incurabili', first of city of Pavia, then the *principato*, and then *forensi*: Malamani, 'L'Ospedale', p. 167. They also had to furnish proof that they had been rejected from the Spedale Maggiore: Malamani, 'L'Ospedale', p. 154
177. ASF, Ospedale degli Incurabili 1: ch. 6, f. 14r (1574 statutes).
178. By the early 1580s this had apparently dropped to 4 per cent: Cavaterra, 'L'ospedalità', pp. 97, 108–9.
179. On this question see Delumeau, *Vie économique*, i, pp. 189–213; E. Lee, 'Foreigners in Quattrocento Rome', *Renaissance and Reformation*, n.s. 7 (1983), pp. 135–46 (see p. 135 for the quotation from Alberini); and A. Esposito, 'Osservazioni sulla popolazione rionale', *Il Rione Parione durante il pontificio sistino: analisi di un'area campione* in *Un pontificio ed una città. Sisto IV (1471–1484). Atti del convegno, Roma, 3–7 dicembre 1984*, Rome, 1985, pp. 651–62.
180. The geographical origins of San Giacomo patients were calculated from ASR, ASG 386, 390–2. Cf. Cavaterra, 'L'ospedalità', pp. 97, 108–9.
181. Cited by Delumeau, *Vie économique*, i, p. 189.
182. Although San Giacomo and the Neapolitan Incurabili hospital came to see themselves as operating a complementary service, offering Holy Wood treatment in alternate years, there is little evidence that this practice – if it had already begun – had a substantial impact on the patient population in these four years (Vanti, *S. Giacomo*, p. 44).
183. On this theme see Delumeau, *Vie économique*, i, pp. 190–213.

184. Delumeau, *Vie économique*, i, pp. 207–9. Cf. also E. Lee, *Descriptio Urbis: the Roman census of 1527*, Rome, 1985.
185. Delumeau, *Vie économique*, i, p. 212.
186. Delumeau, *Vie économique*, i, pp. 199–201.
187. M. Vanti, *San Camillo de Lellis e i suoi Ministri degli Infermi*, Rome, 1957, p. 53.
188. Delicado, *La Lozana Andalusa*, p. 303n.
189. Cicatelli, *Vita di P. Camillo*, pp. 6, 18.
190. Fracastoro, *De Contagione*, p. 139.
191. Guicciardini, *Storia d'Italia*, i, p. 233.
192. Langasco, *Gli spedali*, doct. 20: p. 263; cf. M. Del Lungo, 'Aspetti dell'organizzazione sanitaria nella Genova del settecento: la cura delle Malattie Veneree', *Società e storia*, 22, 1983, pp. 772–3.
193. Fracastoro, *De Contagione*, pp. 152–3, 272–3.
194. A. Kinzelbach, '"Böse Blattern" oder "Franzosenkrankheit": Syphiliskonzept, Kranke und die Genese des Krankenhauses in oberdeutschen Reichsstädten der frühen Neuzeit', in M. Dinges and T. Schlich, eds, *Neue Wege in der Seuchengeschichte*, Stuttgart, 1995, pp. 56–61, esp. p. 59.
195. ASF, Ospedale degli Incurabili 1 (1574 statutes), f. 17r. The 1645 statutes (f. 17r) record that the hospital changed from Legno Santo for Mal Francese to 'the method used by the French doctors'.
196. Palmer, 'L'assistenza medica', p. 40, quotes the records of San Giacomo to the effect that the administrators did not believe it to be very efficacious: 'maxime cum modus sit debilis': ASR, ASG 1, f. 86v: 7.ii.1552.
197. In general see Simoncelli, 'Note', pp. 141–56; Delumeau, *Vie économique*, ii, pp. 529–32, 603–5.
198. Simoncelli, 'Origini', pp. 146–8.
199. Pecchai, *Roma*, pp. 418–19; Fiorani, 'Religione e povertà', p. 84 n. 83.

200. Quoted in Palmer, 'L'assistenza medica', p. 40.

Chapter Nine: Catching the Pox

1. The process of refining Galenic medicine reached a peak with authors like Gentile da Foligno, who died during the first outbreak of plague. He was called 'the theorist', *speculator*, and epitomised a development that had begun with Taddeo Alderotti. His commentary on the *Canon* (the first complete one) was popular enough to warrant printing in the early sixteenth century and its doctrines typify what scholastic medicine was. See *Avicenne medicorum Principis Canonum Liber una cum lucidissima Gentilis Fulg. Expositione, qui merito est Speculator appellatus*, Venice (heirs of Octavian Scot), 1520. This volume is consistent with the *Tertius Can. Avic.* of 1522.

2. For the attractions of university medicine among different parts of society, see M. McVaugh, *Medicine before the Plague: practitioners and their patients in the Crown of Aragon 1285–1345*, Cambridge, 1993, passim. See also L. García-Ballester, 'Medical Ethics in Transition' in A. Wear, J. Geyer-Kordesch and R. K. French, eds, *Doctors and Ethics: the earlier historical setting of professional ethics*, Amsterdam, 1993, pp. 38–71.

3. The authority was Galen's book on the topic, part of the 'new Galen' described by García-Ballester, and the medieval refinement was to treat the qualities of a complexion quantitatively, in degrees. See M. McVaugh, ed., *Arnaldi de Villanova Opera Medica Omnia. II Aphorismi de Gradibus*, Barcelona, 2nd edn 1992.

4. He was in competition with physicians who held to other philosophies and he had to demonstrate the superiority of his own. See P. Brain, *Galen on Bloodletting: a study of the origins, development and validity of his*

opinions, with a translation of the three works, Cambridge, 1986.

5. See L. Deer-Richardson, 'The Generation of Disease: occult causes and diseases of the total substance', in A. Wear, R. French and I. Lonie, eds, *The Medical Renaissance of the Sixteenth Century*, Cambridge, 1985, pp. 175–94.

6. The second, separately paginated part of Fernel's *Universa Medicina* (we have used the edition of Geneva, 1643) is the *Therapeutices Universalis, seu Medendi Rationis libri septem*: see p. 8.

7. H. Cardanus [Girolamo Cardano], *De Subtilitate libri XXI*, Basel, n.d. (address dated 1552).

8. J. Fernel, *De Abditis Rerum Causis libri duo*, in the collected *Universa Medicina*.

9. Fernel, *De Abditis*, p. 8.

10. Fernel, *De Abditis*, p. 9.

11. Fernel, *De Abditis*, p. 12.

12. Fernel, *De Abditis*, p. 13.

13. Fernel, *De Abditis*, p. 17.

14. The pox is dealt with in ch. 20 of his *De Partium Morbis et Symptomatis*, the 6th book of pathology, which opens at p. 486 of the *Universa Medicina*; see p. 604.

15. Fernel, *Universa Medicina*, p. 343

16. J. Fernel, *De Morbis eorumque Causis liber I* (the first of seven books of pathology, at p. 335 of the *Universa Medicina*).

17. See V. Nutton, 'The Reception of Fracastoro's Theory of Contagion: the seed that fell among thorns?', *Osiris*, 6, 2nd ser. (1990), pp. 196–234.

18. On diseases of the whole substance, see Deer-Richardson, 'The Generation of Disease', esp. p. 182.

19. Fernel, *De Luis Venereae Curatione perfectissima*: p. 419 of the second pagination of the *Universa Medicina*.

20. Fernel, *De Luis . . . Curatione*, p. 433.

21. Fernel, *De Luis . . . Curatione*, p. 433.

22. Fernel, *De Luis . . . Curatione*, p. 433.

23. Fernel, *De Luis . . . Curatione*, p. 438.
24. Fernel, *De Luis . . . Curatione*, p. 442.
25. Fernel, *De Luis . . . Curatione*, p. 443.
26. Fernel, *De Luis . . . Curatione*, p. 453.
27. Linda Deer Cf. Deer-Richardson, 'The Generation of Disease', pp. 184ff.
28. Fernel, *Therapeutices*, p. 130.
29. This had been one of the main charges against Vesalius, the attacker of Galen, by his enemies. See R. K. French, *William Harvey's Natural Philosophy*, Cambridge, 1994, ch. 3.
30. Fernel, *De Abditis*, p. 121.
31. Fernel also believed that the standard medical picture did not give enough importance to spirits. Spirits had – like soul – religious connotations for Fernel, and he was not content to accept a purely pagan ancient usage. It seemed therefore that the medicine of the ancients would have to be refined further by reinterpreting, within the Latin tradition, what meaning lay below the surface of words like *spiritus*. See J. J. Bono, 'Reform and the Languages of Renaissance Theoretical Medicine: Harvey versus Fernel', *Journal of the History of Biology*, 23/3 (1990), pp. 341–87.
32. Fernel, *De Abditis*, p. 153.
33. In addition to drawing from the Thomistic tradition, Fernel is using Platonism, at least in his anatomical account of the body (J. Fernel, *De Partium Corporis Humani Descriptio*, in the *Universa Medicina*: it is the opening work of the collection). Piccolomini follows the Platonising Fernel in this. He saw the soul confined in the body as in a workhouse, an *ergastulum*. It is at first blinded with ignorance, but from its divine origin it brings both the seeds of knowledge and a desire to know.
34. See Deer-Richardson, 'The Generation of Disease', p. 178.

35. See French, *Harvey*, chs 1 and 2.
36. J. Riolan (the elder), *Opera cum Physica, tum Medica*, Frankfurt, 1611, ch. 9 (p. 94).
37. See French, *Harvey*, ch. 11.
38. Antonius Fracancianius [Antonio Fracanzano], *De Morbo Gallico fragmenta quaedam elegantissima ex lectionibus anni 1563. Bononiae*, Padua, 1563.
39. Fracancianius, *De Morbo Gallico*, p. 3v.
40. Laurence Joubert, *Medicinae Practicae priores libri tres*, Geneva, 1572.
41. *Institutionum Medicinae libri quinque*, Basel, 1583, p. 522.
42. Riolan, *Opera*, p. 105
43. J. Riolan (the elder), *Praelectiones in libros Physiologicos, et de Abditis Rerum Causis*, Paris, 1601. This contains the *Ad libros de Abditis Rerum Causis Ioannis Riolani Commentarius*, separately paginated.
44. Fernel, *De Abditis*, p. 5.
45. Aloysius Luisinus [Luigi Luigini], *De Morbo Gallico omnia quae extant apud omnes medicos cuiuscunque nationis, qui vel integris libris, vel quoquo alio modo huius affectus curationem methodice aut empirice tradiderunt, diligenter hincinde conquisita, sparsim inventa, erroribus expurgata, et in unum tandem hoc corpus redacta. In quo de ligno Indico, salsa perillia, radice Chynae, argento vivo, caeterisque rebus omnibus ad huius luis profligationem inventis, difusissima tractatio habetur . . . Opus hac nostra aetate, qua Morbi Gallici vis passim vagatur, apprime necessarium*, 2 vols, Venice, 1566–7, ii, p. 44.
46. Leonardus Botallus, *Luis Venereae Curandi Ratio*, in Luigini, *De Morbo Gallico*, ii, a third pagination, p. 9.
47. J. Struthius, *Sphygmicae artis iam mille ducentos annos perditae et desideratae libri V*, Basel, 1555; at p. 273 he argues that it is a new disease.
48. Hieronymus Fracastorius, *Syphilis, sive Morbus Gallicus*, Paris, 1531. There is a convenient text in the edition by Heneage Wynne-Finch, *Fracastor: Syphilis or the French*

Disease. A poem in Latin hexameters by Girolamo Fracastoro with translation, notes and appendix, London, 1935.

49. Girolamo Fracastoro (1470–1553) was taught by Leonico Tomeo and Pomponazzi and took his arts and medicine degree in Padua in 1502.

50. Fracastoro, 1935 edn, p. 56.

51. Fracastoro, 1935 edn, p. 54.

52. Fracastoro, 1935 edn, p. 61.

53. This historiographical view is discussed sensibly by Nutton, 'Fracastoro's Theory of Contagion'.

54. H. Fracastorius [G. Fracastoro], *De Sympathia et Antipathia Rerum liber unus: De Contagione et Contagiosis Morbis et eorum Curatione, libri III*, Venice, 1546. On the latter see also C. W. Wright, ed. and trans., *Hieronymi Fracastorii de Contagione et Contagiosis Morbis et eorum Curatione, libri III*, New York and London, 1930.

55. Sympathetic disorders happened by *communication* (through nerves, blood vessels or membranes); by *similarity of substance* (separate similar parts of the same kind might suffer similarly); *similarity of origin* (when two parts shared a common ancestry); by *similarity of function* (where two parts conspired in a single purpose, like the uterus and breasts in generating and sustaining the child); by *transmission* of substance (like vapours rising from a disordered stomach to produce headaches); and by *contiguity*.

56. As an infant in his mother's arms, he escaped unhurt when his mother was killed by lightning. Such an event, in Fracastoro's mind, may well have directed his attention when reading his Pliny to the story of Marcia, the Roman woman who survived when her child was killed by lightning at the moment of birth (*Naturalis historia*, II/52) or that man is the only animal that can survive lightning (II/55) or about lightning and the money-box (or purse: II/52). Of the sympathies and antipathies listed above, that of adamant/diamond for goat's blood is Pliny,

XX/1, 2. The story of lightning and the gold is common to Seneca (see J. A. Clark, *Physical Science in the Time of Nero*, London, 1910, p. 78) and to Pliny; the lion's fear of the cock is *Naturalis Historia*, VIII.

57. By 1500 there were fifteen. See R. K. French, 'Pliny and Renaissance Medicine,' in French and G. Greenaway, *Science in the Early Roman Empire: Pliny the Elder, his sources and influence*, London, 1986, pp. 252–81: p. 252.

58. In Wittenberg they used in particular book II of the *Naturalis Historia*. This is where Pliny gives his summary view of the heavens and earth, that is, where he covers the same ground as Aristotle in the physical works. See chapter 5, n. 56.

59. *ignotum illud antiquis miraculum navigatoriae pyxidis*. Fracastoro (1546), p. 1r.

60. Fracastoro (1546), p. 1v (ch. 2).

61. Fracastoro (1574), p. 77r.

62. Fracastoro (1550), p. 217.

63. Fracastoro (1550), p. 216.

64. Fracastoro speaks of Lucretius in *De Sympathia*, p. 4v and has a major discussion of atoms.

65. Fracastoro (1574), p. 77.

66. Fracastoro (1574), pp. 7r–v: *contagionem esse consimilem quandam misti secundum substantiam corruptionem, de uno in aliud transeuntem infectione in particulis insensibilis*.

67. Fracastoro (1574), p. 79r.

68. Fracastoro (1574), p. 77v (ch. 2).

69. Fracastoro (1546), p. 10.

70. Fracastoro (1546): the opening of ch. 6, p. 22.

71. Fracastoro (1546), p. 20.

72. See Margaret J. Osler, ed., *Atoms, Pneuma and Tranquillity: Epicurean and Stoic themes in European thought*, Cambridge, 1991.

73. Fracastoro (1546), p. 59; (1574), p. 91r.

74. Fracastoro (1546), p. 136.

75. Fracastoro (1546): ch. 12, p. 143 is concerned with the causes of syphilis.

76. Fracastoro (1546), p. 148.

77. Fracastoro (1546), p. 187.
78. Fracastoro (1546), p. 194.

Chapter Ten: The French Disease Grows Old

1. See the case studies by J. Shatzmiller, *Jews, Medicine and Medieval Society*, Berkeley, 1994, esp. ch. 2; and M. McVaugh, *Medicine before the Plague: practitioners and their patients in the Crown of Aragon, 1285–1345*, Cambridge, 1993, esp. ch. 4.
2. His work, *De Morbo Gallico libellus*, appears in Aloysius Luisinus [Luigi Luigini], *De Morbo Gallico omnia quae extant apud omnes medicos cuiuscunque nationis, qui vel integris libris, vel quoquo alio modo huius affectus curationem methodice aut empirice tradiderunt, diligenter hincinde conquisita, sparsim inventa, erroribus expurgata, et in unum tandem hoc corpus redacta. In quo de ligno Indico, salsa perillia, radice Chynae, argento vivo, caeterisque rebus omnibus ad huius luis profligationem inventis, difusissima tractatio habetur . . . Opus hac nostra aetate, qua Morbi Gallici vis passim vagatur, apprime necessarium*, 2 vols, Venice, 1566–7, i, p. 148.
3. See R. K. French, *William Harvey's Natural Philosophy*, Cambridge, 1994, ch. 2.
4. Borgarucci seems to have been a fairly orthodox Galenist, despite having been taught by Vesalius. Luigini called his text a *Methodus De Morbo Gallico*, for the first time in his collection, *De Morbo Gallico*, vol. ii, p. 150, which suggests a 'methodical' approach (see above). Indeed, he recalls a conversation with an abbot in which they discussed 'subtleties' and hidden causes (see Chapter Nine above) and in which he stayed close to the academic position, promising a 'method' for the pox.
5. Laurentius Phrisius [Lorenz Friese], *De Morbo Gallico Opusculum* (1532) in Luigini, *De Morbo Gallico*, i, p.

299. Friese also wanted Avicenna to be 'the Prince' for German physicians; he had also published on the English Sweats.
6. P. A. Russell, 'Syphilis, God's Scourge or Nature's Vengeance? The German printed response to a public problem in the early sixteenth century', *Archive for Reformation History*, 80 (1989), pp. 286–307: p. 300.
7. See W. Pagel, *Paracelsus: an introduction to philosophical medicine in the era of the renaissance*, Basel, 1958, p. 23.
8. Pagel, *Paracelsus*, pp. 20, 23.
9. Pagel, *Paracelsus*, p. 18.
10. Hock, from Brackenau, had learned his medicine in Bologna. His *De Morbo Gallico Opus* is in Luigini, *De Morbo Gallico*, i, p. 268.
11. Literally 'pushers'; but perhaps 'murderers', *trucidatores*, is intended.
12. See R. K. French, 'The Medical Ethics of Gabriel Zerbi', in A. Wear, J. Geyer-Kordesch and R. K. French, eds, *Doctors and Ethics: the earlier historical setting of professional ethics*, Amsterdam, 1993.
13. Borgarucci, *Methodus de Morbo Gallico* (ch. 2), in Luigini, *De Morbo Gallico*, ii, p. 150.
14. See Antonio Benivieni, *De Morbo Gallico Tractatus*, taken by Luigini, *De Morbo Gallico*, i, p. 345, from Benivieni's well-known book on the hidden causes of disease; Laurentius Phrisius [Lorenz Friese], *De Morbo Gallico Opusculum* (1532), Luigini, *De Morbo Gallico*, i, p. 299; Leonhard Schmaus, *De Morbo Gallico Tractatus* (1518), Luigini, *De Morbo Gallico*, i, p. 331. Luigini had scant regard for the original titles used by the authors whose texts he collected.
15. Ch. 2 of his text: see Luigini, *De Morbo Gallico*, ii, p. 151.
16. Friese, *De Morbo Gallico Opusculum*, in Luigini, *De Morbi Gallico*, i, p. 299.
17. Petrus Trapolinus [Trapolino], *De Morbo Gallico Tractatus*, in Luigini, *De Morbo Gallico*, ii, p. 44.
18. See M. H. Fish, *Nicholaus Pol Doctor 1494: with a critical text of his guaiac*

tract, ed. and trans. D. M. Schullian, New York, 1947.

19. His work appears in *Morbi Gallici Curandi Ratio*, Basel, 1536: the collected tracts of P. A. Mattheoli [sic; Mattioli], J. Almenar, N. Massa, N. Poll and Benedictus de Victoriis; p. 79.

20. Giovanni Pascale uses the term in this sense of 'orthodox': Joannes Paschalis Suessanus, *De Morbo quodam Composito: qui vulgo apud nos Gallicus appellatur liber*, in Luigini, *De Morbo Gallico*, i, p. 192. Massa uses it (in the collection of 1536, p. 119) for 'learned'.

21. 'Canon' is a transcription of the Arabic title (usually rendered now as *Qanun*) by someone who knew that by a judicious selection of vowels (not present in the Arabic) he could construct a title meaningful in the West.

22. Georgius Vella, *De Morbo Gallico Opusculum*, in Luigini, *De Morbo Gallico*, i, p. 179.

23. Marinus Brocardus [Brocardo], *De Morbo Gallico tractatus*, in Luigini, *De Morbo Gallico*, ii, p. 9.

24. Benedictus Rinius, *De Morbo Gallico tractatus*, in Luigini, *De Morbo Gallico*, ii, p. 14. The tract seems to be a *consilium* to the Archbishop of Corcyra. Rinio was involved in preparing editions of Avicenna's *Canon*. See Nancy Siraisi, *Avicenna in Renaissance Italy: the Canon and medical teaching in Italian universities after 1500*, Princeton, 1987, esp. p. 140.

25. Trapolino, *De Morbo Gallico Tractatus*, in Luigini, *De Morbo Gallico*, ii, p. 44.

26. See his *Disputatio utilis de Morbo Gallico*, Luigini, *De Morbo Gallico*, i, p. 110.

27. Da Monte Latinises as Joannes Baptista Montanus. His tract on the pox, *De Morbo Gallico tractatus*, together with letters on the same topic from his 'consultations' of medical cases, appears in Luigini, *De Morbo Gallico*, i, p. 476. His 'method' of teaching the arts appeared in 1558.

28. Tomitano's *De Morbo Gallico libri duo* was published by Luigini, *De Morbo Gallico*, ii, p. 58. Luigini admired his treatment of the French Disease and dedicated the second volume of his collection to him.

29. Prosper Borgarucci, *Methodus de Morbo Gallico*, in Luigini, *De Morbo Gallico*, ii, p. 150.

30. Domenico Leone Latinises as Dominicus Leo. See Jean Astruc, *De Morbis Venereis libri sex*, Paris, 1736, p. 764.

31. Astruc, *De Morbis Venereis*, pp. 764, 819.

32. Nicolaus Macchellus; see Astruc, *De Morbis Venereis*, p. 743.

33. Iacobus a Béthencourt [Jacques de Béthencourt], *Nova Penitentialis Quadragesima, necnon Purgatorium in Morbum Gallicum sive Venereum una cum Dialogo aquae Argenti et Ligni Guaiaci colluctanctium super dicti morbi curationis praelatura opus fructiferum*, Paris, 1527.

34. J. Sylvius, *Vaesani cuiusdam Calumniarum in Hippocratis Galenique rem Anatomicam Depulsio*, Venice, 1555.

35. Benedictus Rinius, *De Morbo Gallico tractatus*, in Luigini, *De Morbo Gallico*, ii, p. 14.

36. Guillaume Rondelet, *De Morbo Gallico liber unus*, in Luigini, *De Morbo Gallico*, ii, p. 77.

37. *Distinctiones reales:* 'distinctions' were different meanings drawn from a term during disputation or commentary. Scanaroli clearly saw the 'things' of medicine as transcending the words that signified them. Scanaroli, *Disputatio utilis de Morbo Gallico*, in Luigini, *De Morbo Gallico*, ii, p. 111.

38. *Sed extra iocum.* Joannes Paschalis Suessanus [Giovanni Pascale], *De Morbo quodam Composito: qui vulgo apud nos Gallicus appellatur liber*, in Luigini, *De Morbo Gallico*, i, p. 192.

39. Hock, *De Morbo Gallico Opus*, in Luigini, *De Morbo Gallico*, i, p. 270.

40. Brocardo, *De Morbo Gallico tractatus*, in Luigini, *De Morbo Gallico*, ii, p. 9.

The 'nominalism' or 'realism' of authors like Brocardo, Hock and Pascale was appropriate for their circumstances, but much of their argument was paraphrased from texts of Avicenna and Galen (the *Canon* and *De Ingenio Sanitatis*).

41. Benedictus Victorius [Benedetto Vittori], *De Morbo Gallico Liber* (with a *consilium*) in Luigini, *De Morbo Gallico*, i, p. 528.

42. Jacobus Cataneus Genuensis [Jacopo Cattaneo], *De Morbo Gallico tractatus*, in Luigini, *De Morbo Gallico*, i, p. 123.

43. Hock, *De Morbo Gallico Opus*, in Luigini, *De Morbo Gallico*, i, p. 268.

44. Hock, *De Morbo Gallico Opus*, in Luigini, *De Morbo Gallico*, i, p. 269.

45. Brocardo, *De Morbo Gallico tractatus*, in Luigini, *De Morbo Gallico*, ii, p. 9.

46. Pascale, *De Morbo quodam Composito*, in Luigini, *De Morbo Gallico*, i, p. 192.

47. Rondelet said occult qualities were a refuge: *De Morbo Gallico liber unus*, in Luigini, *De Morbo Gallico*, ii, p. 79; Da Monte, *De Morbo Gallico tractatus*, in Luigini, *De Morbo Gallico*, i, p. 479.

48. *Opera Omnia*, Frankfurt, 1600, p. 682.

49. Cattaneo, *De Morbo Gallico tractatus*, in Luigini, *De Morbo Gallico*, i, p. 128 .

50. Johannes Benedictus [Giovanni Benedetto], *De Morbo Gallico libellus*, in Luigini, *De Morbo Gallico*, i, p. 148.

51. Brocardo, *De Morbo Gallico tractatus*, in Luigini, *De Morbo Gallico*, ii, p. 9.

52. Trapolino, *De Morbo Gallico tractatus*, in Luigini, *De Morbo Gallico*, ii, p. 47.

53. The doctrine was current before the arrival of the French Disease. See Zerbi's tract on ethics in French, 'Ethics of Gabriel Zerbi'.

54. See J. A. Paniagua, 'Clínica del Renacimiento', in P. Laín-Entralgo, ed.,*Historia Universal de la Medicina*, 7 vols, Barcelona, 1972–5, iv.

55. All these points are taken from Hermann Neuenar (1492–1530) and Simon Riquin, *De Novo hactenusque Germaniae inaudito Morbo ἰδροπυρετοὺ, hoc est sudatoria Febri, quem vulgo Sudorem Britannicum vocant . . . duabus Epistolis contentum*, Cologne, 1529. The effort to fit the disease into a classical pattern also included the device of giving it a critical period. While fevers of traditional medicine had critical days, so the English Sweats was said to have critical hours, of which the ninth was often the termination of the disease. See Jacobus Castricus of Antwerp, *De Sudore Epidemiali quem Anglicum vocant ad medicos Gandenses Epistola*, Antwerp, 1529. Another device was to call upon Galen's notion of poisons acting by their 'whole substance' rather than by their manifest qualities. See J. Sylvius, *Opera Medica*, Geneva, 1630, p. 399. (Sylvius was writing in the middle of the previous century.) We shall see below that 'whole substance' explanations came to figure large in understanding the pox.

56. Trapolino, *De Morbo Gallico Tractatus*, in Luigini, *De Morbo Gallico*, ii, p. 47. The story is also told by Rinio from Montagnana: see Astruc, *De Morbis Venereis*, p. 703.

57. Alexander Trajanus Petronius, *De Morbo Gallico liber primus*, in Luigini, *De Morbo Gallico*, ii, p. 1 of new pagination. Benivieni in contrast saw the servant classes as much more liable to the disease than their masters. See his tract in Luigini, *De Morbo Gallico*, i.

58. Petronius practised in Rome, was a friend of the founder of the Jesuits and became physician to Pope Gregory XIII. Astruc, *De Morbis Venereis*, p. 774.

59. Antonio Musa Brasavola, *De Morbo Gallico liber*, in Luigini, *De Morbo Gallico*, i, p. 564.

60. Borgarucci indicates that he thought Brasavola had over-classified the symptoms of the French Disease, saying that there were as many spe-

cies of pox in his day as there are ways of letting people out of a house. See his *Methodus de Morbo Gallico*, in Luigini, *De Morbo Gallico*, ii, p. 155.

61. A. Laurentius, *Opera Omnia*, 2 vols, Paris, 1628, ii (separately paginated as *Opuscula*), p. 59. Francis Bacon reported a form of the story in which unscrupulous merchants sold human flesh in barrels during the siege of Naples, the consumption of which began the disease. Bacon relates the story to another, that the natives of the West Indies were cannibals and hence suffered from the disease. See J. Fabricius, *Syphilis in Shakespeare's England*, London, 1994, p. 15.

62. We met his textbook in the previous chapter: Laurence Joubert, *Medicinae Practicae priores libri tres*, Geneva, 1572.

63. Quoted by Astruc, *De Morbis Venereis*, p. 797.

64. Astruc, *De Morbis Venereis*, p. 819.

65. See French, *Harvey*, ch. 3.

66. G. Mercurialis, *Medica Practica*, Frankfurt, 1601, p. 568.

67. However, there is very little direct evidence that such thinking influenced actual sanitary practice in cities.

68. See Astruc, *De Morbis Venereis*.

69. See V. Nutton, 'The Reception of Fracastoro's Theory of Contagion: the seed that fell among thorns?', *Osiris*, 6, 2nd ser. (1990), pp. 196–234.

70. Johannes Benedictus, *De Morbo Gallico libellus*, in Luigini, *De Morbo Gallico*, i, p. 150.

71. A. Scanaroli [Scanarolus], *Disputatio utilis de Morbo Gallico*, in Luigini, *De Morbo Gallico*, i, p. 110.

72. Schmaus, *De Morbo Gallico Tractatus*, in Luigini, *De Morbo Gallico*, i, p. 331.

73. Hock, *De Morbo Gallico Opus*, in Luigini, *De Morbo Gallico*, i, p. 269.

74. Trapolino, *De Morbo Gallico Tractatus*, in Luigini, *De Morbo Gallico*, ii, p. 51.

75. J. Struthius, *Sphygmicae artis iam mille ducentos annos perditae et desideratae libri V*, Basel, 1555, p. 271.

76. Post-mortem examination to discover the cause of death was not an uncommon practice. Vella noted from Pietro d'Abano a case where a patient had died from an accidental swallowing of mercury. The anatomists found that the blood around the heart was coagulated. Vella, *De Morbo Gallico Opusculum*, in Luigini, *De Morbo Gallico*, i, pp. 181–2.

77. See the collection of 1536: *Morbi Gallici Curandi Ratio*, Basel.

78. Vella has a fairly standard explanation for the disease, based on putrefaction, but occurring only in a woman. His argument is that, unlike the male, the female genitalia acts as a *cloaca*, excreting menstrual waste. The putrefaction thus generated is transferred to the male organ *ex simboleitate* of the man's natural humours for the woman's corrupted humours; Luigini, *De Morbo Gallico*, i, p. 180.

79. *ab una enim quaque aegritudine materiali malus vapor exhalat*: *Morbi Gallici Curandi Ratio*, p. 105.

80. See Chapter Eight above for the Incurabili hospitals. See also the *Morbi Gallici Curandi Ratio* of 1536.

81. Leonardus Botallus, *Luis Venereae Curandi Ratio*, in Luigini, *De Morbo Gallico*, ii, a third pagination, p. 9.

82. Cattaneo, *De Morbo Gallico tractatus*, ch. 2, in Luigini, *De Morbo Gallico*, i, p. 123.

83. See the *Morbi Gallici Curandi Ratio* of 1536.

84. Daniel Sennert, *Operum Tomus I–III*, Paris, 1641. Although Democritean atomism was part of his natural philosophy, he attempted to reconcile it with Aristotelian matter-theory. See William A. Wallace, 'Traditional Natural Philosophy', in *The Cambridge History of Renaissance Philosophy*, ed. Charles B. Schmitt, Quentin Skinner, Eckhard Kessler and Jill Kraye, Cambridge, 1988, pp. 201–35: p. 215.

85. For an introduction to these issues, see French, *Harvey*, esp. chs 2 and 8.
86. A. G. Debus, *The Chemical Philosophy: Paracelsian science and medicine in the sixteenth and seventeenth centuries*, 2 vols, New York, 1977, i, p. 192.
87. Debus, *Chemical Philosophy*, i, p. 115, discussing the English Paracelsian John Hester.
88. Sennert, *Operum*, iii: *De Morbis Occultis libri VI*, p. 977.
89. *Nouvelle Biographie Universelle*, Paris, 1852.
90. Perhaps Sennert has drawn the notion from Fracastoro's *Contagion* or *Syphilis*. See for example edition by Heneage Wynne-Finch of 1935, p. 53.
91. Sennert, *Operum*, iii, p. 988.
92. Sennert, *Operum*, iii, p. 970.
93. Sennert, *Operum*, iii, p. 1013 (part 4 of book 6).
94. The attempt to by-pass the active Aristotelian qualities was not uncommon. Sennert deals briefly with Luis Mercado (c.1525–1611), who believed that reduction of elements to their smallest parts – literally, atoms – would dissociate them from their qualities and allow for occult action. Sennert's particular enemy, Arnold Freitag (c.1560–

1614), wanted to derive all qualities from matter (says Sennert) by claiming that new forms arise in mixtures and produce new qualities. This seems to have involved matter being reduced to prime matter, *materia prima*, where its association with qualities was lost (like Mercado's atoms). Sennert, *Operum*, iii, p. 1017.

95. Pagel, *Paracelsus*, p. 311.
96. One of Sennert's major arguments against supra-elementary powers arising from mixtures of the elements is that the souls of animals would otherwise be generated simply from the temperament of their bodies. He agreed with Scaliger that such souls, being elementary, would be corruptible, and Sennert believed that this was not the case. It was clear that animals had perception and memory, and so it was clear to Sennert that they had operations of a different and superior kind. Indeed, he became embroiled with Freitag in a dispute over the spiritual nature of animal souls, and had to write to a number of German theological faculties to escape the charge of heresy. Sennert, *Operum*, iii, p. 967.
97. Sennert, *Operum*, iii, p. 967.

Index